Praise for the First Edition of
Learning Objective-C 2.0

"With *Learning Objective-C 2.0*, Robert Clair cuts right to the chase and provides not only comprehensive coverage of Objective-C, but also time-saving and headache-preventing insights drawn from a depth of real-world, hands-on experience. The combination of concise overview, examples, and specific implementation details allows for rapid, complete, and well-rounded understanding of the language and its core features and concepts."

—Scott D. Yelich, Mobile Application Developer

"There are a number of books on Objective-C that attempt to cover the entire gamut of object-oriented programming, the Objective-C computer language, and application development on Apple platforms. Such a range of topics is far too ambitious to be covered thoroughly in a single volume of finite size. Bob Clair's book is focused on mastering the basics of Objective-C, which will allow a competent programmer to begin writing Objective-C code."

—Joseph E. Sacco, Ph.D., J.E. Sacco & Associates, Inc.

"Bob Clair's *Learning Objective-C 2.0* is a masterfully crafted text that provides in-depth and interesting insight into the Objective-C language, enlightening new programmers and seasoned pros alike. When programmers new to the language ask about where they should start, this is the book I now refer them to."

—Matt Long, Cocoa Is My Girlfriend (www.cimgf.com)

"Robert Clair has taken the Objective-C language and presented it in a way that makes it even easier to learn. Whether you're a novice or professional programmer, you can pick up this book and begin to follow along without knowing C as a prerequisite."

—Cory Bohon, Indie Developer and Blogger for *Mac|Life*

"I like this book because it is technical without being dry, and readable without being fluffy."

—Andy Lee, Author of AppKiDo

Learning
Objective-C 2.0

Second Edition

Learning Objective-C 2.0

A Hands-on Guide to Objective-C
for Mac and iOS Developers

Second Edition

Robert Clair

✦✦Addison-Wesley

Upper Saddle River, NJ · Boston · Indianapolis · San Francisco
New York · Toronto · Montreal · London · Munich · Paris · Madrid
Capetown · Sydney · Tokyo · Singapore · Mexico City

The publisher offers excellent discounts on this book when ordered in quantity for bulk purchases or special sales, which may include electronic versions and/or custom covers and content particular to your business, training goals, marketing focus, and branding interests. For more information, please contact:

U.S. Corporate and Government Sales
(800) 382-3419
corpsales@pearsontechgroup.com

For sales outside the United States, please contact:

International Sales
international@pearsoned.com

Visit us on the Web: informit.com/aw

Cataloging-in-Publication Data is on file with the Library of Congress.

ISBN-13: 978-0-321-83208-5
ISBN-10:   0-321-83208-6
Text printed in the United States on recycled paper at Edwards Brothers Malloy, Ann Arbor, Michigan.
First printing, November 2012

Editor-in-Chief
Mark Taub

Senior Acquisitions Editor
Trina MacDonald

Senior Development Editor
Chris Zahn

Managing Editor
John Fuller

Project Editor
Caroline Senay

Copy Editor
Barbara Wood

Indexer
Richard Evans

Proofreader
Lori Newhouse

Technical Reviewers
Duncan Champney
Joseph Sacco
Scott Yelich

Editorial Assistant
Olivia Basegio

Cover Designer
Chuti Prasertsith

Compositor
Rob Mauhar
The CIP Group

❖

To the memory of my parents,
Selma B. and Martin H. Clair,
and to Ekko

❖

Contents at a Glance

Contents

Preface

Objective-C is an object-oriented extension to C. You could call it "C with Objects." If you're reading this book, you're probably interested in learning Objective-C so that you can write applications for Mac OS X or for iOS. But there's another reason to learn Objective-C: It's a fun language and one that is relatively easy to learn. Like anything else in the real world, Objective-C has some rough spots, but on the whole it is a much simpler language than some other object-oriented languages, particularly C++. The additions that Objective-C makes to C can be listed on a page or two.

Objective-C was initially created by Brad J. Cox in the early 1980s. In 1988, NeXT Computer, the company started by Steve Jobs after he left Apple, licensed Objective-C and made it the basis of the development environment for creating applications to run under NeXT's NeXTSTEP operating system. The NeXT engineers developed a set of Objective-C libraries for use in building applications. After NeXT withdrew from the hardware business in 1993, it worked with Sun Microsystems to create OpenStep, an open specification for an object-oriented system, based on the NeXTSTEP APIs. Sun eventually lost interest in OpenStep. NeXT continued selling its version of OpenStep until NeXT was purchased by Apple in early 1997. The NeXTSTEP operating system became the basis of OS X.

In the Apple world, Objective-C does not work alone. It works in conjunction with a number of class libraries called *frameworks*. The two most important frameworks on OS X are the Foundation framework and the AppKit framework. The Foundation framework contains classes for basic entities, such as strings and arrays, and classes that wrap interactions with the operating system. The AppKit contains classes for windows, views, menus, buttons, and the assorted other widgets needed to build graphical user interfaces (GUIs). Together, the two frameworks are called Cocoa. On iOS a different framework called the UIKit replaces the AppKit. Together, Foundation and UIKit are called Cocoa Touch.

While it is technically possible to write complete OS X programs using other languages, writing a program that follows the Apple *Human Interface Guidelines*[1] and has a proper Mac "look and feel" requires the use of the Objective-C Cocoa frameworks. Even if you write the core of a Mac application in a different language, such as plain C or C++, your user interface layer should be written in Objective-C. When writing for iOS, there is no choice: An iOS app's outer layer and user interface must be written in Objective-C.

About This Book

This book concentrates on learning the Objective-C language. It will not teach you how to write Cocoa or Cocoa Touch programs. It covers and makes use of a small part of the Foundation framework and mentions the AppKit and UIKit only in passing. The book's premise is that you will have a much easier time learning Cocoa and Cocoa Touch programming if you first acquire a good understanding of the language on which Cocoa and Cocoa Touch are based.

Some computer books are written in what I like to think of as a "follow me" style. The user is invited to copy or download some code. A brief discussion of the code follows. As new features are introduced, the reader is asked to change the relevant lines of code and observe the results. After a bit of discussion it is on to the next feature. I find this style of book unsatisfying for a language book. Often there is very little explanation of how things actually work. This style of book can create a false sense of confidence that vanishes when the reader is faced with a programming task that is not a small variation on an example used in the book.

This book takes a more pedagogical approach and uses small examples to emphasize how the language works. In addition to learning the syntax of the language, you are encouraged to think about what is happening "under the hood." This approach requires a bit more mental effort on your part, but it will pay off the first time you face a novel programming task.

Who Should Read This Book

This book is intended for people with some prior programming experience who want to learn Objective-C in order to write programs for OS X or iOS. (iOS is used for the iPhone, the iPod touch, and the iPad.)

The book will also be useful for programmers who want to write Objective-C programs for other platforms using software from the GNUStep project,[2] an open-source implementation of the OpenStep libraries.

---

1. http://developer.apple.com/mac/library/documentation/UserExperience/Conceptual/AppleHIGuidelines.

2. www.gnustep.org/.

What You Need to Know

This book assumes a working knowledge of C. Objective-C is an extension of C; this book concentrates on what Objective-C adds to C. For those whose C is rusty and those who are adept at picking up a new language quickly, Chapters 1 and 2 form a review of the essential parts of C; those that you are likely to need to write an Objective-C program. If you have no experience with C or any C-like language (C++, Java, and C#), you will probably want to read a book on C in conjunction with this book. Previous exposure to an object-oriented language is helpful but not absolutely necessary. The required objected-oriented concepts are introduced as the book proceeds.

About the Examples

Creating code examples for an introductory text poses a challenge: how to illustrate a point without getting lost in a sea of boilerplate code that might be necessary to set up a working program. In many cases, this book takes the path of using somewhat hypothetical examples that have been thinned to help you concentrate on the point being discussed. Parts of the code that are not relevant are omitted and replaced by an ellipsis (**...**).

For example:

```
int averageScore = ...
```

The preceding line of code should be taken to mean that **averageScore** is an integer variable whose value is acquired from some other part of the program. The source of **averageScore**'s value isn't relevant to the example; all you need to consider is that it *has* a value.

About the Exercises

Most of the chapters in this book have a set of exercises at the end. You are, of course, encouraged to do them. Many of the exercises ask you to write small programs to verify points that were made in the chapter's text. Such exercises might seem redundant, but writing code and seeing the result provides a more vivid learning experience than merely reading. Writing small programs to test your understanding is a valuable habit to acquire; you should write one whenever you are unclear about a point, even if the book has not provided a relevant exercise. When I finished writing this book, I had a directory full of small test programs. When you finish with this book, you should have the same.

None of the programs suggested by the exercises require a user interface; all of them can be coded, compiled, and run either by writing the code with a text editor and compiling and running it from a command line, as shown before the exercises in Chapter 2, "More about C Variables," or by using a simple Xcode project, as shown in Chapter 4, "Your First Objective-C Program."

Objective-C—A Moving Target

Objective-C is a moving target. For the past several years Apple has been adding new features and syntax to Objective-C on a regular basis. Despite these added features, Apple has decided *not* to continue versioning the language. Objective-C 2.0 is as high as they are going to go. The only way to specify a particular version or feature set of the language is to refer to Objective-C as of a particular version of Xcode or a particular version of the LLVM compiler. This edition of the book covers Objective-C as of Xcode 4.4 (released with Mountain Lion, OS X 10.8), or, equivalently, Objective-C as implemented in the LLVM Compiler/Clang 4.0.

ARC or Not

Objective-C uses a memory management system called *retain counting*. Each object keeps a count of the number of other objects that are using it. When this count falls to zero, the object's memory is returned to the system for reuse. Historically, this system has been "manual"—you had to write code to manipulate an object's retain count at the appropriate times. The rules for this system have proved difficult for many people to follow correctly 100% of the time. The unfortunate consequences of not following the rules are memory leaks and crashes.

In the spring of 2011 Apple introduced *Automatic Reference Counting* (ARC). ARC automates the reference counting system by analyzing programs and automatically inserting code that keeps the retain count correctly. No coding on the part of the programmer is required.

Some people argue that ARC obviates the need to learn about manual memory management and how reference counting works. They say, "You don't need to know how the engine works to drive a car, and you don't need to know manual reference counting to write Objective-C programs with ARC." This is literally true. But just as some knowledge of how the car's engine works can be valuable, there are some situations where understanding manual memory management can be valuable or even essential:

- There is a lot of existing code that has not been converted to use ARC. If you are asked to work on non-ARC code or want to use an open-source project that is non-ARC, you will have to understand manual reference counting.

- There is a set of C language libraries ("Core"-level libraries) below the Objective-C frameworks. These libraries are written in an object-oriented fashion and have their own manual reference counting system. While it is best to use the Objective-C frameworks if you can, there are cases (in graphics, for example) where it is necessary to use the lower-level libraries. To use these libraries properly you must understand the concepts of manual reference counting.

- Some objects are "toll-free bridged" (see Chapter 8, "Frameworks"). A pointer to one of the low-level C objects can be cast to a pointer to an Objective-C framework object and vice versa. Doing this under ARC requires one of several special casts. Deciding which cast to use requires an understanding of manual reference counting and what ARC is automating for you.

- There are some situations (for example, creating large numbers of temporary objects in a tight loop) where you can help keep the memory footprint of your program small by doing some manual tuning. Doing this tuning requires an understanding of how reference counting operates.

- ARC is still relatively new and there is still the odd bug or unexpected behavior in edge cases. If you encounter one of these, you need to understand what is happening behind the scenes in order to reason your way past the obstacle.

ARC presented me with a dilemma in preparing the second edition of this book. Should I abandon the sections on manual reference counting and just use ARC? I felt strongly that this would be a bad choice, but to help me decide I asked the question of a number of my colleagues. Their answers were unanimous: Understanding how reference counting works is important. Teach it first and then introduce ARC. Accordingly, this book teaches manual memory management until Chapter 16, "ARC." After you have absorbed the material in Chapter 16, you can return to the exercises in earlier chapters and do them using ARC. You will find it much easier to learn how to do manual reference counting and then enjoy the freedom of not doing it in most cases, than to have to learn it on an emergency basis because you have encountered one of the situations in the preceding list.

How This Book Is Organized

This book is organized into three sections. The first section is a review of C, followed by an introduction to object-oriented programming and Objective-C. The second section of the book covers the Objective-C language in detail, as well as an introduction to the Foundation framework. The final section of the book covers memory management in Objective-C and Objective-C blocks.

Part I: Introduction to Objective-C

- Chapter 1, "C, the Foundation of Objective-C," is a high-speed introduction to the essentials of C. It covers the parts of C that you are most likely to need when writing Objective-C programs.

- Chapter 2, "More about C Variables," continues the review of C with a discussion of the memory layout of C and Objective-C programs, and the memory location and lifetime of different types of variables. Even if you know C, you may want to read through this chapter. Many practicing C programmers are not completely familiar with the material it contains.

- Chapter 3, "An Introduction to Object-Oriented Programming," begins with an introduction to the concepts of object-oriented programming and continues with a first look at how these concepts are embodied in Objective-C.

- Chapter 4, "Your First Objective-C Program," takes you line by line through a simple Objective-C program. It also shows you how to use Xcode, Apple's integrated development environment, to create a project, and then compile and run an Objective-C program. You can then use this knowledge to do the exercises in the remainder of the book.

Part II: Language Basics

Objects are the primary entities of object-oriented programming; they group variables, called *instance variables*, and function-like blocks of code, called *methods*, into a single entity. *Classes* are the specifications for an object. A class lists the instance variables and methods that make up a given type of object and provides the code that implements those methods. An object is more tangible; it is a region of memory, similar to a C struct, that holds the variables defined by the object's class. A particular object is said to be an *instance* of the class that defines it.

- Chapter 5, "Messaging," begins the full coverage of the Objective-C language. In Objective-C, you get an object to "do something" by sending it a *message*. The message is the name of a method plus any arguments that the method takes. In response to receiving the message, the object executes the corresponding method. This chapter covers methods, messages, and how the Objective-C messaging system works.

- Chapter 6, "Classes and Objects," covers defining classes and creating and copying object instances. It also covers *inheritance*, the process of defining a class by extending an existing class, rather than starting from scratch.

  Each class used in an executing Objective-C program is represented by a piece of memory that contains information about the class. This piece of memory is called the class's *class object*. Classes can also define *class methods*, which are methods executed on behalf of the class rather than instances of the class.

- Chapter 7, "The Class Object," covers class objects and class methods. Unlike classes in some other object-oriented languages, Objective-C classes do not have class variables, variables that are shared by all instances of the class. The last sections of this chapter show you how to obtain the effect of class variables by using static variables.

- Chapter 8, "Frameworks," describes Apple's way of encapsulating dynamic link libraries. It covers the definition and structure of a framework and takes you on a brief descriptive tour of some of the common frameworks that you will encounter when writing OS X or iOS programs.

- Chapter 9, "Common Foundation Classes," covers the most commonly used Foundation classes: classes for strings, arrays, dictionaries, sets, and number objects.

- Chapter 10, "Control Structures in Objective-C," discusses some additional considerations that apply when you use Objective-C constructs with C control structures. It goes on to cover the additional control structures added by Objective-C, including Objective-C 2.0's Fast Enumeration construct. The chapter concludes with an explanation of Objective-C's exception handling system.

- Chapter 11, "Categories, Extensions, and Security," shows you how to add methods to an existing class without having to subclass it and how to hide the declarations of methods and instance variables that you consider private. The chapter ends with a discussion of Objective-C security issues.

- Chapter 12, "Properties," introduces Objective-C 2.0's *declared properties* feature. Properties are characteristics of an object. A property is usually modeled by one of the object's instance variables. Methods that set or get a property are called *accessor methods*. Using the declared properties feature, you can ask the compiler to synthesize a property's accessor methods and its instance variable for you, thereby saving yourself a considerable amount of effort.

- Chapter 13, "Protocols," covers a different way to characterize objects. A *protocol* is a defined group of methods that a class can choose to implement. In many cases what is important is not an object's class, but whether the object's class *adopts* a particular protocol by implementing the methods declared in the protocol. (More than one class can adopt a given protocol, and a class can adopt more than one protocol.) The Java concept of an interface was borrowed from Objective-C protocols.

Part III: Advanced Concepts

The chapters in this section cover memory management in detail and Objective-C blocks.

- Chapter 14, "Memory Management Overview," is a discussion of the problem of memory management and a brief introduction to the two systems of memory management that Objective-C provides.

- Chapter 15, "Reference Counting," covers Objective-C's traditional manual reference counting system. Reference counting is also called *retain counting* or *managed memory*. In a program that uses reference counting, each object keeps a count, called a *retain count*, of the number of other objects that are using it. When that count falls to zero, the object is deallocated. This chapter covers the rules needed to keep your retain counts in good order.

- Chapter 16, "ARC," covers Automatic Reference Counting (ARC). ARC is not a completely different memory management system. Rather, ARC automates Objective-C's traditional reference counting system. ARC is a compile-time process. It analyzes your Objective-C code and inserts the appropriate memory management messages for you.

- Chapter 17, "Blocks," discusses Objective-C 2.0's *blocks* feature. A block is similar to an anonymous function, but, in addition, a block carries the values of the variables in its surrounding context with it. Blocks are a central feature of Apple's Grand Central Dispatch concurrency mechanism.

- Chapter 18, "A Few More Things," covers a few minor items that did not fit elsewhere in the book.

Part IV: Appendices

- Appendix A, "Reserved Words and Compiler Directives," provides a table of names that have special meaning to the compiler, and a list of Objective-C compiler directives. Compiler directives are words that begin with an @ character; they are instructions to the compiler in various situations.

- Appendix B, "Toll-Free Bridged Classes," gives a list of Foundation classes whose instances have the same memory layout as, and may be used interchangeably with, corresponding objects from the low-level C language Core Foundation framework.

- Appendix C, "32- and 64-Bit," provides a brief discussion of 32-bit and 64-bit environments.

- Appendix D, "The Fragile Base Class Problem," describes a problem that affects some object-oriented programming languages and how Objective-C avoids that problem.

- Appendix E, "Resources for Objective-C," lists books and websites that have useful information for Objective-C developers.

We Want to Hear from You!

As a reader of this book, you are our most important critic and commentator. We value your opinion and want to know what we're doing right, what we could do better, what areas you'd like to see us publish in, and any other words of wisdom you're willing to pass our way.

You can e-mail or write me directly to let me know what you did or didn't like about this book—as well as what we can do to make our books stronger.

Please note that I cannot help you with technical problems related to the topic of this book, and that due to the high volume of mail I receive, I might not be able to reply to every message.

When you write, please be sure to include this book's title and author as well as your name and phone or e-mail address. I will carefully review your comments and share them with the author and editors who worked on the book.

E-mail: trina.macdonald@pearson.com

Mail: Trina MacDonald
          Senior Acquisitions Editor
          Addison-Wesley/Pearson Education, Inc.
          1330 6th Avenue
          New York, NY 10019

Reader Services

Visit our website and register this book at informit.com/register for convenient access to any updates, downloads, or errata that might be available for this book.

Acknowledgments

As anyone who has ever written one knows, even a single-author book is a group effort. This book is no exception. Scott D. Yelich, Andy Lee, Matt Long, Cory Bohon, and Joachim Bean read and commented on the manuscript for the first edition. Scott and Duncan Champney performed the same services for the second edition. The readers not only found mistakes but also forced me to think more carefully about some issues that I had originally glossed over. Steve Peter started me on the path to writing this book, and Daniel Steinberg helped me with an earlier incarnation of it. At Addison-Wesley, I'd like to thank Romny French, Olivia Basegio, and my editors: Chuck Toporek (first edition) and Trina MacDonald (second edition). Chuck was especially sympathetic to my frustrations and grumpiness as a (then) first-time user of MS Word.

Everyone needs a sympathetic ear when things seem not to be going well. My friends Pat O'Brien, Michael Sokoloff, and Bill Schwartz lent one, both while I was writing this book and for several decades before I began it.

Two people deserve special mention:

- Joseph E. Sacco, Ph.D., read several drafts of this book and field-tested the exercises. Joe enthusiastically found some of the darker corners of Objective-C and encouraged me to explore them. He also provided the proverbial "many valuable technical discussions," as well as many valuable non-technical discussions, during the writing of both editions of this book.

- Ekko Jennings read some of the chapters and, in addition, provided moral support and diversions, cooked dinner even when it was my turn, and just generally put up with me while I was writing. When I finished the first edition of this book I told Ekko that if I ever did anything like that again, she could hit me with a brick. To her great credit, she graciously refrained from doing so as I wrote the second edition. Thanks, Chérie.

About the Author

Robert Clair holds a B.A. in Physics from Oberlin College, and an M.A. and Ph.D. in Physics from the University of California, Berkeley. He has more than twenty years of experience in commercial software development, working mainly in CAD, modeling, graphics, and mobile applications. For the past eleven years he has worked primarily in Objective-C on the Mac and now on iOS. Among other programs, he has written ZeusDraw, a vector drawing program for Mac OS X, and ZeusDraw Mobile, a drawing and painting program for iOS. Robert has been the lead programmer on several large commercial iOS apps, including The Street's iPad app. He has also made additions to, and performed surgery and repair work on, various other iOS apps. Robert lives in New York City, where he is the principal of Chromatic Bytes, LLC, an independent consulting and software development company.

Part I

Introduction to Objective-C

Part I of this book is an introduction to Objective-C 2.0. Objective-C is an extension of the C language, so Part I begins with two chapters that provide a review of C. The C review is followed by an introduction to the concepts of object-oriented programming and how those concepts are implemented in Objective-C. The final chapter in this part takes you on a line-by-line tour of a simple Objective-C program.

The chapters in Part I are

- Chapter 1, "C, the Foundation of Objective-C"
- Chapter 2, "More about C Variables"
- Chapter 3, "An Introduction to Object-Oriented Programming"
- Chapter 4, "Your First Objective-C Program"

1

C, the Foundation of Objective-C

Objective-C is an extension of C. Most of this book concentrates on what Objective-C adds to C. But in order to program in Objective-C, you have to know the basics of C. When you do such mundane things as add two numbers together, put a comment in your code, or use an `if` statement, you do them the identical way in both C and Objective-C. The non-object part of Objective-C isn't *similar to C*, or *C-like*, it *is* C. Objective-C 2.0 is currently based on the C99 standard for C.

This chapter begins a two-chapter review of C. The review isn't a complete description of C; it covers only the basic parts of the language. Topics such as bit operators, the details of type conversion, Unicode characters, macros with arguments, and other arcana are not mentioned. It is intended as an aide-mémoire for those whose knowledge of C is rusty, or as a quick reference for those who are adept at picking up a new language from context. The following chapter continues the review of C and treats the topics of declaring variables, variable scope, and where in memory C puts variables. If you are an expert C/C++ programmer, you can probably skip this chapter. (However, a review never hurts. I learned some things in the course of writing the chapter.) If you are coming to Objective-C from a different C-like language, such as Java or C#, you should probably at least skim the material. If your only programming experience is with a scripting language, or if you are a complete beginner, you will probably find it helpful to read a book on C in parallel with this book.

Note
I recommend that everyone read Chapter 2, "More about C Variables." In my experience, many who should be familiar with the material it contains are not familiar with that material.

There are many books on C. The original Kernighan and Ritchie book, *The C Programming Language*, is still one of the best.[1] It is the book many people use to learn C. For a language lawyer's view of C, or to explore some of the darker corners of the language, consult *C: A Reference Manual* by Harbison and Steele.[2]

Think for a moment about how you might go about learning a new natural language. The first thing to do is look at how the language is written: Which alphabet does it use? (If it uses an alphabet at all; some languages use pictographs.) Does it read left to right, right to left, or top to bottom? Then you start learning some words. You need at least a small vocabulary to get started. As you build your vocabulary, you can start making the words into phrases, and then start combining your phrases into complete sentences. Finally, you can combine your sentences into complete paragraphs.

This review of C follows roughly the same progression. The first section looks at the structure of a C program, how C code is formatted, and the rules and conventions for naming various entities. The subsequent sections cover variables and operators, which are roughly analogous to nouns and verbs in a natural language, and how they are combined into longer expressions and statements. The last major section covers control statements. Control statements allow a program to do more interesting things than execute statements in a linear sequence. The final section of the review covers the C preprocessor, which allows you to do some programmatic editing of source files before they are sent to the compiler, and the `printf` function, which is used for character output.

The Structure of a C Program

This chapter begins by looking at some structural aspects of a C program: the `main` routine, formatting issues, comments, names and naming conventions, and file types.

`main` Routine

All C programs have a `main` routine. After the OS loads a C program, the program begins executing with the first line of code in the `main` routine. The standard form of the `main` routine is as follows:

```
int main(int argc, const char *argv[])
{
  // The code that does the work goes here
  return 0;
}
```

1. Brian W. Kernighan and Dennis M. Ritchie, *The C Programming Language,* Second Edition (Englewood Cliffs, NJ: Prentice Hall, 1988).

2. Samuel P. Harbison and Guy L. Steele, *C: A Reference Manual,* Fifth Edition (Upper Saddle River, NJ: Prentice Hall, 2002).

The key features are:

- The leading `int` on the first line indicates that `main` returns an integer value to the OS as a return code.
- The name `main` is required.
- The rest of the first line refers to command line arguments passed to the program from the OS. `main` receives `argc` number of arguments, stored as strings in the array `argv`. This part isn't important for the moment; just ignore it.
- All the executable code goes between a pair of curly brackets.
- The `return 0;` line indicates that a zero is passed back to the OS as a return code. In Unix systems (including Mac OS X and iOS), a return code of zero indicates "no error" and any other value means an error of some sort.

If you are not interested in processing command line arguments or returning an error code to the OS (for example, when doing the exercises in the next several chapters), you can use a simplified form of `main`:

```
int main( void )
{

}
```

The `void` indicates that this version of `main` takes no arguments. In the absence of an explicit `return` statement, a return value of zero is implied.

Formatting

Statements are terminated by a semicolon. A whitespace character (blank, tab, or newline) is required to separate names and keywords. C ignores any additional whitespace: Indenting and extra spaces have no effect on the compiled executable; they may be used freely to make your code more readable. A statement can extend over multiple lines; the following three statements are equivalent:

```
distance = rate*time;

    distance    =    rate  *  time;

distance =
    rate *
        time;
```

Comments

Comments are notations for the programmer's edification. The compiler ignores them.

C supports two styles of comments:

- Anything following two forward slashes (//) and before the end of the line is a comment. For example:

```
// This is a comment.
```

- Anything enclosed between /* and */ is also a comment:

```
/* This is the other style of comment */
```

The second type of comment may extend over multiple lines. For example:

```
/* This is
        a longer
            comment. */
```

It can be used to temporarily "comment out" blocks of code during the development process.

This style of comment cannot be nested:

```
/*  /* WRONG - won't compile */ */
```

However, the following is legal:

```
/*
    // OK - You can nest the two slash style of comment
*/
```

Variable and Function Names

Variable and function names in C consist of letters, numbers, and the underscore character (_):

- The first character must be an underscore or a letter.
- Names are case sensitive: `bandersnatch` and `Bandersnatch` are different names.
- There cannot be any whitespace in the middle of a name.

Here are some legal names:

```
j
taxesForYear2012
bananas_per_bunch
bananasPerBunch
```

These names are not legal:

```
2012YearTaxes
rock&roll
bananas per bunch
```

Naming Conventions

As a kindness to yourself and anyone else who might have to read your code, you should use descriptive names for variables and functions. `bpb` is easy to type, but it might leave you pondering when you return to it a year later; whereas `bananas_per_bunch` is self-explanatory.

Many plain C programs use the convention of separating the words in long variable and function names with underscores:

`apples_per_basket`

Objective-C programmers usually use *CamelCase* names for variables. CamelCase names use capital letters to mark the beginnings of subsequent words in a name:

`applesPerBasket`

Names beginning with an underscore are traditionally used for variables and functions that are meant to be private, or for internal use:

`_privateVariable`
`_leaveMeAlone`

However, this is a convention; C has no enforcement mechanism to keep variables or functions private.

Files

The code for a plain C program is placed in one or more files that have a *.c* filename extension:

`ACProgram.c`

> **Note**
>
> Mac OS X filenames are not case sensitive. The filesystem will remember the case you used to name a file, but it treats *myfile.c*, *MYFILE.c*, and *MyFile.c* as the same filename. However, filenames on iOS *are* case sensitive.

Code that uses the Objective-C objects (the material covered starting in Chapter 3, "An Introduction to Object-Oriented Programming") is placed in one or more files that have a *.m* filename extension:

`AnObjectiveCProgram.m`

> **Note**
>
> Because C is a proper subset of Objective-C, it's OK to put a plain C program in a *.m* file.

There are some naming conventions for files that define and implement Objective-C classes (discussed in Chapter 3), but C does not have any formal rules for the part of the name preceding the filename extension. It is silly, but not illegal, to name the file containing the code for an accounting program

`MyFlightToRio.m`

C programs also use *header files*. Header files usually contain various definitions that are shared by many *.c* and *.m* files. Their contents are merged into other files by using an **#include** or **#import** preprocessor directive. (See *Preprocessor* later in this chapter.) Header files have a *.h* filename extension as shown here:

`AHeaderFile.h`

> **Note**
>
> It is possible to mix Objective-C and C++ code in the same program. The result is called Objective-C++. Objective-C++ code must be placed in a file with a *.mm* filename extension:
>
> `AnObjectiveCPlusPlusProgram.mm`
>
> The topic is beyond the scope of this book.

Variables

A variable is a name for some bytes of memory in a program. When you assign a value to a variable, what you are really doing is storing that value in those bytes. Variables in a computer language are like the nouns in a natural language. They represent items or quantities in the problem space of your program.

C requires that you tell the compiler about any variables that you are going to use by declaring them. A variable declaration has the form

`variabletype name;`

C allows multiple variables to be declared in a single declaration:

`variabletype name1, name2, name3;`

A variable declaration causes the compiler to reserve storage (memory) for that variable. The value of a variable is the contents of its memory location. The next chapter describes variable declarations in more detail. It covers where variable declarations are placed, where the variables are created in memory, and the lifetimes of different classes of variables.

Integer Types

C provides the following types to hold integers: **char**, **short**, **int**, **long**, and **long long**. Table 1.1 shows the size in bytes of the integer types on 32- and 64-bit executables on Apple systems.

The **char** type is named *char* because it was originally intended to hold characters, but it is frequently used as an 8-bit integer type.

Table 1.1   **The Sizes of Integer Types on iOS and Mac OS X**

Type	32-Bit	64-Bit
char	1 byte	1 byte
short	2 bytes	2 bytes
int	4 bytes	4 bytes
long	4 bytes	8 bytes
long long	8 bytes	8 bytes

Note

iOS executables are 32-bit. Mac OS X executables can be either 32-bit or 64-bit with 64-bit as the default. 32-bit and 64-bit executables are discussed in Appendix C, "32- and 64-Bit."

An integer type can be declared to be `unsigned`:

```
unsigned char a;
unsigned short b;
unsigned int c;
unsigned long d;
unsigned long long e;
```

When used alone, `unsigned` is taken to mean `unsigned int`:

```
unsigned a;  // a is an unsigned int
```

An `unsigned` variable's bit pattern is always interpreted as a positive number. If you assign a negative quantity to an `unsigned` variable, the result is a very large positive number. This is almost always a mistake.

Floating-Point Types

C's floating-point types are `float`, `double`, and `long double`. The sizes of the floating-point types are the same in both 32- and 64-bit executables:

```
float aFloat;   // floats are 4 bytes
double aDouble; // doubles are 8 bytes
long double aLongDouble;  // long doubles are 16 bytes
```

Floating-point values are always signed.

Truth Values

Ordinary expressions are commonly used for truth values. Expressions that evaluate to zero are considered false, and expressions that evaluate to non–zero are considered true (see the following sidebar).

___

_Bool, bool, and BOOL

Early versions of C did not have a defined Boolean type. Ordinary expressions were (and still are) used for Boolean values (truth values). As noted in the text, an expression that evaluates to zero is considered false and one that evaluates to non-zero is considered true. A majority of C code is still written this way.

C99, the current standard for C, introduced a _Bool type. _Bool is an integer type with only two allowed values, 0 and 1. Assigning any non-zero value to a _Bool results in 1:

```
_Bool  b = 35;    // b is now 1
```

If you include the file *stdbool.h* in your source code files, you can use bool as an alias for _Bool and the Boolean constants true and false (true and false are just defined as 1 and 0, respectively):

```
#include <stdbool.h>
bool b = true;
```

You will rarely see either _Bool or bool in Objective-C code, because Objective-C defines its own Boolean type, BOOL. BOOL is covered in Chapter 3, "An Introduction to Object-Oriented Programming."

___

Initialization

Variables can be initialized when they are declared:

```
int a = 9;

int b = 2*4;

float c = 3.14159;

char d = 'a';
```

A character enclosed in single quote marks is a character constant. It is numerically equal to the encoding value of the character. Here, the variable **d** has the numeric value of 97, which is the ASCII value of the character **a**.

Pointers

A pointer is a variable whose value is a memory address. It "points" to a location in memory.

You declare a variable to be a pointer by preceding the variable name with an * in the declaration. The following code declares **pointerVar** to be a variable pointing to a location in memory that holds an integer:

```
int *pointerVar;
```

The unary & operator ("address–of" operator) is used to get the address of a variable so it can be stored in a pointer variable. The following code sets the value of the pointer variable **b** to be the address of the integer variable **a**:

```
1  int a = 9;
2
3  int *b;
4
5  b = &a;
```

Now let's take a look at that example line by line:

- Line 1 declares a to be an int variable. The compiler reserves 4 bytes of storage for a and initializes them with a value of 9.
- Line 3 declares b to be a pointer to an int.
- Line 5 uses the & operator to get the address of a and then assigns a's address as the value of b.

Figure 1.1 illustrates the process. (Assume that the compiler has located a beginning at memory address 1048880.) The arrow in the figure shows the concept of pointing.

The unary * operator (called the "contents of" or "dereferencing" operator) is used to set or retrieve the contents of a memory location by using a pointer variable that points to that location. One way to think of this is to consider the expression *pointerVar to be an alias, another name, for whatever memory location is stored in the contents of pointerVar. The expression *pointerVar can be used to either set or retrieve the contents of that memory location. In the following code, b is set to the address of a, so *b becomes an alias for a:

```
int a;
int c;
int *b;
a = 9;
b = &a;
c = *b;  // c is now 9
*b = 10; // a is now 10
```

Pointers are used in C to reference dynamically allocated memory (see Chapter 2, "More about C Variables"). Pointers are also used to avoid copying large chunks of

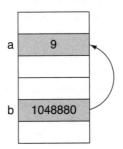

Figure 1.1   Pointer variables

memory, such as arrays and structures (discussed later in this chapter), from one part of a program to another. For example, instead of passing a large structure to a function, you pass the function a pointer to the structure. The function then uses the pointer to access the structure. As you will see later in the book, Objective-C objects are always referenced by pointer.

Generic Pointers

A variable declared as a pointer to **void** is a generic pointer:

```
void *genericPointer;
```

A generic pointer may be set to the address of any variable type:

```
int a = 9;
void *genericPointer;
genericPointer = &a;
```

However, trying to obtain a value from a generic pointer is an error because the compiler has no way of knowing how to interpret the bytes at the address indicated by the generic pointer:

```
int a = 9;
int b;
void *genericPointer;
genericPointer = &a;
b = *genericPointer;  // WRONG - won't compile
```

To obtain a value through a **void*** pointer, you must *cast* it to a pointer to a known type:

```
int a = 9;
int b;
void *genericPointer;
genericPointer = &a;
b = *((int*) genericPointer) ;  // OK - b is now 9
```

The cast operator **(int*)** forces the compiler to consider **genericPointer** to be a pointer to an integer. (See *Conversion and Casting* later in the chapter.)

C does not check to see that a pointer variable points to a valid area of memory. Incorrect use of pointers has probably caused more crashes than any other aspect of C programming.

Arrays

A C array is an ordered collection of elements of the same type. C arrays are declared by adding the number of elements in the array, enclosed in square brackets ([ ]), to the declaration, after the type and array name:

```
int a[100];
```

Individual elements of the array are accessed by placing the index of the element in `[]` after the array name:

```
a[6] = 9;
```

The index is zero-based. In the previous example, the legitimate indices run from 0 to 99. Access to C arrays is not bounds checked on either end. C will blithely let you do the following:

```
int a[100];
a[200] = 25;
a[-100] = 30;
```

Using an index outside of the array's bounds lets you trash memory belonging to other variables, resulting in either crashes or corrupted data. Taking advantage of this lack of checking is one of the pillars of mischievous malware.

The bracket notation is just a nicer syntax for pointer arithmetic. The name of an array, without the array brackets, is a pointer variable pointing to the beginning of the array. These two lines are completely equivalent:

```
a[6] = 9;
```

```
*(a + 6) = 9;
```

When compiling an expression using pointer arithmetic, the compiler takes into account the size of the type the pointer is pointing to. If `a` is an array of `int`, the expression `*(a + 2)` refers to the contents of the 4 bytes (one `int` worth) of memory at an address 8 bytes (two `int`) beyond the beginning of the array `a`. However, if `a` is an array of `char`, the expression `*(a + 2)` refers to the contents of 1 byte (one `char` worth) of memory at an address 2 bytes (two `char`) beyond the beginning of the array `a`.

Multidimensional Arrays

Multidimensional arrays are declared as follows:

```
int b[4][10];
```

Multidimensional arrays are stored linearly in memory by rows. Here, `b[0][0]` is the first element, `b[0][1]` is the second element, and `b[1][0]` is the eleventh element.

Using pointer notation:

```
b[i][j]
```

may be written as

```
*(b + i*10 + j)
```

Strings

A C string is a one-dimensional array of bytes (type `char`) terminated by a zero byte. A constant C string is coded by placing the characters of the string between double quote marks (""):

```
"A constant string"
```

When the compiler creates a constant string in memory, it automatically adds the zero byte at the end. But if you declare an array of `char` that will be used to hold a string, you must remember to include the zero byte when deciding how much space you need. The following line of code copies the five characters of the constant string `"Hello"` and its terminating zero byte to the array `aString`:

```
char aString[6] = "Hello";
```

As with any other array, arrays representing strings are not bounds checked. Over-running string buffers used for program input is a favorite trick of hackers.

A variable of type `char*` can be initialized to point to a constant string. You can set such a variable to point at a different string, but you can't use it to modify a constant string:

```
char *aString = "Hello";
aString = "World";
aString[4] = 'q';  // WRONG - causes a crash, "World" is a constant
```

The first line points `aString` at the constant string `"Hello"`. The second line changes `aString` to point at the constant string `"World"`. The third line causes a crash, because constant strings are stored in a region of protected, read-only memory.

Structures

A structure is a collection of related variables that can be referred to as a single entity. The following is an example of a structure declaration:

```
struct dailyTemperatures
  {
    float high;
    float low;
    int   year;
    int   dayOfYear;
};
```

The individual variables in a structure are called *member variables* or just *members* for short. The name following the keyword `struct` is a *structure tag*. A structure tag identifies the structure. It can be used to declare variables typed to the structure:

```
struct dailyTemperatures today;

struct dailyTemperatures *todayPtr;
```

In the preceding example, **today** is a **dailyTemperatures** structure, whereas **todayPtr** is a pointer to a **dailyTemperatures** structure.

The dot operator (**.**) is used to access individual members of a structure from a structure variable. The pointer operator (**->**) is used to access structure members from a variable that is a pointer to a structure:

```
todayPtr = &today;

today.high = 68.0;

todayPtr->high = 68.0;
```

The last two statements do the same thing.

Structures can have other structures as members. The previous example could have been written like this:

```
struct hiLow
{
    float high;
    float low;
};

struct dailyTemperatures
{
    struct hiLow tempExtremes;
    int    year;
    int    dayOfYear;
};
```

Setting the high temperature for **today** would then look like this:

```
struct dailyTemperatures today;
today.tempExtremes.high = 68.0;
```

> **Note**
>
> The compiler is free to insert padding into a structure to force structure members to be aligned on a particular boundary in memory. You shouldn't try to access structure members by calculating their offset from the beginning of the structure or do anything else that depends on the structure's binary layout.

typedef

The **typedef** declaration provides a means for creating aliases for variable types:

```
typedef float Temperature;
```

Temperature can now be used to declare variables, just as if it were one of the built-in types:

```
Temperature high, low;
```

`typedef`s just provide alternate names for variable types. Here, `high` and `low` are still floats. The term *typedef* is often used as a verb when talking about C code, as in "Temperature is typedef'd to float."

Enumeration Constants

An `enum` statement lets you define a set of integer constants:

```
enum woodwind { oboe, flute, clarinet, bassoon };
```

The result of the previous statement is that `oboe`, `flute`, `clarinet`, and `bassoon` are constants with values of 0, 1, 2, and 3, respectively.

If you don't like going in order from zero, you can assign the values of the constant yourself. Any constant without an assignment has a value one higher than the previous constant:

```
enum woodwind { oboe=100, flute=150, clarinet, bassoon=200 };
```

The preceding statement makes `oboe`, `flute`, `clarinet`, and `bassoon` equal to 100, 150, 151, and 200, respectively.

The name after the keyword `enum` is called an *enumeration tag*. Enumeration tags are optional. Enumeration tags can be used to declare variables:

```
enum woodwind soloist;
soloist = oboe;
```

Enumerations are useful for defining multiple constants, and for helping to make your code self-documenting, but they aren't distinct types and they don't receive much support from the compiler. The declaration `enum woodwind soloist;` shows your intent that `soloist` should be restricted to one of `oboe`, `flute`, `clarinet`, or `bassoon`, but unfortunately, the compiler does nothing to enforce the restriction. The compiler considers `soloist` to be an `int`, and it lets you assign any integer value to `soloist` without generating a warning:

```
enum woodwind { oboe, flute, clarinet, bassoon };
enum woodwind soloist;
soloist = 5280;  // No complaint from the compiler!
```

> **Note**
> You can't have a variable and an enumeration constant with the same name.

Operators

Operators are like verbs. They cause things to happen to your variables.

Arithmetic Operators

C has the usual binary operators +, −, *, and / for addition, subtraction, multiplication, and division, respectively.

> **Note**
>
> If both operands to the division operator (/) are integer types, C does integer division. Integer division truncates the result of doing the division. The value of 7/2 is 3.
>
> If at least one of the operands is a floating-point type, C promotes any integers in the division expression to float and performs floating-point division. The values of 7.0/2, 7/2.0, and 7.0/2.0 are all 3.5.

Remainder Operator

The remainder or *modulus* operator (%) calculates the remainder from an integer division. The result of the following expression is 1:

```
int a = 7;
int b = 3;
int c = a%b;   // c is now 1
```

Both operands of the remainder operator must be integer types.

Increment and Decrement Operators

C provides operators for incrementing and decrementing variables:

```
a++;
```

```
++a;
```

Both lines add 1 to the value of **a**. However, there is a difference between the two expressions when they are used as a part of a larger expression. The prefix version, **++a**, increments the value of **a** *before* any other evaluation takes place. It is the incremented value that is used in the rest of the expression. The postfix version, **a++**, increments the value of **a** after other evaluations take place. The original value is used in the rest of the expression. This is illustrated by the following example:

```
int a = 9;
int b;
b = a++; // postfix increment
```

```
int c = 9;
int d;
d = ++c; // prefix increment
```

The postfix version of the operator increments the variable after its initial value has been used in the rest of the expression. After the code has executed in this example, the value of **b** is 9 and the value of **a** is 10. The prefix version of the operator increments the variable's value before it is used in the rest of the expression. In the example, the value of both **c** and **d** is 10.

The decrement operators **a--** and **--a** behave in a similar manner.

Code that depends on the difference between the prefix and postfix versions of the operator is likely to be confusing to anyone but its creator.

Precedence

Is the following expression equal to 18 or 22?

```
2 * 7 + 4
```

The answer seems ambiguous because it depends on whether you do the addition first or the multiplication first. C resolves the ambiguity by making a rule that it does multiplication and division before it does addition and subtraction; so the value of the expression is 18. The technical way of saying this is that multiplication and division have higher *precedence* than addition and subtraction.

If you need to do the addition first, you can specify that by using parentheses:

```
2 * (7 + 4)
```

The compiler will respect your request and arrange to do the addition before the multiplication.

> **Note**
> C defines a complicated table of precedence for all its operators (see http://en.wikipedia.org/wiki/Order_of_operations). But specifying the exact order of evaluation that you want by using parentheses is much easier than trying to remember operator precedences.

Negation

The unary minus sign (–) changes an arithmetic value to its negative:

```
int a = 9;
int b;
b  = -a;  // b is now -9
```

Comparisons

C also provides operators for comparisons. The value of a comparison is a truth value. The following expressions evaluate to 1 if they are true and 0 if they are false:

```
a > b // true, if a is greater than b
```

```
a < b // true, if a is less than b
```

```
a >= b // true, if a is greater than or equal to b
```

```
a <= b // true, if a is less than or equal to b
```

```
a == b // true, if a is equal to b
```

```
a != b // true, if a is not equal to b
```

> **Note**
>
> As with any computer language, testing for floating-point equality is risky because of rounding errors, and such a comparison is likely to give an incorrect result.

Logical Operators

The logical operators for AND and OR have the following form:

```
expression1 && expression2  // Logical AND operator

expression1 || expression2  // Logical OR operator
```

C uses *short circuit evaluation*. Expressions are evaluated from left to right, and evaluation stops as soon as the truth value for the entire expression can be deduced. If *expression1* in an AND expression evaluates to false, the value of the entire expression is false and *expression2* is not evaluated. Similarly, if *expression1* in an OR expression evaluates to true, the entire expression is true and *expression2* is not evaluated. Short circuit evaluation has interesting consequences if the second expression has any side effects. In the following example, if **b** is greater than or equal to **a**, the function `CheckSomething()` is not called (`if` statements are covered later in this chapter):

```
if ( b < a && CheckSomething() )
  {
    ...
  }
```

Logical Negation

The unary exclamation point (`!`) is the logical negation operator. After the following line of code is executed, **a** has the value `0` if *expression* is true (non-zero), and the value `1` if *expression* is false (zero):

```
a = ! expression;
```

Assignment Operators

C provides the basic assignment operator:

```
a = b;
```

a is assigned the value of **b**. Of course, **a** must be something that is capable of being assigned to. Entities that you can assign to are called *lvalues* (because they can appear on the *left* side of the assignment operators). Here are some examples of lvalues:

```
/* set up */
float a;
float b[100]
float *c;
struct dailyTemperatures today;
struct dailyTemperatures *todayPtr;
c = &a;
```

```
todayPtr = &today;

/* legal lvalues */
a = 76;
b[0] = 76;
*c = 76;
today.high = 76;
todayPtr->high = 76;
```

Some things are not *lvalues*. You can't assign to an array name, the return value of a function, or any expression that does not refer to a memory location:

```
float a[100];
int x;

a = 76; // WRONG
x*x = 76; // WRONG
GetTodaysHigh() = 76; // WRONG
```

Conversion and Casting

If the two sides of an assignment are of different variable types, the type of the right side is converted to the type of the left side. Conversions from shorter types to longer types don't present a problem. Going the other way, from a longer type to a shorter type, or converting between a floating-point type and an integer type, requires care. Such a conversion can cause loss of significant figures, truncation, or complete nonsense. For example:

```
int a = 14;
float b;
b = a;  // OK, b is now 14.0
        // A float can hold approximately 7 significant figures

float c = 12.5;
int d;
d = c;  // Truncation, d is now 12

char e = 99;
int f;
f = e;  // OK, f is now 99

int g = 333;
char h;
h = g;  // Nonsense, h is now 77
        // The largest number a signed char can hold is 127

int h = 123456789;
float i = h;  // loss of precision
              // A float cannot keep 9 significant figures
```

You can force the compiler to convert the value of a variable to a different type by using a *cast*. In the last line of the following example, the **(float)** casts force the compiler to convert **a** and **b** to **float** and do a floating-point division:

```
int a = 6;
int b = 4;
float c, d;

c = a / b;  // c is equal to 1.0 because integer division truncates

d = (float)a / (float)b; // Floating-point division, d is equal to 1.5
```

You can cast pointers from pointer to one type to pointer to another. Casting pointers can be a risky operation with the potential to trash your memory, but it is the only way to dereference a pointer passed to you typed as **void***. Successfully casting a pointer requires that you understand what type of entity the pointer is "really" pointing to.

Other Assignment Operators

C also has shorthand operators that combine arithmetic and assignment:

```
a += b;
```

```
a -= b;
```

```
a *= b;
```

```
a /= b;
```

These are equivalent to the following, respectively:

```
a = a + b;
```

```
a = a - b;
```

```
a = a * b;
```

```
a = a / b;
```

Expressions and Statements

Expressions and statements in C are the rough equivalent of phrases and sentences in a natural language.

Expressions

The simplest expressions are just single constants or variables:

```
14
bananasPerBunch
```

Every expression has a *value*. The value of an expression that is a constant is just the constant itself: The value of 14 is 14. The value of a variable expression is whatever value the variable is holding: The value of **bananasPerBunch** is whatever value it was given when it was last set by initialization or assignment.

Expressions can be combined to create other expressions. The following are also expressions:

```
j + 14
a < b
distance = rate * time
```

The value of an arithmetic or logical expression is just whatever you would get by doing the arithmetic or logic. The value of an assignment expression is the value given to the variable that is the target of the assignment.

Function calls are also expressions:

```
SomeFunction()
```

The value of a function call expression is the return value of the function.

Evaluating Expressions

When the compiler encounters an expression, it creates binary code to evaluate the expression and find its value. For primitive expressions, there is nothing to do: Their values are just what they are. For more complicated expressions, the compiler generates binary code that performs the specified arithmetic, logic, function calls, and assignments.

Evaluating an expression can cause *side effects*. The most common side effects are the change in the value of a variable due to an assignment, or the execution of the code in a function due to a function call.

Expressions are used for their value in various control constructs to determine the flow of a program (see *Program Flow*). In other situations, expressions may be evaluated only for the side effects caused by evaluating them. Typically, the point of an assignment expression is that the assignment takes place. In a few situations, both the value and the side effect are important.

Statements

When you add a semicolon (;) to the end of an expression, it becomes a *statement*. This is similar to adding a period to a phrase to make a sentence in a natural language. A statement is the code equivalent of a complete thought. A statement is finished executing when all of the machine language instructions that result from the compilation of the statement have been executed, and all of the changes to any memory locations the statement affects have been completed.

Compound Statements

You can use a sequence of statements, enclosed by a pair of curly brackets, any place where you can use a single statement:

```
{
  timeDelta = time2 — time1;
  distanceDelta = distance2 — distance1;
  averageSpeed = distanceDelta / timeDelta;
}
```

There is no semicolon after the closing bracket. A group like this is called a *compound statement* or a *block*. Compound statements are very commonly used with the control statements covered in the next sections of the chapter.

Note

The use of the word *block* as a synonym for *compound statement* is pervasive in the C literature and dates back to the beginnings of C. Unfortunately, Apple has adopted the name *block* for its addition of closures to C (see Chapter 17, "Blocks"). To avoid confusion, the rest of this book uses the slightly more awkward name *compound statement*.

Program Flow

The statements in a program are executed in sequence, except when directed to do otherwise by a **for**, **while**, **do-while**, **if**, **switch**, or **goto** statement or a function call.

- An **if** statement conditionally executes code depending on the truth value of an expression.
- The **for**, **while**, and **do-while** statements are used to form loops. In a loop, the same statement or group of statements is executed repeatedly until a condition is met.
- A **switch** statement chooses a set of statements to execute based on the arithmetic value of an integer expression.
- A **goto** statement is an unconditional jump to a labeled statement.
- A function call is a jump to the code in the function's body. When the function returns, the program executes from the point after the function call.

These control statements are covered in more detail in the following sections.

Note

As you read the next sections, remember that every place it says *statement*, you can use a compound statement.

if

An `if` statement conditionally executes code depending on the truth value of an expression. It has the following form:

```
if ( expression )

    statement
```

If *expression* evaluates to true (non-zero), *statement* is executed; otherwise, execution continues with the next statement after the `if` statement. An `if` statement may be extended by adding an **else** section:

```
if ( expression )

    statement1

else

    statement2
```

If *expression* evaluates to true (non-zero), *statement1* is executed; otherwise, *statement2* is executed.

An `if` statement may also be extended by adding **else if** sections, as shown here:

```
if ( expression1 )

    statement1

else if ( expression2 )

    statement2

else if ( expression3 )

    statement3

...

else

    statementN
```

The expressions are evaluated in sequence. When an expression evaluates to non-zero, the corresponding statement is executed and execution continues with the next statement following the `if` statement. If the expressions are all false, the statement following the **else** clause is executed. (As with a simple `if` statement, the **else** clause is optional and may be omitted.)

Conditional Expression

A conditional expression is made up of three sub-expressions and has the following form:

```
expression1 ? expression2 : expression3
```

When a conditional expression is evaluated, *expression1* is evaluated for its truth value. If it is true, *expression2* is evaluated and the value of the entire expression is the value of *expression2*. *expression3* is not evaluated.

If *expression1* evaluates to false, *expression3* is evaluated and the value of the conditional expression is the value of *expression3*. *expression2* is not evaluated.

A conditional expression is often used as shorthand for a simple **if** statement. For example:

```
a = ( b > 0 ) ? c : d;
```

is equivalent to

```
if ( b > 0 )

  a = c;

else

  a = d;
```

while

The **while** statement is used to form loops as follows:

```
while ( expression ) statement
```

When the **while** statement is executed, *expression* is evaluated. If it evaluates to true, *statement* is executed and the condition is evaluated again. This sequence is repeated until *expression* evaluates to false, at which point execution continues with the next statement after the **while**.

You will occasionally see this construction:

```
while (1)
  {
    ...
  }
```

Since the constant 1 evaluates to true, the preceding is an infinite loop from the **while**'s point of view. Presumably, something in the body of the loop checks for a condition and breaks out of the loop when that condition is met.

do-while

The **do-while** statement is similar to the **while**, with the difference that the test comes after the statement rather than before:

```
do statement while ( expression );
```

One consequence of this is that *statement* is always executed once, independent of the value of *expression*. Situations where the program logic dictates that a loop body be executed at least once, even if the condition is false, are uncommon. As a consequence, **do-while** statements are rarely encountered in practice.

for

The **for** statement is the most general looping construct. It has the following form:

```
for (expression1; expression2; expression3) statement
```

When a **for** statement is executed, the following sequence occurs:

1. *expression1* is evaluated once before the loop begins.
2. *expression2* is evaluated for its truth value.
3. If *expression2* is true, *statement* is executed; otherwise, the loop ends and execution continues with the next statement after the loop.
4. *expression3* is evaluated.
5. Steps 2, 3, and 4 are repeated until *expression2* becomes false.

expression1 and *expression3* are evaluated only for their side effects. Their values are discarded. They are typically used to initialize and increment a loop counter variable:

```
int j;

for (j=0; j < 10; j++)
  {
    // Something that needs doing 10 times
  }
```

> **Note**
>
> You can also declare the loop variable inside a **for** statement:
>
> ```
> for ( int j=0; j < 10; j++ )
>   {
>   }
> ```
>
> When you declare the loop variable inside a **for** statement, it is valid only inside the loop. It is undefined once the loop exits. If you are breaking out of a loop on some condition (see the next section) and you want to examine the loop variable to see what its value was when the condition was met, you must declare the loop variable outside the **for** statement as shown in the earlier example.

Any of the expressions may be omitted (the semicolons must remain). If *expression2* is omitted, the loop is an infinite loop, similar to `while( 1 )`:

```
int i;

for (i=0; ; i++)
  {
    ...
    // Check something and exit if the condition is met
  }
```

> **Note**
>
> When you use a loop to iterate over the elements of an array, remember that array indices go from zero to one less than the number of elements in the array:
>
> ```
> int j;
> int a[25];
>
> for (j=0; j < 25; j++)
>   {
>     // Do something with a[j]
>   }
> ```
>
> Writing the **for** statement in the preceding example as
>
> ```
> for (j=1; j <= 25; j++)
> ```
>
> is a common mistake.

break

The **break** statement is used to break out of a loop or a **switch** statement:

```
int j;

for (j=0;  j < 100; j++)
  {
    ...

    if ( someConditionMet ) break; //Execution continues after the loop
  }
```

Execution continues with the next statement after the enclosing **while**, **do**, **for**, or **switch** statement. When used inside nested loops, **break** only breaks out of the innermost loop. Coding a **break** statement that is not enclosed by a loop or a switch causes a compiler error:

```
error: break statement not within loop or switch
```

continue

`continue` is used inside a `while`, `do-while`, or `for` loop to abandon execution of the current loop iteration. For example:

```
int j;

for (j=0;  j < 100; j++)
 {

    ...

    if ( doneWithIteration ) continue; // Skip to the next iteration
    ...
}
```

When the `continue` statement is executed, control passes to the next iteration of the loop. In a `while` or `do-while` loop, the control expression is evaluated for the next iteration. In a `for` loop, the iteration (third) expression is evaluated and then the control (second) expression is evaluated. Coding a `continue` statement that is not enclosed by a loop causes a compiler error.

Comma Expression

A comma expression consists of two or more expressions separated by commas:

```
expression1, expression2, ..., expressionN
```

The expressions are evaluated in order from left to right, and the value of the entire expression is the value of the right-most sub-expression.

The principal use of the comma operator is to initialize and update multiple loop variables in a `for` statement. As the loop in the following example iterates, `j` goes from 0 to `MAX-1` and `k` goes from `MAX-1` to 0:

```
int j, k;

for (j=0, k=MAX-1; j < MAX; j++, k--)
  {
    // Do something
  }
```

When a comma expression is used like this in a `for` loop, only the side effects of evaluating the sub-expressions are important. The value of the comma expression is discarded. In the preceding example a comma expression is also used to increment `j` and decrement `k` after each pass through a `for` loop.

switch

A `switch` branches to different statements based on the value of an integer expression. The form of a `switch` statement is shown here:

```
switch ( integer_expression )
  {
     case value1:
        statement
        break;

     case value2:
        statement
        break;

     ...

     default:
        statement
        break;
  }
```

In a slight inconsistency with the rest of C, each case may have multiple statements without the requirement of a compound statement.

`value1`, `value2`, `...` must be either integers, character constants, or constant expressions that evaluate to an integer. (In other words, they must be reducible to an integer at compile time.) Duplicate cases with the same integer are not allowed.

When a `switch` statement is executed, `integer_expression` is evaluated and the switch compares the result with the integer case labels. If a match is found, execution jumps to the statement after the matching case label. Execution continues in sequence until either a `break` statement or the end of the switch is encountered. A `break` causes the execution to jump out to the first statement following the switch.

A `break` statement is not required after a case. If it is omitted, execution falls through to the following case. If you see the `break` omitted in existing code, it can be either a mistake (it is an easy one to make) or intentional (if the coder wanted a case and the following case to execute the same code).

If `integer_expression` doesn't match any of the case labels, execution jumps to the statement following the optional `default:` label, if one is present. If there is no match and no `default:`, the `switch` does nothing, and execution continues with the first statement after the switch.

Note

If you use an `enum` variable as the argument for a `switch` statement, do not supply a case for each value of the `enum`, and do not supply a `default:` case, some compilers will complain with a warning. The Clang (LLVM) compiler currently used by Apple is among those that complain.

goto

C provides a `goto` statement:

```
goto label;
```

When the `goto` is executed, control is unconditionally transferred to the statement marked with `label:`, as here:

```
label: statement
```

- Labels are not executable statements; they just mark a point in the code.
- The rules for naming labels are the same as the rules for naming variables and functions.
- Labels always end with a colon.

Using `goto` statements with abandon can lead to tangled, confusing code (often referred to as *spaghetti code*). The usual boilerplate advice is "Don't use `goto` statements." Despite this, `goto` statements are useful in certain situations, such as breaking out of nested loops (a `break` statement only breaks out of the innermost loop):

```
int i, j;

for (i=0; i < MAX_I; i++)
  for (j=0; j < MAX_J; j++)
    {
      ...
      if ( finished ) goto moreStuff;

    }


moreStuff:  statement      // more statements
```

> **Note**
>
> Whether to use `goto` statements is one of the longest-running debates in computer science. For a summary of the debate, see http://david.tribble.com/text/goto.html.

Functions

Functions have the following form:

```
returnType functionName( arg1Type arg1, ..., argNType argN )
{

  statements

}
```

An example of a simple function looks like this:

```
float salesTax( float purchasePrice, float taxRate )
{
  float tax = purchasePrice * taxRate;
  return tax;
}
```

> **Note**
>
> Variables that are declared inside a function are called *local variables*. Local variables are generally valid only from the point they are declared until the end of the function. The range of code for which a variable is valid is called the variable's *scope*. Variable scope is treated in detail in the next chapter.

A function is called by coding the function name followed by a parenthesized list of expressions, one for each of the function's arguments. Each expression type must match the type declared for the corresponding function argument. The following example shows a simple function call:

```
float carPrice = 20000.00;
float stateTaxRate = 0.05;

float carSalesTax = salesTax( carPrice, stateTaxRate );
```

When the line with the function call is executed, control jumps to the first statement in the function body. Execution continues until a **return** statement is encountered or the end of the function is reached. Execution then returns to the calling context. The value of the function expression in the calling context is the value set by the **return** statement.

> **Note**
>
> Functions are not required to have any arguments or to return a value. Functions that do not return a value are typed **void**:
>
> ```
> void FunctionThatReturnsNothing( int arg1 )
> ```
>
> You may omit the **return** statement from a function that does not return a value.
>
> Functions that don't take any arguments are indicated by using empty parentheses for the argument list:
>
> ```
> int FunctionWithNoArguments()
> ```

Functions are sometimes executed solely for their side effects. This function prints out the sales tax but changes nothing in the program's state:

```
void printSalesTax ( float purchasePrice, float taxRate )
{
  float tax = purchasePrice * taxRate;

  printf( "The sales tax is: %f.2\n", tax );

}
```

C functions are *call by value*. When a function is called, the expressions in the argument list of the calling statement are evaluated and their *values* are passed to the function. A function cannot directly change the value of any of the variables in the calling context. This function has no effect on anything in the calling context:

```
void salesTax( float purchasePrice, float taxRate, float carSalesTax )
{
  // Changes the local copy of carSalesTax but not the value of
  // the variable in the calling context

    carSalesTax = purchasePrice * taxRate;
    return;
}
```

To change the value of a variable in the calling context, you must pass a pointer to the variable and use that pointer to manipulate the variable's value:

```
void salesTax( float purchasePrice, float taxRate, float *carSalesTax)
{
  *carSalesTax = purchasePrice * taxRate; // this will work

  return;
}
```

> **Note**
> The preceding example is still call by value. The *value* of a pointer to a variable in the calling context is passed to the function. The function then uses that pointer (which it doesn't alter) to set the value of the variable it points to.

Declaring Functions

When you call a function, the compiler needs to know the types of the function's arguments and return value. It uses this information to set up the communication between the function and its caller. If the code for the function comes before the function call (in the source code file), you don't have to do anything else. If the function is coded after the function call or in a different file, you must declare the function before you use it.

A function declaration repeats the first line of the function, with a semicolon added at the end:

```
void printSalesTax ( float purchasePrice, float taxRate );
```

It is a common practice to put function declarations in a header file. The header file is then included (see the next section) in any file that uses the function.

> **Note**
> Forgetting to declare functions can lead to insidious errors. If you call a function that is coded in another file, and you don't declare the function, neither the compiler nor the linker will complain. But the function will receive garbage for any floating-point argument and return garbage if the function's return type is floating-point. In the absence of a declaration the compiler assumes that argument types and the return type are integers. It then interprets the bit patterns of floating-point arguments or return values as integers, resulting in (wildly) erroneous results.

Preprocessor

When C (and Objective-C) code files are compiled, they are first sent through an initial program, called the *preprocessor*, before being sent to the compiler proper. Lines that begin with a # character are directives to the preprocessor. Using preprocessor directives, you can:

- Import the text of a file into one or more other files at a specified point.
- Create defined constants.
- Conditionally compile code (compile or omit statement blocks depending on a condition).

Including Files

The following line:

```
#include "HeaderFile.h"
```

causes the preprocessor to insert the text of the file *HeaderFile.h* into the file being processed at the point of the **#include** line. The effect is the same as if you had used a text editor to copy and paste the text from *HeaderFile.h* into the file being processed.

If the included filename is enclosed in quotation marks (""):

```
#include "HeaderFile.h"
```

the preprocessor will look for *HeaderFile.h* in the same directory as the file being compiled, then in a list of locations that you can supply as arguments to the compiler, and finally in a series of system locations.

If the included file is enclosed in angle brackets (<>):

```
#include <HeaderFile.h>
```

the preprocessor will look for the included file only in the standard system locations.

> **Note**
>
> In Objective-C, **#include** is superseded by **#import**, which produces the same result, except that it prevents the named file from being imported more than once. If the preprocessor encounters further **#import** directives for the same header file while working on a given file, the additional **#import** directives are ignored.

#define

#define is used for textual replacement. The most common use of **#define** is to define constants, such as

```
#define MAX_VOLUME 11
```

The preprocessor will replace every occurrence of **MAX_VOLUME** in the file being compiled with an 11. A **#define** can be continued on multiple lines by placing a backslash (\) at the end of all but the last line in the definition.

> **Note**
>
> If you do this, the \ must be the last thing on the line. Following the \ with something else (such as a comment beginning with //) results in an error.

A frequently used pattern is to place the **#define** in a header file, which is then included by various source files. You can then change the value of the constant in all the source files by changing the single definition in the header file. The traditional C naming convention for defined constants is to use all capital letters. A traditional Apple naming convention is to begin the constant name with a **k** and CamelCase the rest of the name:

```
#define kMaximumVolume 11
```

You will encounter both styles, sometimes in the same code.

Conditional Compilation

The preprocessor allows for conditional compilation:

```
#if condition

  statements

#else

  otherStatements

#endif
```

Here, *condition* must be a constant expression that can be evaluated for a truth value at compile time. If *condition* evaluates to true (non-zero), *statements* are compiled, but *otherStatements* are not. If *condition* is false, *statements* are skipped and *otherStatements* are compiled.

The **#endif** is required, but the **#else** and the alternative code are optional. A conditional compilation block can also begin with an **#ifdef** directive:

```
#ifdef name

  statements

#endif
```

The behavior is the same as the previous example, except that the truth value of **#ifdef** is determined by whether *name* has been **#define**'d.

One use of **#if** is to easily remove and replace blocks of code during debugging:

```
#if 1
  statements
#endif
```

By changing the 1 to a 0, *statements* can be temporarily left out for a test. They can then be replaced by changing the 0 back to a 1.

    #if and **#ifdef** directives can be nested, as shown here:

```
#if 0
#if 1
statements
#endif
#endif
```

In the preceding example, the compiler ignores all the code, including the other compiler directives, between the **#if 0** and its matching **#endif**. *statements* are not compiled.

    If you need to disable and re-enable multiple statement blocks, you can code each block like this:

```
#if _DEBUG

statements

#endif
```

The defined constant **_DEBUG** can be added or removed in a header file or by using a **–D** flag in the compile command.

printf

Input and output (I/O) are not a part of the C language. Character and binary I/O are handled by functions in the C standard I/O library.

> **Note**
>
> The standard I/O library is one of a set of libraries of functions that is provided with every C environment.

To use the functions in the standard I/O library, you must include the library's header file in your program:

```
#include <stdio.h>
```

The only function covered here is **printf**, which prints a formatted string to your terminal window (or to the Xcode console window if you are using Xcode). The **printf** function takes a variable number of arguments. The first argument to **printf** is a *format string*. Any remaining arguments are quantities that are printed out in a manner specified by the format string:

```
printf( formatString, argument1, argument2, ... argumentN );
```

The format string consists of ordinary characters and *conversion specifiers*:

- Ordinary characters (not %) in the format string are sent unchanged to the output.
- Conversion specifiers begin with a percent sign (%). The letter following the % indicates the type of argument the specifier expects.
- Each conversion specification consumes, in order, one of the arguments following the format string. The argument is converted to characters that represent the value of the argument, and the characters are sent to the output.

The only conversion specifiers used in this book are %d for `char` and `int`, %f for `float` and `double`, and %s for C strings. C strings are typed as `char*`.

Here is a simple example:

```
int myInt = 9;
float myFloat = 3.145926;
char* myString = "a C string";

printf( "This is an integer: %d, a float: %f, and a string: %s.\n",
    myInt, myFloat, myString );
```

> **Note**
>
> The \n is the *newline character*. It advances the output so that any subsequent output appears on the next line.

The result of the preceding example is

```
This is an Integer: 9, a float: 3.145926, and a string: a C string.
```

If the number of arguments following the format string doesn't match the number of conversion specifications, `printf` ignores the excess arguments or prints garbage for the excess specifications.

> **Note**
>
> This book uses `printf` only for logging and debugging non-object variables, not for the output of a polished program, so this section presents only a cursory look at format strings and conversion specifiers.
>
> `printf` handles a large number of types, and it provides very fine control over the appearance of the output. A complete discussion of the available types of conversion specifications and how to control the details of formatting is available via the Unix *man* command. To see them, type the following at a terminal window:
>
> ```
> man 3 printf
> ```

> **Note**
>
> The Objective-C Foundation framework provides `NSLog`, another logging function. It is similar to `printf`, but it adds the capability to print out object variables. It also adds the program name, the date, and the time in hours, minutes, seconds, and milliseconds to the output. This additional information can be visually distracting if all you want to know is the value of a variable or two, so this book uses `printf` in some cases where `NSLog`'s additional capability is not required. `NSLog` is covered in Chapter 3, "An Introduction to Object-Oriented Programming."

Command Line Compiling and Debugging

When you write programs for Mac OS X or iOS, you should write, compile, and debug your programs using Xcode, Apple's integrated development environment (IDE). You'll learn how to set up a simple Xcode project in Chapter 4, "Your First Objective-C Program." However, for the simple C programs required in the exercises in this chapter and the next chapter, you may find it easier to write the programs in your favorite text editor and then compile and run them from a command line.

Compilers and Debuggers

Historically, Apple has used the open-source GNU compiler, gcc, for building iOS and OS X programs. However, in the past several years they have transitioned to using compilers from the open-source LLVM (Low Level Virtual Machine) project. LLVM is not a single compiler; it is a set of modules that can be used to build compilers, debuggers, and related tools. In the first part of the transition Apple used a compiler called llvm-gcc-4.2 that combined the front end from gcc 4.2 with the LLVM code generator and optimizer. The current compiler is the Clang compiler, which combines a new unified parser for C, Objective C, C++, and Objective C++ with the LLVM code generator and optimizer.

Note that Apple refers to the Clang compiler as "LLVM Compiler *N*," where *N* is the current version number—4.0 as of Xcode 4.4.

The Clang compiler has many advantages over llvm-gcc-4.2:

- Clang provides much more informative error messages when you make a mistake.
- Clang is faster than gcc.
- Certain newer features of Objective-C, such as automatic reference counting (ARC), are available only by using the Clang compiler.

Clang is the default compiler in the current version of Xcode. Apple has announced that llvm-gcc-4.2 is "frozen" (no new features or bug fixes) as of Xcode 4.4 and will be removed in a future version of Xcode.

The LLVM project also includes LLDB, a new debugger.

You can find more information on Clang, LLDB, and the LLVM project on the LLVM website: http://llvm.org.

To compile from the command line, you will need:

1. A terminal window. You can use the Terminal app (*/Applications/Utilities/ Terminal*) that comes with Mac OS X. If you are coming from another Unix environment, and you are used to xterms, you may prefer to download and use iTerm, an OS X native terminal application that behaves similarly to an xterm (http://iterm.sourceforge.net/).

2. A text editor. Mac OS X comes with both *vi* and *emacs*, or you can use a different editor if you have one.

3. The Apple Developer tools. You can get the current version of Xcode and the Developer tools from the OS X App Store (they're free).

The first step is to check whether the command line tools are installed on your system. At the command prompt type

```
which clang
```

If the response is

```
/usr/bin/clang
```

your command line tools are already installed. If the response is

```
clang: Command not found.
```

the command line tools are not installed on your system and you must use Xcode to install them. To install the command line tools:

1. Open Xcode.

2. Choose *Xcode > Preferences...* from the menu.

3. When the *Preferences* panel opens, click the *Downloads* tab and then click on *Components*.

4. Finally, click the *Install* button for *Command Line Tools*.

5. When the installation is finished, you may close Xcode.

You are now ready to compile. If your source code file is named *MyCProgram.c*, you can compile it by typing the following at the command prompt:

```
clang -o MyCProgram MyCProgram.c
```

The −o flag allows you to give the compiler a name for your final executable. If the compiler complains that you have made a mistake or two, go back to fix them, and then try again. When your program compiles successfully, you can run it by typing the executable name at the command prompt:

```
MyCProgram
```

If you want to debug your program using gdb, the GNU debugger, or LLDB, you must use the −g flag when you compile:

```
clang -g -o MyCProgram MyCProgram.c
```

The **-g** flag causes `clang` to attach debugging information to the final executable.
    To use gdb to debug a program, type **gdb** followed by the executable name:

```
gdb MyCProgram
```

Similarly, to use lldb you type **lldb** followed by the executable name:

```
lldb MyCProgram
```

Documentation for gdb is available at the GNU website, www.gnu.org/software/
gdb/, or from Apple at http://developer.apple.com/mac/library/#documentation/
DeveloperTools/gdb/gdb/gdb_toc.html. In addition, there are many websites with
instructions for using gdb. Search for "gdb tutorial."
You can learn more about LLDB by watching the Apple video at http://devimages.
apple.com/llvm/videos/LLDB_Debugging_Infrastructure.mov or by going to the
LLDB website, http://lldb.llvm.org/.

Summary

This chapter has been a review of the basic parts of the C language. The review continues in Chapter 2, "More about C Variables," which covers the memory layout of a
C program, declaring variables, variable scope and lifetimes, and dynamic allocation
of memory. Chapter 3, "An Introduction to Object-Oriented Programming," begins
the real business of this book: object-oriented programming and the object part of
Objective-C.

Exercises

1. Write a function that returns the average of two floating-point numbers. Write
   a small program to test your function and log the output. Next, put the function
   in a separate source file but "forget" to declare the function in the file that has
   your main routine. What happens? Now add the function declaration to the file
   with your main program and verify that the declaration fixes the problem.

2. Write another averaging function, but this time try to pass the result back in one
   of the function's arguments. Your function should be declared like this:

   ```
   void average( float a, float b, float average )
   ```

   Write a small test program and verify that your function doesn't work. You
   can't affect a variable in the calling context by setting the value of a function
   parameter.

Now change the function and its call to pass a pointer to a variable in the calling context. Verify that the function can use the pointer to modify a variable in the calling context.

3. Assume that you have a function, `int flipCoin()`, that randomly returns a 1 to represent heads or a 0 to represent tails. Explain how the following code fragment works:

```
int flipResult;
if ( flipResult = flipCoin() )
  printf( "Heads is represented by %d\n", flipResult );
else
  printf( "Tails is represented by %d\n", flipResult );
```

As you will see in Chapter 6, "Classes and Objects," an `if` condition similar to the one in the preceding example is used in the course of initializing an Objective-C object.

4. An identity matrix is a square array of numbers with ones on the diagonal (the elements where the row number equals the column number) and zero everywhere else. The 2×2 identity matrix looks like this:

$$\begin{bmatrix} 1 & 0 \\ 0 & 1 \end{bmatrix}$$

Write a program that calculates and stores the 4×4 identity matrix. When your program is finished calculating the matrix, it should output the result as a nicely formatted square array.

5. Fibonacci numbers (http://en.wikipedia.org/wiki/Fibonacci_number) are a numerical sequence that appears in many places in nature and in mathematics. The first two Fibonacci numbers are defined to be 0 and 1. The nth Fibonacci number is the sum of the previous two Fibonacci numbers:

$$F_n = F_{n-1} + F_{n-2}$$

Write a program that calculates and stores the first 20 Fibonacci numbers. After calculating the numbers, your program should output them, one on a line, along with their index. The output lines should be something like this:

```
Fibonacci Number 2 is: 1
```

Use a `#define` to control the number of Fibonacci numbers your program produces, so that it can be easily changed.

6. Rewrite your program from the previous exercise to use a `while` loop instead of a `for` loop.

7. What if you are asked to calculate the first 75 Fibonacci numbers? If you are using `int`s to store the numbers, there is a problem. You will find that the 47th Fibonacci number is too big to fit in an `int`. How can you fix this?

8. Judging by the number of tip calculators available in the iOS App Store, a substantial fragment of the population has forgotten how to multiply. Help out those who can't multiply but can't afford an iPhone. Write a program that calculates a 15% tip on all check amounts between $10 and $50. (For brevity, go by $0.50 increments.) Show both the check amount and the tip.

9. Now make the tip calculator look more professional. Add a column for 20% tips (Objective-C programmers eat in classy joints). Place the proper headers on each column and use a pair of nested loops so that you can output a blank line after every $10 increment.

   Using the conversion specification `%.2f` instead of `%f` will limit the check and tip output to two decimal places. Using `%%` in the format string will cause `printf` to output a single `%` character.

10. Define a structure that holds a rectangle. Do this by defining a structure that holds the coordinates of a point and another structure that represents a size by holding a width and a height. Your rectangle structure should have a point that represents the lower-left corner of the rectangle and a size. (The Cocoa frameworks define structures like these, but make your own for now.)

11. One of the basic tenets of efficient computer graphics is "Don't draw if you don't have to draw." Graphics programs commonly keep a bounding rectangle for each graphic object. When it is time to draw the graphic on the screen, the program compares the graphic's bounding rectangle with a rectangle representing the window. If there is no overlap between the rectangles, the program can skip trying to draw the graphic. Overall, this is usually a win; comparing rectangles is much cheaper than drawing graphics.

   Write a function that takes two rectangle structure arguments. (Use the structures that you defined in the previous exercise.) Your function should return 1 if there is a non-zero overlap between the two rectangles, and 0 otherwise. Write a test program that creates some rectangles and verify that your function works.

2

More about C Variables

When you write a program in most common scripting languages, you rarely have to spend much time thinking about variables. You create variables just by using them, and you don't have to worry about what happens to your variables when you are finished with them. The language's interpreter takes care of all the details for you.

When you code in a compiled language, life is not so simple. You must declare any variables that you use in your program by telling the compiler the type and name of each variable. The compiler then looks at the declared type of the variable, reserves the appropriate number of bytes, and associates the variable name with those bytes.

In this chapter we'll look at the form of variable declarations in C and where the compiler arranges storage for different kinds of variables.

Memory Layout of a C Program

To understand the material in the rest of the chapter, it's helpful to know how a C program is arranged in memory. Figure 2.1 shows a simplified diagram of a running program's virtual address space.

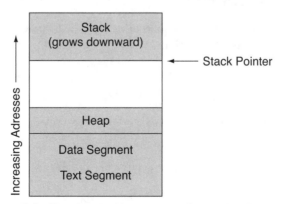

Figure 2.1 The virtual address space of a running C program

> **Note**
>
> The virtual address space is the address space that a program "sees." The translation between virtual address space and the actual physical addresses is handled invisibly by the OS and the computer's memory management unit (MMU).

Going in order from low to high virtual address:

- The text segment contains the program's executable code and read-only data.
- The data segment contains read/write data, including global variables.
- The heap contains blocks of memory that can be dispensed to the program on request. (See *Dynamic Allocation* later in this chapter.) When more memory is required, the system may expand the heap upward.
- The stack is used for calling functions. When you call a function, the system constructs a stack frame for the called function. The stack frame is a region of memory built on the bottom (lowest address) of the stack. The stack pointer (which points to the lowest address of the stack) moves downward. The stack frame contains space for the called function's parameters and local variables, space for saving the values of any registers that need to be saved across the function call, and some control information. When the function returns, the stack pointer is restored to its previous (higher address) value and control returns to the calling function. The important point to remember about this process is: After a function returns, the contents of its stack frame are no longer valid.

> **Note**
>
> Some people like to think of the stack as expanding upward, analogous to a pile of physical papers on their desk. They refer to the stack pointer as pointing to the "top of the stack." However you choose to think about it, the stack grows downward in terms of memory addresses. Calling a function moves the stack pointer to a lower address, and returning from a function moves it back to a higher address.

Automatic Variables

Variables you declare in a function or subroutine are called *automatic* or *local* variables. Consider the following simple function:

```
void logAverage( float a, float b )
{
  float average;
  average = 0.5 * (a + b);
  printf( "The average is %f\n", average );
}
```

In the preceding example, **average** is an automatic variable.

These are the important things to remember about automatic variables:

- Automatic variables are created on the stack. They are valid only from the point where they are declared to the end of the function (see *Scope* later in the chapter). When the function returns, the system moves the stack pointer back to the bottom of the previous frame. Subsequent calls to other functions create new stack frames and most likely overwrite the memory locations assigned to earlier functions' automatic variables. If you call **logAverage()** with the arguments 10.0 and 12.0, the variable **average** has the value 11.0 when you reach the **printf** statement. If you later call **logAverage()** again, **average** is unlikely to be 11.0 at the top of the routine.

- Automatic variables are not initialized by the system. Until you assign them a value, they contain whatever random junk was left in that memory location from the last time it was used.

- Automatic variables are associated with a single call of a function. If you have recursive code where a function calls itself, each call of the function has its own stack frame and its own copy of the automatic variables. Changing the value of the variable in one call will not change its value in any of the other calls on the stack.

- Taking the address of an automatic variable with the **&** operator and assigning the address to a pointer variable held outside of the function is a very bad idea— the pointer variable points to junk as soon as the function exits.

Note

Under ARC (see Chapter 16) automatic variables that hold pointers to Objective-C objects are initialized to **nil** (**nil** is a "pointer to no object"). Other types of automatic variables such as basic C types and other types of pointers remain uninitialized under ARC.

Note

Automatic variables are automatic in the sense that their storage is allocated on the stack when you call the function in which they are used. However, you still have to tell the compiler about them with a declaration.

Function Parameters

Function parameters are essentially automatic variables that have been initialized with the values supplied when the function was called. They are created on the stack, and they become invalid when the function returns. You can reset their value in the function body but, as noted in the previous chapter, changing their value has no effect on the corresponding variables in the calling function.

External Variables

Variables that are declared in a source file outside the scope of `main` or any subroutine are called *external* variables. In the following example, `pageCount` is an external variable:

```
int pageCount;

main()
{
...
  printf( "The current page count is: %d\n", pageCount );
}

void addpage()
{
  pageCount++;
  ...
}

void deletePage
{
  pageCount--;
  ...
}
```

Although it is not always a good design choice, external variables are sometimes used as global variables to share information between different functions and different source files. These are the important things to remember about external variables:

- The compiler assigns external variables memory locations in the data segment of the virtual address space. External variables persist for the lifetime of the program—they never go out of scope or disappear, and their value changes only when you assign a new value to them.

- The compiler initializes external variables to zero if you do not provide an explicit initialization.

- External variables are visible (usable) beyond the scope of a single function. In fact, external variables are global symbols. Unless you declare an external variable to be `static` (see the upcoming section by that name), it is potentially visible to any function in any source file.

Declaration Keywords

C defines several keywords that modify declarations.

auto

The `auto` keyword is only used within a function to tell the compiler that the variable is an automatic variable. Because this is the default, it is rarely used. You will probably never see it.

extern

The `extern` keyword is used when you want to reference an external variable that is declared in a different file. A declaration beginning with `extern` makes the name and type of the variable known to the compiler but does not cause the compiler to reserve any storage for that variable.

The following statement tells the compiler that `pageCount` is an `int`, and that you have reserved storage for it with a declaration somewhere else in the program:

```
extern int pageCount;
```

If you haven't declared `pageCount` as an external variable (without an `extern` keyword) somewhere else in your program with a statement like the following:

```
int pageCount;
```

your program will compile, but it won't link. The compiler is satisfied by the `extern` declaration, but the linker fails, looking for the non-existent `pageCount`.

static

The `static` keyword has different meanings depending on whether it is used with a variable inside a function or with an external variable. When used inside a function, the `static` keyword creates a variable that is similar to an external variable:

```
void countingFunction()
{
  static int timesCalled;
  timesCalled++;
  ...
}
```

In the preceding example, `timesCalled` keeps a count of the number of times `countingFunction` has been called.

These are the important things to remember about function static variables:

- The compiler creates storage for a function static variable in the data segment.
- A function static variable is initialized to zero unless you provide an explicit initialization.
- The value of a function static variable persists between calls to the function.
- References to a function static variable in multiple calls to the function (even if the function recursively calls itself) refer to the same memory location.

The only difference from an external variable is that a function static variable is visible only within the scope of the function that declared it.

When the **static** keyword is used with an external variable, it limits the visibility of the variable to the file in which it is declared and hides it from other source files. If you code

```
static int pageCount;
```

outside of a function body, **pageCount** can be referenced only by functions in the same source file. If you attempt to use **pageCount** in a different source file by declaring it with an **extern** statement:

```
extern int pageCount;
```

the linker will fail.

register

The **register** keyword is a hint to the compiler that the variable it precedes is heavily referenced:

```
register int count;
```

As a result, the compiler may choose to store the variable in a register (for faster access) rather than in RAM. However, the compiler is not obligated to honor the hint.

const

The **const** keyword tells the compiler that a variable should be considered as constant. The compiler flags any attempt to change the variable as an error:

```
const int maxAttempts = 100;
maxAttempts = 200;   // This will cause a compiler error.
```

When **const** is used with pointer variables, the order is important. The declaration should be read from left to right. The following example declares that **ptr** is a constant pointer to an **int**:

```
int a = 10;
int b = 15;

int *const ptr = &a;

*ptr = 20;   // OK. a is now 20.
 ptr = &b; // Error, ptr is a constant
```

ptr cannot be modified to point at a different location in memory, but it can be used to modify the variable it points to.

Putting the `const` in front of the rest of the declaration has a different meaning. `ptr` is then a pointer to a constant `int`:

```
int a = 10;
int b = 15;

const int *ptr = &a;

*ptr = 20; // Error, ptr's contents are constant.

a = 20;    // OK, a itself has not been declared as const.

ptr = &b;  // OK, ptr now points at b.
```

`ptr` can be modified to point to a different variable, but whatever variable it points to cannot be modified through `ptr`. This is true even if, as in the preceding example, the variable itself is not declared `const`. (But because `a` has not been declared as `const` in the preceding example, it may be changed if it is accessed directly.)

volatile

The `volatile` keyword declares that a variable's contents may be changed by something outside of the program's execution. The compiler will then avoid optimizations that it would otherwise make. This can happen, for example, if the variable's storage is actually a hardware register belonging to an external device that has been memory-mapped into the program's address space.

Consider a case where `shouldContinue` is mapped to a control line on a hardware device:

```
int shouldContinue = 1;  // initialization
// Check the control line before each pass through the loop.
while ( shouldContinue ) doStuff;
```

The intent of this code is that when the hardware device sets the control line to zero, the condition (`shouldContinue`) evaluates to false and the loop terminates. But if the code represented by `doStuff` doesn't modify `shouldContinue`, an optimizing compiler would conclude that `shouldContinue` never changes, and it would optimize the code to the equivalent of the following:

```
while (1) doStuff;
```

Unfortunately, the preceding is an infinite loop. It ignores the variable set by the hardware device to signal when to break out of the loop. Declaring `shouldContinue` as `volatile` prevents the compiler from making that optimization:

```
volatile int shouldContinue;
```

Scope

The *scope* of a variable is the range of statements over which the variable is active. Here *active* means that a statement can reference the variable without the compiler giving you an error complaining that it doesn't know anything about the variable in question.

The Scope of Automatic Variables

Automatic variables can be declared at any point in a function body. The scope of an automatic variable goes from the point at which it is declared until the end of the function. You can't use a variable before it has been declared:

```
void someFunction()
{
  int a;
  a = 7; // OK, a is in scope
  ...
  b = 7; // WRONG, b is not in scope at this point
  int b;
  ...
}
```

After the function in which an automatic variable is declared returns, the variable is out of scope. It is not visible from outside the function.

Compound Statements and Scope

A *compound statement* is a sequence of statements enclosed between curly brackets. The interior of a compound statement is a separate scope. You can declare a variable at any point inside a compound statement; the variable is active from the point where it is declared until the end of the compound statement. The scope in which a compound statement itself occurs is called the compound statement's *enclosing scope*. Variables declared in the enclosing scope are visible inside a compound statement, but variables declared in the compound statement are not visible in the enclosing scope:

```
void someFunction()
{
  int a = 7;
    {
      int b = 2;
      int c;

      c = a * b;  // OK, a is visible inside the compound statement
    }

  int d = 2 * c;  // WRONG,  c is not visible at this point
}
```

Compiling a program that contains the preceding code fragment results in a compiler error:

```
someFunction.c:12: error: 'c' undeclared (first use in this function)
someFunction.c:12: error: (Each undeclared identifier is reported only
someFunction.c:12: error: once for each function it appears in.)
```

If you declare a variable inside a compound statement that has the same name as a variable in the enclosing scope, the inside variable hides the variable in the enclosing scope for the duration of the inside variable's scope:

```
void someFunction()
{
  int a = 7;
  int b = 2;
    {
      int c;
      c = a * b;  // c is 14, enclosing scope a is still visible;

      int a = 10; // This hides the enclosing scope's variable a
      c =  a * b; // c is now 20
    }
}
```

The Scope of External Variables

An external variable (a variable declared outside of a function) is visible from the point in the file where it is declared until the end of that file. An external variable's visibility can be extended to a different file by declaring that variable in the other file with an **extern** keyword, as described earlier in this chapter. Going in the direction of less visibility, beginning the declaration of an external variable with the **static** keyword restricts the variable's scope to the file in which it is declared. The **static** keyword overrules any **extern** declarations in other source files that refer to the same variable.

Dynamic Allocation

The variable declarations covered up to this point in the chapter are examples of *static allocation*. You have to tell the compiler the number and type of the variables that you need at compile time.

Static and static

The word *static* is overloaded here. Don't confuse the general term *static allocation* with either meaning of the **static** keyword discussed in the previous section. Yes, it can be confusing. When I'm awarded control of the Universe, I will do better.

Specifying the required amount of memory at compile time is a problem in many cases. Let's say you want to read in pixels of a grayscale (8 bits per pixel) image. You'll need an array of bytes to hold them:

```
#define MAX_WIDTH 1000
#define MAX_HEIGHT 1000
unsigned char pixels[MAX_WIDTH * MAX_HEIGHT];
```

But what should **MAX_HEIGHT** and **MAX_WIDTH** really be? If you make them too small, there will be images you can't read in. You could make them really huge, but there are problems with that: For the average case, you waste a lot of memory, and your program's footprint will be unnecessarily large, which affects performance. It's also an invitation to be bitten by Murphy's Law—as soon as you hard-code the size, someone, somewhere, will make an image file bigger than the hard-coded size and expect your program to read it.

The answer to this problem is to use *dynamic allocation*. Dynamic allocation allows you to request more memory at run time, when your program is executing. When you need some more storage, you ask the system for a block of memory. When you're finished using the memory, you give it back. The bytes used for dynamic allocation are located in the region labeled "Heap" in Figure 2.1.

> **Note**
>
> *Heap* is the generic Unix term for this region. Mac OS X actually has a more complicated system. In OS X, this region is technically called a *malloc zone* (see the sidebar *Malloc Zones*). In most cases, the rest of the book will continue to use the generic term *heap*.

Dynamic allocation is handled with two functions: **malloc** and **free**. You request memory by calling **malloc** with an argument that specifies the required number of bytes. **malloc** returns a pointer to a requested number of bytes, which you then cast as a pointer to the required data type and assign to a variable that is typed as a pointer to the requested type.

> **Note**
>
> Historically, **malloc** returned **NULL** when there was no more memory available to be allocated. However, both OS X and iOS use *lazy allocation*. Using lazy allocation, **malloc** returns a pointer to the requested memory, but the system doesn't commit the memory resources for that request until you execute a piece of code that accesses that memory. As a result, if you make multiple requests for memory and don't use or free that memory, **malloc** may return a non-**NULL** value, even when there is no more memory available. In this situation, using the returned pointer may result in a crash. Given the current typical values for RAM and swap space, you should rarely, if ever, see this happen on an OS X system. On iOS, an app will most likely receive a low memory warning from the system well before encountering this situation.

To calculate the number of bytes that you need, you can determine the number of bytes in each item by using the `sizeof` function and multiplying the result by the number of items you need. The number of bytes required for an 8-bit grayscale image is (assuming you've read the image height and width from some information in the file's header)

```
numBytesNeeded = imageHeight * imageWidth * sizeof( unsigned char );
```

The allocation is written as follows:

```
numBytesNeeded = imageHeight * imageWidth * sizeof( unsigned char );
unsigned char *pixels =
    (unsigned char*) malloc( numBytesNeeded );
```

Note that you should cast the return value of `malloc` to the appropriate pointer type.

When you are finished using the memory you allocated with `malloc`, you return it by calling `free`:

```
free( pixels );
pixels = NULL;
```

The call to `free` allows the program to reuse the memory. After the bytes are freed, they can be handed out for a different use with a subsequent call to `malloc`. The Golden Rule of dynamic allocation is: If you allocate something, you're responsible for giving it back when you are finished. Otherwise, your application will "leak" memory. Your process size will be bigger than it needs to be, and the performance of your program and any others running at the same time may suffer.

Note

Each `free` must balance a corresponding `malloc`. Freeing a pointer that you have not `malloc`'d or freeing the same pointer twice causes an immediate crash.

Note

Using a pointer to bytes that have been freed can corrupt your program's memory and cause seemingly random crashes that are very difficult to debug. Setting `pixels` to NULL provides a measure of safety. If you make a mistake in your code and attempt to use the NULL pointer, your program will likely crash. The problem and its location will be obvious.

Malloc Zones

Instead of a unified heap, OS X has one or more *malloc zones*. The first malloc zone, called the *default malloc zone*, is created at the time of the first call to `malloc`. The standard `malloc` function gets its bytes from the default malloc zone. It is possible to create additional malloc zones using the function `malloc_create_zone`.

Using additional zones is an advanced technique that can be used in special cases to optimize performance. It allows you to give groups of frequently accessed variables adjacent memory locations or to release many variables at once (by releasing an entire zone).

While not officially deprecated,[1] Apple now highly discourages using zones other than the default malloc zone for Objective-C objects (see http://developer.apple.com/library/mac/documentation/Performance/Conceptual/ManagingMemory/Articles/MemoryAlloc.html).

Summary

This chapter covered how C variables are declared. The main points are:

- You must declare any variable that you use in a C program. The declaration tells the compiler the variable type and optionally some other information. In response to the declaration, the compiler arranges storage (some bytes in memory) for the variable and associates the variable name with the storage.

- There are three places that the compiler can place variables: on the stack, in part of the data segment, and in the heap.

- Variables declared inside a function are automatic variables. Automatic variables are created on the stack when the function is called. The compiler does not initialize automatic variables, and they are valid only for the scope of the function in which they are declared.

- Variables declared outside the scope of any function are called external variables. External variables are created in the data segment at compile time and are initialized to zero (unless you provide an explicit initialization). They persist for the life of the program.

- C provides the following keywords that modify variable declarations: `auto`, `static`, `extern`, `register`, `const`, and `volatile`.

- You can request additional memory while your program is running using the function `malloc`. Memory obtained with `malloc` comes from the heap.

- When you are finished with memory that you obtained with `malloc`, you must return it to the heap using the function `free`.

This chapter concludes the rapid review of the non-object part of Objective-C. In the next chapter the book moves on to objects with an introduction to object-oriented programming and the basics of the object part of Objective-C.

---

1. A function whose status is changed to deprecated in a given major OS release is still available in that release but may be withdrawn in a future major OS release. For example, a function marked as deprecated in Mac OS X 10.6 may not be available in Mac OS X 10.7.

Exercises

1. Write a small program that declares an external variable and also calls a function that declares and uses an automatic variable. (It is not important what the function does for this exercise. You can just declare and initialize a local variable and then log the value of both variables with a `printf` statement.) Build the program and then run it in gdb. Set a break point inside the function. When you reach the break point, look at the addresses of both the automatic variable and the external variable. You can show the address of a variable by typing

   `p &variableName`

   at the prompt. Do the results agree with what you learned in this chapter?

2. Modify your program from Exercise 1 by adding a second function that also declares an automatic variable. Modify the original function so that it calls the new function. Verify that the stack does grow toward lower addresses: Set a break point and stop inside the new function. Show the address of the new function's automatic variable. Then type

   `up 1`

   at the gdb prompt. This will move gdb's attention to the previous stack frame so you can display the address of the calling function's automatic variable.

3. Write a function that logs the number of times it has been called. Store the count in a function-scope static variable. Call the function several times to verify that the count is correctly recorded. Is there a way to make the count start at a value other than zero?

4. This exercise uses two source files. In the first file, declare an external variable and initialize it to some value. Put a function that logs the value of the external variable in the second source file. (Don't forget the **extern** declaration in the second file.) Build and run the program to verify that it works. What happens if you omit the **extern** declaration? Restore the **extern** declaration to the second source file and add the keyword **static** to the variable declaration in the first file. What happens?

5. Write a program that calculates and stores the squares of the first 10 integers. When it is done calculating all 10, the program should display the results using `printf`. Instead of declaring an array of 10 `ints`, use `malloc` to obtain the memory to hold the calculated values. Don't forget to `free` the memory when you are finished.

3

An Introduction to Object-Oriented Programming

The earliest high-level computer languages, such as Fortran, COBOL, and C, are procedural. The natural organization of a program written in a procedural language is a series of sequential tasks to execute. Procedural programming is eminently suitable for some types of problems, such as solving mathematical equations. However, there are many types of problems—for example, user interface programming—for which procedural programming is not a good fit. In many areas of computing today, the dominant programming paradigm is a different one, called *object-oriented programming*. Objective-C is an example of an object-oriented language. It extends the procedural C language, adding constructs and syntax to support object-oriented programming.

This chapter begins with an introduction that describes the fundamentals of object-oriented programming. The following section illustrates how these concepts are implemented in Objective-C. The final section of the chapter lists the additions that Objective-C makes to the C language.

Object-Oriented Programming

Object-oriented programming is a style of programming that organizes programs into collections of objects that interact with each other. An object is a group of related variables that models something in your problem space, and some procedures, called methods, that represent the actions that the object knows how to perform. In Objective-C objects communicate by sending and receiving *messages*. A message to an object is a request to the object, asking it to execute one of its methods.

As an example, a drawing program might have a `Shape` object to represent free-form shapes (such as those shown in Figure 3.1) that a user can draw on the screen. A `Shape` object would have variables to store the points that define its outline, its color, and its position in the drawing. It would have methods to set and retrieve those

Figure 3.1   Some shapes

quantities and a method to draw itself on the screen. To draw the `Shape` on the screen, you would send the `Shape` a `draw` message. In response, the `Shape` would execute its `draw` method (which contains the code to do the actual drawing).

Classes and Instances

Objects are typed by their class. Every object belongs to some class; it is an *instance* of that class. In a real-world analogy, the information contained in the plans and specifications of a Porsche sports car is a class. That information defines what it means to be a Porsche and how to construct one. The actual car in your driveway (lucky you) is an instance of the class Porsche. Back in the world of computer programs, a class is a template or recipe that defines a set of variables, called *instance variables*, and a set of methods, including the code to implement those methods. An object (an instance of a class) is an actual chunk of memory that provides storage for the set of the variables defined in the class. There can be more than one instance of a given class. Each instance is a separate area of memory and has its own copy of the instance variables defined by the class.

Methods

Methods are similar to functions but they are not quite the same thing. Methods are executed on behalf of an instance of the class that defines them. When an object executes a method, that method has access to the object's data. If you send a `draw` message to a `Shape` object, the `draw` method will use that `Shape` object's outline, position, and color. If you send the same `draw` message to a different `Shape` object, the `draw` method will use the other `Shape`'s outline, position, and color.

Encapsulation

Encapsulation, sometimes called *information hiding*, refers to hiding the inner workings of a class from the users of a class. It is a way of reducing complexity by reducing the connections between different parts of a program. Objects can be manipulated only by a defined interface: the set of publicly declared methods its class implements.

A programmer writing code that uses the **Shape** class does not need to know how the **Shape**'s data is stored internally or how the drawing code works. He or she only needs to know that when a **Shape** instance receives a **draw** message, it will draw itself.

Encapsulation gives the developer of a class the freedom to tinker with its implementation without disturbing code that uses the class. The developer of the **Shape** class might, for example, change the coordinate system the **Shape** uses to store the points describing its outline, or improve the performance of the **draw** method by caching a bitmap representation of the shape. As long as the new coordinate system and the new, improved **draw** method produce the same result as the old version in all cases, no other code has to be changed. Code that uses the **Shape** class automatically benefits from the improved **draw** method the next time the program is compiled and linked.

Inheritance

Inheritance provides a way to create new classes by extending or modifying the behavior of an existing class. Suppose that you want to add an **AnnotatedShape** class to the drawing program. An **AnnotatedShape** draws a shape and a text annotation below the shape, as shown in Figure 3.2.

You could code **AnnotatedShape** from scratch, but that would be wasteful. Most of the code in **AnnotatedShape** would duplicate the code in **Shape**. It would be much better if you could specify that **AnnotatedShape** was the same as **Shape** except:

- An **AnnotatedShape** has one more variable, a string variable to hold the text of the annotation.

- An **AnnotatedShape** has two extra methods that set and retrieve the text of the annotation.

- **AnnotatedShape**'s **draw** method has a different implementation from **Shape**'s **draw** method. It has to draw the annotation as well as the shape.

Acheulean Hand-axe

Figure 3.2 An **AnnotatedShape**

If you define `AnnotatedShape` like this, then in object-oriented speak:

- `AnnotatedShape` *inherits* from `Shape`.
- `AnnotatedShape`'s implementation of the `draw` method *overrides* `Shape`'s implementation of `draw`.
- `AnnotatedShape` is a *subclass* of `Shape`.
- `Shape` is `AnnotatedShape`'s *superclass*.

Polymorphism

Polymorphism is the capability of objects belonging to different classes to respond to the same message. For example, you could add an `Image` class to the drawing program so the program can also render images (bitmaps). Like the `Shape` class, the `Image` class defines a `draw` method. Each class's implementation of the `draw` method is different: `Shape`'s `draw` method knows how to draw a `Shape` and `Image`'s `draw` method knows how to draw images. If you have a list of graphic objects that represent a drawing, you can render it on the screen by sending each object in the list a `draw` message. Even though the message is the same in each case, the `Shape` objects on the list will execute `Shape`'s version of `draw` and the `Image` objects will execute `Image`'s version of `draw`.

What Is the Point of an Object-Oriented Language?

It is possible, but difficult and somewhat unpleasant, to implement an object-oriented style of programming using a procedural language. Using C as an example, you could use structures as objects and regular C functions as methods. To add methods to your objects you could add fields to the object structure to hold pointers to the method functions. You could also add an argument to each method function that would allow you to pass in a pointer to the object on whose behalf it was being executed. But you will rapidly run into problems. Even something as simple as storing different classes of objects in a single array and looping over them requires awkward use of the cast operator.

There are other drawbacks. Building your own object system can result in fragile code and perhaps unintended consequences if you haven't thought through all the implications of your design. A more serious problem is that a homemade object system is likely to be a one-off design. A one-off custom design makes it difficult to incorporate code or libraries from other sources into your program. You would have to build everything from scratch, at a cost of longer development times and an expanded opportunity for bugs.

It is much easier to code an object-oriented design in a language that has the constructs for object-oriented programming built in to the language.

An Introduction to Objective-C

Objective-C is an object-oriented extension to C. As you will see in this section and the next, Objective-C's additions to C are quite minimal. The additions are primarily a way to define classes, a way to invoke methods, and a dozen or so keywords and directives to the compiler. The concepts are subtle and very powerful, but there is relatively little syntax to memorize.

In adding an object system to C, Objective-C doesn't eliminate the procedural parts of C. This gives you the best of both worlds. You can use objects for those tasks where they are appropriate and use the procedural part of Objective-C (plain C) where it is the best fit to the problem. Having plain C as a base for the language also makes it easy for Objective-C programs to use existing libraries and code that are written in plain C.

This section shows, in overview fashion, how Objective-C implements the concepts of object-oriented programming. The core part of Objective-C is covered in detail in Chapter 5, "Messaging," Chapter 6, "Classes and Objects," and Chapter 7, "The Class Object."

Defining a Class

By convention, Objective-C class names begin with an uppercase letter. The rest of the class name is *CamelCased*: Each of the remaining words in the name begins with a capital letter, and the words are not separated with an underscore character (_).

An Objective-C class definition has two parts: the *interface section* and the *implementation section*. The interface section declares the class's instance variables and its methods. The implementation section contains the code that implements the class's methods. The interface section is usually placed in a header file that is, by convention, named after the class. The implementation section goes in a file with a *.m* file extension, also named after the class. The *.m* file extension tells the compiler that the file contains Objective-C source code.

Interface Section

The interface section of a class definition looks like this:

```
@interface  className : superclassName
{
    Instance variable declarations
}

Method declarations

@end
```

- @interface and @end are used to mark the beginning and end of the interface section. Objective-C words that begin with an @ character are *compiler directives*, instructions to the compiler, not executable code.

- @interface is followed by the class name, a colon, and the name of the class's superclass.

- The class's instance variable declarations go between a set of curly brackets, following the `@interface` line.
- The class's methods are declared following the instance variable declarations.

> **Note**
>
> The method declarations must come after the instance variable declarations. If you place a method declaration before the curly brackets, the code will not compile.

To make this more concrete, consider a class, `Accumulator`, that holds a running total. The `Accumulator` class has an instance variable to hold the total, and methods to add to the total, report the total, and reset the total to zero. This is a fairly trivial example, but it lets you concentrate on the syntax. Here is `Accumulator`'s interface section:

```
1   @interface Accumulator : NSObject
2   {
3     int total;
4   }
5
6   - (void) addToTotal:(int) amount;
7   - (int) total;
8   - (void) zeroTotal;
9
10  @end
```

Following the naming convention, this code goes in a file named *Accumulator.h*.

- Line 1: The class is named `Accumulator`. By convention, Objective-C class names begin with a capital letter. `Accumulator`'s superclass is `NSObject`.
- Line 3: The `Accumulator` class has a single instance variable, `total`. The variable declarations in a class's interface section don't reserve any storage. When you create an instance of `Accumulator`, the new instance gets its own copy of `total`, but there is no storage associated with the class itself.
- Lines 6–8: These are method declarations. The form of a method declaration is

  - (*return type*) *method_name*:(*argument_type*) *argument*;

  The leading hyphen (–) indicates that these are instance methods, methods that will be executed by an instance of the class. The hyphen is followed by the type of the value returned by the method, encased in parentheses. Methods that do not return a value have a return type of **void**. If the method takes an argument, the method name is followed by a colon (:), the type of the argument encased in parentheses, and the argument name. Note that the colon is part of the method's name. `addToTotal:` and `addToTotal` are different method names. The declarations for methods that take more than one argument are slightly more complicated. They are covered in Chapter 5, "Messaging."

It is also possible to define class methods that are executed by the class itself. Class methods begin with a plus sign (+):

```
+ (return type) class_method_name:(argument_type) argument;
```

Class methods are explained later in this chapter and in Chapter 7, "The Class Object."

By convention, Objective-C method names are also CamelCased. However, unlike class names, the initial letter of a method name is lowercased.

Implementation Section

The implementation section contains a class's method implementations. `Accumulator`'s implementation section is shown here:

```
1   #import "Accumulator.h"
2
3   @implementation Accumulator
4
5   - (void) addToTotal:(int) amount
6   {
7     total = total + amount;
8   }
9
10  - (int) total
11  {
12    return total;
13  }
14
15  - (void) zeroTotal
16  {
17    total = 0;
18  }
19
20  @end
```

This code goes in a file named *Accumulator.m*.

- Line 1: The compiler needs information from a class's interface section when it compiles the corresponding implementation section, so *Accumulator.m* imports *Accumulator.h*. Recall that `#import` is like `#include`; it adds the text of the imported file at the point of the `#import`.

- Lines 3 and 20: The method implementations go between an `@implementation` directive (followed by the class name) and an `@end` directive.

- Lines 5–8: A method implementation consists of a repeat of the method declaration (without the terminating semicolon) followed by the code that implements the method, encased in curly brackets. The body of a method implementation is coded in the same way that you would code an ordinary C function.

- Line 7: Notice that a method implementation has direct access to the object's instance variables, even though it does not declare them.

Inheritance

All Objective-C classes, except for root classes, inherit from some other class. Except in some special circumstances, like distributed object systems, the only root class you need to be concerned with is NSObject. Almost all Objective-C classes are direct or indirect subclasses of NSObject. NSObject defines the class factory method, alloc, which is responsible for allocating memory for object instances, and the instance methods that define basic behaviors for all objects. Other classes, like the Accumulator class, acquire these methods by inheriting them from NSObject. Inheritance is covered in more detail in Chapter 6, "Classes and Objects."

Class Names as Types

Objective-C objects are created on the heap. This means that when you create an object instance (you'll see how to do this later in the chapter), what you receive is a pointer to some bytes on the heap. When people say, "This variable holds an Accumulator," or "This variable holds an Accumulator object," what they really mean is "This variable holds a pointer to an instance of the Accumulator class."

Variables that hold pointers to object instances are declared using the class name as the type. This line of code declares that the variable anAccumulator holds a pointer to an instance of the Accumulator class:

```
Accumulator *anAccumulator;
```

The explicit asterisk (*) that marks anAccumulator as a pointer is required. Omitting the asterisk:

```
Accumulator anAccumulator;   //WRONG
```

results in a compiler error. (The compiler thinks that you are trying to create the object on the stack, which is not allowed in Objective-C.)

Messaging (Invoking a Method)

Having objects isn't of much use unless you can get them to do something for you. You need a way to get an object to execute one of its methods. In some objected-oriented languages, such as Java and C++, method invocations are function calls that are associated with a particular object by appending the function call to the object variable with a period. If Accumulator were written in C++, you would write something like this to add a number to anAccumulator's total:

```
anAccumulator.addToTotal( 137 );
```

Objective-C uses a different system, called *messaging*, that was borrowed from the computer language Smalltalk (http://en.wikipedia.org/wiki/Smalltalk). Using messaging, you send the object a message rather than calling a function. The following line shows the form of a message expression:

```
[receiver message]
```

The *receiver* is the object that you would like to have execute a method. It's called the receiver because it receives the message. The *message* is the name of the method that you want executed, plus any arguments to the method. When the message expression is evaluated, the receiver executes the method that corresponds to the name in the message. (Chapter 5, "Messaging," explains how this is accomplished.)

Using an instance of the **Accumulator** class as an example, the following line of code adds 137 to **anAccumulator**'s total:

```
[anAccumulator addToTotal: 137];
```

Note that the argument goes after the colon.

The following line gets the current value of **anAccumulator**'s total and stores it in a variable named **currentTotal**:

```
int currentTotal = [anAccumulator total];
```

At first, messaging may seem to be just another way of writing a function call. It's not. The difference is subtle but powerful. The receiver and the message are not bound together at compile time. The message only contains a method name. It does not associate that method name with any particular class or method implementation. Different classes may provide different implementations of the same method name. When the message expression is evaluated at execution time, the receiver object executes the version of the method that is defined in its class.

Messaging also allows for dynamic techniques that are not possible with a language like C++ that requires method calls to be bound (determined) at compile time. For example, it is possible for the message part of an Objective-C message expression to be a variable. The actual message that is sent in such a message expression is determined at execution time, not at compile time. It is also possible to programmatically construct message expressions and save them as objects for execution at a later time (see the section *NSInvocation* in Chapter 17, "Blocks").

Polymorphism

As noted earlier in the chapter, the capability to send the same message to objects that are members of different classes and have them act on that message in a class-specific manner is called *polymorphism*.

As an example, consider a simple drawing program. The program defines classes **Shape** and **Image** to represent the various items that the program can draw. Both classes implement a method named **draw**, but each class's implementation of **draw** is different. To draw a picture on the screen, the program loops over a list of objects and draws each one in turn:

```
while( /* check for loop ending condition goes here */ )
  {
    id graphic = [graphicEnumerator nextObject];
    [graphic draw];
  }
```

`graphicEnumerator` is an instance of a class that hands out objects in a collection one by one. (Enumerators are covered in Chapter 10, "Control Structures in Objective-C.")

`id` is an Objective-C type, defined as a generic "pointer to object." It is used when a variable will hold objects of different classes at different times, or when you don't know at compile time what type of object will be stored in the variable at run time. You may assign an object of any type to an `id` variable without complaint from the compiler.

> **Note**
>
> `id` is inherently a pointer type. There is no need to add an asterisk (*).

In this example, `graphic` may hold a `Shape` object during one iteration of the loop and an `Image` during another iteration. When `graphic` contains a `Shape`, the `draw` message results in the execution of `Shape`'s implementation of `draw`. When it contains an `Image`, the `draw` message results in the execution of `Image`'s implementation of `draw`.

Although `id` makes writing polymorphic code convenient, the real source of polymorphism is the Objective-C messaging system. As long as at execution time `graphic` contains a `Shape`, an `Image`, or an instance of any other class that implements a `draw` method, the code works. Ultimately, what matters is the object type at run time, not the variable type.

Class Objects and Object Creation

Each class in Objective-C is represented by a class object that can execute methods on behalf of the class. An Objective-C class object is an actual piece of memory that contains information about the instance variables and the methods of the class it represents. Class objects are instances of a special class named `Class`.

You can message a class object by using the class name as the receiver in a message expression:

```
[classname classmessage]
```

When you message a class object, the method name in the message must be the name of a class method.

The primary use of a class object is as a factory to create instances of the class. Object instances are created with the class method `alloc`, which all classes inherit from the `NSObject` class:

```
Accumulator *anAccumulator = [Accumulator alloc];
```

`alloc` allocates the memory for the instance, fills in a special instance variable created by the compiler called `isa`, which is a pointer to the object's class object, zeros out all the other instance variables, and returns a pointer to the object.

> **Warning**
> The preceding line of code was for pedagogical purposes; in a real program you should always nest the `alloc` message with an initialization message, as shown in the next example.

All Objective-C objects need to be initialized. The syntax for creating an initialized instance of `Accumulator` is

```
Accumulator *anAccumulator = [[Accumulator alloc] init];
```

When the preceding line of code is executed:

1. An `alloc` message is sent to the class object for the `Accumulator` class.
2. The `alloc` class method allocates the memory for an `Accumulator` object and returns a pointer to the uninitialized object.
3. The uninitialized `Accumulator` object becomes the receiver for an `init` message. `init` is an instance method that `Accumulator` inherits from `NSObject`.
4. `init` returns a pointer to the now initialized `Accumulator` object, which is then assigned to the variable `anAccumulator`.

To learn more about class objects and class methods, see Chapter 7, "The Class Object."

> **Note**
> You don't have to worry about creating class objects. The compiler creates the class objects for you.

Memory Management

Whenever you allocate memory on the heap, you are responsible for returning that memory when it is no longer needed. If you allocate a chunk of memory using `malloc`, you must `free` it when you are finished with it. Objective-C uses a slightly different system for managing object memory called *reference counting* (also called *retain counting* or *managed memory*). Each Objective-C object has a *retain count*, which tracks the number of places the object is being used. When an object's retain count becomes zero, the object is deallocated and its bytes are returned to the heap.

The methods `retain` and `release` increment and decrement an object's retain count:

```
[anObject retain];  //Increments anObject's retain count
[anObject release]; //Decrements anObject's retain count
```

Objects are created with a retain count of one. If you create an object with a method whose name begins with `alloc`, `new`, `copy`, or `mutableCopy`, you "own" the object. When you are finished with the object, you must balance its creation and relinquish your ownership by sending it a `release` message. If you receive an object from a method whose name does *not* begin with `alloc`, `new`, `copy`, or `mutableCopy`, you do *not* own the object. In most circumstances, the object will remain valid for the remainder of the scope in which you acquired it. But if you want to use the object longer—for example, by storing it in an instance variable—you must "take ownership" of the object by sending it a `retain` message. This prevents the object's retain count from falling to zero if the object's creator releases it. You must eventually balance the `retain` message by sending the object a `release` message when you are finished with it.

Chapter 15, "Reference Counting," covers reference counting in detail. Chapter 16, "ARC," covers Automatic Reference Counting. When you use ARC, the compiler automates the system described in the preceding paragraphs. The compiler analyzes your code and inserts the appropriate `retain` and `release` messages for you.

Objective-C Additions

This section is a brief summary of the additions that Objective-C makes to C.

Runtime

Objective-C requires a *runtime* that does the work of setting up and operating the Objective-C messaging system. The runtime does its work silently, behind the scenes. The runtime is implemented as a dynamic link library of C functions that is provided on all systems that support Objective-C. In normal circumstances, there is no need to interact with the runtime directly by calling one of its functions.

Apple provides two different versions of the Objective-C runtime: "legacy" and "modern." The legacy runtime is used only for 32-bit Mac OS X programs, and the modern runtime is used for iOS applications (on both the simulator and iOS devices) and 64-bit applications (the default) running on Mac OS X 10.5 or later. There are some minor differences in the behavior of the two runtimes, which are covered as they are encountered later in the book.

Names

As in plain C, names in the object part of Objective-C are case sensitive. Objective-C has a number of naming conventions such as the naming conventions for class names and method names noted earlier in the chapter. These conventions are not an enforced part of the language, but they are almost universally followed. If you violate them, people familiar with Objective-C will have a difficult time following your code.

Some other name rules:

- A class can declare an instance variable that has the same name as an instance variable in a different class.
- A class can declare a method that has the same name as a method in a different class, as was shown in the section on polymorphism earlier in the chapter.

- A method can have the same name as an instance variable. (This is common for methods that return the value of an instance variable. See Chapter 12, "Properties.")
- An instance method of a class can have the same name as a class method of the same class.
- Apple considers method names that begin with an underscore character (_) to be reserved for internal Apple use.

Message Expressions

The most important addition that Objective-C makes to C is the *message expression*:

```
[receiver message]
```

The `receiver` is an object or, strictly speaking, a pointer to an instance of a class. The `message` is the name of one of the methods defined by the receiver's class plus any arguments that the method takes. When a statement containing a message expression is executed, the Objective-C runtime determines the receiver's class, looks up the method name contained in `message` in the class's list of methods, and executes the code corresponding to that method. Message expressions are covered in detail in Chapter 5, "Messaging."

> **Note**
>
> When the method in the message is a class method, the receiver is the class object or the class name (which can stand in for the class object in message expressions).

Compiler Directives

Words that begin with the character @ are compiler directives, not executable code. You've already seen `@interface`, which marks the beginning of the interface section of a class definition; `@implementation`, which marks the beginning of the implementation section; and `@end`, which is used to mark the ends of those sections. A complete list of Objective-C compiler directives is given in Appendix A, "Reserved Words and Compiler Directives."

Literal Strings

Literal strings are constants that hold the text of a string. Objective-C uses constant instances of `NSString`, a class defined in the Foundation framework (see *Frameworks* later in this chapter), instead of plain C strings. You create a literal `NSString` the same way that you create a literal C string except that you add an @ at the beginning of the string:

```
"The Big Apple"   // Literal C string
@"The Big Apple"  // Literal NSString
```

> **Note**
>
> Strictly speaking, @"The Big Apple" is a compiler directive that tells the compiler to create a literal NSString with the text "The Big Apple."

Objective-C Keywords

id

id is a type that holds a "pointer to object." A variable that is declared as id can hold a pointer to any Objective-C object, independent of the object's class.

The declaration

```
id myObject;
```

tells you (and the compiler) that **myObject** is a pointer to an object. The bytes at that address are the memory representation of an instance of some class.

You can assign a variable of a more specific type to a variable of type id, and vice versa, without an explicit cast; for example:

```
NSString *string1 = @"The Big Apple";
id  something;
NSString *string2;
something = string1;
string2 = something;
```

The compiler will silently assume that you know what you are doing. Note that the fact that id holds pointers is built in to the type. There is no need for an asterisk (*):

```
id *myObject;  // WRONG !
```

Finally, don't confuse id with **void***. The declaration

```
void *someBytes;
```

says nothing about what **someBytes** is. It's just a pointer to some bytes. What those bytes represent is unknown to the compiler.

nil

nil is a defined constant that represents a "pointer to no object." While nil is defined to be zero, it is universally used instead of the bare zero whenever an object pointer to nothing is required.

Using a bare zero will not cause any actual problems:

```
[anObject setObjectInstanceVariable: 0];  // Bad form
```

However, it is considered bad form. Using nil instead reminds you that what is being set to nothing is an object pointer. Code this instead:

```
[anObject setObjectInstanceVariable: nil];  // Correct form
```

In Objective-C, you can send messages to a receiver whose value is `nil`. Messages to `nil` are no-ops: They do nothing and execution continues with the next line of code. They do not cause a crash. This feature spares you from writing guard code such as the following:

```
// This check is unnecessary
if ( anObject )
  {
    [anObject someMethod];
  }
```

BOOL

For most of its history, C has lacked a defined Boolean type. Truth value is determined by evaluating expressions. If an expression evaluates to zero, it is considered false; otherwise, it is true. The C99 standard adds a Boolean type, `bool`, and the truth values `true` and `false`.

Objective-C has its own Boolean type, `BOOL`, and the truth constants `YES` and `NO`. `BOOL` is not a fundamental type. It is a typedef (alias) for `unsigned char`. `YES` and `NO` are just defined constants for 1 and 0.

Because Objective-C inherits all of C's types, you could use the `bool` type in your Objective-C programs. However, the Cocoa frameworks and most existing Objective-C code use `BOOL`. Although you could convert back and forth between `bool` and `BOOL`, it's easier to just forget about `bool` unless your program is using a library or framework that uses `bool`.

> ### Note
> Although the current version of Objective-C is based on the C99 standard, Objective-C was originally developed as an extension to an earlier version of C that lacked a Boolean type. Most of the Objective-C community uses the Objective-C `BOOL` despite the availability of the C99 `bool` type.

SEL

`SEL` is a type that holds a representation of an Objective-C method name. `SEL` is short for *selector*. Method names are sometimes called selectors because the runtime uses them to select the block of code to execute in response to a message (see Chapter 5, "Messaging").

A `SEL` is used for this determination, instead of the actual string name of the method, for performance reasons. Strings are awkward to manipulate; just comparing two strings for equality is a slow, multistep process. Comparing two `SEL`s is much faster.

You can use the compiler directive `@selector()` to convert a method name into its `SEL`:

```
SEL aSelector = @selector( aMethodName );
```

IMP

`IMP` is a typedef for "pointer to a function taking the arguments `id`, `SEL`, and possibly some other arguments, and returning `id`."

The compiler ultimately turns an Objective-C method into a regular C function. When you execute a method, the runtime uses the method's selector to find the actual function that implements the method and then executes that function. But occasionally, for purposes of efficiency or some behind-the-scenes trickiness, you may want to call the function that implements a method directly. You can do this by getting a pointer to the function and using that pointer to call the function. The methods and runtime functions you can use to get such a pointer return it typed as `IMP`:

```
IMP methodImplementation =
   [anObject methodForSelector: @selector( aMethodName )];
```

> **Note**
>
> IMP is also used as a slang term for "method implementation" in documentation and books, as in "use `methodForSelector:` to get the IMP."

Class

`Class` is a type that holds a reference to an Objective-C class. In Objective-C, classes are themselves objects. Because they are objects, classes must be instances of some class. That class, which is the class of classes, is named (drum roll, please) `Class`. Like `id` and `IMP`, and unlike any other class type, `Class` is inherently a pointer type and doesn't require an asterisk (`*`), for example:

```
Class *myClass; //WRONG !
```

Class objects are the topic of Chapter 7.

Frameworks

Objective-C works closely with a number of dynamic link libraries, called *frameworks*, which are not, strictly speaking, part of the Objective-C language (see Chapter 8, "Frameworks"). The Foundation framework provides classes for basic types such as strings, arrays, sets, and dictionaries (see Chapter 9, "Common Foundation Classes") on both iOS and OS X. The AppKit framework provides classes for windows, views, controls, and other user interface items on OS X. The UIKit framework provides these items for iOS. The combination of Foundation and AppKit is called Cocoa. The combination of Foundation and UIKit is called Cocoa Touch.

Framework Numeric Types

The types in this section are not part of the Objective-C language. They are defined in various header files, but you will see them often enough that they are mentioned here. Apple has replaced most occurrences of `int` and `float` in their framework code with defined types whose length depends on whether the code is being compiled as a 32-bit executable or a 64-bit executable (see Appendix C, "32- and 64-Bit").

NSInteger

NSInteger replaces most occurrences of int in the frameworks. It is defined to be an int (32-bit integer) in a 32-bit environment and a long (64-bit integer) in a 64-bit environment.

NSUInteger

NSUInteger is the unsigned analog of NSInteger. It replaces most occurrences of unsigned int in the frameworks. It is an unsigned 32-bit integer in a 32-bit environment and an unsigned long (unsigned 64-bit integer) in a 64-bit environment.

CGFloat

CGFloat replaces float. It is a float (32 bits) when compiling for a 32-bit environment and a double (64 bits) when compiling for a 64-bit environment. The Foundation framework provides a defined constant, CGFLOAT_IS_DOUBLE, to use if you need to know programmatically whether CGFloat is a float or a double in the current environment:

```
if ( CGFLOAT_IS_DOUBLE )
    NSLog( @"Double !" );
else
    NSLog( @"Float !" );
```

NSLog

NSLog is a function for character output defined by the Foundation framework. NSLog is not a part of the Objective-C language itself, but it is described here because it is used for many of the examples and exercises in this book.

NSLog is similar to printf, but it has these differences:

- NSLog writes to the console log as well as to a terminal window. The console log is a log of messages maintained by the operating system. On OS X, you can view the console log with the Console application (*/Applications/Utilities/Console.app*).

- NSLog's format string is a literal NSString rather than a literal C string.

- NSLog automatically advances to a new line after printing. There is no need to add \n to the end of the format string.

- NSLog uses an additional conversion specifier, %@, which takes an Objective-C object as its argument. During the conversion, NSLog invokes the argument object's description method. The description method returns an NSString describing the object. The returned NSString replaces the %@ in the output, as shown in this example:

```
NSString *aString = @"Hello New York!";
NSLog( @"The object description is: %@", aString );
```

The description of an `NSString` is just the string itself. Executing the preceding code produces this output:

```
The object description is: Hello New York!
```

When you create your own classes, you can override the **description** method to provide custom descriptions for your classes.

Note

If you use a format string with a `%@` specifier, but forget to provide a corresponding object argument, `NSLog` attempts to send a description message to the bytes at the address where the object argument should have been located. This usually results in a crash.

You shouldn't leave `NSLog` statements in a shipping program (it's rude to scribble in a customer's console log), but it is useful for simple output while you are learning and for debugging.

`NSLog` has one feature that can be annoying: It prefixes what you ask it to print with a long string of information, including the time and date the statement was executed (down to the millisecond), the executable name, and the process ID of the program that executes it. The following `NSLog` statement:

```
NSLog( @"Greetings from NSLog" );
```

produces the following output:

```
2010-02-01 11:41:26.556 a.out[33955:903] Greetings from NSLog
```

For visual clarity, in the rest of the book this extra information has been stripped from examples showing the output of `NSLog`.

Summary

This chapter began with a general discussion of object-oriented programming. After reading it, you should have a basic understanding of the following concepts: classes, objects, instance variables, methods, encapsulation, inheritance, polymorphism, and messaging.

The second part of the chapter began the task of illustrating how these concepts are implemented in Objective-C. The next chapter builds on this one by taking you, step by step, through a small but complete Objective-C program. You will also learn how to build and run programs using Xcode, Apple's integrated development environment.

4

Your First Objective-C Program

The previous chapter introduced the concepts of object-oriented programming and covered the basic syntax of Objective-C. This chapter puts those concepts and syntax to work in a simple program. Following tradition, this program will be a "Hello World" program, but with a twist: It will be an object-oriented "Hello World" program. The chapter will examine the program line by line. You should follow along by building the program yourself using Xcode, Apple's integrated development environment (IDE).

> **Note**
>
> An IDE is a program that manages all aspects of application development, including file management, code writing and editing, compiling, linking, and debugging. Xcode, Apple's IDE, runs on Mac OS X and is used for building programs for both Mac OS X and iOS. Compiling and debugging from the command line is useful for quick test programs, but it becomes impractical for large applications. If you are developing for iOS, you need to use Xcode to access the iOS iPhone and iPad simulator, and to load and debug applications on an iOS device.
>
> You can get Xcode from the Mac App Store (it's free). If you are a member of either the iOS Developer Program or the Mac Developer Program, you can download prerelease versions of Xcode as a disk image (*.dmg* file) from the Apple developer website (https://developer.apple.com/).

Building with Xcode

Xcode is a big application, but this chapter looks only at what you need to build a simple program. Before starting, you should make a directory to hold your projects, something like *~/ObjectiveCProjects* or *~/Code/ObjectiveCProjects*.

Note

The tilde (~) is Mac OS X (and Unix) shorthand for your home directory. For example, in my case:

`~/ObjectiveCProjects`

is equivalent to

`/Users/rclair/ObjectiveCProjects`

Open Xcode (located in your */Applications* directory if you installed it from the Mac App Store) and start a new project by using *File > New > New Project...* (Shift-⌘-N). You should see the *New Project* sheet, shown in Figure 4.1.

Note

The default arrangement of Xcode's windows and views takes up most of the screen. To save space the screen pictures in this chapter show only the area that is relevant to the topic being discussed.

In the *New Project* sheet, do the following:

1. Select *Application* under *Mac OS X* in the left pane.
2. Click the *Command Line Tool* icon in the upper-right pane to select it.
3. Click the *Next* button (or press the Return key).
4. A new sheet appears (Figure 4.2) that lets you select some options for your project.

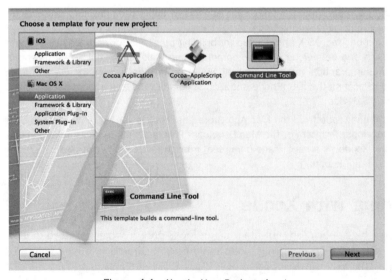

Figure 4.1   Xcode *New Project* sheet

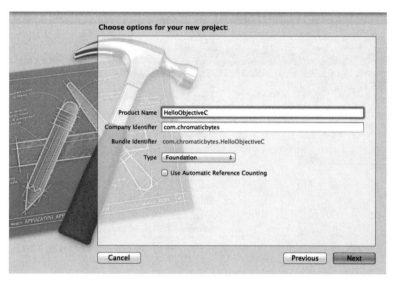

Figure 4.2   Xcode *New Project Options* sheet

In the *New Project Options* sheet, do the following:

1. Enter *HelloObjectiveC* (or whatever you like) in the *Product Name* text field.

2. Enter something in the *Company Identifier* text field. Since you are not going to be selling HelloObjectiveC, it doesn't matter what you enter here. If this were a real product, you would enter a unique identifier of some sort. A common choice for a unique identifier is a domain that you own, entered in reverse DNS order, such as com.mydomain.

3. Make sure the *Type* pop-up menu is set to *Foundation*.

4. Make sure the *Use Automatic Reference Counting* check box is left unchecked. You will be using manual reference counting for this example. As I mentioned in the Preface, the book will teach you how reference-counted memory management works by using manual reference counting until Automatic Reference Counting is covered in Chapter 16.

5. Click the *Next* button (or press the Return key).

6. Another sheet appears that lets you select the directory where your project will be stored. Choose the directory you just created for projects and click *Create* (or press the Return key).

When you are finished, you should see the project window for HelloObjectiveC, as shown in Figure 4.3. By default the left pane shows the *Project Navigator* view. This is a tree view showing all the files associated with the project. Since we will look at the files in detail, I opened a number of the disclosure triangles in the tree view before taking the screen picture.

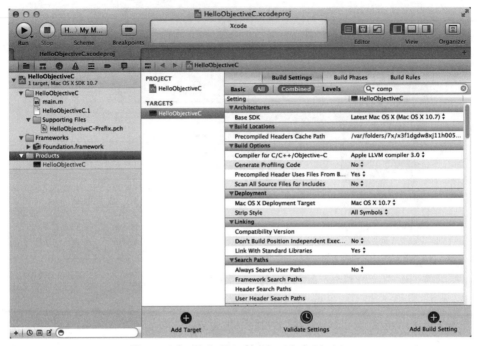

Figure 4.3   HelloObjectiveC project window

> **Note**
>
> The disclosure triangle is the small triangle to the left of a folder in a tree structure. When it points to the right, the contents of the corresponding folder are hidden. When you click on the disclosure triangle, it rotates to point downward and the contents of the folder are revealed. Clicking on the disclosure triangle a second time returns the triangle to its original position and hides the contents of the folder.

> **Note**
>
> Xcode is very (some might say excessively) configurable. The screen pictures in this chapter show what you should see with the default configuration. To learn more about how to set up and use Xcode choose *Xcode User Guide* from the *Help* menu.

The contents of the various panes will change as you do different things. In its initial state the pane on the right shows settings that control how the project is built. You can ignore these; for this project the default values are what you need.

The left pane shows many different things depending on which of the small icons just above it is selected. When you first create your project, the far left icon is selected. This shows a tree view of all the files in your project.

- The top item on the left, *HelloObjectiveC*, represents the project and all the items needed to build the project.

- *main.m* is an Objective-C file for your program, containing a skeleton **main** routine. Recall that every Objective-C program must have a **main** routine. The next section looks at this file in detail.

- *HelloObjectiveC.1* is the file for a Unix **man** page for HelloObjectiveC. Xcode added *HelloObjectiveC.1* to the project because it thinks you are making a Unix tool. Just ignore this item.

- *HelloObjectiveC_Prefix.pch* is a precompiled header file, something that helps make the compiler more efficient when dealing with large numbers of header files. Xcode configures *HelloObjectiveC_Prefix.pch* for you so you don't need to do anything with it.

- *Foundation.framework* is the framework that contains the non-GUI Cocoa classes. (A framework is a directory structure that wraps a dynamic link library; see Chapter 8, "Frameworks.") Because you told Xcode that you are building a Foundation (command line) tool, Xcode assumes that you are going to use classes or functions defined in Foundation. Xcode adds *Foundation.framework* to the project so that your program can link against it.

- *HelloObjectiveC* is your finished program. It is shown in red (on your monitor, not in the book) because Xcode can't find it. (Xcode can't find the program HelloObjectiveC because you haven't built it yet.)

Objective-C Program Structure

Click *main.m* in the left pane to open it in an editor in the right pane. (You can open files in a separate window by double-clicking instead of single-clicking.) When the file opens, your window should look like the example shown in Figure 4.4.

The code that Xcode generates is shown in Listing 4.1.

Listing 4.1   *main.m* (**first version**)

```
1   #import <Foundation/Foundation.h>
2
3   int main (int argc, const char * argv[])
4   {
5
6       @autoreleasepool {
7
8           // insert code here...
9           NSLog(@"Hello, World!");
10
11      }
12      return 0;
13  }
```

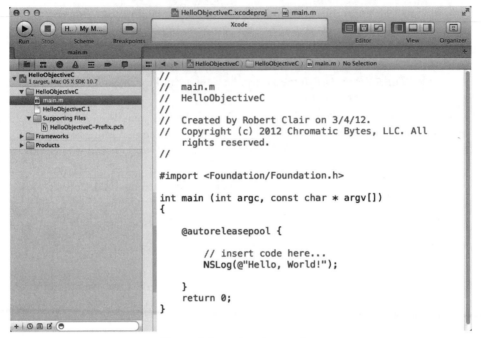

Figure 4.4   *main.m* in an editor

> **Note**
>
> Xcode puts a lot of comments at the top of newly created files, listing the project name, the filename, the author, and a copyright notice. These comments aren't shown in the listings in this chapter. Like all comments, they have no effect on compiling or executing the program.

Notice that Xcode has created a trivial "Hello World" program for you. The `NSLog` statement in Line 9 prints out `Hello World`. This is convenient if your only goal is to acquire a "Hello World" program, but it doesn't provide much of a learning experience. In the next section you'll create an object-oriented version of HelloObjectiveC by removing the `NSLog` statement and replacing it with an object that issues greetings.

Looking at the rest of the code:

- Line 1: This line imports the header files for the classes in the Foundation framework. The Foundation contains classes for strings, arrays, dictionaries, and other necessities. To use any of these classes, you must import the corresponding header files, so most programs import them as a group, as shown here.

- Line 3: This line begins the program's `main` function (the lines between the curly brackets). Every Objective-C program requires a `main` function. When the program is started, the OS transfers control to the `main` function. The program begins executing statements in the `main` function body and continues until it reaches the `return` statement at the bottom of the `main` function.

The `int` preceding the `main` indicates that `main` should return an integer.

`int argc` and `const char *argv[]` are the arguments to `main`. `argv` (for *argument variables*) is an array of C strings. `argc` (for *argument count*) is the number of elements in `argv`. The first element of `argv`, `argv[0]`, is always present. It is the name of the program. If `argc` is greater than one, the remaining elements of `argv` are arguments passed in to the program from the command line. You don't need these for most programs, including HelloObjectiveC, but Xcode puts them in for you when it generates the files for a new application.

- Line 6: The compiler directive `@autoreleasepool` creates an *autorelease pool*. The pool is in effect from the opening bracket following the `@autoreleasepool` directive until the matching closing bracket on Line 11. Autorelease pools are an advanced feature of Objective-C's reference-counted memory management system. Autorelease pools are covered in Chapter 15, "Reference Counting," but you don't need to worry about them for the examples in this chapter. Just ignore Lines 6 and 11 for now.

- Line 12: On Mac OS X and other Unix systems, a return value of 0 indicates that the program completed without an error; any other value means an error. Unless you are writing a command line utility that has meaningful error conditions, you should just `return 0` as shown in Line 12.

Build and Run the Program

Before going on to the next section, build and run this version of HelloObjectiveC (*Product > Run*, or ⌘-R).

After it has compiled the program, Xcode opens another pane below the right pane. To see the console window (which shows the output of the `NSLog` statement) you must click on the center button in the strip at the top right of the new pane as shown in Figure 4.5. You can then resize the console by dragging the vertical divider on its left side.

GUI Applications and `main`

In the rest of the chapter you will be adding code in `main` to make a simple application. In the world of GUI applications the `main` routine is very simple. It is used to call a function that starts an event loop that handles interactions with the user. This is the `main` routine of a Cocoa GUI application:

```
int main(int argc, char *argv[])
{
    return NSApplicationMain(argc,
                        (const char **) argv);
}
```

The `main` routine simply calls the function `NSApplicationMain`.
`NSApplicationMain` starts the event loop. When you quit a Cocoa GUI application, it pops out of the event loop and `NSApplicationMain` returns.

The `main` routine of an iOS app is similar:

```
int main(int argc, char *argv[])
{
    @autoreleasepool {
        return UIApplicationMain(argc, argv, nil,
                    NSStringFromClass([AppDelegateClassName class]));
    }
}
```

In iOS `UIApplicationMain` performs the same duties as `NSApplicationMain` does on Mac OS X. It also sets up the app's app delegate. (It identifies the app delegate class by name. `NSStringFromClass()` is a Foundation function that returns the name of a class as a string object.)

In both cases Xcode generates `main` for you. In a GUI application, you rarely need to modify the generated `main`. However, in this example we are writing a command line tool and not a GUI app, so we will be adding code to `main`.

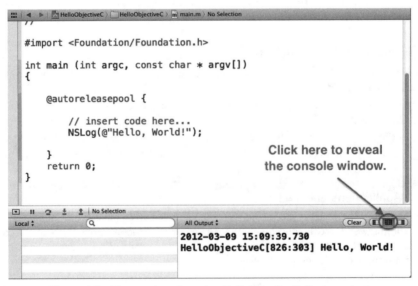

Figure 4.5 The results of running HelloObjectiveC (first version)

An Object-Oriented "Hello World"

This section takes you through creating an object-oriented version of HelloObjectiveC. It defines a class, named `Greeter`, which has the capability to remember the text of a greeting and to issue the greeting on command. The `main` routine of the new version of HelloObjectiveC creates an instance of the `Greeter` class, sets the text of the greeting, and then asks the `Greeter` to issue its greeting. Like all Objective-C classes, the `Greeter` class has an interface section that declares the class's instance variables and methods, and an implementation section that contains the code that implements those methods. The `Greeter` class's interface section goes in a header file named *Greeter.h*, and the implementation section goes in a file named *Greeter.m*. You can use Xcode to create skeleton versions of these files.

Choose *File > New > New File...* (⌘-N). You should see the *New File* sheet, shown in Figure 4.6.

In the *New File* window, do the following:

1. Select *Cocoa* under *Mac OS X* in the left pane.

2. Click the *Objective-C class* icon in the upper-left pane to select it.

3. Click the *Next* button (or press the Return key). The *New File* sheet should be replaced by a second sheet that allows you to set the name and superclass of your new class, as shown in Figure 4.7.

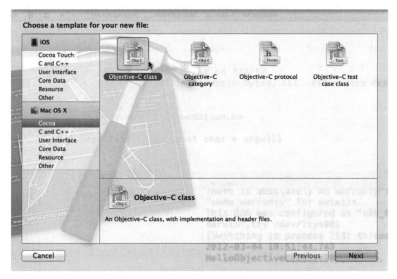

Figure 4.6   Xcode *New File* sheet

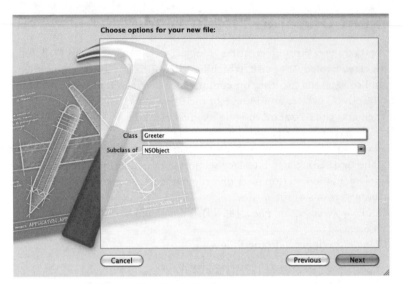

Figure 4.7   Xcode *New File* second sheet

In the second sheet, do the following:

1. Enter *Greeter* in the *Class* text field.

2. Make sure that the *Subclass of* pop-up menu is set to *NSObject*.

3. Click *Next* or use your Return key.

4. Another sheet appears that lets you select where to store the newly created file. It initially offers you the directory where the other files for your project are stored. Click on *Create* or use the Return key.

Look at the tree list in the left pane of your project window and notice that Xcode has added the files *Greeter.h* and *Greeter.m* to your project. In the next two sections you will fill in these two files.

Greeter.h

Click on *Greeter.h* in your project window to open an editing view, and change the contents of the file so that it looks like Listing 4.2.

Listing 4.2   *Greeter.h*

```
1   #import <Foundation/Foundation.h>
2
3   @interface Greeter : NSObject
4   {
5     NSString *greetingText;
```

```
 6   }
 7
 8   - (NSString*) greetingText;
 9   - (void) setGreetingText:(NSString*) newText;
10   - (void) issueGreeting;
11
12   @end
```

Line 1 imports the Foundation headers. This single import makes the headers for all the classes in the Foundation framework available to your program.

The compiler directives—`@interface` on Line 3 and `@end` on Line 12—mark the beginning and end, respectively, of the interface section.

The `@interface` line contains the name of the class being defined, followed by a colon and the name of that class's superclass. Line 3 tells the compiler that this section defines the class `Greeter`, which is a subclass of `NSObject`. The `NSObject` class provides some basic behaviors that are required for all Objective-C classes. All the classes that are considered in this book are subclasses of `NSObject` or some other class that is directly or indirectly a subclass of `NSObject`. Classes and inheritance are covered in Chapter 6, "Classes and Objects."

When you define a class, the compiler requires information about the class's superclass. You provide this information by importing the superclass's header file. In this example, *Foundation.h* automatically imports *NSObject.h*, so you don't have to do anything extra.

The lines between the curly brackets list the class's *instance variables*. Instance variables are sometimes referred to as *ivars*. Each instance of a class has its own copy of each instance variable. The `Greeter` class defines a single instance variable, `greetingText`. `greetingText` is typed as a pointer to an `NSString` object. `NSString` is a Foundation class that holds a string of characters (see Chapter 9, "Common Foundation Classes"). Instance variables may be either pointers to objects or C types.

> **Note**
>
> The pointer part of the declaration of `greetingText` is important. All Objective-C objects are created on the heap and referenced by a pointer. The blocks feature (added to Objective-C in Mac OS X 10.6 and iOS 4) introduces a single exception to this rule for the block class. Now that you know about this exception, please forget about it until Chapter 17, "Blocks."

Lines 8, 9, and 10 declare the `Greeter` class's methods. The form of a method declaration is

```
- (returnType) methodName;
```

If the method has an argument, a value to be passed to the method, its form is

```
- (returnType) methodName:(ArgumentType) argumentName;
```

If the method doesn't return anything, the return type is **void**. The leading hyphen (–) indicates that these methods are instance methods.

setGreetingText: and **greetingText** set and retrieve the **NSString** object held in the instance variable **greetingText**. Methods like these are called *accessor* methods or, more casually, *setter* and *getter* methods. It is a custom (and a necessity for using an advanced feature of Cocoa called key-value coding) to name the accessors for an instance variable after the instance variable's name. The setter and getter for an instance variable named **someObject** would be named **setSomeObject:** and **someObject**, respectively (with the capitalizations shown here).

> **Note**
>
> In the case where the property is a Boolean value, the getter may also be named *isPropertyName*. The getter for a Boolean property named **visible** may be named either **visible** or **isVisible**.

The use of accessor methods illustrates *information hiding* (also known as *encapsulation*), an important concept in object-oriented programming. Code that uses the **Greeter** class does not touch the instance variable **greetingText** directly. This leaves the maintainer of the class free to modify the class's implementation as long as the accessor methods still work properly after the modification. For example, an updated **Greeter** class might choose to store the greeting text in an **NSDictionary** object instead of a separate instance variable. (An **NSDictionary** is a type of container object, an object that holds other objects; see Chapter 9, "Common Foundation Classes.") As long as the methods **greetingText** and **setGreetingText** are updated to store and retrieve the greeting text using the dictionary, any code that uses a **Greeter** object will be unaffected by the change.

The final method, **issueGreeting**, is the method that causes the **Greeter** to proclaim its greeting.

Greeter.m

The implementation section of a class definition contains the code that does the actual work. Close the editing window for *Greeter.h*, and then return to the project window and click *Greeter.m* to open it in an editing window. Change the contents of the file to what is shown in Listing 4.3.

Listing 4.3   *Greeter.m*

```
1  #import "Greeter.h"
2
3  @implementation Greeter
4
5  - (NSString*) greetingText
6  {
7    return greetingText;
```

```
 8   }
 9
10   - (void) setGreetingText:(NSString*) newText
11   {
12      [newText retain];
13      [greetingText release];
14      greetingText = newText;
15   }
16
17   - (void) issueGreeting
18   {
19      NSLog(@"%@", [self greetingText]);
20   }
21
22   - (void) dealloc
23   {
24      [greetingText release];
25      [super dealloc];
26   }
27
28   @end
```

A class's implementation file imports the header file that contains the class's interface. *Greeter.m* begins by importing *Greeter.h*. Enclosing the header filename in quote marks (") tells the compiler to look for the header file in a local directory, in this case your project directory. There is no need to add an import statement for the framework headers. Because *Greeter.h* already imports the framework headers, importing *Greeter.h* into *Greeter.m* automatically imports the framework headers into *Greeter.m*.

The implementation section begins with an **@implementation** compiler directive, followed by the class name on the same line. It ends with an **@end** directive. The method implementations go between the two directives.

A method implementation consists of the text of the method's declaration without the ending semicolon, followed by a pair of curly brackets enclosing the code that does the actual work. The following sections go through **Greeter**'s method implementations in order.

greetingText

greetingText is a very simple method; it just returns a pointer to the **NSString** stored in the instance variable **greetingText**.

setGreetingText:

setGreetingText: has some new things. It takes an argument, a pointer to an **NSString** object that holds the greeting text that we want the **Greeter** to remember. The colon is part of the name; the method name is

setGreetingText:

not

```
setGreetingText
```

Lines 12 and 13 are message expressions. The form of a messaging expression is

```
[receiver message]
```

The *receiver* is the object that is being asked to execute a method. The *message* is the name of that method, plus any arguments that the method takes. When a message expression is executed, the runtime system determines the class of the receiver, looks up the method in the class's list of method names, and then executes the code that corresponds to the method name. This process is covered in more detail in Chapter 5, "Messaging."

`retain` and `release` are methods that `NSString` inherits from `NSObject`. They are part of Objective-C's reference counting system. In a program using reference counting, each object has a *retain count* or *reference count*.[1] An object's retain count keeps track of how many *other* objects are using the object. When an object is first created, it has a retain count of one. Sending an object a `retain` message increments the object's retain count; sending a `release` message decrements the retain count. When an object's retain count drops to zero, the object is removed; its memory is returned to the heap and any further references to the object are invalid.

> **Note**
>
> As noted in the Preface, Apple has now introduced Automatic Reference Counting (ARC). When you use ARC, the compiler analyzes your code and inserts any required `retain` and `release` messages for you. Because it is important to have a good understanding of the underlying reference counting system, this book uses the existing manual reference counting system until ARC is covered in Chapter 16. Once you are comfortable with the basics of Objective-C and have read Chapter 16, you can come back and go through the examples again, this time using ARC.

The `Greeter` didn't create the object passed in the argument `newText`, and it has no information about if or when other code might cause `newText`'s retain count to drop to zero. To prevent `newText` from being deallocated while the `Greeter` is still using it, the `Greeter` takes ownership of `newText` by sending it a `retain` message. This assures that `newText`'s retain count remains at least one while the `Greeter` is using it.

In this setter method, the `Greeter` has finished with the `NSString` object currently held in `greetingText`. In Line 13, it relinquishes its ownership of that object by sending it a `release` message to balance the `retain` message that was sent to the object when it was first stored. Sending a `release` message does not necessarily mean

---

1. The two terms are used interchangeably in the Objective-C literature.

that an object will be deallocated. The **release** message only decrements the object's retain count. If the new retain count is zero, the object will be deallocated.

> **Note**
>
> The compiler initializes all instance variables to zero (for numeric types) or **nil** (for object pointers). The first time that **setGreetingText** is called, **greetingText** will be **nil**. Executing a message expression with a **nil** receiver is not an error. It is just a no-op; nothing happens.

Finally, Line 14 stores the new **NSString** in **greetingText**.

The order of Lines 12 and 13 is important. Releasing **greetingText** before retaining **newText** could cause a crash if they were both the same object. The **release** message might decrement the object's retain count to zero and cause it to be deallocated. The subsequent **retain** message would then be sent to an invalid receiver. You might think it unlikely that someone would invoke **setGreetingText:** twice in a row with the same argument, but you have no guarantee that it won't happen. It is best to code defensively.

issueGreeting

issueGreeting is the method that delivers the greeting. It uses the Foundation function **NSLog** to print the greeting string. In Line 19, the second argument to **NSLog** is a message expression, not an object. When Line 19 is executed, the message expression is evaluated and the expression's **return** value (an **NSString** containing the greeting) is used as the argument corresponding to the **%@** specifier in the **NSLog** format string.

Where did **self** come from and what is it? **self** is a special variable that is automatically created for you by the compiler and the runtime system. **self** is a pointer to the object that was the receiver when the method was invoked. When Line 19 is executed, **self** points to the object that was used as a receiver when the method **issueGreeting** was invoked. Inside the **issueGreeting** method **self** is used as the receiver to retrieve the object's **greetingText**.

dealloc

When an object's reference count drops to zero, the object's **dealloc** method is called before its bytes are returned to the heap. This gives the object a chance to perform any necessary cleanup tasks. **dealloc** is declared in **Greeter**'s superclass, **NSObject**. The **Greeter** class *overrides* the superclass implementation of **dealloc** by providing its own implementation. When a **dealloc** message is sent to an instance of the **Greeter** class, it is **Greeter**'s implementation that is executed.

Greeter's cleanup consists of releasing the object held in **greetingText**. One of the rules of reference counting is that every time you send an object a **retain** message, you must eventually balance the **retain** with a **release** message. If a **Greeter** object didn't release the **NSString** held in **greetingText**, it might hang around after the Greeter object was gone. If there were no other references to the string, it would be a memory leak.

Line 25 is interesting. Unlike self, super is not an actual variable or pointer. When super is used as a receiver, it tells the runtime to execute the implementation of the message provided by the object's superclass. Here, [super dealloc] invokes NSObject's implementation of dealloc. It is NSObject's dealloc that actually returns an object's bytes to the heap.

If your class implements a dealloc method, you must always remember to invoke the superclass dealloc from within your class's implementation of dealloc. If you forget to do this, NSObject's implementation of dealloc will never be called and the bytes allocated for the object will never be released. The message [super dealloc] should be the *last* line in a class's dealloc method. When it returns, the object has been deallocated and is no longer valid.

> **Note**
>
> Other than invoking [super dealloc] as described in the preceding paragraph, you should never invoke dealloc yourself. dealloc is automatically invoked when an object's retain count falls to zero.

main.m

Now it's time to put the Greeter class to use. The code in the main routine creates an object of type Greeter, configures it, and then asks it to greet you. Click *main.m* in the project window. When the editing view opens, edit the file so that it looks like Listing 4.4.

Listing 4.4 *main.m* (second version)

```
1   #import <Foundation/Foundation.h>
2   #import "Greeter.h"
3
4   int main (int argc, const char * argv[])
5   {
6     @autoreleasepool {
7
8         Greeter* myGreeter = [[Greeter alloc] init];
9
10        [myGreeter setGreetingText: @"Hello Objective-C!!"];
11
12        [myGreeter issueGreeting];
13        [myGreeter release];
14    }
```

```
15   return 0;
16   }
```

Line 2 imports the header file for the `Greeter` class. Because this file creates an instance of `Greeter`, it must import `Greeter`'s header file.

Line 8 allocates an instance of the `Greeter` class, initializes the instance, and stores the pointer to it in the local variable `myGreeter`. Look at the innermost message on the right side:

```
[Greeter alloc]
```

The receiver in this message expression is the class `Greeter`. Objective-C classes are themselves objects and can have methods, called *class methods*. The `alloc` method is a class method that allocates storage for an (uninitialized) instance of `Greeter` and returns a pointer to it. The uninitialized `Greeter` instance then becomes the receiver for the `init` message. Because you didn't override `init` to provide your own implementation, `NSObject`'s implementation of `init` will be called. `NSObject`'s `init` returns the pointer to the initialized object but does nothing else.

Line 10 sets `myGreeter`'s greeting text. The directive

```
@"Hello Objective-C!!"
```

tells the compiler to create a constant `NSString` object with the requested text. This becomes the argument for the `setGreetingText:` message.

> **Note**
> The sharp-eyed reader may wonder what happens when the constant `NSString` object here encounters `retain` and `release` in the `setGreetingText:` method. The answer is: nothing. They are no-ops for a constant string. So why bother? Because `setGreetingText:` doesn't know anything about what type of `NSString` object will be passed in to it. If you use the `Greeter` class in a different program, it may be passed a normal allocated `NSString` object. If you want the class to behave properly, you shouldn't make assumptions about the type of input it will get.

Line 12 is the payoff. It causes `myGreeter` to actually issue the greeting by invoking `Greeter`'s `issueGreeting` method.

Finally, Line 13 releases the object held in `myGreeter`. Because you created the object (with `alloc`), you are responsible for releasing it when you are finished with it.

Build and Run the Program

Build the program and run it (*Product > Run*, or ⌘-R). You should see the greeting in the console window, as shown in Figure 4.8.

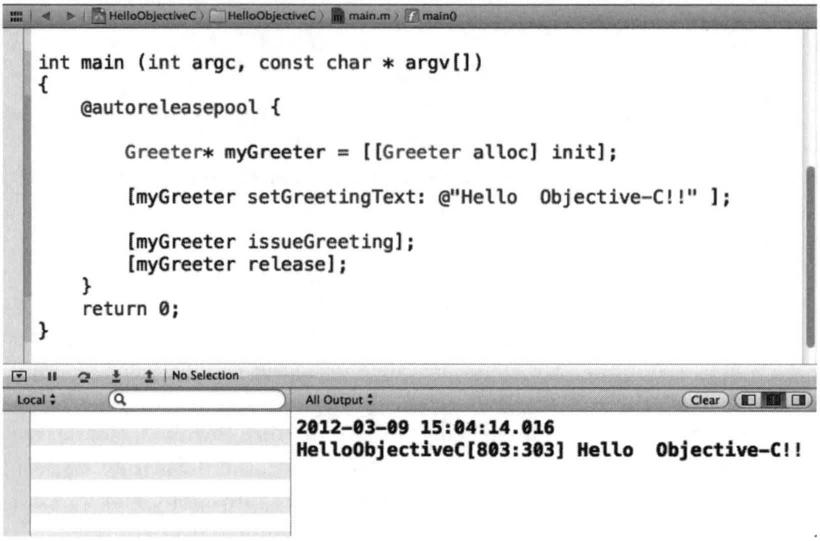

```
int main (int argc, const char * argv[])
{
    @autoreleasepool {

        Greeter* myGreeter = [[Greeter alloc] init];

        [myGreeter setGreetingText: @"Hello  Objective-C!!" ];

        [myGreeter issueGreeting];
        [myGreeter release];
    }
    return 0;
}
```

```
2012-03-09 15:04:14.016
HelloObjectiveC[803:303] Hello  Objective-C!!
```

Figure 4.8   The results of running HelloObjectiveC (second version)

Summary

This chapter has been a lot of words about a very small program. If you've followed along and worked through HelloObjectiveC using Xcode, you should now have the skills to build and run a non-GUI Objective-C program. You can put those skills to use doing the exercises in the remainder of the book.

This chapter concludes Part I of the book: a review of C and an introduction to Objective-C. The next section is a more detailed treatment of the Objective-C language. It begins with Chapter 5, "Messaging," which covers method names and declarations, message expressions, and how the Objective-C messaging system works.

Exercises

1. Modify the HelloObjectiveC program used as the example in this chapter:

    a. Define a `Greeting` class with `NSString` instance variables to hold the text of the greeting and a description of the greeting. (A sample description might say something like "This is the everyday greeting" or "This is the VIP greeting.") Be sure to supply methods to set and retrieve both the text of the greeting and the description. Name the files for the interface and implementation sections of the `Greeting` class *Greeting.h* and *Greeting.m*. Even if you are not completely comfortable with Objective-C at this point, you should be able to define the `Greeting` class by analogy, looking at the `Greeter` class.

b. Modify the `Greeter` class to use a `Greeting` object instead of an `NSString` for its greeting. To make this work, you have to place the following line of code at the top of the *Greeter.h* file:

```
#import "Greeting.h"
```

This line is necessary so that the compiler knows about the `Greeting` class while it is compiling the `Greeter` class (see Chapter 6, "Classes and Objects").

c. Modify *main.m* to allocate an instance of `Greeting` and pass it to the `Greeter` object.

d. Build and run your program to verify that it works correctly.

2. Extend your program from Exercise 1:

a. Modify the `Greeter` class so that it holds a second `Greeting` object. Name the new instance variable `vipGreeting`. Be sure to provide methods to set and get the new variable.

b. Modify `Greeter`'s `issueGreeting` method so that it takes an integer argument:

```
-(void) issueGreeting:(int) whichGreeting;
```

If `whichGreeting` is 0, issue the normal greeting; if it is 1, issue the VIP greeting. For any other value, log an error.

c. Modify *main.m* to allocate a second `Greeting` object and pass it to the `Greeter` object as the `vipGreeting`. Then, add a statement asking the `Greeter` to issue the `vipGreeting` as well as the original greeting.

d. Build and run your program to verify that it works correctly.

Part II

Language Basics

Part II of this book covers the Objective-C 2.0 language in detail. The first three chapters of Part II cover the core of what you need to know about Objective-C. The remaining chapters cover additional topics that are necessary for you to learn in order to gain a broad understanding of the language. When you have finished this section, you should be well on your way to becoming a skilled Objective-C programmer.

Chapters in this part of the book are

- Chapter 5, "Messaging"
- Chapter 6, "Classes and Objects"
- Chapter 7, "The Class Object"
- Chapter 8, "Frameworks"
- Chapter 9, "Common Foundation Classes"
- Chapter 10, "Control Structures in Objective-C"
- Chapter 11, "Categories, Extensions, and Security"
- Chapter 12, "Properties"
- Chapter 13, "Protocols"

5

Messaging

In Objective-C, when you want an object to do something, you send the object a message. In response, the object executes one of its methods. This is not quite the same thing as calling a function. Functions are usually statically bound—the code that the function executes is determined when the program is compiled. Using messaging, the actual code that is executed in response to a message is determined at execution time.

In this chapter you will learn how Objective-C messaging works. The chapter covers methods, message expressions, and the machinery of the messaging system.

Methods

The structure of an Objective-C method is very similar to that of a C function (in fact, the compiler eventually turns the methods into C functions). There are three major differences:

- Methods are executed on behalf of a particular instance of the class that defines them. The method receives a pointer to the object instance in the form of the hidden variable `self`. (*Hidden* means you can use the variable `self` in the method even though it is not declared in the method's argument list or anywhere else in the method's code.)

- Methods can directly access the object's instance variables without having to declare them.

- The syntax for naming the method and its arguments is different from that of a function.

A Simple Method

Imagine that you are writing a drawing program and one of your classes is a `Shape` class, as shown in this header file:

```
@interface Shape : Graphic
{
  NSColor *outlineColor;
```

```
  NSColor *fillColor;
  ...  // Other instance variables
}

...  // Method declarations

@end
```

> **Note**
>
> **NSColor** is a class that is defined in the OS X AppKit framework. For the examples in this book, the only thing that you need to know about **NSColor** is that it is a class that represents a color used for drawing on the screen or to a printer. If you are writing for iOS, you would use the UIKit class **UIColor** instead.

Shape should provide a method to return the object's fill color. Such a method would look like this:

```
1 - (NSColor*) fillColor
2 {
3   return fillColor; // fillColor is an instance variable
4 }
```

Looking at the preceding example:

- Line 1: The leading hyphen (–) indicates that this is an instance method. When this method is used in a message expression, the receiver is an instance of the **Shape** class. Methods that begin with a plus sign (+) are class methods and are used with a receiver that is a class name. Class methods are covered in Chapter 7, "The Class Object."
- Line 1: The method's return type is enclosed in parentheses. Here, **fillColor**'s return type is **NSColor***, a pointer to an **NSColor** object.
- Line 3: The **return** statement is the same as in a C function.
- Lines 2 and 4: The body of a method consists of one or more statements enclosed by curly brackets ({ ... }).

Methods with Arguments

Sometimes you have to pass information into a method, so you need methods that take arguments. One of the things that newcomers find most surprising about Objective-C is the way that method names are formed. The argument type, surrounded by parentheses, and the argument name go in the method declaration, preceded by a colon. The declaration of a method to set a **Shape**'s fill color looks like this:

```
- (void) setFillColor:(NSColor*) newFillColor;
```

The colon is part of the method name. The name of the preceding method is

```
setFillColor:
```

not

```
setFillColor
```

What if a method has multiple arguments? This is where things may begin to seem strange: When a method has more than one argument, the arguments are interspersed with parts of the method name. A method to set a **Shape**'s outline and fill color at the same time would be declared like this:

```
- (void) setOutlineColor:(NSColor*) outlineColor
          fillColor:(NSColor*) fillColor;
```

The preceding method's name is:

```
setOutlineColor:fillColor:
```

Note that each argument comes after a colon.

The parts of a method name are not argument labels, and you are not allowed to rearrange them.

```
setOutlineColor:fillColor:
```

and

```
setFillColor:outlineColor:
```

are different methods. Although you may find this way of naming methods odd at first, it makes it easy to write descriptive, self-documenting method names.

Methods, like functions, can take a variable number of arguments. Methods that take a variable number of arguments are declared like this:

```
- (void) methodWithVariableNumberOfArguments:(id) arg1, ...;
```

The comma and ellipsis are not part of the name. The name of the preceding method is

```
methodWithVariableNumberOfArguments:
```

Method Name Conventions

It is not a formal part of the Objective-C language specification, but it is an almost universal naming convention in Objective-C that each part of a method name begins with a lowercase letter, and that any subsequent words in that part of the name begin with capital letters, like this:

```
// Good form
- (void) setOutlineColor:(NSColor*) outlineColor
        fillColor:(NSColor*) fillColor;
```

The following method name is considered bad form because it does not follow the convention:

```
// Bad form
- (void) SetOutlineColor:(NSColor*) outlineColor
        FillColor:(NSColor*) fillColor;
```

Strictly speaking, it is not necessary to have any name characters before the colons. You could write

```
// Very bad form
- (void) setColors:(NSColor*)outlineColor
            :(NSColor*) fillColor;
```

The name of the preceding method would then be `setColors::`.

Names like `setColors::` are legal, but they are *very* bad form. They make your code extremely hard to read.

Messaging

Asking an Objective-C object to execute one of its methods is not the same thing as calling a function. Function calls are usually statically bound: What happens at run time is determined at compile time. When the compiler encounters a function call, it inserts a jump instruction into the code that makes up the function body. Objective-C uses a more dynamic system called *messaging*. When you want an Objective-C object to execute one of its methods, you send the object a message. The object responds by executing the method that corresponds to the message.

A message expression has the following form:

```
[receiver message]
```

The message expression is enclosed in square brackets. The receiver is the object that will execute a method. It *receives* the message. The message is the name of the method that you want the receiver to execute, plus any arguments that the method takes.

```
NSColor *newColor = ...
Shape  *aShape = ...
[aShape setFillColor: newColor];
```

In the preceding example, the message is

```
setFillColor: newColor
```

How does this work? When you execute a message expression, the Objective-C runtime examines the receiver and determines its class. The runtime has a table for each class that lists the methods that the class defines and associates the name of each method with a pointer to the code that implements the method. The runtime takes the method name from the message expression, finds the corresponding pointer in the receiver's class table, and then uses the pointer to execute the method's code. This process is discussed in more detail in the section *Under the Hood*, later in this chapter.

> **Note**
>
> Constantly using phrases like "send the `setFillColor:` message to `aShape`" can become tiresome. As a result, people (the author included) often speak loosely and say, "invoke `setFillColor:`" or even "call `setFillColor:`."

What Is the Runtime?

Who, or what, is this "runtime" that is doing all these things? It's not really mysterious. The runtime is just a shared library of plain C functions and data structures. Some of these functions are called when your program starts. These functions build tables based on information placed in your executable by the compiler. Other functions are called at various points in the execution of the program to look up and act on information in these tables. These function calls are automatically created for you by the compiler.

Polymorphism

Polymorphism is the capability of objects of different classes to respond to the same message. Suppose that your drawing program has the classes **Shape**, for drawing line art, **Text**, for drawing text, and **Image**, for drawing images. Each of the classes **Shape**, **Text**, and **Image** implements a method named **draw**. Although the method name, **draw**, is the same in each case, each class's implementation of **draw** is different. **Shape**'s **draw** method knows how to draw shapes, **Text**'s **draw** method knows how to draw text, and **Image**'s **draw** method draws images.

Drawing programs typically keep a list, called a *display list*, of the items in a drawing. To draw the screen, the program loops over the display list, drawing each item in the list in turn. In the following example, the display list is an instance of the Foundation class **NSMutableArray**. Assume that it contains a mixture of **Shape**, **Text**, and **Image** objects. The looping construct shown here is described in Chapter 10, "Control Structures in Objective-C." All you need to know for this example is that **enumerator** is an object that returns the objects stored in **displayList**, one by one, each time it receives a **nextObject** message. When the end of the array is reached, the **enumerator** returns **nil**.

```
1  NSMutableArray *displayList = ...
2  NSEnumerator *enumerator =[displayList objectEnumerator];
3  id graphic;
4
5  while (graphic = [enumerator nextObject] )
6  {
7    [graphic draw];
8  }
```

In Line 3, the variable `graphic` is typed as `id`, the generic "pointer to object" type. This allows `graphic` to hold whatever type of graphic, `Shape`, `Text`, or `Image`, the `nextObject` method returns.

The loop in Lines 5 through 8 is deceptively simple, but very powerful. It lets you draw a heterogeneous list of objects without knowing the class of each object or doing any extra work. As you loop, the variable `graphic` holds different objects belonging to different classes, each of which may implement the method `draw` in a completely different way. Each time Line 7 is executed, the runtime looks at the class of the object held in `graphic` and executes that class's version of `draw`. The classes used in this loop don't have to be subclasses of a common superclass, or related in any other way. The only requirement is that each class used in the loop must implement a method named `draw`.

Polymorphism helps you to write flexible, non-fragile code. Suppose at a later time you decide to add new graphics classes to the drawing program—for example, a `BrushStroke` class. You can add the new class to the program with minimal disturbance to the rest of the code. As long as the new `BrushStroke` class implements a `draw` method, instances of `BrushStroke` can be used with the existing display list and drawing loop without modifying or even recompiling the code.

Who Is Sending the Message?

In ordinary speech, the notion of "sending a message" implies three things: a sender, receiver, and message—some information that is transferred from the sender to the receiver. You've just seen the receiver and message, but who is the sender in this scheme? To be honest, the analogy breaks down here. In some vague sense, the function or block of code that contains the message expression is the sender, but the Objective-C messaging syntax has no formal notion of a "sender."

One thing that can confuse newcomers is the way that buttons, sliders, and other controls work in GUI applications that use the AppKit or UIKit (the UI frameworks for OSX and iOS, respectively). For example, when you configure a button, you register an object as the target of the button. When the user clicks the button, the button object sends the target a message, and the target object performs whatever action is supposed to happen in response to the button click. The message that is sent to the target is declared as

```
- (void) somethingChanged:(id) sender
```

The message sent has the single argument `sender`. The control (in this example, the button) passes a pointer to itself as the value of `sender`. The controlled object (the registered target of the button) can then use this value as a receiver to send messages back to the control to get, for example, the numerical value of a slider or the on-off state of a button. Note that this is just a quirk in the way arguments in the AppKit and the UIKit are named. `sender` is an ordinary method argument, not a part or feature of the Objective-C messaging system. The argument name `sender` is a convention, but it could just as well have been `widgetWhoseValueChanged`.

Messaging Details

Now that you've seen how basic message expressions work, it's time to look at how they are used in some common situations.

Nesting

Any message argument can be replaced by a message expression that returns the appropriate type.

```
1  Shape *shape1 = ...
2  Shape *shape2 = ...
3  NSColor *tmpFillColor;
4
5  // Set shape2's fill color to be the same as shape1's fill color
6  tmpFillColor = [shape1 fillColor];
7  [shape2 setFillColor: tmpFillColor];
```

The preceding lines of code and the following lines of code both produce the same result:

```
Shape *shape1 = ...
Shape *shape2 = ...

// Set shape2's fill color to be the same as shape1's fill color
[shape2 setFillColor: [shape1 fillColor]];
```

Although it is more verbose, using an intermediate variable, as in the first example, is useful when you are debugging. It gives you a chance to set a break point on Line 7 (after Line 6 has been executed) and get the value of `tmpFillColor`, which you can then interrogate with the debugger without having to step into the method `fillColor`.

The message receiver can also be replaced by a message expression that returns an appropriate object:

```
NSMutableArray *displayList = ...
id graphic;

// Draw the last object on the display list
graphic = [displayList lastObject];
[graphic draw];
```

can be rewritten as

```
NSMutableArray *displayList = ..

// Draw the last object on the display list
[[displayList lastObject] draw];
```

Nesting can extend to multiple levels. Evaluating nested message expressions proceeds in the obvious way: The innermost message expressions are evaluated and the message expressions are replaced by their return values. The process is then repeated until the outermost message expression is evaluated.

Naturally, all your brackets must balance. (Lisp veterans will feel right at home.) A very common typo when writing expressions nested several levels deep is to have one more or one less closing bracket than you have opening brackets. If your brackets are unbalanced, the compiler will complain and decline to compile the code. The default text editor used in Xcode helps you out with this problem by temporarily highlighting the matching opening bracket whenever you type a closing bracket.

Messaging `nil`

Objective-C is designed so that sending a message to a `nil` receiver has no effect. When a message expression with a `nil` receiver is evaluated, no method is executed. Silently ignoring a `nil` receiver instead of raising an exception or crashing allows you to write cleaner code. Instead of protecting yourself by cluttering your code with constructions like this:

```
Shape *aShape = ...

if ( aShape!= nil )
{
  [aShape draw];
}
```

you can simply write

```
[aShape draw];
```

If **aShape** happens to be `nil`, nothing is drawn and execution continues with the next line of code.

The return value of a message sent to a `nil` receiver is zero if the return type of the method in the message expression is a pointer or a numeric type. For other return types (structures, for example), the rules are complicated and the return value is undefined in some cases.

There might be places where you would prefer a `nil` receiver to raise an exception, but in most situations, avoiding the guarding `if` statement results in cleaner code. If trapping a `nil` receiver is important in a particular situation, you can always test for it explicitly.

Why Isn't the Method Being Executed?

If you are having a problem with a method that is not being executed—you're sure it *should* be executed, but the program skips over the method—check the receiver. It is probably `nil` at the point of execution. This can be a puzzling consequence of forgetting to initialize a variable someplace in your code.

Sending Messages to `self`

If you want to invoke one of an object's methods from within another method belonging to the same object, you must use the variable `self` as the message receiver. `self` is a hidden variable that the compiler passes to your method implementation. It's a pointer to the object that was the receiver when the original method was invoked. (`self` is not explicitly shown as an argument in the method signature, but it is always available.)

```
- (void) someMethod
{
  [self someOtherMethod]; // Different method in the same class
}
```

This pattern is commonly used in conjunction with accessor methods, methods that set or get the value of an instance variable. Although methods have direct access to an object's instance variables, there are times when you should use the instance variable's accessors instead. If the accessor methods have *side effects*, such as retaining or releasing an object stored in an instance variable, limiting the range of a numeric variable, or performing some bookkeeping, directly accessing the instance variable inside a method would bypass the side effects.

  `self` is also useful when you need to repeat the same functionality in more than one method. Instead of repeating the code, you can put the common code in a "helper" method and then invoke the helper method (with `self` as the receiver) from the other methods. This makes your code cleaner and makes debugging easier. If you find a bug in the common code, you have to fix it in only one place.

Overriding and Messages to `super`

A class can override a method defined in its superclass by providing a different implementation of the method in its `@implementation` section. When the overridden method is invoked with an instance of the subclass as the receiver, it is the subclass's implementation of the method that is executed.

  As an example, imagine defining a class **AnnotatedShape** that is a subclass of **Shape**. **AnnotatedShape** draws a text annotation next to its shape. This capability is useful for charting tasks. **AnnotatedShape** adds an instance variable to hold the text of the annotation, and it overrides some of **Shape**'s methods. The following code shows part of **AnnotatedShape**'s interface section:

```
@interface AnnotatedShape : Shape
{
  NSString *annotationText;
}

- (NSRect) boundingBox;
- (void) draw;

...

@end
```

Assume **Shape** has a method **boundingBox** that returns a rectangle that just contains the shape. A smart graphics program will test this rectangle against the program's window rectangle before trying to draw the shape. If the shape's rectangle is outside the window rectangle, the program can save some CPU cycles and skip the shape's drawing code. **AnnotatedShape** overrides **boundingBox** because it must return a bigger rectangle that includes the annotation.

```
1   Shape *aShape = ...
2   AnnotatedShape *anAnnotatedShape = ...
3   NSRect shapeBounds;
4   NSRect annotatedShapeBounds;
5
6   shapeBounds = [aShape boundingBox];
7   annotatedShapeBounds = [anAnnotatedShape boundingBox];
```

In the preceding code, when Line 6 is executed, it is **Shape**'s implementation of **boundingBox** that is executed. In Line 7, it is **AnnotatedShape**'s implementation of **boundingBox** that is executed.

In some cases, a subclass overrides a method to obtain different behavior. In the previous example, **AnnotatedShape**'s and **Shape**'s versions of **boundingBox** return different rectangles. In other cases, the overridden method needs to provide additional behavior. **AnnotatedShape**'s **draw** method has to draw the shape just as **Shape**'s **draw** method does, but it also has to draw the text annotation. One way to arrange this is to copy the drawing code inside **Shape**'s **draw** method into **AnnotatedShape**'s **draw** method. However, this is a bad idea. Not only does it needlessly increase your program's size, but it is also fragile: If you need to modify the drawing code for **Shape**, you have to remember to make the same changes in two different places. Instead, you should code **AnnotatedShape**'s **draw** method like this:

```
1   - (void) draw
2   {
3       [super draw]; // Draw the shape
4
5       // Code to draw the annotation text
6       ...
7   }
```

When an expression of the form

```
[super message]
```

is evaluated, the runtime uses the current object (the one pointed to by **self**) as the real receiver but executes the superclass implementation of the method named in the *message*. In Line 3 of the preceding example, the real receiver is an instance of **AnnotatedShape**, but it is **Shape**'s implementation of **draw** that is executed. **AnnotatedShape**'s **draw** method draws the **Shape** part of the **AnnotatedShape** using the code in **Shape**'s implementation of **draw**. It then goes on and draws the text annotation part before returning.

> **Note**
>
> Using `self` or `super` as a receiver makes sense only in the context of a method where there is an object (`self`) on whose behalf the method is being executed. You can't use `self` or `super` inside an ordinary C function.

There is an important difference between `self` and `super`: `self` is a legitimate pointer variable; `super` is not. `self` points to an actual location in memory that represents an instance of the object in question. You can pass it on as an argument in a method call:

```
- (void) passItOn
{
 [someOtherObject doSomethingWithMe: self];
}
```

`super`, on the other hand, is not a real variable. It is just an indication to the runtime to use `self` as the receiver, but to use the implementation of the method from the object's superclass rather than its own.

> **Note**
>
> When you invoke the superclass implementation of a method via `super`, any reference to `self` in the superclass implementation still refers to the original receiver, which is an instance of the subclass. If the superclass implementation goes on to invoke another of the class's methods, and that method is overridden by the subclass, it is the subclass implementation that will be invoked.

Selectors

The method name part of a message is sometimes referred to as the *selector* or *method selector* because it is used by the runtime to select which of the receiver's methods to execute. Selectors are just names; they don't carry any type information.

Objective-C defines a type, `SEL`, for holding a representation of a selector. A `SEL` has a one-to-one relationship with the selector name, but a `SEL` is not itself a string. All selectors with the same name have the same `SEL`, and different names always correspond to different `SEL`s. Internally, Objective-C uses the `SEL` type to identify methods for reasons of efficiency. Using strings would be slow; just testing to see if two strings are the same requires looping over all the characters in the string.

> **Note**
>
> Currently, a method's `SEL` is defined as a pointer to a unique structure that holds the string name of the method. However, this is an implementation detail, not something that you should use in any way. It could change in a future release.

The compiler directive `@selector()` converts a method name into a `SEL`:

```
SEL aSelector = @selector( someMessageName );
```

If the method has any arguments, you must remember to include the colons when you create a SEL. They are part of the method name.

```
@selector( aMethod )
```

and

```
@selector( aMethod: )
```

are different SELs.

> **Note**
>
> The Foundation framework provides two functions that convert back and forth between SEL and NSString:
>
> ```
> SEL aSelector =
>     NSSelectorFromString( @"SelectorStringName" );
> NSString *selectorStringName =
>     NSStringfromSelector( aSelector );
> ```
>
> These functions are useful if you need to store a selector in a container object or a file.

SELs can be used to make the message part of a message expression dynamic. NSObject defines the following method:

```
- (id)performSelector:(SEL)aSelector
```

When **performSelector:** is executed, the object executes the selector that is its argument. The following two lines of code are equivalent:

```
[aShape draw];
[aShape performSelector: @selector( draw )];
```

Writing the same thing in a longer way isn't very useful; the real usefulness of **performSelector:** comes when its argument is a variable. For example, when the user selects an object in a drawing program, the program draws that object with a highlight to indicate that it is selected. If the graphic object has a different method, **drawHighlighted**, to draw itself in the selected state, the drawing code might be written like this:

```
BOOL isHighlightDraw = ...
SEL  shapeDrawingSelector;

if ( isHighlightDraw )
  {
  shapeDrawingSelector = @selector( drawHighlighted );
  }
else
  {
  shapeDrawingSelector = @selector( draw );
  }
```

...

```
Shape *aShape = ...
```

```
[aShape performSelector: shapeDrawingSelector];
```

NSObject also defines `performSelector:withObject:` and
`performSelector:withObject:withObject:` for selectors that take one or two
object arguments. They work the same way as `performSelector:` except that they
pass their additional arguments on to the method named by the selector argument.

Methods with the Same Name

If you are using dynamic typing (variables typed as `id`), all methods with the same
name should have the same argument types and return values, even if they are
declared by unrelated classes. If you violate this rule, you will get a compiler warning;
if you ignore the warning, your program may have very subtle bugs.

For example, suppose you have a class, `ClassWithInt`, that declares this method:

```
- (void) setNumber:(int) newInt;
```

and another class, `ClassWithFloat`, that declares a method with the same name, but
with a different argument type:

```
- (void) setNumber:(float) newFloat;
```

Then, you import the header files for both classes by coding the following:

```
1  // DON'T DO THIS
2  #import "ClassWithFloat.h"
3  #import "ClassWithInt.h"
4
5  id numberObj = [[ClassWithInt alloc] init];
6  [numberObj setNumber: 21];
```

The compiler will warn you:

```
MethodNameTest.m:6:1: warning: multiple methods named 'setNumber:'
```

If you heedlessly push ahead and run the program, you are in trouble: When Line 6 is
executed, `numberObj` contains an instance of `ClassWithInt` and it is (as expected)
`ClassWithInt`'s implementation of `setNumber:` that is executed. But the value the
method receives in the `newInt` argument is not 21.

The problem occurs because the compiler now has two different sets of type information for the method name `setNumber:`. Because `numberObj` is typed as `id`,
there is nothing to tell the compiler whether it is the integer or the float version of
`setNumber:` that will be executed at run time. (The compiler needs to know the
variable type so it can set up the arguments in the stack frame properly.) In the preceding example the compiler encountered *ClassWithFloat.h* first, so it picks `float`. When

Line 6 is executed, the 21 argument (an int) is promoted to float. The bits of that float are passed to the ClassWithInt implementation of the method, which then interprets those bits as an int. The result is not the value you started with. (The exact wrong value you wind up with depends on whether the program is compiled as 32-bit or 64-bit.) Note that if you reverse the order of the import statements, the bug does not occur because the compiler picks int as the argument type.

This problem is a more insidious bug than a crash. You might not notice the corrupt value at first, and the bug's occurrence is controlled by something that really shouldn't matter, the order of the import statements.

> **Note**
>
> Unlike C++, Objective-C does not have method *overloading*. A C++ class can have methods that have the same name and are distinguished by having different argument types or return types. This is not allowed in Objective-C.

Dynamic and Static Typing

A variable typed as id declares that it holds a pointer to an object, but it says nothing about what class the object belongs to. It is legal to assign a pointer to an object of any class to a variable of type id. Although this is very useful in cases where you want to take advantage of polymorphism, it has the drawback that it sacrifices compiler type checking. If you don't need the flexibility of id, you can use static typing and the compiler will obligingly type check your assignments:

```
Shape *aShape = [[Shape alloc] init];
```

In this example, all AnnotatedShapes are Shapes but not all Shapes are AnnotatedShapes. A variable declared as Shape* can hold a pointer to an object of class Shape or any subclass that descends from Shape.

```
Shape *aShape;
AnnotatedShape *anAnnotatedShape = [[AnnotatedShape alloc] init];
aShape = anAnnotatedShape; //OK
```

The converse isn't true—you shouldn't assign an instance of a superclass to a variable typed as a pointer to one of its subclasses.

```
AnnotatedShape *anAnnotatedShape;
Shape *aShape = [[Shape alloc] init];
anAnnotatedShape = aShape; // NOT OK !
```

The preceding code results in this warning message:

```
warning: incompatible pointer types assigning to
    'AnnotatedShape *' from 'Shape *'
```

Ignoring the warning and sending a message that is defined only in the subclass to an instance of its superclass results in a crash.

Using static typing also relaxes, somewhat, the rule that all methods with the same name must have the same argument types and return value. If you aren't going to assign objects to variables typed id, the rule becomes "Two methods, defined by different classes, may have the same name but different argument types or return type, as long as neither of the defining classes is a subclass of the other." However, doing so is potentially confusing and is best avoided.

If you don't need the flexibility of id, you should use static typing and let the compiler type check for you. Then, if you assign an object to an incompatible variable, the mistake will appear as a compiler warning rather than a runtime crash.

Under the Hood

When the following line of code is executed, the object **anObject** receives the message **doSomething** and responds by executing its method named **doSomething**:

```
id anObject;
[anObject doSomething];
```

How does it know how to do this? How does it know which code to actually execute when **anObject** could be an instance of different classes at different points in time, each one with a different implementation of **doSomething**? The short answer is "You don't need to know—it just works." But for those who are unhappy with magic, the rest of this section explains how the Objective-C messaging system works.

When a message expression is evaluated, the runtime looks at the receiver and determines the receiver's class. It then looks at the class information for that class to find the method that corresponds to the method name in the message. Finally, it executes that method.

Here are the details:

- All Objective-C objects know their class. To accomplish this, the compiler adds an instance variable, called **isa**, to every object instance. As the name implies, **isa** tells what kind of object an instance is. At run time, **isa** points to the class's class structure, an opaque type that contains information about the class, including what instance variables and methods the class defines, and a pointer to the class information for its superclass. This information is filled in by the runtime when your application starts.

- The compiler converts methods into actual compiled C functions. In the process, it adds two extra arguments, **self** and **_cmd**, to the beginning of the argument list. **self** is a pointer to the object that was the receiver when the message was sent, and **_cmd** is the selector corresponding to the message's method name.

Consider the following Objective-C method:

```
-(void) doSomethingWithArg:(int) anArg
{
  // ...
}
```

During compilation, the compiler turns `doSomethingWithArg:` into a C function with the following argument list:

```
(id self, SEL _cmd, int anArg)
```

- Each Objective-C class has a table that connects a method's selector to a pointer to the function that implements the method. Given a selector, the runtime can use the table to find a pointer to the matching function. Each class also has an associated caching mechanism that speeds up subsequent searches for a given method.

Now you can follow the sequence from a message expression to an actual function. When the compiler encounters a message expression like this:

```
Shape *aShape = ...
NSColor *newFillColor = ...

[aShape setFillColor: newFillColor];
```

it replaces the message expression with a call to the runtime function `objc_msgSend`:

```
objc_msgSend( aShape, @selector( setFillColor: ), newFillColor );
```

The first argument to `objc_msgSend` is the receiver object. The second argument is the method name, converted to `SEL`. The remaining arguments are the arguments (if any) to be passed to the method.

When the call to `objc_msgSend` is executed at run time:

1. `objc_msgSend` looks at the pointer stored in `aShape`'s `isa` variable and follows the pointer to the class structure for the `Shape` class.

2. It then looks in `Shape`'s method cache to see if it can quickly find a pointer to the function implementing `setFillColor:`.

3. If the function pointer for `setFillColor:` is not in the cache, `objc_msgSend` looks in the `Shape` class's table of methods to find the function pointer.

4. After it has the function pointer, the runtime calls the function with the arguments

   ```
   (aShape, @selector( setFillColor: ), newFillColor)
   ```

Each class structure also contains a pointer to the class structure for its superclass. If the runtime doesn't find the selector it is looking for in either the class structure's cache or its table of methods, it follows the pointer to the class structure for the class's superclass and repeats the search. This process continues until either the runtime finds a matching function pointer or it reaches the top of the object hierarchy and runs out of places to look. The latter case is the subject of the next section.

Runtime Changes for Objective-C 2.0

There are major changes in implementation of the runtime for Objective-C 2.0. One of the main changes is that the structures representing the runtime information for classes and methods that were defined in earlier versions of Objective-C have been replaced with opaque types and a set of functions to manipulate these types. This is essentially a primitive object system in itself, implemented directly in C. Functionally, it works as it did before, but you can no longer peek inside or directly play with the structures.

Message Forwarding

What happens if `objc_msgSend` gets to the top of the object hierarchy without finding a method implementation that corresponds to the selector in the message? If that happens, `objc_msgSend` calls the `forwardInvocation:` method of `NSObject` with an `NSInvocation` argument (see the sidebar *NSInvocation*) formed from the original message expression. `NSObject`'s implementation of `forwardInvocation:` invokes the `NSObject` method `doesNotRecognizeSelector:`.

`NSObject`'s implementation of `doesNotRecognizeSelector:` raises an exception and logs an error message, and then your program crashes.

But it doesn't have to be this way. You can override `forwardInvocation:` and then use the information contained in the invocation argument to send the message to a different object, one that can handle the message properly. This is called *forwarding*. Forwarding can be used, for example, to borrow behavior from a different object. The original object handles some messages, but other messages are passed on to a helper object.

NSInvocation

An `NSInvocation` is an Objective-C message expression encapsulated as an object. An `NSInvocation` object's instance variables hold an object (the receiver of the original expression, called a *target* here) and a message to send to the object (in the form of a selector and any arguments that the method takes). It can be stored for later use or passed as an argument to a method just like any other object.

When you want to execute the message expression that the invocation encapsulates, you send the `invoke` message to the `NSInvocation` object:

```
NSInvocation *anInvocation = ...
[anInvocation invoke];
```

The `NSInvocation` class defines methods for setting and retrieving the receiver, the selector, and the arguments of the encapsulated message expression, and for getting the return value. `NSInvocation` is covered in Chapter 17, "Blocks."

Efficiency

You are probably saying to yourself: "All this lookup business has to be much slower than a plain function call." It is. The runtime code goes to great lengths to make the method lookup as fast as possible, but it is still slower than a C function call. However, this usually doesn't make much practical difference. In almost every case, the time required to execute the body of a method will dwarf the time required to dispatch the message. There are rare cases where the dispatch overhead could be an issue. These are usually cases where you are doing something a huge number of times in a tight loop. If you find one of these cases, you can use the **NSObject** method **methodForSelector:** to get a pointer to the C function that implements the method:

```
IMP anIMP = [aShape methodForSelector: @selector( draw )];
```

Recall from Chapter 3, "An Introduction to Object-Oriented Programming," that **IMP** is defined as a pointer to a function. After you have the function pointer, you can use it to call the function, like this:

```
(*anIMP) (aShape, @selector( draw ));
```

Remember that when the compiler turns your method into a C function, it adds the arguments **self** and **_cmd** to the front of the argument list. When you call the function through its **IMP**, you must remember to fill in those arguments. If the method takes arguments, those arguments follow **self** and **_cmd** in the function call.

How much faster is a direct function call? The following code executes **testMethod** one million times, first using a normal method dispatch, and then by calling the function that implements **testMethod** directly:

```
int j;
// Loop 1, regular message dispatch

for (j=0; j < 1000000; j++)
 {
  [testObject testMethod];
 }


IMP testIMP = [testObject methodForSelector: @selector( testMethod )];

// Loop 2, calling the function with its IMP

for (j=0; j < 1000000; j++)
 {
  (*testIMP) (testObject, @selector( testMethod ));
 }
```

If `testMethod` contains only a `return` statement, the ratio of the execution times for the two loops is[1]

```
(time for Loop 1) / (time for Loop 2)  ~ 2.63
```

The direct function call is a bit more than two and a half times as fast as the message dispatch. A dramatic improvement! Unfortunately, a method that just returns isn't very useful. If `testMethod` contains four floating-point multiplication instructions, the ratio is ~1.25; if `testMethod` has a single `sin()` evaluation, the ratio is ~1.04. You shouldn't put too much stock in the exact numbers, but the trend is clear. As soon as you start to do anything substantial in a method, the time spent executing the method's code overwhelms the time spent in the method dispatch.

> **Note**
>
> There is one thing that you must be careful of when you get a method's `IMP` and call it directly. `IMP` is defined with the following typedef:
>
> ```
> typedef  id  (*IMP)(id, SEL, ...);
> ```
>
> This typedef assumes that all the method's arguments and its return value are either pointers or integer types. If your method has floating-point arguments or a floating-point return value, you must take the returned `IMP` and cast it to the proper function pointer type. If you don't do this, the compiler sets up the stack frame for the function call incorrectly and your function receives or returns garbage.
>
> For the following method declaration:
>
> ```
> - (void) setLinewidth: (float) input;
> ```
>
> the proper calling code looks like this:
>
> ```
> void (*functionPtr)(id, SEL, float) =
> (void (*)(id, SEL, float))[aShape methodForSelector:
> @selector(setLinewidth:)];
>
> // Set line width to 1.5
> *functionPtr( aShape, @selector(setLinewidth:), 1.5 );
> ```
>
> The intricacies of function pointer declarations are covered in Chapter 17, "Blocks."

Introspection and Other Runtime Fun

Objective-C's runtime support allows you to discover various properties of objects at execution time. This process is called *introspection*. You can find out an object's class and superclass using the methods `class` and `superclass`, as follows:

```
Class objectsClass;
Class objectsSuperClass;
id anObject;
```

---

1. Times were measured on a Fall 2009 iMac with a 3.06 GHz Core 2 Duo processor, running Mac OS X Snow Leopard (version 10.6.2).

```
objectsClass = [anObject class];
objectsSuperClass = [anObject superclass];
```

There may be times when you are unsure if an object can respond to a given message. In those cases you can use the method `respondsToSelector:` to check whether the object can respond to a message before you send it. For example, some classes advertise that they conform to a particular protocol.

> **Note**
>
> A *protocol* is a defined set of methods. When a class conforms to a protocol, it promises that it implements all of the required methods in the set. Protocols are covered in Chapter 13, "Protocols."

However, methods in a protocol can be declared as optional. A class that conforms to a protocol is free to implement or not implement an optional method. You don't want to invoke an optional method if the receiver's class doesn't implement that method. Doing so will cause a crash. You can avoid this problem by using `respondsToSelector:` as shown in the following code:

```
id anObject = ...  // object that conforms to a protocol
SEL optionalSelector = @selector( optionalMethod );

if ( [anObject respondsToSelector: optionalSelector] )
  {
    [anObject optionalMethod];
  }
```

`class`, `superclass`, and `respondsToSelector:` are methods defined by `NSObject` and inherited by any object that descends from `NSObject`.

Beyond these examples, you can call the C language runtime functions directly in order to do more interesting (and sometimes dangerous) tasks, such as getting a list of a class's instance variables or methods, or replacing a method implementation with a different implementation at run time. I'm not going to cover this material, but if you are curious or adventurous, you should look at the *Objective-C 2.0 Runtime Reference*: https://developer.apple.com/library/mac/#documentation/Cocoa/Reference/ObjCRuntimeRef/Reference/reference.html.

> **Note**
>
> If you are very curious and really want to know how the runtime machinery works, the runtime is open-source. The code can be downloaded from www.opensource.apple.com. (But be forewarned: The code is not easy reading.)

The dynamism of the Objective-C messaging system is very powerful and makes it easier to build flexible, innovative software. This dynamism does come at a price—it limits the capability of the compiler to perform some kinds of validity checking. As a consequence, some errors will show up only at run time. This bothers a certain fraction of the population that considers it dangerous and prefers stricter type checking, as found in languages such as C++. To these people I'd like to offer the following analogy: A well-maintained 8- to 12-inch chef's knife (or its Asian equivalent) is dangerous, even lethal, if used carelessly or maliciously. But very little in the way of truly interesting food is prepared without its use.

Summary

Objective-C methods are invoked by messaging, rather than by direct function calls. A message expression consists of a receiver (the object whose method is being called) and a message (the name of the method to be executed, plus any arguments that the method takes) enclosed in square brackets. When a message expression is evaluated, the runtime determines the receiver's class and then looks in the class's class structure to find a pointer to the code that implements the method. The runtime then fills in the hidden variables **self** (a pointer to the receiver) and **_cmd** (the name of the method, converted to a **SEL**) and uses the pointer to execute the code.

This arrangement has several advantages. Both parts of the message expression can be dynamic; they can be determined at run time rather than compile time. It also allows for complete polymorphism. If the receiver is typed as **id** (pointer to object), it can hold any object as long as the object's class implements a method with a name that corresponds to the name in the message. Polymorphism is used when you need to elicit the same type of behavior from a heterogeneous collection of objects—for example, asking each object in a heterogeneous collection to draw itself.

The keywords **self** and **super** are used inside a method to invoke other methods in the class or its superclass, respectively.

The flexibility of the Objective-C messaging system comes at some cost in performance. For time-critical code, it is possible to bypass the messaging system and call the method directly, although in practice this is rarely necessary. The time spent in the message dispatch is usually much less than the time spent executing the method body.

Exercises

1. Modify the version of the HelloObjectiveC program that you created for Exercise 2 in the previous chapter.

   a. Add a method to the **Greeter** class that sets both the regular greeting and the VIP greeting at the same time. Don't forget to retain the new values of **greeting** and **vipGreeting** and release the old values in the proper order.

   b. Modify *HelloObjectiveC.m* to use this new method.

   c. Build and run your program to verify that it works correctly.

2. Modify the new method you created in Exercise 1:

    a. Instead of setting the instance variables **greeting** and **vipGreeting** directly in your new method, use the keyword **self** with the existing setter methods **setGreetingText:** and **setVIPGreetingText:** to set the new values.

    b. Build and run your program to verify that it works correctly.

Notice that when you code your new method using the existing setter methods, they automatically take care of the memory management for you.

3. Practice using selectors:

    a. In *HelloObjectiveC.m* replace the message expression

```
[myGreeter issueGreeting];
```

    with a message expression that uses **performSelector:**.

    b. Build and run your program to verify that it still works correctly.

There is no real reason to use **performSelector:** in this case. The point of the exercise is to make sure that you understand how to get and use a selector.

4. Verify that sending a message to **nil** does nothing (and in particular that it doesn't cause a crash):

    a. Add a second variable of type **Greeter*** to *HelloObjectiveC.m*:

```
Greeter* greeter2;
```

    b. Assign **nil** to **greeter2**.

    c. Use **greeter2** as the receiver for an **issueGreeting** message.

    d. Build and run your program. Verify that it works as you expect.

5. C++ allows *method overloading*. A C++ class can define two (or more) different methods that have the same name, but that are distinguished by having arguments or return values of different types. Use what you have learned about how the Objective-C message dispatch system works to explain why it would be difficult to implement C++-style method overloading in Objective-C.

6

Classes and Objects

Objects are the basis for object-oriented programming. This chapter gets down to the business of making objects. The chapter is divided into five main sections:

- Defining classes
- Extending classes by subclassing
- Creating objects (instances of a class)
- Destroying objects
- Copying objects

Some of these topics were covered briefly in Chapter 3, "An Introduction to Object-Oriented Programming." They are presented here in greater detail.

Defining a Class

When you define an Objective-C class, you have to provide the compiler with two sets of information. The first set is essentially a blueprint for constructing instances of the class. You have to specify the class's name, the class's superclass, a list of the names and types of the class's instance variables, and finally the declarations of the class's methods. The second set of information is the code that implements the class's methods. The first set goes in the class's *interface section*. The second set goes in the class's *implementation section*.

The two sections are normally placed in separate files, both named after the class. If you were defining a `Guitar` class, you would put the interface section in a header file named *Guitar.h* and the implementation section in a file named *Guitar.m*.

The Interface Section

Imagine that you are going to create a `RockStar` class for a simulation game. A `RockStar` instance does all the usual rock star things: sing, play guitar, trash hotel rooms. The interface section for `RockStar` looks like this:

```
#import <Foundation/Foundation.h>

@class Band;
@class Guitar;

@interface  RockStar : NSObject

{
  NSString *name;
  Band *band;
  Guitar  *guitar;

   // More instance variables

}

- (void) sing;
- (void) playGuitar;
- (void) trashHotelRoom:(float) damagePercent;

// More method declarations

@end
```

The interface section contains

- An **@interface** compiler directive followed by the name of the class being defined (**RockStar** in this example), a colon, and the class's superclass (**NSObject** in this example).
- Declarations of the class's instance variables. An instance variable declaration gives the type and name of the instance variable and ends with a semicolon. The instance variable section is enclosed in curly brackets. If the class doesn't define any instance variables, the curly brackets may be omitted.
- A list of method declarations. The method declarations must come after the instance variable declarations.

  Methods that have a declaration beginning with a hyphen (–) are instance methods; they are used with an instance of the class as a receiver. Methods whose declaration begins with a plus sign (+) are class methods; they are used with the class name as the receiver. Class methods are covered in Chapter 7, "The Class Object."
- A final **@end** directive, to close the section.

The compiler needs some information about a class's superclass, so a class's **@interface** section must import the header file that contains its superclass's interface section. In this example, **RockStar**'s superclass, **NSObject**, is a Foundation framework class. Importing *Foundation/Foundation.h* automatically imports the super-class header file, *NSObject.h*.

> **Note**
>
> Beginning with Xcode 4.2, you can also declare your instance variables inside a class extension (see Chapter 11, "Categories, Extensions, and Security") or between a set of curly brackets directly inside the class's `@implementation` section. This is useful for instance variables that you don't want to expose to users of your class.

`@class` Directive

If you use a class type, such as `Band` or `Guitar`, in an instance variable declaration or a method declaration, you must inform the compiler that the type is a class. If that class's interface is defined in any of the imported header files (a Cocoa framework header, the superclass header file, or any header file that they, in turn, import), you don't have to do anything else. Otherwise, you need to use a `@class` directive.

The `RockStar` class has instance variables of type `Band` and `Guitar`. But *RockStar.h* doesn't import *Band.h* or *Guitar.h*, so you need to put the following lines in the file:

```
@class Band;
@class Guitar;
```

The `@class` directive, which must precede any use of the type being declared, is an example of a *forward declaration*. In this example, `@class Band;` tells the compiler that `Band` is a class, and that something typed `Band*` is a pointer to an instance of the class, but it provides no other information about `Band`.

Technically, in many cases you could just import the relevant header file directly to make the type known to the compiler. But using a `@class` directive is a better design choice:

- Using a `@class` directive can cut down on compile times by reducing dependencies. Suppose that you import *Band.h* into *RockStar.h*. If you then make a change to *Band.h*, you have to recompile all the files that import *RockStar.h*, as well as all the files that import *Band.h*. If you use `@class Band;` instead, only the files that import *Band.h* need recompiling.

- Using a `@class` directive is *required* in some rare cases. Imagine that the `Band` class has a `leadGuitarist` instance variable that is typed as a `RockStar*`:

    ```
    RockStar *leadGuitarist;
    ```

    You now have a case where *RockStar.h* needs to know that `Band` is a class and *Band.h* needs to know that `RockStar` is a class. If you try to handle this by importing *Band.h* into *RockStar.h*, and importing *RockStar.h* into *Band.h*, the code will not compile. You must use a `@class` directive in at least one of the two header files.

The Implementation Section

The implementation section contains the code that implements the class's methods. The structure of an implementation section is very simple. It begins with a line containing an @implementation directive and the class name, and ends with an @end directive. You place all your method implementations between these two lines.

Here is the RockStar class's implementation file:

```
#import "RockStar.h"
#import "Guitar.h"


@implementation RockStar

-(void) playGuitar
{
  [guitar tune];

    ...
}


// More method implementations

@end
```

If you declare a method in a class's interface section and then forget to provide an implementation for that method, the compiler warns you that you forgot the implementation. If you forget to implement trashHotelRoom:, you get this warning when you compile *RockStar.m*:

```
warning: incomplete implementation of class RockStar
warning: method definition for '-trashHotelRoom:' not found
```

If you ignore the scolding and try to invoke the non-existent method, your program will, of course, crash.

Imports

A class's implementation file imports the header file that contains the corresponding interface section. It must also import the header file for any other class that will be used by the implementation. In the RockStar example, the implementation of playGuitar invokes Guitar's tune method, so, to avoid compiler warnings, *RockStar.m* must import *Guitar.h*. This is true even if *RockStar.h* has a @class directive for Guitar. The compiler needs to look at *Guitar.h* to see the method declaration for the tune method.

If you omit importing *Guitar.h*, the code works at run time as long as the Guitar class is part of your Xcode project and Guitar actually implements tune. But compiler warnings are there for your program's health, and acquiring the habit of ignoring them is a large step on the road to buggy software.

> **Note**
>
> If you are using ARC, omitting *Guitar.h* causes an error, not a warning. See Chapter 16, "ARC."

The Interface and Implementation Sections Go in Separate Files

A class's interface section is placed in a separate header file so that the interface section (which provides the compiler information about the class) can be imported into code that uses the class. For example, if you want to create an instance of `RockStar`, invoke one of `RockStar`'s methods, or subclass `RockStar`, your code must import *RockStar.h*. If the interface section and the implementation section are in the same file, importing the interface section also imports the code that implements the class, resulting in multiple copies of the implementation code. Doing this causes a compiler error with a complaint about duplicate symbols.

There is one situation where it is OK to place both sections of a class definition in one file. If you have a helper class that is used *only* inside another class, you can place both sections of the helper class inside the implementation file of the main class. The interface section of the helper class should come before the implementation sections of both the helper class and the main class.

Subclassing a Class

It would be very time-consuming (not to mention very boring) if you had to start from scratch every time you wrote a program. Object-oriented languages like Objective-C let you avoid some of this effort and tedium by reusing code. You can create new classes by modifying or adding to existing classes. Although you can reuse code at the source level in any language, the important point here is that object-oriented languages let you build on an existing class, even if you don't have the source code for the original class.

Here is some terminology that is used when talking about this subject:

- A class defined by extending an existing class is called a *subclass* of the original class.
- The existing class is the *superclass* of the new class.
- Aside from the modifications noted in the next section, a subclass has the same instance variables and methods as its superclass. The subclass is said to *inherit* its superclass's instance variables and methods.

Defining a Subclass

A subclass can extend or modify an existing class in one or more of three ways:

1. A subclass can add instance variables to those present in its superclass. A subclass cannot, however, *remove* any instance variables defined by its superclass.

2. A subclass can add methods to those present in its superclass.

3. A subclass can provide its own implementation of a method that is declared in its superclass. This is called *overriding* a method.

Note

To be technically correct, a subclass isn't required to do any of the preceding three things. But a subclass that didn't add instance variables or methods, or override a method, would be fairly pointless. It would merely be an alias for its superclass.

An Example of Subclassing

As an example, this section defines a subclass of the `Accumulator` class shown in Chapter 3, "An Introduction to Object-Oriented Programming." The original `Accumulator` class keeps a running total and has methods to add to the total, report the current total, and reset the total to zero. The new class, `NamedAccumulator`, makes the following changes to the original `Accumulator` class:

- `NamedAccumulator` has the capability to store a name.

- `NamedAccumulator` has methods to set and get the name.

- `NamedAccumulator` overrides `Accumulator`'s version of the method `addToTotal:`. The new version of `addToTotal:` logs each addition.

To refresh your memory, Listings 6.1 and 6.2 contain the code for the original `Accumulator` class.

Listing 6.1   *Accumulator.h*

```
#import <Foundation/Foundation.h>

@interface Accumulator : NSObject
{
  int total;
}

- (void) addToTotal:(int) amount;
- (int) total;
- (void) zeroTotal;

@end
```

Listing 6.2   *Accumulator.m*

```
#import "Accumulator.h"

@implementation Accumulator

- (void) addToTotal:(int) amount
{
  total = total + amount;
}

- (int) total
{
  return total;
}

- (void) zeroTotal
{
  total = 0;
}

@end
```

Listing 6.3 shows the interface file for the subclass **NamedAccumulator**.

Listing 6.3   *NamedAccumulator.h*

```
1   #import <Foundation/Foundation.h>
2   #import "Accumulator.h"
3
4   @interface NamedAccumulator : Accumulator
5   {
6      NSString *name;
7   }
8
9   - (NSString*) name;
10  - (void) setName:(NSString*) newName;
11  - (void) addToTotal:(int) amount;
12
13  @end
```

Note the following about Listing 6.3:

- Line 2: A subclass interface file imports its superclass's header file. To create a subclass, the compiler must see the definition of its superclass.

- Line 4: The name before the colon on the **@interface** line is the subclass; the name after the colon is the superclass.

- Line 6: The instance variable section of the subclass lists only the instance variables that the subclass adds to the original class. Here, **NamedAccumulator** adds a single new instance variable, **name**.

- Lines 9–10: These are new methods that **NamedAccumulator** defines; they get and set the **name** instance variable.

- Line 11: **NamedAccumulator** overrides **addToTotal:**. Redeclaring an overridden method in a subclass's interface section isn't required, but it is good practice for documentation purposes. It tells users of the subclass that the subclass has provided its own implementation of the method.

There is no reason to redeclare inherited methods that are not overridden.

A subclass implementation file contains only the implementations of methods that have been added or overridden by the subclass. Listing 6.4 shows **NamedAccumulator**'s implementation file.

Listing 6.4   *NamedAccumulator.m*

```
1  #import "NamedAccumulator.h"
2
3  @implementation NamedAccumulator
4
5  - (void) setName:(NSString*) newName
6  {
7   NSString *tmp = [newName copy];
8   [name release];
9    name = tmp;
10  }
11
12  - (NSString*) name
13  {
14    return name;
15  }
16
17  - (void) addToTotal:(int) amount
18  {
19    NSLog(@"Adding %d to the %@ Accumulator", amount, [self name]);
20    [super addToTotal: amount];
21  }
22
23  - (void) dealloc
24  {
25    [name release];
26    [super dealloc];
27  }
28
29  @end
```

Note the following about Listing 6.4:

- Line 1: As with any other class definition, a subclass implementation file imports its corresponding interface file.

- Lines 5–10 and 12–15: These are the implementations of the methods that set and get NamedAccumulator's name instance variable.

- Lines 17–21: This is the new version of addToTotal:. It logs the transaction and then calls the superclass (Accumulator) version of addToTotal: to do the actual addition. The pattern shown here is a very common pattern in subclassing. When a subclass needs to *add* behavior to a superclass method, it overrides the method. The new implementation codes the new behavior and then invokes the superclass version of the method with the keyword super.

- Lines 23–27: When an object's reference count drops to zero, its dealloc method is called to give the object a chance to do any required cleanup work before the object is returned to the heap. An Accumulator object does not have any instance variables that hold objects, so it does not require any cleanup. The dealloc method that Accumulator inherits from NSObject is sufficient.

NamedAccumulator is different: It stores an NSString object in an instance variable name. The object stored in name was copied when it was assigned to name; the copy must be balanced by a release before NamedAccumulator goes away. To do this, NamedAccumulator overrides dealloc. In its dealloc method, it releases the object held in name and then invokes the superclass implementation of dealloc. dealloc methods are discussed in more detail later in this chapter.

> **Note**
>
> Notice that the definition of the NamedAccumulator class did not make any reference to the source code of its superclass, Accumulator. When you create a subclass, the only information needed from the superclass is the superclass name and the superclass header file. You do not need the superclass's source code. (You must, of course, have the compiled object code for the superclass at the time your program is linked.)

You can now put the NamedAccumulator class to work, as shown in this code snippet:

```
NamedAccumulator *myAccumulator = [[NamedAccumulator alloc] init];

[myAccumulator zeroTotal];
[myAccumulator setName: @"Game Points"];

[myAccumulator addToTotal: 100];
[myAccumulator addToTotal: 37];
```

```
NSLog( @"The total in the %@ Accumulator is... %d",
       [myAccumulator name],[myAccumulator total] );
...

[myAccumulator release];
```

Executing the preceding code results in the following output:

```
Adding 100 to the Game Points Accumulator
Adding 37 to the Game Points Accumulator
The total in the Game Points Accumulator is... 137
```

Class Hierarchies

Repeated subclassing results in a chain of classes, each one built on the previous class, called a *class hierarchy*. Classes that come earlier than a given class in a class hierarchy are called *ancestor classes*. (The term isn't used, but you could call a class's superclass its immediate ancestor class.)

The class at the top of a class hierarchy is called a *root* class. A root class has no superclass. Except in some very rare cases involving the class NSProxy, the root class for all Objective-C objects is NSObject.

Note

NSProxy is a skeletal class that is used as the root class for objects that function as stand-ins for other objects. For example, when you build a system that uses distributed objects (a system that uses more than one process), you use a subclass of NSProxy to stand in for an object in another process. When the proxy object receives a message, the proxy forwards the message to the object it is representing. For more information on distributed objects, see http://developer.apple.com/library/mac/#documentation/Cocoa/Conceptual/DistrObjects/DistrObjects.html.

NSObject defines and implements the basic methods necessary for an object to interact properly with the Objective-C runtime and otherwise be a good Objective-C citizen. Some examples of these methods are methods for object allocation and memory management, and methods for introspection. You are spared the effort of implementing these methods yourself when you create a class—they come for free when you inherit from NSObject.

Note

Introspection refers to the ability to determine an object's class at run time.

A Class Hierarchy Example

Figure 6.1 shows a class hierarchy for a part of a hypothetical restaurant operations program.

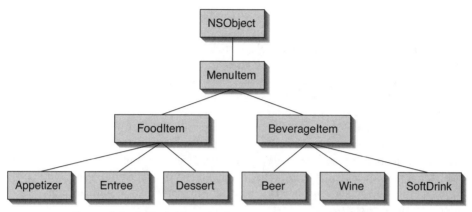

Figure 6.1   A class hierarchy for a restaurant operations program

As you move down a class hierarchy from the root class, you move from the general to the specific. In Figure 6.1, the **MenuItem** class would have instance variables for items, such as price and total calories, that are common to every item that the restaurant serves.[1] The **BeverageItem** class would add instance variables that are specific to drinks, such as whether refills are free. If there were nothing to distinguish between food and beverages, you wouldn't need the intermediate **FoodItem** and **BeverageItem** classes. The lowest classes in the hierarchy are the most specific. For example, the **Wine** class would hold information relevant only to wine: varietal, vintage, and winery name.

Note

Although inheritance is a powerful tool, you shouldn't use it indiscriminately. Long inheritance chains can make a program fragile. If you have to modify one of the classes near the top of a long inheritance chain, the effects will propagate through your entire program with possibly unforeseen results. A different technique, adding a *category*, lets you add methods to a class without subclassing it. See Chapter 11, "Categories, Extensions, and Security."

Abstract Classes

In the restaurant example in the previous section, **MenuItem**, **FoodItem**, and **BeverageItem** are *abstract* classes. An abstract class is a class that is intended to be used as a template for subclassing. You do not normally create an instance of an abstract class.

---

1. This part isn't hypothetical. As of July 2008, many restaurants in New York City are required by law to list the calories for food and drink items on their menus.

Directly creating a `MenuItem` instance would make no sense. You can't eat or drink the abstract concept of a menu item. But if you implement the functionality for storing a menu item's price and calories in an abstract class, that functionality is automatically available to all of the abstract class's subclasses. In this example, you would have to write the code to set and get an item's price and number of calories only once. Without the abstract class, you would have to write the code six times. Using the abstract class not only saves effort, it is also far less error prone.

Some abstract classes declare methods that they intend their subclasses to implement (called *abstract methods* or *virtual methods*). The `MenuItem` class might define a `menuBlurb` method to provide the text that describes the menu item. The `MenuItem` class would provide an empty (do nothing) implementation of `menuBlurb` and expect its non-abstract descendants to override its empty implementation with an implementation that supplies class-specific text.

There is no way to *require* that a subclass override an abstract method. However, you can warn users of the abstract class if they forget to override an abstract method when they subclass, by logging any attempts to invoke the abstract class's implementation of that method.

In that case, `MenuItem`'s implementation of `menuBlurb` would look like this:

```
- (NSString*) menuBlurb
{
  NSLog(@"Warning: concrete subclass of class MenuItem must override
↵    -menuBlurb.");

  return nil;
}
```

It is also possible to create "semi-abstract" classes. These are classes that have some usefulness when instantiated by themselves but require subclassing to perform more advanced functions.

A prominent example of such a class in the Cocoa frameworks is `NSView`, which represents an area of the screen. An instance of a pure `NSView` provides some functionality: It can be used as a container for other views, called *subviews*. But to draw anything in a view, you must define a custom subclass of `NSView` and override the method `drawRect:`. Similarly, if you need a view to respond to user input, your view must be a subclass of `NSView` that overrides one or more of the event handling methods, such as `mouseDown:`.

There Is No Special Syntax for Abstract Classes or Methods

Objective-C has no explicit syntax for abstract classes. If you have a class that is effectively an abstract class, you should note this in your documentation (in the class header file and any class documentation). Unlike abstract classes in Java or C++, there is no way to prevent someone from actually instantiating a class you consider abstract.

Objective-C also has no syntax to declare a method abstract or virtual. If you are creating an abstract class, you should provide an empty implementation of the methods that you require the abstract class's subclasses to implement. If your abstract class declares these methods but doesn't provide an implementation for them, you will get a compiler warning. If you then subclass the abstract class and still forget to provide an implementation, you will get a runtime error if the method is called.

Creating Objects

Creating an Objective-C object requires two steps: allocation and initialization. The allocation step obtains the memory for an object from the heap; the initialization step fills in any instance variables that require initial values, acquires any resources the object requires, and returns a pointer to the finished object. The two steps are customarily combined in a single statement:

```
Foo *myFoo = [[Foo alloc] init];
```

The next sections follow these steps in more detail.

Object Allocation

Object allocation is handled by a class method, `alloc`, which all classes inherit from `NSObject`.

Note
You'll learn more about class objects and class methods in the next chapter. For now, all you need to know is that you use the name of the class as the receiver when you invoke a class method.

`alloc` does several things:

- `alloc` allocates memory for the new object and returns a pointer to that memory.
- `alloc` fills in the object's `isa` instance variable. The compiler automatically adds an instance variable named `isa` to every object instance. `isa` points to a structure of information about the object's class.
- `alloc` zeros out the rest of the object's memory. All instance variables other than `isa` start out with a value of zero.
- `alloc` sets the newly created object's retain count to one. The code that created the object by sending the `alloc` message is responsible for balancing the `alloc` by eventually sending the object a `release` or an `autorelease` message. (Autorelease is covered in Chapter 15, "Reference Counting.")

The object returned by `alloc` becomes the receiver for an `init` message. `init` performs any required initializations and returns a pointer to a fully constructed object.

new

new is mostly a holdover from the earlier Objective-C days. You might see it if you are asked to work on some legacy code. It is a class method that combines allocation and initialization in a single step:

```
Foo *myFoo = [Foo new];
```

+new is equivalent to (and currently implemented as) alloc followed by init. new is not deprecated, but it is rarely used today. It can't be used when initializing an object requires information passed in by argument to an init routine. Most people prefer to use a consistent alloc ... init pattern for all their object allocations.

---

alloc and allocWithZone:

Mac OS X divides its heap, the area of memory that is the source of bytes for dynamic allocation, into regions called *malloc zones*. One malloc zone, called the *default malloc zone*, is always available; other zones can be created and destroyed.

There is an NSObject class method, allocWithZone:, which allocates an object and allows you to specify the zone used as the source of the allocated object's bytes. The idea behind allocWithZone: was to allow you to allocate objects from custom zones. If you had a group of objects allocated from the same custom zone, you could free them all at once by destroying that zone. alloc is implemented as allocWithZone: nil. The nil argument tells allocWithZone: to obtain its bytes from the default malloc zone. In practice, the use of custom zones does not work very well. Apple now discourages using malloc zones other than the default malloc zone in Objective-C. In fact, beginning with Objective-C 2.0, the zone parameter is ignored. The returned object is always allocated from the default malloc zone. You should use plain alloc for your object allocations.

Object Initialization

Objective-C initialization methods are instance methods that by convention begin with the word init. If you are designing a class whose objects do not require any specific initialization, you can use the initialization method init, which all classes inherit from NSObject. NSObject's implementation of init does nothing other than return self. But if instances of your class require custom initialization, such as setting instance variables to particular values, registering callbacks, or acquiring resources, you must override init and provide your own implementation.

The Form of init

Here is the typical form of an init implementation:

```
1  - (id) init
2  {
```

```
3    if ( self = [super init] )
4      {
5         // Class-specific initializations
6      }
7    return self;
8  }
```

Looking at the preceding code:

- Line 3: (Yes, that is a *single* = .) This line of code invokes the superclass `init` method to initialize the superclass part of the object. The object returned by the superclass initialization is then assigned to the variable `self`. Recall that `self` is a hidden argument that is added by the compiler to all methods.

  The assignment to `self` is necessary. The value of `self` when `init` is invoked is a pointer to the original receiver (the object returned by `alloc`). However, the superclass `init` may fail and return `nil`, or it may release the original receiver and allocate and return a different object. Because `self` is eventually used to return a pointer to the initialized object, you must set it to the object returned by the superclass `init`.

- Line 5: If the superclass has returned a non-`nil` object, you can proceed with any required initialization.

- Line 7: Finally, you must remember to return the pointer to the newly created object. If you forget, the return value of the method will be garbage.

Return Type of `init`

You may have noticed (and been surprised) that `init` methods are typed as returning an `id` rather than a pointer to an instance of a specific class. There are two reasons for this:

- As noted earlier, an `init` method may release its receiver and substitute an object belonging to a subclass of the original receiver. This commonly happens with classes that are implemented as class clusters.

  A class cluster is designed so that a public-facing abstract class manages a group of private subclasses. When you allocate and initialize an instance of the public class, what you actually receive is an instance of one of the private subclasses. Many common Foundation objects such as `NSString`, `NSArray`, and `NSDictionary` are examples of class clusters. See Chapter 9, "Common Foundation Classes."

- The same `init` method may be used with receivers of different classes. Typing the return value of an `init` method as `id` allows the method to be inherited and used by classes that inherit from the original class that declared it.

Combining `alloc` and `init`

It is a universal idiom to combine allocation and initialization into a single statement:

```
Foo *myFoo = [[Foo alloc] init]; // Correct
```

Doing so protects against this error:

```
Foo *myFoo = [Foo alloc]; // WRONG!
[myFoo init];
```

What's wrong with this code? It discards the return value of `init`. If `init` substitutes an object that belongs to a subclass of the requested class (which can happen if `Foo` is a class cluster), or if initialization fails and `init` returns `nil`, `myFoo` will be left holding a pointer to memory that has been returned to the heap.

The following code is technically correct, but it is verbose and a poor practice because it might lead you to forget to assign the return value of `init` to `myFoo`:

```
// Technically correct but verbose and poor practice

Foo *myFoo = [Foo alloc];
myFoo = [myFoo init];
```

Initializers with Arguments

What if you want to initialize one of your class's instance variables to a specific value? Then you need an initializer that takes an argument, so you can pass in the value. (There is nothing special about the default initializer `init`, other than the fact that every class inherits it from `NSObject`. A class can have as many initializers as it needs.)

> **Note**
>
> Using an initializer with an argument isn't necessary if you want the initial value of an instance variable to be zero or `nil`. Unlike function or method automatic variables, instance variables are initialized to zero (by `alloc`) when the object is created.

As an example, assume that you are designing a `TeeShirt` class. The `TeeShirt` class should have an `NSUInteger` instance variable `shirtSize` to hold the shirt size. An initialization method to set the shirt size when a `TeeShirt` object is created looks like this:

```
- (id) initWithShirtSize:(NSUInteger) inShirtSize
{
  if ( self = [super init] )
    {
      shirtSize = inShirtSize;
    }
  return self;
}
```

> **Note**
>
> It is a universal custom to give initializers names that begin with `init`. Initializers that take arguments usually have names with the form `initWithFoo:` where `Foo` is the property that the initializer sets. (I'll use the expression `init...` as an abbreviation for "an initialization method.")

Initializers can have more than one argument. If you redesign the `TeeShirt` class to have an additional instance variable to hold the shirt color, you should discard the original `initWithShirtSize:` and add an initializer that sets both the shirt size and the shirt color:

```
1   - (id) initWithShirtSize:(NSUInteger) inShirtSize
2          color:(NSColor*)  inShirtColor
3   {
4     if ( self = [super init] )
5       {
6         shirtSize = inShirtSize;
7         shirtColor = [inShirtColor retain];
8       }
9     return self;
10  }
```

In Line 7, the **retain** message is necessary to make sure that the **NSColor** object is not deallocated while the **TeeShirt** object is using it. The **retain** message must be balanced by a **release** message in **TeeShirt**'s **dealloc** method.

When there is more than one instance variable to be initialized, you can design initializers that set only some of the variables to values passed in as arguments. The other variables are set to default values. Here is an initializer for **theTeeShirt** class that sets the **shirtSize** directly but sets the **shirtColor** to a default color:

```
- (id) initWithShirtSize:(int) inShirtSize
{
  NSColor *defaultShirtColor = [NSColor whiteColor];
  return      [self initWithShirtSize: inShirtSize
                   color: defaultShirtColor];
}
```

Notice that the preceding code follows a different pattern: `initWithShirtSize:` gets a default value for the shirt color and then calls another one of `TeeShirt`'s initializers, `initWithShirtSize:color:`, to do the real work of initializing the object.

Designated Initializers

Every class must have one initializer that is the *designated initializer*. The designated initializer is an initializer that will completely initialize an instance of the class. The designated initializer is usually the initializer that has the most arguments or that does the most work in setting up the object. For classes that do not require initializers with arguments, the designated initializer is `init`.

In the preceding `TeeShirt` example, `initWithShirtSize:color:` is the `TeeShirt` class's designated initializer. Using `initWithShirtSize:color:` produces a fully initialized instance of `TeeShirt`.

There are two rules that you have to follow when you design initializers for a class:

1. All other class initializers must eventually invoke that class's (*not* the superclass's) designated initializer. `TeeShirt`'s `initWithShirtSize:` invokes `initWithShirtSize:color:`, `TeeShirt`'s designated initializer.

2. A class's designated initializer must invoke its superclass's designated initializer. The designated initializer is the *only* initializer that invokes the superclass's designated initializer.

`TeeShirt` follows those rules:

1. `initWithShirtSize:` invokes `initWithShirtSize:color:`, `TeeShirt`'s designated initializer.

2. `initWithShirtSize:color:` invokes the superclass designated initializer (`NSObject`'s) `init`.

Note

You should (as the Cocoa frameworks do) note which initializer is the designated initializer in the documentation for your class. However, despite the need to follow the preceding rules, there is no formal notion of a designated initializer in the Objective-C syntax.

As it stands, the `TeeShirt` class has one problem that requires attention: `TeeShirt` has a different designated initializer from its superclass, `NSObject` (`initWithShirtSize:color:` versus `init`). What would happen if you coded the following?

```
TeeShirt *aTeeShirt = [[TeeShirt alloc] init];
```

`TeeShirt` doesn't override `init`, so it is `NSObject`'s implementation of `init` that will be invoked in the preceding line of code. `NSObject` doesn't know anything about `TeeShirt`s. The newly created `TeeShirt` instance with instance variables `shirtSize` and `shirtColor` will be left, incorrectly, uninitialized. To make sure that the `TeeShirt` instance is properly initialized in this case, you must override `init` and then invoke `TeeShirt`'s designated initializer from within the override:

```
- (id) init
{
  NSUInteger *defaultShirtSize = 36;
  NSColor *defaultShirtColor = [NSColor whiteColor];
  return
    [self
      initWithShirtSize: defaultShirtSize color: defaultShirtColor];
}
```

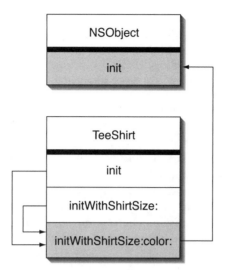

Figure 6.2   Initializers for the **TeeShirt** class. The shaded boxes are designated initializers.

Figure 6.2 shows the pattern of initializer calls for the **TeeShirt** class. The boxes with the shaded background are the class's designated initializers.

If your class's designated initializer is different (has a different name) from that of its superclass, you must override any **init...** methods declared in your class's ancestor classes and invoke your class's designated initializer from the overrides. In practice, this is less onerous than it sounds. Objective-C class hierarchies are usually not very deep, and in most cases there will be only a few initializers that need attention.

Failed Initialization

What happens if you can't successfully initialize an object? Perhaps some resource that your object needs to function is not available. If that happens, you should clean up the failure gracefully:

1. Do any cleanup that is not handled by **dealloc**. For example, if you have created a temporary object or connection that would normally be released later in the **init** method, it needs to be released before returning.

2. Release **self**. Because **self** was created by **alloc** with a retain count of one, you must balance the **alloc** with a **release**.

3. Return **nil**. This indicates to the invoking code that the initialization failed and that no object was created.

> **Note**
>
> Executing [self release] inside an initialization method causes the object's retain count to drop to zero, which causes the object's dealloc method to be called (see the following section, *Destroying Objects*). If the design of your class requires that you handle an initialization failure, you must also make sure that it is safe to invoke the class's dealloc method at the point(s) of failure.

As an example, suppose that you have an object that has two instance variables that are array objects, anArray1 and anArray2. (NSArray and NSMutableArray are covered in Chapter 9, "Common Foundation Classes"; you don't need to know any details about them for this example.) Further, suppose that both arrays must be properly initialized for the object to function correctly.

anArray1 is allocated as an empty array, and anArray2 is initialized from the contents of a file using the NSArray initialization method initWithContentsOfFile:. But if there is no file at the specified path, initWithContentsOfFile: fails and returns nil. If that happens, your object can't be properly initialized, so your init should clean up and return nil.

The following code shows how to handle this situation:

```
1   - (id) init
2   {
3     if ( self = [super init] )
4       {
5         anArray1 = [[NSMutableArray alloc] init];
6
7         if ( anArray1 == nil )
8           {
9             [self release];
10            return nil;
11          }
12
13        anArray2 =
14              [[NSArray alloc]
15                  initWithContentsOfFile: @"/Users/rclair/stuff"];
16
17        if ( anArray2 == nil )
18          {
19            [self release];
20            return nil;
21          }
22      }
23    return self;
24  }
25
26  - (void) dealloc
27  {
28    [anArray1 release];
```

```
29   [anArray2 release];
30   [super dealloc];
31   }
```

Now let's walk through the code in this example:

- Line 3: Call the superclass `init`, assign the return value to `self`, and check to see that it is not `nil`.

- Line 5: Allocate and initialize `anArray1`.

- Line 7: The allocation of `anArray1` can fail only if you are completely out of memory. If that happens, you are going to have many other problems and your program will probably crash very soon. However, to be proper and practice good code hygiene, this line of code checks for a `nil` value of `anArray1`.

- Line 9: If `anArray1` is `nil`, the object cannot be initialized, so the code releases `self`. If you don't release `self`, the bytes allocated for `self` are leaked. They aren't used for anything and they aren't returned to the heap.

  Releasing `self` causes the object's `dealloc` method to be invoked. Lines 28 and 29 do not cause any problems because `anArray1` and `anArray2` are both `nil` at this point. Line 30 invokes the superclass implementation of `dealloc`, which releases any objects stored in instance variables declared by the superclass.

- Line 10: Returning `nil` indicates that the initialization failed.

If `anArray1` is successfully created, the `init` method continues:

- Line 13: Allocate `anArray2` and initialize it from the contents of the file */Users/rclair/stuff.*

- Line 17: Check to see if `anArray2` was successfully created.

- Line 19: If `anArray2` could not be created, `self` is released, causing `dealloc` to be invoked. Line 28 releases `anArray1`, which was allocated in Line 5.

- Line 20: Returning `nil` indicates that the initialization failed.

- Line 23: If `anArray1` and `anArray2` are non-nil, and the superclass initialization did not fail, this line returns a fully initialized object.

> **Note**
>
> After `[self release]` is executed, the object held in `self` is no longer valid. You should not execute any code that references `self` between invoking `release` on `self` and returning `nil`. If you don't follow this rule, and the offending code is executed, it may cause your program to crash.

Destroying Objects

How do you get rid of objects when you are finished with them? It is important to properly dispose of unneeded objects so their bytes can be returned to the heap for reuse. In Objective-C, you don't explicitly destroy objects.

When you are finished with an object you created or retained, you send it a release message. If that release message drops the object's retain count to zero, the release method calls the object's dealloc method. The object's dealloc method should

1. Send a release message to any objects that the disappearing object has created or retained

2. Invoke the superclass's dealloc method

The dealloc method for the TeeShirt class from the preceding section looks like this:

```
- (void) dealloc
{
  [shirtColor release];
  [super dealloc];  // Important!
}
```

In the preceding code, shirtColor holds an object (an NSColor) that was retained when the TeeShirt instance was created. When it is about to disappear, the TeeShirt object must balance that retain with a release message. Otherwise, the object held in shirtColor becomes a potential memory leak.

The line [super dealloc] is very important. It is NSObject's implementation of dealloc that returns the object's bytes to the heap. If any class in the inheritance chain between your class and NSObject forgets to call [super dealloc] in its own dealloc, NSObject's implementation won't be invoked. The bytes used for the object's storage will be leaked. The compiler helps you by warning you if you forget the [super dealloc].

> **Note**
>
> Be careful of spelling. If you mistype and accidentally name your dealloc method deallloc or some other misspelling, it is the superclass dealloc that will be called. Any objects that your implementation of dealloc should release will be leaked. The compiler doesn't warn you about this. It thinks deallloc is just another method that you have declared for your subclass.

When you write a dealloc method, the [super dealloc] message should be the last line of the method. After [super dealloc] returns, the object has been destroyed; any references to self are invalid.

For example, consider adding a final logging statement to the NamedAccumulator class dealloc method (refer to Listing 6.4).

If you code the dealloc method like this:

```
- (void) dealloc
{
  // WRONG!
  [super dealloc];
```

```
  NSLog(@"The final total of %@ is %d", [self name], [self total]);
  [name release];
}
```

the program will likely crash when the **dealloc** method is executed:

```
*** -[NamedAccumulator name]:
        message sent to deallocated instance 0x10010d6b0
```

The correct way to code this method is as follows:

```
- (void) dealloc
{
  // Correct
  NSLog(@"The final total of %@ is %d", [self name], [self total]);
  [name release];

  [super dealloc];
}
```

In the preceding code, note also that the [self name] message precedes the [name release] message. Releasing an instance variable may cause it to be deallocated.

Copying Objects

Copying objects is more difficult than it might seem at first glance, thanks to a bit of what could be termed deceptive advertising. **NSObject** implements a method named **copy**. Seeing this, you might be tempted to go ahead and use the inherited **copy** method to copy one of your objects:

```
SomeClass *anObject = [[SomeClass alloc] init];
SomeClass *anObjectCopy = [anObject copy];
```

This compiles without a warning, but unless **SomeClass** has been coded properly, it results in an immediate crash.

   NSObject's implementation of **copy** invokes a method named **copyWithZone:** with a **nil** argument. The problem is that **NSObject** does *not* implement **copyWithZone:**. **NSObject** can't implement **copyWithZone:** because it has no way of knowing what type of copy a particular subclass should implement or if that subclass should even allow copying at all.

> **Note**
>
> As with **allocWithZone:**, the zone argument in **copyWithZone:** was designed to allow you to specify which malloc zone to use when obtaining the bytes for a copy. As described earlier, Apple now discourages the use of any zone other than the default malloc zone (the zone that is used when you invoke **copyWithZone:** with a **nil** argument).

Classes that permit copying adopt the **NSCopying** protocol. Protocols are covered in Chapter 13, but for now it's sufficient to note that all this means is that the class is required to implement **copyWithZone:**. When attempting to copy a Cocoa framework object, make sure the object's class does adopt **NSCopying** (this is noted in the documentation for the class). There are many framework classes that cannot be copied.

If you want to copy objects of a class that you define, you must implement **copyWithZone:** yourself. Before proceeding, you need to make some decisions about what sort of copy your class should provide. The next two sections look at some of the things that you should take into account when designing a **copyWithZone:** for your class.

Shallow and Deep Copies

If any of the instance variables in the object you are copying hold pointers (to other objects or to **malloc**'d memory), you must decide whether to fill in the corresponding instance variables of your newly created copy with the same pointers that are held in the original object. If you give your new copy the original pointers, you are making a *shallow* copy. The alternative is to copy any sub-objects in turn and give the sub-object copies to your new object. This type of copy is called a *deep* copy.

Which should you do? This question can't be answered in the abstract. It is something you must decide, based on the requirements of your program, when you design your classes. Here are the issues:

- A shallow copy leaves the copy and the original object entangled. If you make a change to one object by altering the state of a commonly held sub-object, the change is reflected in both the original object and the copy.

- A deep copy leaves two completely independent objects (as long as any copied sub-objects themselves implement a deep copy), but making a deep copy is a much more expensive operation (in both execution time and memory) than making a shallow copy.

- A copy need not be exclusively a deep copy or a shallow copy. You can implement copying to deep copy some instance variables and shallow copy others.

- If a class's instance variables are all primitive C types, there is no difference between a deep copy and a shallow copy.

Most Cocoa framework classes that implement copying implement a shallow copy.

Mutable and Immutable Copies

As you will see in Chapter 9, "Common Foundation Classes," some Cocoa framework classes create immutable instances. An immutable object's instance variables cannot be changed after the object has been created. For example, instances of **NSNumber** and **NSColor** are immutable. If you want an **NSNumber** with a different value or an **NSColor** with different color components, you must create new objects.

How is this enforced? The classes simply do not provide any methods for modifying their internal state.

Other framework classes such as NSString and the collection classes (NSArray, NSDictionary, and NSSet) create immutable instances but have subclasses that can create mutable instances. For classes like these, NSObject provides the mutableCopy method.

> **Note**
>
> In a similar fashion to copy, NSObject's mutableCopy method just invokes mutableCopyWithZone: with a nil argument. As you've probably guessed, NSObject does not implement mutableCopyWithZone:. Implementing mutableCopyWithZone: is left to any immutable class that provides a mutable subclass. A class that implements mutableCopyWithZone: is said to adopt the NSMutableCopying protocol.

For example, NSArray allows both copying and mutable copying. To get a mutable copy of an NSArray (one that has the same contents as the original array but permits you to add objects to or delete objects from the array), you can code this:

```
NSArray *anArray = ...
NSMutableArray *aMutableCopyOfAnArray = [anArray mutableCopy];
```

Of course, you should check the documentation to make sure the class of the object you are copying supports mutable copying before attempting to make a mutable copy.

> **Note**
>
> The Foundation documentation is located at https://developer.apple.com/library/ios/#documentation/Cocoa/Reference/Foundation/ObjC_classic/_index.html/, the AppKit documentation is located at https://developer.apple.com/library/mac/#documentation/Cocoa/Reference/ApplicationKit/ObjC_classic/_index.html, and the UIKit documentation is located at https://developer.apple.com/library/ios/#documentation/UIKit/Reference/UIKit_Framework/_index.html.

Implementing Copying in Your Own Classes

If instances of your class are supposed to be immutable, you can implement copyWithZone: by sending the object you are copying an additional retain message:

```
- (id) copyWithZone:(NSZone*) zone
{
  return [self retain];  // self is an instance of an immutable class
}
```

Because an immutable object cannot be modified, there will never be any difference between the original and a copy. You can use the original as the copy as long as you add a retain, as shown in this example, so that the object will not disappear on you until you are ready to release it.

In the more typical case, where the object you are copying is mutable, you must allocate storage for a new object and then initialize the new object with values derived from the original object.

The usual recommendation for implementing `copyWithZone:` is to call the superclass implementation of `copyWithZone:` to create the new copy and fill in any instance variables defined in the superclass. The rest of the subclass implementation of `copyWithZone:` then fills in any instance variables defined in the subclass and returns the copy.

Unfortunately, you can't do this if your class is a direct subclass of `NSObject` or any other class that doesn't implement `copyWithZone:`. In that case, you must allocate and initialize the copy yourself. Using the `TeeShirt` class example, a first attempt at a `copyWithZone:` method might look like Listing 6.5.

Listing 6.5   `TeeShirt copyWithZone:` **(version 1)**

```
- (id) copyWithZone:(NSZone*) zone
{
  id copiedTeeShirt =
    [[TeeShirt alloc]  // Bug in waiting!
        initWithShirtSize: [self shirtSize] color: [self color]];

  return copiedTeeShirt;
}
```

This works for copying `TeeShirt` instances, but it is a bug in waiting if you ever decide to subclass `TeeShirt`. To see why, define a `SloganTeeShirt` class that extends `TeeShirt` by adding a string to print on the front of the shirt, as shown in the following code:

```
#import "TeeShirt.h"

@interface SloganTeeShirt : TeeShirt
{
  NSString *slogan;
}

-(void) setSlogan:(NSString*) slogan;
-(NSString*) slogan;

...

@end
```

You can then implement `copyWithZone:` for the `SloganTeeShirt` class, as shown in Listing 6.6.

Listing 6.6 `SloganTeeShirt copyWithZone:`

```
1  - (id) copyWithZone:(NSZone*) zone
2  {
3    // This is a BUG because the superclass copyWithZone is
4    // incorrectly coded
5
6    id copiedSloganTeeShirt = [super copyWithZone: zone];
7    [copiedSloganTeeShirt setSlogan: [self slogan]];
8    return copiedSloganTeeShirt;
9  }
```

However, there is a problem: When Line 6 is executed, it causes a crash with an unrecognized selector exception. The problem is with the **TeeShirt** implementation of **copyWithZone:** (refer to Listing 6.5). When [super copyWithZone: zone] is invoked in Line 6 of Listing 6.6, **TeeShirt**'s **copyWithZone:** returns a **TeeShirt** object, not a **SloganTeeShirt** object.

When Line 7 is executed, the **TeeShirt** object held in **copiedSloganTeeShirt** is sent a **setSlogan:** message. Because **TeeShirt** doesn't implement a **setSlogan:** method, this line causes a crash.

The solution is to modify Listing 6.5 so that **TeeShirt**'s **copyWithZone:** returns an object that is the same class as the receiver it was called with: If it is called with a **TeeShirt** object as the receiver, it returns a completed **TeeShirt** copy; if it is called with a **SloganTeeShirt** object as the receiver, it returns a **SloganTeeShirt** object with the superclass instance variables filled in.

The corrected version of **TeeShirt**'s **copyWithZone:** is shown in Listing 6.7.

Listing 6.7 `TeeShirt copyWithZone:` **(version 2)**

```
1  -(id) copyWithZone:(NSZone*) zone
2  {
3    id copiedTeeShirt =
4      [[[self class] alloc]
5        initWithShirtSize: [self shirtSize]
                      color: [self shirtColor]];
6
7    return copiedTeeShirt;
8  }
```

The key here is Line 4. [self class] is a message that returns the class of the object that **self** points to. When **TeeShirt**'s implementation of **copyWithZone:** is called with a **TeeShirt** object as the receiver, [self class] returns **TeeShirt** and the object returned by the method is a **TeeShirt** object. But when the **TeeShirt** implementation of **copyWithZone:** is called with a **SloganTeeShirt** object as the receiver, as in Line 6 of Listing 6.6, **self** is an instance of **SloganTeeShirt**. [self class] yields **SloganTeeShirt**. (Recall that when a method is invoked using **super**, the method is the superclass implementation, but the *receiver* is the original object.) The newly created object is a **SloganTeeShirt** ready to have its **slogan** instance variable set.

Finally, as part of the Objective-C naming convention, you own any object returned to you by a method that contains the word *copy* in its name. As a consequence, you must send the copied object a **release** message when you are finished using it. You should be careful to respect this convention when writing your own **copyWithZone:** methods, by making sure to return an object that has a retain count of one. In the common cases, this is satisfied when you return a newly **alloc**'d object for the copy (as in Listing 6.7) or an object that was obtained from another copy method (as in Listing 6.6).

Summary

After reading this chapter, you should understand how to define a class and how to allocate, initialize, destroy, and copy objects. The material from this chapter and the previous chapter on messaging forms the core of Objective-C. At this point, you should be able to write a modest but complete Objective-C program.

Exercises

1. Create skeleton versions of a **RockStar** class and a **Band** class. The **RockStar** class should have an instance variable typed as **Band**, and the **Band** class should have an instance variable typed as **RockStar**.

   a. Verify that if you import *Band.h* into *RockStar.h* and *RockStar.h* into *Band.h*, the classes don't compile.

   b. Verify that you can fix the situation by replacing one or both of the imports with a **@class** directive.

2. Create a small testbed program and use it to verify that the **NamedAccumulator** class works as expected. (Use the code from Listings 6.1, 6.2, 6.3, and 6.4 in your project.)

3. Define and code some initializers for the **NamedAccumulator** class. One initializer should have an **NSString** argument to set the name and an **int** argument to set the total to an initial value. A second initializer should take an **NSString** argument for the name but set the total to a default value of zero. Make sure your initializers follow the Objective-C naming conventions.

   a. One of your new initializers must be the class's designated initializer. Which one should it be?

   b. Make sure all initializers eventually call the designated initializer.

   c. Don't forget to fix `init`.

   d. Use your testbed program from Exercise 2 to verify that your initializers work correctly.

4. Implement copying for the `Accumulator` and `NamedAccumulator` classes. Use your testbed program from Exercise 2 to verify that your copy methods work correctly.

5. Create a new subclass of `Accumulator` called `AveragingAccumulator`. An `AveragingAccumulator` should keep a running total of the number of times its `addToTotal:` method has been called. It should also have a method to return that number and a method, `averagePerTransaction`, that can report the average value of all the `addToTotal:` transactions. Using a test program, verify that your new class works correctly.

The Class Object

In Objective-C, unlike Java or C++, classes are themselves objects. Objective-C classes are instances of a special class called **Class**. You can send classes messages, and they can execute methods. This chapter looks at the technical details of class objects and class methods and then takes a brief look at some examples of class methods. The last section of this chapter is an extended example where you'll learn how to implement variables that are global to all instances of a given class.

Class Objects

Each class in an Objective-C program is represented by a single class object that contains the information that defines the class. You don't have to do anything to instantiate class objects; the compiler creates them for you from information in the class definition.

Class objects can receive messages and execute methods called *class methods*. You have already seen the most common example of this, the **alloc** class method:

```
[SomeClass alloc]
```

The receiver in a class message is a class object. The class name may be used to represent the class object in a message expression as shown in the preceding example.

> **Note**
>
> The receiver in a class message expression is the only place that a class name can substitute for its corresponding class object.

Class objects are not instances of the class they represent. You can't use a class object as the receiver with any of the class's instance methods. For example, **count** is an instance method of the **NSArray** class. It returns the number of objects in an **NSArray**. If you try to use **count** with the **NSArray** class object as the receiver:

```
[NSArray count];
```

you will get the following compiler warning:

```
testbed.m:6: warning: 'NSArray' may not respond to '+count'
testbed.m:6: warning: (Messages without a matching method signature
testbed.m:6: warning: will be assumed to return 'id' and accept
testbed.m:6: warning: '...' as arguments.)
```

If you ignore the warning and execute the code, the program crashes:

```
*** Terminating app due to uncaught exception
  'NSInvalidArgumentException',
reason: '+[NSArray count]:
  unrecognized selector sent to class 0x7fff707ebd28'
```

Although Objective-C classes are objects, class objects do not have instance variables. Objective-C has no equivalent of the class variables found in some other object-oriented languages.

> **Note**
>
> Class variables (in languages that have them) are variables that are global to a class. In contrast to normal instance variables, there is only one copy of a class variable that is shared by all instances of the class.

However, in the section *Mimicking Class Variables* later in this chapter, you'll learn how to imitate the functionality of class variables using ordinary C external variables.

The Class Type

Variables typed as `Class` are used for pointers to class objects. You can get a pointer to a class object by invoking the class method `class` with the class name as the receiver:[1]

```
Class aClass = [NSString class];

// aClass now holds a pointer to the NSString class object
```

> **Note**
>
> `Class` is inherently a pointer type. There is no need for an * when declaring a `Class` variable:
>
> ```
> Class *someClass;    // WRONG!
> ```
>
> Similarly, you can use the class method `superclass` to get the class object of a class's superclass:
>
> ```
> Class aClass = [NSString superclass];
>
> // aClass now holds a pointer to NSString's superclass, NSObject
> ```

---

1. I apologize for the necessary overuse of the word *class* in the preceding sentence. It gives me a headache, too.

<table>
<tr><td>

Note

There are also NSObject instance methods, `class` and `superclass`, that return the class and superclass of an object. You should be very careful when using these instance methods with classes that you did not code yourself. Many common framework classes are actually *class clusters*. When you request an instance of a class that is a class cluster, you may receive an instance of a private subclass of the original class. The result of invoking `class` or `superclass` on an instance of a class cluster may be different from what you expect. (See Chapter 9, "Common Foundation Classes.")

</td></tr>
</table>

A variable of type **Class** can be used instead of the class name as the receiver with class methods. This is useful in situations where you need to create an object, but the class of the new object is not known until run time. As an example, you can create a new object based on a type stored as a string in a configuration file:

```
NSString *classNameAsString = ... // Read string from file
Class classToInstantiate = NSClassFromString( classNameAsString );
id newObject = [[classToInstantiate alloc] init];
```

In the preceding code, **NSClassFromString** is a regular C function, defined in the Foundation framework, which takes an **NSString** argument and returns a pointer to the corresponding class object. The returned pointer is stored in the **Class** variable **classToInstantiate**. Finally, **classToInstantiate** is used as the receiver with the class method **alloc** to create a new object of the requested class.

Type Introspection

You can ask an Objective-C object about its class membership using the NSObject methods `isMemberOfClass:` and `isKindOfClass:` as shown here:

```
[mysteriousObject isMemberOfClass: [Dog class]];
```

The preceding returns YES if `mysteriousObject` is an instance of the Dog class and returns NO otherwise; whereas the following line:

```
[mysteriousObject isKindOfClass: [Dog class]];
```

returns YES if `mysteriousObject` is an instance of the Dog class or *any class that inherits from Dog*. If you have defined a class RescueDog that is a subclass of Dog, the preceding statement returns YES if `mysteriousObject` is an instance of either Dog or RescueDog.

You should rarely need to rely on these methods. If you find yourself using one of them, you should stop, think for a moment, and see if there is a better way to accomplish the same goal. For example, if you have been handed an object typed as id, and you are trying to find out its class to see if it is safe to send the object a particular message, you should use `respondsToSelector:` instead:

```
id mysteriousObject = ...
if ( [mysteriousObject respondsToSelector: @selector( rollOver )] )
  {
```

```
    [mysteriousObject rollOver];
  }
```

The preceding example tests for behavior (whether the object responds to the message you want to send) rather than class (which you shouldn't care about). (Also see Exercise 2 at the end of this chapter.)

Class Methods

Class methods are methods defined on a class's class object. Another way of saying this is that the class object, not an instance of the class, is the receiver for a message corresponding to a class method. Here are the rest of the details:

- The declaration of a class method begins with a plus sign. For example, the declaration of **alloc** is

  ```
  + (id) alloc
  ```

- Class method declarations and implementations go in the class's **@interface** section and **@implementation** section, respectively, just like instance methods. They are often placed ahead of the instance methods, but this is just a convention and isn't required.

- A class method does not have direct access to any of the instance variables defined for an instance of the class. (It wouldn't make sense if it did. Imagine that you've created four instances of a class, each with a different value for one of the instance variables. If a class method accessed that instance variable, which value would it get?)

- Like instance methods, class methods are inherited by subclasses. A subclass can override an inherited class method. For example, if you create a new class, your class can override the **NSObject** implementation of the class method **description** and return a string with a custom description.

- It is possible to have a class method with the same name as an instance method of that class. The runtime handles this just like any other method dispatch. The message is sent to the receiver. If the receiver is the class object, it is the class method that is eventually called. If the receiver is an instance of the class, it is the instance method that is called.

- There is one very important point to remember when writing class methods: *self in a class method refers to the class object, not to an instance of the class*. If you forget this, not only will you most likely have a bug or crash, you will also have a very difficult time discovering the cause of your troubles.

Autorelease

When you create an object with a method whose name begins with `alloc`, `new`, `copy`, or `mutableCopy`, the object is returned with a retain count of one. You are eventually responsible for balancing the object creation by sending the newly created object a `release` message. In some situations, this requirement causes an awkward problem. If you have a method that creates an object to pass on as a return value, and you send the object a `release` message before the `return` statement is executed, the object is immediately deallocated. The returned pointer points to a dead object. If you don't send the object a `release` message, you are depending on the method's caller to remember to release the object. If the caller fails to release the object, the object's memory is leaked. You need a way to register a release but delay the execution of that release. This is what an `autorelease` message does.

When an object receives an `autorelease` message, a pointer to the object is added to the current *autorelease pool*. All the objects in an autorelease pool receive a `release` message when the pool is drained at some future time. If an object has received more than one `autorelease` message, it receives one `release` message for each `autorelease` message it received. In a GUI program, the pool is typically drained at the bottom of the run (event) loop. For the purposes of retain count bookkeeping, an autorelease counts as a release. It's just one that happens at an unspecified future time. Reference counting is covered in detail in Chapter 15, "Reference Counting."

Other Class Methods

The primary function of a class object is to act as a factory object to create instances of the class. As we saw in the previous chapter, you create object instances by using the class method `alloc`. The next two sections cover areas where classes often define additional class methods. *Convenience constructors* and *singletons* are common patterns in the Cocoa frameworks, and you may want to use them in some of your own classes.

Convenience Constructors

Many of the Cocoa framework classes define convenience constructors, which combine allocation and initialization in a single method. The `NSString` class method `string` is a typical example. It returns an initialized but empty string:

```
NSString *emptyString = [NSString string];
```

`NSString` provides a number of other convenience constructors such as `stringWithFormat:`, `stringWithString:`, and `stringWithCharacters:length:`. (For a complete list, see https://developer.apple.com/library/mac/#documentation/Cocoa/Reference/Foundation/Classes/NSString_Class/Reference/NSString.html.) When a class defines a number of different `init...` methods, it usually matches each `init...` method with a convenience constructor that takes the same arguments.

There is one very important thing to be aware of when using convenience constructors with reference counting: *You do not own an object returned by a convenience constructor.* (The name of a convenience constructor does not begin with `alloc`, `new`, `copy`, or `mutableCopy`.) If you want to use an object that you received from a convenience constructor beyond the current context (for example, by storing it in an instance variable), you must take ownership of the object by retaining it. If you don't take ownership, the object may disappear at some future time, leaving you with a pointer to a deallocated object.

Consider the following example:

```
NSArray *arrayOne =
  [[NSArray alloc] initWithObjects: @"iPhone", @"iPod", nil];
NSArray *arrayTwo =
  [NSArray arrayWithObjects: @"iPhone", @"iPod", nil];
```

You own `arrayOne` because you created it with `alloc`. When you are finished with `arrayOne`, you must send it a `release` message to balance the `alloc`. In contrast, you do *not* own `arrayTwo` because you obtained it from a convenience constructor. If you need `arrayTwo` to remain alive beyond the current calling context, you have to send a `retain` message to `arrayTwo` (and, of course, a balancing `release` when you are finished with it).

Creating a Convenience Constructor

Imagine that you have a class `Dog`. You can create a convenience constructor that returns an initialized instance of a `Dog` like this:

```
+ (id) dog
{
  return [[[Dog alloc] init] autorelease];
}
```

The `alloc` creates an instance of a `Dog` with a retain count of one. The `autorelease` fulfills your obligation to balance the `alloc` with a `release`. (Remember, an `autorelease` schedules a `release` for sometime in the future. See the previous sidebar, *Autorelease*.)

When you use your convenience constructor, you must remember to take ownership of the returned `Dog` if you plan to keep it:

```
Dog *spot = [Dog dog];
[spot retain];
```

As it stands, `dog` functions properly with the class `Dog`, but a problem appears if you subclass `Dog`. If you create a subclass of `Dog`, `RescueDog`, your subclass will inherit `dog`. The current version of `dog` doesn't work correctly with `RescueDog`. For example:

```
[RescueDog dog]
```

returns an instance of `Dog`, not an instance of `RescueDog`. You can fix this problem by using `self` as the receiver for `alloc` instead of `Dog`:

```
+ (id) dog
{
  return [[[self alloc] init] autorelease];
}
```

Because `dog` is a class method, `self` refers to the class object that is used as the receiver. The revised convenience constructor now works properly for both `Dog` and `RescueDog`.

```
[Dog dog]
```

returns an instance of `Dog` and

```
[RescueDog dog]
```

returns an instance of `RescueDog`.

> **Note**
>
> Convenience constructors are customarily typed as returning `id` rather than an instance of a specific class, so that they can be inherited by subclasses.

Convenience constructors are usually employed when the returned object is going to be used only in the context where the convenience constructor was invoked. You get an object from a convenience constructor and then use it for the remainder of the method. Because you are not keeping the object, you do not have to retain it. The returned object's memory management was taken care of when the convenience constructor put the object in an autorelease pool. However, if the object is very large, or if you are running into memory problems in an iOS program, it is better practice to create the object with an `alloc ... init` sequence and then release the object as soon as you are finished with it. This minimizes the memory impact of using the object by minimizing the amount of time the object occupies memory.

Singletons

A *singleton* is a class with only a single shared instance. Singleton classes are commonly used to wrap operating system services or for UI items such as inspector panels. Here is a typical setup for a singleton:

```
+ (InspectorPanel*) sharedInspectorPanel
{
  static InspectorPanel *inspectorPanel = nil;

  if ( ! inspectorPanel )
    {
      inspectorPanel = [[InspectorPanel alloc] init];
```

```
    }
    return inspectorPanel;
}
```

You create the single shared **InspectorPanel** instance and store it in a static variable. When you send a **sharedInspectorPanel** message to the class object, it returns the pointer stored in the static variable.

This code also illustrates *lazy instantiation*. You don't create the shared instance until it is requested the first time. This is a common pattern in Cocoa programs. Lazy instantiation reduces the startup time of a program. You create objects as they are needed rather than creating them all at once when the program is launched.

> **Note**
>
> To learn more about design patterns and how to use them to improve your code, see *Cocoa Design Patterns*, by Erik M. Buck and Donald A. Yacktman.[2]

Initializing Classes

The Objective-C runtime gives you a chance to initialize a class before it is used. The first time a class object is sent a message (typically an **alloc** message creating the first instance of that class), the runtime intercedes and sends an **initialize** message to the class object. The **initialize** message is sent before the original message is delivered.

> **Note**
>
> Using **initialize** to initialize a class is different from using an **init...** method to initialize an instance of a class.

The default **initialize** method inherited from **NSObject** does nothing. Most classes don't require any initialization, but there are a few situations where you might want to override the **initialize** method:

- The Foundation framework provides a singleton class, **NSUserDefaults**, that manages a program's interactions with the defaults system on iOS and OS X. (The defaults system manages user preferences and other values.) You can use the shared **NSUserDefaults** instance inside an **initialize** method to set default values or retrieve the current values for any preference items used by your class.

- If your class is using external variables to mimic class variables, you can do any work required to initialize those variables in **initialize**.

As an example, imagine that you have a game that simulates a team of traders working from a common money pool. The **Trader** class itself manages the money

2. Erik M. Buck and Donald A. Yacktman, *Cocoa Design Patterns* (Boston: Addison-Wesley, 2010.

pool using an external variable. You can use the **NSUserDefaults** system to store the value of the money pool between game sessions. When the game is restarted, you use the **Trader** class's **initialize** method to restore the value of **currentMoneyPool** from the defaults:

```
static NSInteger currentMoneyPool;

@implementation Trader

+ (void) initialize
{
 currentMoneyPool =
    [[NSUserDefaults standardUserDefaults]
        integerForKey: @"MoneyPool"];
}

...

@end
```

The first time the **Trader** class is sent a message, the **initialize** method retrieves the saved value of the money pool and stores it in the external variable **currentMoneyPool**.

A Problem with `initialize`

There is a potential problem with **initialize** to watch out for. If you have a class that overrides **initialize**, and that class has a subclass that *doesn't* override **initialize**, the original class will receive the **initialize** message twice: once when the original class is first used and again when the subclass is first used. Because this is probably not the behavior you want, you can restrict the initialization to the original class (call it **Dog**) by coding the **initialize** method as follows:

```
+ (void) initialize
{
  if ( self == [Dog class] )
    {
      // Do the initialization for Dog
    }
}
```

> **Note**
>
> In theory, in the preceding code you could skip the check shown in the **if** statement and just require that all subclasses of **Dog** implement an **initialize** method. But that would be a bad idea. It would leave the proper functioning of the **Dog** class dependent on the proper coding of all its subclasses. Coding the **Dog** class as shown ensures that its initialization occurs only once, even if a subclass does not implement **initialize**.

Mimicking Class Variables

As mentioned earlier in the chapter, Objective-C does not have class variables. For the most part, you can mimic class variables by using ordinary file scope variables in the class's implementation file. You can then define class methods that allow you to set or get the value of the external variable without requiring you to have an instance of the class.

To illustrate this, Listings 7.1 and 7.2 show how to create a **Coupon** class that can issue only a fixed number of coupons.

Listing 7.1   **CouponDispenser**/*Coupon.h*

```
#import <Foundation/Foundation.h>

@interface Coupon : NSObject
{
   ...
}

+ (int) numberCouponsLeft; // Class method
+ (void) resetCoupon;      // Class method

@end
```

Listing 7.2   **CouponDispenser**/*Coupon.m*

```
#import "Coupon.h"

#define INITIAL_COUPON_ALLOCATION 100

// The static keyword here limits the visibility
// of the name availableCoupons to this file

static int availableCoupons = INITIAL_COUPON_ALLOCATION;

@implementation Coupon

-(id) init
{
  if (self = [super init])
    {
      if ( availableCoupons == 0 )
        {
          [self release];
          return nil;
        }
```

```
      availableCoupons--;
    }
  return self;
}


+ (int) numberCouponsLeft
{
  return availableCoupons;
}


+ (void) resetCoupon
{
  availableCoupons = INITIAL_COUPON_ALLOCATION;
}

...


@end
```

`availableCoupons` keeps track of the total number of coupons available for the `Coupon` class. Each time `init` is called, it checks `availableCoupons` for the number of coupons remaining. If `availableCoupons` is zero, `init` releases `self` and returns `nil`. Otherwise, `init` decrements `availableCoupons` and returns an initialized `Coupon` instance.

The weak part of this arrangement is that it doesn't handle inheritance properly. If you blindly subclass `Coupon`, both `Coupon` and its subclass (call it `NewCoupon`) will share the same static variable `availableCoupons`. If you make several subclasses, they all will share the variable with the original `Coupon` class. This is probably not what you want. Both `Coupon` and `NewCoupon` need to keep their own separate totals of the number of coupons they have issued. You can fix the problem, but the repair requires a bit of extra handwork:

1. Declare separate static variables `availableCoupons` and `availableNewCoupons` for `Coupon` and `NewCoupon`, respectively. This gives each class its own count of the number of available coupons.

2. Implement the following class accessors in *both* implementation files:

   ```
   + (int) availableCoupons;
   + (void) setAvailableCoupons:(int) inAvailableCoupons;
   ```

   The accessors implemented in `Coupon` access `availableCoupons`. The accessors implemented in `NewCoupon` (which override those implemented in `Coupon`) access `availableNewCoupons`.

3. In both the class and the subclass, rewrite any methods (class or instance) that access the coupon count to use the class accessors. In instance methods, the accessors should be called like this:

```
[[self class] availableCoupons];
[[self class] setAvailableCoupons: newNumber];
```

This ensures that the proper version of the accessors is called. (You don't need to use [self class] in a class method, because in that case self already refers to the proper class object—the one used as the receiver.)

Listing 7.3 shows the repaired version. The changes to the code are shown in **bold**. Coupon can be subclassed as long as you follow the preceding recipe. It declares the accessors for the static variable in an extension. They are for internal use only and shouldn't be visible in the public header file.

> **Note**
>
> Extensions, which are covered in Chapter 11, "Categories, Extensions, and Security," move method declarations into the implementation file. They provide a way to hide the declarations of methods that are intended for internal use from public view. An extension interface section begins with @interface, followed on the same line by the name of the class being extended and a set of empty parentheses. It ends in the usual way with an @end. Methods that are declared in extensions are implemented in the normal way in the class's @implementation section.

Listing 7.3   **CouponDispenserFixed**/*Coupon.m*

```
#import "Coupon.h"

#define INITIAL_COUPON_ALLOCATION 100

//  The static keyword here just limits the visibility
//  of availableCoupons to this file

static int availableCoupons = INITIAL_COUPON_ALLOCATION;

// Declare private accessors in an extension

@interface Coupon ()

+ (int) availableCoupons;
+ (void) setAvailableCoupons:(int) inAvailableCoupons;

@end

@implementation Coupon
```

```
+ (int) availableCoupons
{
  return availableCoupons;
}


+ (void) setAvailableCoupons:(int) inAvailableCoupons
{
  availableCoupons = inAvailableCoupons;
}


- (id) init
{
  if (self = [super init])
    {
      if ( [[self class] availableCoupons] == 0 )
        {
          [self release];
          return nil;
        }
      [[self class] setAvailableCoupons:
          [[self class] availableCoupons]-1];
    }
  return self;
}


+ (int) numberCouponsLeft
{
  return [self availableCoupons];
}


+ (void) resetCoupon
{
  [self setAvailableCoupons: INITIAL_COUPON_ALLOCATION];
}

@end
```

Listings 7.4 and 7.5 show the NewCoupon subclass. Giving NewCoupon its own static variable, availableNewCoupons, and overriding the private accessor methods availableCoupons and setAvailableCoupons: to refer to availableNewCoupons lets Coupon and NewCoupon have independent values of the maximum number of coupons.

Listing 7.4   *NewCoupon.h*

```objc
#import <Foundation/Foundation.h>
#import "Coupon.h"


@interface NewCoupon : Coupon
{

}

@end
```

Listing 7.5   *NewCoupon.m*

```objc
#import "NewCoupon.h"

#define INITIAL_NEW_COUPON_ALLOCATION 50

static int availableNewCoupons = INITIAL_NEW_COUPON_ALLOCATION;

@interface NewCoupon ()

+ (int) availableCoupons;
+ (void) setAvailableCoupons:(int) inAvailableCoupons;

@end


@implementation NewCoupon

+ (int) availableCoupons
{
  return availableNewCoupons;
}

+ (void) setAvailableCoupons:(int) inAvailableCoupons
{
  availableNewCoupons = inAvailableCoupons;
}


// This method overrides the superclass implementation so each
// class can have its own value for the initial allocation.

+ (void) resetCoupon
{
```

```
    [self setAvailableCoupons: INITIAL_NEW_COUPON_ALLOCATION];
}
...
```

```
@end
```

In Listings 7.3 and 7.5 `Coupon` and `NewCoupon` have separate static variables, `availableCoupons` and `availableNewCoupons`, respectively. Each class also has its own implementation of the class accessor methods `availableCoupons` and `setAvailableCoupons:` to access the class's static variable.

In Listing 7.3, `init` gets and sets the number of remaining coupons by calling the class accessor methods `availableCoupons` and `setAvailableCoupons:` instead of directly accessing the static variable. The construction

```
[[self class] availableCoupons]
```

ensures that the correct version of `availableCoupons` is called for both:

```
[[Coupon alloc] init]
```

and

```
[[NewCoupon alloc] init]
```

Summary

Objective-C classes are objects and have methods, called class methods. The key things to remember about class objects and class methods are:

- Class methods are indicated by a declaration that begins with a + rather than a –.
- You use the class name or a pointer to the class object as the message receiver when you invoke a class method.
- A pointer to the class object can be stored in a variable of type `Class`.
- Class objects do not have instance variables, and they cannot use the instance variables or methods of an instance of the class.
- The most common class method is `alloc`, which is a factory method that creates instances of the class.
- The second most common use for class methods is for convenience constructors. Convenience constructors return initialized instances of the class.
- The functionality of class variables can be duplicated using static variables, but extra work is required to correctly subclass a class that uses external variables.

Exercises

1. Create a class, **Train**, and a subclass, **BulletTrain**, of your original class. (The classes don't have to do anything for the purposes of this exercise.)

    a. Write a convenience constructor for **Train** that will be inherited by **BulletTrain**.

    b. Write a small program that gets an instance of **Train** and an instance of **BulletTrain**, using the convenience constructor in both cases.

    c. Log the returned instances to prove that your convenience constructor functions properly.

2. Assume that you have an abstract class, **Dog**, with subclasses **AmericanDog**, **JapaneseDog**, and **ItalianDog**. You are asked to write a small piece of code that logs the sound of a **Dog** barking. What is wrong with the following code? (This is a design question, not a syntax question.)

```
Dog *myDog = ...

if ( [myDog isMemberOfClass: [AmericanDog class]] )
   {
     NSLog(@"woof woof");
   }
else if ( [myDog isMemberOfClass: [JapaneseDog class]] )
   {
     NSLog(@"wan wan");
   }
else if ( [myDog isMemberOfClass: [ItalianDog class]] )
   {
     NSLog(@"bau bau");
   }
```

    How would you improve the design? How would the code (both the old and new versions) have to be modified if you added a **FrenchDog** subclass?

3. Write a program that uses the first version of the **Coupon** class (refer to Listings 7.1 and 7.2):

    a. Create a naive version of the subclass **NewCoupon** (without the improvements shown in Listings 7.3, 7.4, and 7.5).

    b. In your program, obtain an instance of **Coupon** and then log the number of remaining **Coupon**s and **NewCoupon**s.

    c. Then obtain an instance of **NewCoupon** and again log the number of remaining **Coupon**s and **NewCoupon**s.

    d. Verify that the classes **Coupon** and **NewCoupon** are sharing a single number of remaining coupons.

4. In your program from Exercise 3, replace the versions of Coupon and NewCoupon with the corrected versions (refer to Listings 7.3, 7.4, and 7.5). Verify that the classes Coupon and NewCoupon now keep track of their remaining coupons independently.

5. Take your program from Exercise 4 and add a new type of coupon, NewCoupon2, that is a subclass of NewCoupon. Verify that Coupon, NewCoupon, and NewCoupon2 all have independent versions of their remaining coupons.

6. Take your program from Exercise 5 and move the initialization of the static variables holding the remaining number of coupons into class initialize methods. You need an initialize method for each class. (There is no benefit from doing this in the case of a simple assignment, but in a real program you would probably use the initialize method to read the initial number of coupons from the defaults system or some other resource.)

8

Frameworks

Imagine that you have some good carpentry skills and need to build a house. You could take your tools into the woods and build your house by cutting down trees, hewing timber, and making everything that you need, by hand, from the raw materials. The resulting cabin might be a gem of craftsmanship, but this is hardly an efficient way to obtain a usable dwelling. A more efficient procedure would be to go to your local builder's supply store and investigate the fine collection of premade doors, windows, and other components. The Objective-C equivalent of your local builder's supply store is a set of frameworks. Frameworks are repositories of predefined classes and useful functions that you can use in building your applications. They are the Objective-C equivalent of Java or C++ class libraries.

An important attribute of frameworks is that they are dynamically loaded shared resources. Only one copy of the executable code or resources that a framework contains needs to be present on the system. Whenever possible, only one copy is loaded into memory and shared among all the running applications that require it. Although disk space seems like less and less of an issue these days, memory is still at a premium, especially on iOS devices.

If you are building a GUI application, using framework objects for your UI preserves a degree of uniformity between your UI and that of other applications. This helps users because experience gained with other applications transfers to your application.

This chapter covers what a framework is and how to use frameworks with your program. It then goes on to take a high-level, descriptive look at some of the frameworks you are likely to encounter while writing iOS or Mac OS X programs. The next chapter delves into the Foundation framework in more detail. The Foundation framework defines `NSObject`, the root class for Objective-C objects, classes for strings, arrays, sets, dictionaries, and number objects, as well as objects that wrap interactions with the OS.

What Is a Framework?

A framework is a type of *bundle*—a directory hierarchy with a specified layout that groups shared dynamic libraries, header files, and resources (images, sounds, nib files) in a single place. The shared dynamic libraries that you need for iOS and Mac OS X development are wrapped as frameworks. The name of a framework bundle always has the form *frameworkName.framework*.

A framework can wrap a dynamic library written in any language, but all the frameworks that you are most likely to encounter have either Objective-C or plain C interfaces.

> **Note**
>
> Frameworks are very common in iOS and Mac OS X programming, but you can also link Objective-C code to any regular static or dynamic libraries that your program requires.

Using a Framework

To use an Objective-C or C framework, you have to import the header files for any framework-defined classes or functions that you are going to use in your code. Most frameworks have a group header that imports all the individual header files for the framework. Some frameworks are *umbrella frameworks*. Umbrella frameworks are frameworks that contain two or more other frameworks.

The following line imports all the relevant header files for the classes in the Foundation framework:

```
#import <Foundation/Foundation.h>
```

A group import doesn't cause program bloat; it just makes all the classes in the framework available. Importing the proper header files keeps the compiler happy. You also have to keep the linker happy by telling it to add the framework to its list of places to look for bits of executable code. Xcode automatically adds the basic required frameworks (based on the project type) to your project when you create it. If you are compiling your program from the command line, using the Clang (LLVM) compiler, you have to pass Clang the names of any frameworks you are using. You do this with a –framework flag followed by the name of the framework minus the *.framework* extension, for example:

```
clang myProgram.m -framework Foundation
```

If you are using multiple frameworks, you have to list them all on the **clang** command line, each with its own **-framework** flag:

```
clang myProgram.m -framework Cocoa -framework CoreFoundation
```

Cocoa and Cocoa Touch

Cocoa is the name Apple uses to refer to Mac OS X programs written with the Objective-C technology that they acquired with the purchase of NeXTSTEP. Similarly, iOS programs are called Cocoa Touch programs. iOS and OS X have similar versions of the basic Foundation framework but have different UI frameworks. The OS X UI framework is called AppKit and the iOS UI framework is called UIKit.

OS X

OS X has an umbrella framework, called the Cocoa framework, that consists of the three primary frameworks used in building Cocoa applications:

- *Foundation framework:* Foundation contains the basic objects needed for almost any application. The next chapter covers some of the important Foundation classes.

- *AppKit framework:* AppKit is short for Application Kit. AppKit contains the classes that are needed to build GUI applications on OS X.

- *Core Data:* Core Data is the most recent addition (with Mac OS X 10.4). It is a framework for managing collections of persistent (that is, saved out to disk between invocations of the program) objects.

You can get the headers for all three of these frameworks by importing:

```
#import <Cocoa/Cocoa.h>
```

If you are writing a command line program that doesn't use Core Data or AppKit, you can just use the Foundation group header:

```
#import <Foundation/Foundation.h>
```

The relationship between the Objective-C language and the Cocoa frameworks is similar to the relationship between the Java language and the Java class libraries: The language itself is compact and relatively easy to learn, but the real work is learning the details of the libraries. It would be nice if just learning Objective-C made you a competent Cocoa programmer, but unfortunately it's only a first step. After you've mastered the material in this book, you need to spend some quality time with the documentation for the Cocoa frameworks or a book like *Cocoa Programming for Mac OS X*, by Aaron Hillegass,[1] or *Cocoa Programming Developer's Handbook*, by David Chisnall, [2] before you create your killer app.

1. Aaron Hillegass, *Cocoa Programming for Mac OS X, Third Edition* (Boston: Addison-Wesley, 2008).
2. David Chisnall, *Cocoa Programming Developer's Handbook* (Boston: Addison-Wesley, 2009).

iOS

iOS provides the Foundation and Core Data (on iOS 3 and later) frameworks. However, on iOS the UIKit framework replaces the AppKit and supplies the classes that make up an iPhone or iPad app's user interface.

Together, the UIKit, Foundation, and Core Data frameworks are called *Cocoa Touch*.

Note

Despite the name similarity with Cocoa, there is no actual Cocoa Touch umbrella framework and no *CocoaTouch.h* header file.

Note

The iOS and OS X versions of the Foundation framework are almost, but not quite, identical. When you look at the documentation for Foundation, make sure you are looking at the version that applies to the system you are working on. The documentation will say either *iOS Developer Library* or *Mac OS X Developer Library* at the top left of the page.

AppKit

The AppKit is a large framework of almost 200 interrelated classes used for building Mac OS X GUI apps. A detailed treatment of the AppKit is beyond the scope of this book, but this section gives a brief description of some of the AppKit's prominent classes.

In its simplest form, a GUI application displays some information (text, images) in one or more areas of the screen. The user then interacts with the application by using a mouse, keyboard, or some other input device. The operating system takes these interactions, packages them up in a container called an *event*, and forwards the event to the application. The application then uses the events to modify its internal state and display the changes back to the screen.

These are some of the AppKit classes you'll need to learn about to write a GUI app:

- **NSApplication** is the central class for a Cocoa GUI application—every application must contain a single instance of it. Rather than subclassing **NSApplication**, any required customization is handled by creating a separate object and assigning it as **NSApplication**'s delegate.

- **NSWindow** represents a window on the screen.

- **NSView** represents a region of a window. Most windows have a hierarchy of **NSView**s.

- **NSEvent** carries the information about the user's interactions with an application: the type of event, the location on the screen where the event occurred, a timestamp recording when the event occurred, and whether a modifier key was depressed during the event.

- Controls such as **NSButton**, **NSSlider**, **NSMenu**, **NSSegmentedControl**, and **NSColorWell** provide the means for the user to interact with the application.

- **NSDocument** is the principal class used for building applications where the user can open and work on more than one set of data at a time.

The AppKit also provides Objective-C classes that wrap much of the functionality of the low-level C language Core Graphics library. You can use the AppKit classes to draw vector graphics (**NSBezierPath**) or bitmapped images (**NSImage**).

Many of the AppKit classes are quite complex and have extensive catalogs of methods. For example, much of the editing functionality of the TextEdit program that comes with Mac OS X comes directly from the class **NSTextView** (a subclass of **NSView**). You can see the full source code for the TextEdit program in the examples provided with the Xcode tools: */Developer/Examples/TextEdit.*

UIKit

The UIKit supplies the classes that are used to build the GUI of an iOS application. The UIKit is similar in many ways to the AppKit. However, there are differences due to the nature of iOS devices: On an iOS device only a single application is visible at a time. The active application has only a single window that covers the entire screen. Instead of using a mouse, the user interacts with an iOS program by using one or more fingers to touch the screen. These are some of the basic UIKit classes:

- **UIApplication** is the central class for a Cocoa Touch application. As with a Cocoa application, any required customization is handled by creating a separate object and assigning it as the **UIApplication**'s delegate.
- **UIWindow** represents a window on the screen.
- **UIView** represents a region of a window. **UIView** has a subclass, **UIImageView**, which can display an image on the screen.
- A **UIViewController** manages a **UIView** hierarchy. iOS programs have at least one **UIViewController**, called the *root view controller.*
- The **UIEvent** and **UITouch** classes encapsulate information about the user's interactions with the device's touch screen.
- **UIImage** and **UIBezierPath** provide a means to draw bitmaps and vector graphics on the screen.
- User interface controls are provided by classes such as **UIButton**, **UISlider**, **UISegmentedControl**, and **UISwitch**.

For information on using UIKit and building iOS apps see *Learning iPad Programming: A Hands-on Guide to Building iPad Apps with iOS 5,* by Kirby Turner and Tom Harrington.[3]

3. Kirby Turner and Tom Harrington, *Learning iPad Programming: A Hands-on Guide to Building iPad Apps with iOS 5* (Boston: Addison-Wesley, 2011).

Core Foundation

Core Foundation is a low-level C language framework that (partially) parallels the Objective-C Foundation framework. It defines data types and provides services that are used by many of the other C language frameworks. Core Foundation is mentioned here because it is sometimes necessary to use Core Foundation types in Cocoa or Cocoa Touch programs. This is frequently necessary if your program uses one of the other low-level C frameworks, such as Core Graphics. (Core Graphics is described in the next section.)

Although it is written in plain C, Core Foundation is organized into objects. Some of the common Core Foundation types are **CFString**, **CFArray**, **CFMutableArray**, **CFDictionary**, **CFMutableDictionary**, **CFData**, and **CFNumber**.

> **Note**
>
> Although C isn't an object-oriented language, it can be used to implement a custom object system.

Core Foundation objects are accessed using an opaque pointer (see the upcoming sidebar *Opaque Pointers*). The pointer declarations for Core Foundation objects are hidden by typedefs that use the type name with **Ref** added to the end. The declaration **CFMutableArray*** is hidden by the typedef **CFMutableArrayRef**.

As an example of a Core Foundation object, the following line of code creates a Core Foundation mutable array:

```
CFMutableArrayRef cfMutableArray =
    CFArrayCreateMutable ( CFAllocatorRef allocator,
                           CFIndex capacity,
                           const CFArrayCallBacks *callBacks
                         );
```

The **allocator** argument specifies how the dynamic allocation for the object's memory is handled, **capacity** is the maximum number of entries in the array (a zero indicates no limit on the capacity), and **callBacks** is a pointer to a structure of callback functions. The callback functions are used to perform tasks like retaining and releasing objects when they are stored in or removed from the array.

Don't worry about these details right now; the point of the preceding code is just to show you a concrete example of a Core Foundation object.

Compare the Core Foundation mutable array with creating the equivalent Foundation object:

```
NSMutableArray *nsMutableArray =
  [[NSMutableArray alloc] initWithCapacity: capacity];
```

The main thing to notice is that the Core Foundation object is more complicated and harder to use than its Foundation equivalent. There may be times when you are forced to use a Core Foundation object, but, whenever you can, staying at the Objective-C level is an easier, less error-prone way to code.

Opaque Pointers

Core Foundation object references are *opaque pointers*. An opaque pointer is a pointer to a structure whose declaration is placed in a private header file that is not supplied to the user. Without the header file, structure members can be accessed only with a set of supplied functions. The contents of the structure cannot be accessed directly by dereferencing a pointer to the structure, nor can the object be interrogated in the debugger. The point of opaque pointers is information hiding. Opaque pointers let the owner of the code modify the (private) internal implementation of the object without changing its public interface. Core Foundation does provide a function, CFShow, that can be used in the debugger to display information about a Core Foundation object, but the use of opaque pointers can make debugging code that uses Core Foundation objects a frustrating experience.

Memory Management for Core Foundation Objects

Core Foundation objects have a reference-counted memory management system similar to Objective-C's reference counting:

- You own any Core Foundation object that you create by calling Core Foundation functions that have **Create** or **Copy** in the name.

- You *do not* own any Core Foundation object that you get from any other function (typically a Core Foundation function with **Get** somewhere in its name). If you want the object to remain valid past the current scope, you must take ownership of the object by calling the function **CFRetain** with the object as the function argument.

- When you are finished with a Core Foundation object that you own, you must relinquish ownership of that object by calling the function **CFRelease** with the object as the function argument.

- Objective-C's Automatic Reference Counting (ARC) system does not manage Core Foundation objects. (ARC is covered in Chapter 16.)

The Objective-C **release** and **retain** methods are like any other Objective-C methods; using **retain** or **release** with a **nil** receiver is a no-op. However, calling **CFRetain** or **CFRelease** with a **NULL** argument will cause a crash. If you use **CFRetain** or **CFRelease**, make sure that you check for a non-**NULL** argument first.

> **Note**
>
> Some of the other low-level C frameworks such as Core Graphics (described in the next section) have the same object and memory management system as Core Foundation. Some of these classes provide their own retain and release functions. For example, `CGColor`, the Core Graphics color class, provides `CGColorRetain()` and `CGColorRelease()`. These custom retain and release functions are all equivalent to `CFRetain()` and `CFRelease()`, except that they do not crash when called with a `NULL` argument.

Toll-Free Bridging

Some Foundation classes have a memory layout that is almost identical to the memory layout of the corresponding Core Foundation class. For these classes, a pointer to the Foundation object can be used as a reference to the corresponding Core Foundation object and vice versa. All you need is the appropriate cast. Apple calls this feature *toll-free bridging*.

Listing 8.1 shows an example of toll-free bridging using **NSString** and **CFString**.

Listing 8.1   *TollFreeBridge.m*

```
#import <Foundation/Foundation.h>
#import <CoreFoundation/CoreFoundation.h>

int main( void )
{
  @autoreleasepool
  {

  // Create an NSString

    NSString *nsString = @"Toll-Free";

  // Cast nsString to a CFString and get its length with a CF function

    CFStringRef cfString;
    cfString = (CFStringRef) nsString; // Cast it to a CFString
    int length = CFStringGetLength ( cfString );
    NSLog( @"CFString length is: %d", length );

  // Create a CFString

    CFStringRef cfString2 =
          CFStringCreateWithCString( NULL,
                                     "Bridge",
                                     kCFStringEncodingASCII );

  // Cast cfString to an NSString and log it
```

```
    NSString *nsString2;
    nsString2 = (NSString*) cfString2;
    NSLog( @"NS string is: %@", nsString2 );

  }
}
```

When the preceding program is run, the result is

```
CFString length is: 9
NS string is: Bridge
```

A complete list of toll-free bridged classes is shown in Appendix B, "Toll-Free Bridged Classes."

> **Note**
>
> All Core-level objects are toll-free bridged at the level of NSObject. This means that any Core-level object can be cast to a variable of type id and the result will respond correctly to retain, release, and autorelease messages. Going the other way, any Objective-C object can be cast to the generic core type CFType. The result will work correctly with the Core Foundation functions CFRetain() and CFRelease().
>
> This is convenient because it allows you to store Core-level objects in Objective-C Foundation collection classes. When you add an object to a Foundation collection class such as NSArray, the object receives a retain message. When the object is removed from the collection, it receives a release message. The Foundation collection classes are covered in the next chapter.

Core Graphics

Core Graphics is the low-level API for Quartz 2D graphics. Like Core Foundation, it is object-oriented but it is written directly in C. Quartz implements a device-independent 2-D imaging model that is almost exactly the same as the PDF (formerly PostScript) imaging model. *Device-independent* here means that all positions and dimensions in the framework refer to a defined floating-point coordinate system, not to device pixels or points. Eventually, most graphics are turned into pixels, but unless you are creating a bitmap for output, you rarely have to think directly about pixels.

Core Graphics provides facilities for setting colors, transparency, and blends; creating paths (lines and Bezier curves); stoking and filling paths; creating and drawing images and PDFs; drawing text; and clipping. It also manages color spaces and the current drawing coordinate system.

Much of the functionality of Core Graphics has been wrapped in Objective-C objects and is available in the AppKit framework. A smaller subset of Core Graphics has been wrapped in Objective-C in the UIKit for iOS. But not everything is wrapped. If you are doing more advanced drawing, you may need to dip into Core

Graphics directly. Fortunately, you can alternate between AppKit- or UIKit-level object messages and Core Graphics function calls without a problem. Do as much as you can at the AppKit or UIKit level and then go to Core Graphics for the rest.

> **Note**
>
> Core Graphics is covered in detail in David Gelphman and Bunny Laden, *Programming with Quartz.*[4]

Core Animation

Adding animation to your app is your chance to "out-Disney" Disney. Some animation has always been a part of Mac OS X. The "puff of smoke" effect when you pull an app out of the dock and the "genie" effect when you minimize something to the dock have been around for years. But beginning with OS X 10.5 and iOS, many previously stationary things are beginning to get up and dance. This movement is courtesy of Core Animation, an Objective-C framework, which takes much of the effort out of doing animations. At the simplest level, you just specify what is going to be animated, where it is going to go (or what the final value will be if you're animating an attribute), and tell Core Animation to go. Core Animation handles the rest.

> **Note**
>
> For an in-depth treatment of Core Animation, see Marcus Zarra and Matt Long, *Core Animation.*[5]

Other Apple-Supplied Frameworks

Apple provides many other frameworks, both high- and low-level. A few of the ones you might need to use are

- *WebKit:* An Objective-C framework for adding Web-based content and browser features to an application
- *ImageIO:* A C language framework for reading and writing more different image file formats than you knew existed
- *Core Image:* An Objective-C framework for doing fast image processing using the GPU
- *Core Audio:* A C language framework for audio processing

4. David Gelphman and Bunny Laden, *Programming with Quartz: 2D and PDF Graphics in Mac OS X* (San Francisco: Morgan Kaufmann, 2006).

5. Marcus Zarra and Matt Long, *Core Animation: Simplified Animation Techniques for Mac and iPhone Development* (Boston: Addison-Wesley, 2009).

Although these frameworks are not written by Apple, Mac OS X and iOS also provide

- *OpenGL (Mac OS X) and OpenGL-ES (iOS):* C language frameworks for doing fast, hardware-accelerated 3-D graphics
- *OpenAL:* A C language framework for the open-source OpenAL audio library
- *OpenCL (Mac OS X):* A C language framework for high-performance computing using the power of GPUs and multicore CPUs

> **Note**
>
> You can see more of the frameworks available on Mac OS X by examining the contents of the directory */System/Library/Frameworks*.

Third-Party Frameworks

Some companies and individual developers offer Objective-C or C frameworks for doing specialized tasks. These frameworks may be either commercially licensed or one of the various degrees of "free." You can use these frameworks the same way that you use any of the Apple-supplied frameworks—you link against a third-party framework by adding it to the *Frameworks* folder in the project window of your Xcode project.

There's only one complication: If you link an application against a framework, a copy of that framework must be available at run time on any system on which that application runs. This isn't a problem with the Apple-supplied frameworks. Those frameworks are guaranteed to be installed on any functional OS X or iOS system. But that isn't the case for third-party frameworks.

If the OS can't find a copy of a framework that is used by an application, the application will crash at startup:

```
Dyld Error Message:
  Library not loaded:
@executable_path/../Frameworks/VitalStuff.framework/Versions/A/VitalStuff
  Referenced from: /Applications/KillerApp.app/Contents/MacOS/KillerApp
  Reason: image not found
```

To prevent a crash, you must add a copy phase to the application's Xcode project to copy any third-party frameworks into the *Frameworks* directory of the application's bundle.

> **Note**
>
> If you are on OS X and creating multiple applications that use the same framework, your applications' install procedure should copy the framework to */Library/Frameworks* so that it can be shared.

It is possible to create your own frameworks for OS X. You might do this if you develop a set of classes that you are going to use in more than one application. You would design, code, and test the classes and then build them into a framework using Xcode. After you have built your framework, you can use it like any other third-party framework—add the new framework to your application's Xcode project and make sure that the framework is copied to the application's bundle. For more information on frameworks and creating your own frameworks see https://developer.apple.com/library/mac/#documentation/macosx/Conceptual/BPFrameworks/Frameworks.htm.

> **Note**
>
> You cannot create your own frameworks or dynamic link libraries on iOS. You can, however, create your own static link libraries and link your app against them.

Under the Hood

Technically, frameworks are *versioned bundles*. The directory structure of a versioned bundle is set up so that different versions of the content can coexist. This allows the maintainer of the framework to add to the framework but still have the original version of the framework available for use by older code. Here is the structure of a typical framework directory:

```
SomeFramework.framework/
  SomeFramework@ -> Versions/Current/SomeFramework
    Headers@ -> Versions/Current/Headers
    Resources@-> Versions/Current/Resources
    Versions/
        A/
            SomeFramework*
            Headers/
            Resources/
        Current@ -> A
```

The framework in the preceding example is still at the initial (**A**) version. The top-level entries **SomeFramework**, **Headers**, and **Resources** are symbolic links that eventually lead to the current versions of the directories.

> **Note**
>
> In the directory shown, symbolic links are indicated by an @ character at the end of the directory name. The file containing the executable code is indicated with a trailing asterisk (*):
>
> SomeFramework*
>
> You can see the @ and * characters as you explore a framework directory by using the —F option of ls from a command line:
>
> % ls —F

Most of the time you don't have to poke around in a framework directory, but it is often useful to look at a framework's header files. This is particularly true if the documentation accompanying the framework isn't clear (or if the author of a third-party framework has rudely neglected to supply you with documentation).

Some frameworks are *umbrella frameworks*—frameworks that contain other frameworks. The Cocoa framework, described earlier in this chapter, is an example of an umbrella framework. The added level of indirection provided by an umbrella framework allows its maintainer some freedom to reorganize the framework's child frameworks without disturbing the framework's clients.

The Apple-supplied frameworks are found in the */System/Library/Frameworks* directory. Frameworks installed by applications for use by all the users on a system are found in the */Library/Frameworks* directory. Applications can also include private frameworks for their own use. These frameworks are found in the *Frameworks* directory inside the application's bundle: *MyApp.app/Contents/Frameworks*.

Mac OS X and iOS also have a number of private frameworks for internal use. If you discover one of these frameworks, there is nothing to prevent you from using it. However, using private frameworks is a bad idea. They may change or disappear in a future OS release. In addition, using a private framework will result in your app being rejected from the App Store or the Mac App Store.

Summary

Frameworks are bundles (directory hierarchies) that provide convenient access to the executable code and resources of dynamic libraries. All Objective-C programs use the Foundation framework, which defines basic classes needed for any non-trivial program. Mac OS X GUI programs use classes from the AppKit framework to construct their UI; iOS programs use classes from the UIKit framework. Apple supplies many other frameworks for specialized tasks such as audio and graphics. Some of these are C language frameworks that use an object system and memory management functions defined in the Core Foundation framework.

Common Foundation Classes

Objective-C is a very compact language. Much of Objective-C's power resides in its associated class libraries, called *frameworks*. The previous chapter covered the general topic of frameworks. In this chapter we'll look at several of the classes in the Foundation framework.

The Foundation framework provides classes for basic entities such as strings, arrays, dictionaries, and number objects. Although it is possible to write an Objective-C program that doesn't use classes from the Foundation framework, using the Foundation classes rather than creating your own equivalent classes results in shorter development times and fewer bugs.

This chapter begins with some general information about Foundation classes that have both immutable and mutable versions, and classes that are implemented as class clusters. It continues with overview treatments of some of the most widely used Foundation classes: `NSString`, `NSMutableString`, `NSArray`, `NSMutableArray`, `NSDictionary`, `NSMutableDictionary`, `NSSet`, `NSMutableSet`, `NSData`, `NSMutableData`, `NSNull`, `NSNumber`, and `NSURL`. It also covers the container class literals, number literals, and boxed expressions introduced in Xcode 4.4. The chapter concludes with a look at some non-object structures that the Foundation defines: `NSRange`, `NSPoint`, `NSSize`, and `NSRect`.

> **Note**
>
> You can find a complete list of Foundation classes and their documentation at https://developer.apple.com/library/mac/#documentation/Cocoa/Reference/ Foundation/ObjC_classic/_index.html.

Immutable and Mutable Classes

The Foundation classes that are containers (for Objective-C objects, for characters, or for bytes) come in two flavors: immutable and mutable. The basic classes are immutable. After you create an instance of an immutable class, you cannot change its contents. For example, if you create an instance of `NSArray` (which is immutable) and you want to add an object to the array, you must create a new array that contains the additional object and release the original array.

Creating separate mutable and immutable classes for containers allows for some behind-the-scenes efficiency in how the immutable classes are implemented. When you create an immutable array, the number of objects it holds is fixed at creation time. The actual storage for the objects can be a simple fixed-size block of memory. A mutable array must use a more complicated storage system that allows its contents to grow or shrink. The pairs of immutable and mutable classes considered in this chapter are `NSString` and `NSMutableString`, `NSArray` and `NSMutableArray`, `NSDictionary` and `NSMutableDictionary`, `NSSet` and `NSMutableSet`, and `NSData` and `NSMutableData`.

Class Clusters

The classes `NSString`, `NSArray`, `NSDictionary`, `NSSet`, `NSNumber`, and `NSData` are implemented as *class clusters*. Class clusters are a means of hiding complexity behind a simple interface. In a class cluster, the publicly visible class is an abstract class. The actual implementation of the class is provided by a group of private "concrete" subclasses that hide behind the publicly visible class. The private subclasses all implement the interface defined by the publicly visible class, but their internal implementation may vary to optimize storage or performance. When you ask for an instance of the public class, you receive an instance of one of the cluster's private subclasses. The choice is determined by the `init` method you use.

> **Note**
>
> For a complete discussion of class clusters, see *Cocoa Design Patterns*, by Erik M. Buck and Donald A. Yacktman.[1]

Implementing a class as a class cluster has several consequences:

- The `init` method of a class that is implemented as a cluster substitutes a different object of the appropriate concrete subclass for the object returned by `alloc`. The cluster's `alloc` method returns a temporary object that belongs to a special placeholder class. The `init` method releases the temporary object and returns an instance of one of the cluster's concrete subclasses. This sequence has an important implication: You should never retain a reference to the object returned by `alloc`. Code your `alloc` and `init` as a single nested statement:

  ```
  SomeClassCluster *classCluster = [[SomeClassCluster alloc] init];
  ```

  As noted in Chapter 6, "Classes and Objects," a nested `alloc ... init` is the standard idiom for object creation. If you get in the habit of using the standard idiom, you don't have to think about this issue.

---

1. Erik M. Buck and Donald A. Yacktman, *Cocoa Design Patterns* (Boston: Addison-Wesley, 2010).

- The NSObject introspection method isMemberOfClass: should not be used on instances of a class that is implemented as a cluster:

```
NSString *string = [NSString stringWithFormat: @"%d", 137];
BOOL test = [string isMemberOfClass: [NSString class]];
```

  After executing the preceding lines of code, test is NO, because string is an instance of NSCFString, a private subclass of NSString, and not an instance of NSString.

- The introspection method isKindOfClass: is also problematic when used with instances of a class that is implemented as a cluster. (Recall that isKindOfClass: returns YES if the receiver is a member of the class used as an argument or any subclass of the class used as an argument.)

```
NSString *string = [NSString stringWithFormat: @"%d", 137];
BOOL test =
    [string isMemberOfClass: [NSMutableString class]];
```

  Surprisingly, in this case test is YES. The inheritance chain for NSCFString is NSObject-> NSString-> NSMutableString-> NSCFString.

  If you use isKindOfClass: to decide if a pointer you receive is a mutable array, you might wind up causing a crash by attempting to modify an immutable string.

- Subclassing a class that is implemented as a class cluster is a more complicated procedure than subclassing a simple class. It is an advanced technique that is beyond the scope of this book.

Is This Class a Class Cluster?

How do you know that a given class is implemented as a class cluster? The only way to tell is to read the documentation for the class. Perhaps there should be a class method, inherited from NSObject, that you could use to test if a class is implemented as a class cluster:

```
+(BOOL)[SomeClass isClassCluster]
```

However, there isn't such a method at present.

NSString

Strings in plain C are just an array of bytes representing characters, followed by a NULL (zero) byte. The NULL byte is an on-the-cheap way of determining where the string ends. A C string has no other structure.

C strings work well enough for simple tasks, but the lack of any real structure makes them prone to all sorts of problems and mischief—buffer overflows, unexpected zero bytes in what is supposed to be text, forgetting to leave room for the NULL byte—and they are just generally painful to use for any kind of string processing.

Foundation bypasses C strings (and their associated troubles) by creating a string class, NSString. There are two types of NSString: A literal NSString is a constant object created by the compiler, and an ordinary NSString object is a dynamically allocated object, like other Objective-C objects.

You create a literal NSString by placing your text between double quote marks and preceding it with an @:

```
NSString *greeting = @"Hello";
```

The preceding line declares greeting to be a pointer to an NSString and initializes it with the address of a constant NSString with the text "Hello."

Aside from literal strings, you can create NSString objects by the usual alloc ... init sequence, or by using one of NSString's many convenience constructors. The following example uses a convenience constructor to create an NSString from characters stored in a file:

```
NSString *textOfFile =
    [NSString stringWithContentsOfFile: @"/Users/you/textfile.txt"
            encoding: NSUTF8StringEncoding
          error: NULL]; // Ignore errors for now
```

Notice that the file path argument is itself an NSString.

> **Note**
>
> Character encodings are a complicated subject and off-topic for this book. The examples use plain ASCII characters. ASCII characters are legal one-byte UTF-8 (Unicode) characters.

NSString is a large class (over 100 methods) with methods for creating strings from files, URLs, and other strings. It has methods for comparing strings, getting substrings, writing strings to a file or URL, formatting strings, and a number of specialized methods for working with strings that are filesystem paths. NSString objects are used throughout Objective-C. In addition to the obvious use for manipulating text and filesystem paths, NSString objects are heavily used as keys with the Foundation dictionary classes.

NSString Examples

This section shows a few examples of some of the things you can do with NSString objects. Each code snippet is followed by the results of executing the code it contains.

NSLog

```
NSLog( @"The sky is %@.", @"blue" );
```

The preceding line of code results in this output:

```
The sky is blue.
```

Notice:

- NSLog's format string is itself an **NSString**.

- NSLog sends the argument corresponding to the **%@** specifier a **description** message. The text of the **NSString** returned by the **description** method replaces the **%@** in the output. **NSString**'s implementation of **description** just returns **self**.

Finding the Length of an NSString

```
NSString *string = @"A string to measure";
NSUInteger stringLength = [string length];
NSLog("The length is: %lu.", stringLength);
```

results in

```
The length is: 19.
```

Obtaining an Uppercase NSString

```
NSString *string1 = @"Make me taller.";
NSString *string2 = [string1 uppercaseString];
NSLog(@"Uppercased string: %@", string2);
```

results in

```
Uppercased string: MAKE ME TALLER.
```

There is a corresponding **lowercaseString** method. Notice that the **uppercaseString** method doesn't convert **string1** to an uppercase string. It returns a new (autoreleased) string, **string2**, which is the uppercase version of **string1**. **string1** remains unchanged.

> **Note**
>
> You will sometimes see code that contains lines like the following:
>
> ```
> string1 = [string1 uppercaseString];
> ```
>
> This does not mean that the original **NSString** has been converted to uppercase. **NSString** objects are immutable. The meaning of the preceding line of code is: The variable **string1**, which is typed as "pointer to **NSString**," is assigned a new value, the address of the string returned by the **uppercaseString** method. If the original value of **string1** was a string literal or an autoreleased string, there is no problem. However, if the original **string1** is not a literal, not autoreleased, and there is no other reference to it, the original **string1** is leaked.

Appending an NSString to Another NSString

```
NSString *string1 = @"The First Part ";
NSString *string2 = @"The Second Part";
NSString *result = [string1 stringByAppendingString: string2];
NSLog(@"Resulting string: %@", result);
```

results in

```
Resulting string: The First Part The Second Part
```

As in the previous example, string1 is not modified. stringByAppendingString returns a new (autoreleased) string.

Breaking a Sentence into Individual Words

```
NSString *string1 = @"This sentence is falling apart";
NSArray *words =
  [string1 componentsSeparatedByCharactersInSet:
    [NSCharacterSet whitespaceCharacterSet]];
NSLog(@"Word array: %@", words);
```

results in

```
Word array: (
    This,
    sentence,
    is,
    falling,
    apart
)
```

The method componentsSeparatedByCharactersInSet returns an NSArray that contains each word in the sentence as a separate NSString. componentsSeparatedByCharactersInSet uses the characters specified in its argument as the separators that delimit individual words. NSCharacterSet is a Foundation class that represents sets of characters. The whitespaceCharacterSet is a convenience constructor that returns a set of characters that consists of the blank and the tab characters.

C String to NSString and Back

If your program interfaces with a pure C library or the Unix level of the operating system, you may need to convert back and forth between C strings and NSString objects. The following code makes an NSString from a C string:

```
char *cString = "Hello Universe";
NSString *nsString = [NSString stringWithUTF8String: cString];
```

This code does the reverse:

```
NSString *nsString = @"Anybody Home?";
char *cString = [nsString UTF8String];
```

UTF8String returns an array of UTF-8 Unicode characters. UTF-8 is a superset of ASCII. The values 0–127 represent the same characters in both UTF-8 and ASCII. The older **NSString** methods **stringWithCString:** and **cString** are now deprecated.

> **Note**
>
> The system owns the memory for the characters returned by the **UTF8String** method. The system frees that memory when the current autorelease pool is emptied. If you need the C string to remain valid beyond the current function scope, you should make your own copy of the bytes.

NSMutableString

NSString objects are immutable. After you create an **NSString**, you cannot change it. If you want to change the text in an **NSString**, you must use **NSString**'s mutable subclass **NSMutableString**. The following code:

```
NSMutableString *mutableString =
  [NSMutableString stringWithString: @"Shun the Bandersnatch."];

[mutableString insertString: @"frumious " atIndex: 9];

NSLog( @"%@", mutableString );
```

results in

```
Shun the frumious Bandersnatch.
```

The index used to specify a character position in an **NSString** or **NSMutableString** starts at zero, like all C indices.

Literal Strings

Literal **NSString** instances are static objects created by the compiler in read-only memory. You can use a literal string anyplace you would use a pointer to an **NSString** instance.

```
NSString *string = [@"speak louder!" uppercaseString];
NSLog( @"Uppercased string: %@", string );
```

results in

```
Uppercased string: SPEAK LOUDER!
```

Literal strings persist for the lifetime of the program. They are not affected by the Objective-C memory management system. However, because you usually do not know whether a variable typed as **NSString*** is pointing to a literal **NSString** or an allocated **NSString**, you should always follow the memory management rules. If, by following the rules, you end up sending a **retain** or **release** message to a literal string, it is harmless. Such a message has no effect.

Collection Classes

NSArray, **NSDictionary**, **NSSet**, and their mutable subclasses are collection classes. They provide containers for handling groups of objects. In other languages you may be familiar with (particularly scripting languages), containers are part of the language. In Objective-C, though, containers are provided by the Foundation framework. **NSDictionary** and **NSArray** are widely used throughout Foundation, AppKit, and UIKit to pass in multiple objects to a method or to get multiple objects back as a return value.

NSArray

Regular C arrays are just regions of contiguous bytes large enough to hold the requested number of items of the specified type; for example:

```
unsigned char name[25];
```

just sets aside 25 bytes beginning at the address of **name[0]**. There is no runtime information on the length of the array and no bounds checking. Nothing prevents you from doing the following:

```
unsigned char name[25];
name[100] = 200;
```

The assignment in the preceding code will overwrite whatever is stored at the memory location **&name+100**, possibly resulting in corrupted data or a crash. This sort of mistake, whether accidental or intentional (a buffer overrun attack), is one of the major headaches in C programming.

The **NSArray** class (and its mutable subclass, **NSMutableArray**) provides arrays of objects that eliminate these problems. **NSArray** has these characteristics:

- **NSArray** objects hold only Objective-C objects. You cannot put a basic C type in an **NSArray**.
- **NSArray** objects are bounds checked. Any attempt to access an array location with an index that is less than zero or beyond the end of the array results in a runtime error.
- **NSArray** objects are *dense*. The valid indices run in sequence from zero to the length of the array minus one. There are no slots that do not contain an object.
- **NSArray** objects retain their contents. Objects receive a **retain** message when they are placed in an array and a **release** message when they are removed from an array.

Length of an NSArray

The **count** method returns the number of items in an **NSArray**:

```
NSArray *fruitBasket =
 [NSArray arrayWithObjects:
    @"Apple", @"Orange", @"Banana", nil];

NSUInteger numFruits = [fruitBasket count];
NSLog (@"Number of fruits in the basket: %lu", numFruits);
```

arrayWithObjects is a convenience constructor that returns an array with the specified objects. Its argument is a comma-separated list of the objects to put in the array. The list is terminated by a **nil**. When the preceding code is run, the result is

```
Number of fruits in the basket: 3
```

NSArray Bounds Checking

Any attempt to reference an array location with a negative index or an index beyond the end of the array results in a runtime error. The following code:

```
NSArray *fruitBasket =
 [NSArray arrayWithObjects:
    @"Apple", @"Orange", @"Banana", nil];

id myFruit = [fruitBasket objectAtIndex: 5];
```

causes the following error:

```
*** Terminating app due to uncaught exception 'NSRangeException',
reason: '*** -[NSCFArray objectAtIndex:]: index (5) beyond bounds (3)
```

> **Note**
>
> The **NSCFArray** referred to in the error message is a private subclass of **NSArray**. Recall that **NSArray** is a class cluster. When you ask for an instance of a class cluster, you receive an instance of a private subclass of the cluster's public class.

Adding an Object to an NSMutableArray

Adding an object to an **NSMutableArray** lengthens the array by one. You can only insert objects in the existing range of indices or add them at the end of the array. You can't add an object at an arbitrary index.

If you try the following:

```
NSMutableArray *mutableFruitBasket =
 [NSMutableArray arrayWithObjects:
    @"Apple", @"Orange", @"Banana", nil];

[mutableFruitBasket insertObject: @"Kiwi" atIndex: 6];
```

you will get an out-of-bounds error just as in the previous example.

If you insert an object in the middle of an array, all the objects at the insertion index and above move over by one:

```
NSMutableArray *mutableFruitBasket =
 [NSMutableArray arrayWithObjects:
    @"Apple", @"Orange", @"Banana", nil];

NSLog( @"Fruit basket before adding kiwi: %@", mutableFruitBasket );

[mutableFruitBasket insertObject: @"Kiwi" atIndex: 1];

NSLog( @"Fruit basket after adding kiwi: %@", mutableFruitBasket );
```

The result of the previous code is

```
Fruit basket before adding kiwi: (
    Apple,
    Orange,
    Banana
)
Fruit basket after adding kiwi: (
    Apple,
    Kiwi,
    Orange,
    Banana
)
```

Similarly, if you remove an object from a mutable array, all the objects at indices higher than the index of the removed object move over by one to fill in the hole. The length of the array decreases by one.

Memory Management for Objects in an NSArray

Objects are sent a **retain** message when they are added to an **NSArray**, and they are sent a **release** message when they are removed or when the array is deallocated. This means you have to be careful when you intend to use an object that you have removed from an **NSMutableArray**. If the array is the only thing retaining the object, the object's retain count will drop to zero when it is removed from the array. The object will be deallocated before you ever have a chance to use it:

```
// Dangerous!

id objectOfInterest = [myMutableArray objectAtIndex: 0];

[myMutableArray removeObject: objectOfInterest];

// objectOfInterest may have just been deallocated

[objectOfInterest someMessage];
```

The final line of code in the preceding example might message a deallocated object and cause a crash.

If you are going to use an object that you are removing from an array, you should retain it before removing it:

```
// Better!

id objectOfInterest = [[myMutableArray objectAtIndex: 0] retain];

[myMutableArray removeObject: objectOfInterest];

[objectOfInterest someMessage];
```

If you do retain the object, you must remember to balance the **retain** with a **release** or an **autorelease** when you are finished with it.

NSDictionary

NSDictionary and **NSMutableDictionary** provide a way to handle collections of key-value pairs. (Dictionaries are sometimes referred to as *associative arrays* in other languages.) The values are the objects that you are trying to group or keep track of, and the keys are objects you use as handles or names to keep track of them. The key-value pair is referred to as an *entry*.

When you add an entry to a dictionary, the dictionary makes a *copy* of the key. This means that if you use an object as a key, the object's class must implement **copyWithZone:** (see Chapter 6, "Classes and Objects"). Other than this restriction, keys can be any type of object, but in practice keys are usually **NSString** objects.

The following example shows creating a mutable dictionary, adding some entries to it, and using a key to retrieve a stored object:

```
NSMutableDictionary *favoriteFruits =
    [NSMutableDictionary dictionaryWithCapacity: 3];

// Add some entries
[favoriteFruits setObject: @"Orange" forKey: @"FavoriteCitrusFruit"];
[favoriteFruits setObject: @"Apple"  forKey: @"FavoritePieFruit"];
[favoriteFruits setObject: @"Blueberry"  forKey: @"FavoriteBerry"];

NSLog(@"Favorite fruits are: %@", favoriteFruits);

// Replace an entry
[favoriteFruits setObject: @"Raspberry"  forKey: @"FavoriteBerry"];

NSLog(@"Favorite fruits are: %@", favoriteFruits);


// Retrieve an entry by key
id pieFruit = [favoriteFruits objectForKey: @"FavoritePieFruit"];

NSLog(@"Favorite pie fruit is: %@", pieFruit);
```

The result of running the preceding example is

```
Favorite fruits are: {
    FavoriteBerry = Blueberry;
    FavoriteCitrusFruit = Orange;
    FavoritePieFruit = Apple;
}
Favorite fruits are: {
    FavoriteBerry = Raspberry;
    FavoriteCitrusFruit = Orange;
    FavoritePieFruit = Apple;
}
Favorite pie fruit is: Apple
```

The argument to the convenience constructor `dictionaryWithCapacity` just specifies the dictionary's initial capacity. An `NSMutableDictionary` will automatically grow to the required size as entries are added.

The method `setObject:forKey:` is used to add entries to a mutable dictionary. A key can be used only once in a given dictionary. If you add an entry using a key that is already used in the dictionary, the original value associated with the key is replaced with the new value. In the preceding example, reusing the key @"FavoriteBerry" causes the value @"Blueberry" to be replaced with @"Raspberry".

The method `objectForKey:` is used to retrieve the values from an `NSDictionary` or `NSMutableDictionary`. If there is no entry corresponding to the key supplied as the argument, the method returns `nil`.

Values are sent a `retain` message when they are added to a dictionary, but the corresponding key is copied, not sent a `retain` message. Both the key (the dictionary's copy, not the original) and the value are sent a `release` message when an entry is removed or the dictionary is released. As with `NSMutableArray`, if you want to use an object that you remove from an `NSMutableDictionary`, you should retain the object before you remove it. If you don't retain the object, removing the object from the dictionary may cause it to be deallocated.

NSSet

`NSSet` and `NSMutableSet` implement a collection of objects as a mathematical set. The main characteristics of the collection are:

- The members of a set are not ordered. There is no way to retrieve a particular object from a set. You can request an array containing all the objects in a set with the `allObjects` method or loop over the set using an `NSEnumerator` object (see Chapter 10, "Control Structures in Objective-C"). The order of the objects in the array returned by `allObjects` or obtained by successive calls to the set's enumerator is unspecified.
- A given object appears in the set only once, no matter how many times it is added to the set.

- As with **NSArray** and **NSDictionary**, objects are sent a **retain** message when they are added to a set and a **release** message when they are removed from a set or when the set is deallocated.

The following example shows the result of adding an object to an **NSMutableSet** that already contains that object:

```
NSMutableSet *favoriteAnimals =
    [NSMutableSet setWithCapacity: 3];

NSString *dog = @"Dog";
NSString *cat = @"Cat";


// Add some objects
[favoriteAnimals addObject: dog];
[favoriteAnimals addObject: cat];

NSLog(@"Favorite animals are: %@", favoriteAnimals);

// Add the same object again
[favoriteAnimals addObject: dog];
NSLog( @"Favorite animals are: %@", favoriteAnimals );
```

The result of running the preceding code is

```
Favorite animals are: {(
    Dog,
    Cat
)}
Favorite animals are: {(
    Dog,
    Cat
)}
```

Despite being added twice, **Dog** appears in the set only once.

NSNumber

One thing that may surprise newcomers to Objective-C (at least those who are not coming from Java) is that you can't put a C numeric type directly into an Objective-C array, dictionary, or set. In fact, you can't use a regular C type (numeric or structure) or a pointer to a regular C type anywhere that requires an object. Basic C types are not objects.

If you try to put a **float** in an **NSArray**:

```
float x = 99.9;
NSMutableArray *array = [NSMutableArray array];
[array addObject:  x];
```

the code doesn't compile:

```
error: incompatible type for argument 1 of 'addObject:'
```

If you try the same thing with an **int** instead of a **float**:

```
int n = 99;
NSMutableArray *array = [NSMutableArray array];
[array addObject:  n];
```

the code compiles with a warning about confusing **int**s and pointers:

```
warning: incompatible integer to pointer conversion sending
      'int' to parameter of type 'id'
```

But it crashes at run time:

```
Segmentation fault
```

To store a number in an Objective-C collection class or to use a number anywhere that requires an object, you must wrap the number in an instance of the **NSNumber** class:

```
float aFloat = 99.9;
NSNumber *floatAsAnObject = [NSNumber numberWithFloat: aFloat];

NSMutableArray *array = [NSMutableArray array];
[array addObject:  floatAsAnObject];

NSLog(@"Array contains: %@", array);
```

Running the preceding code produces this result:

```
Array contains: (
    "99.9"
)
```

When you need the actual number back, the **NSNumber** returns it to you:

```
float y;

y  = [floatAsAnObject floatValue];  // y now = 99.0
```

NSNumber can store and return all your favorite numeric types, as well as **BOOL**s and **chars**. Although **NSNumber** objects can be created with the usual **alloc ... init**, it is more common to use the class convenience constructors:

```
NSNumber *fiveAsNSNumber = [NSNumber numberWithInt: 5];
```

Instances of **NSNumber** are immutable. After an **NSNumber** object has been created, there is no way to change the numeric value that it represents. If you need to wrap a different numeric value, you must create a new **NSNumber**.

NSNull

Another surprising thing about Foundation is that it takes a bit of work to store something that represents "no object" in a collection object. You might want to put a "no object" in an array as a placeholder or enter "no object" with a key in a dictionary to indicate that there is nothing presently associated with that key. Although nil functions as a pointer to no object for most purposes, it is not an object instance. You can't put nil in an array, dictionary, or set.

The following example is even more insidious than trying to put an int or a float into an array:

```
id someObject = nil;

NSMutableArray *myArray = [NSMutableArray array];

[myArray addObject: someObject];
```

The example compiles without even a warning (because the compiler has no way of knowing that someObject will be nil when you try to insert it in the array), but it results in an error when executed:

```
*** Terminating app due to uncaught exception
    'NSInvalidArgumentException',
reason:
  '*** -[NSCFArray insertObject:atIndex:]: attempt to insert nil'
```

To work around this problem, Foundation supplies the NSNull class. NSNull has only the single class method, null, which returns the null object:

```
+(NSNull*) null
```

You can safely put the null object into a collection class:

```
NSMutableArray *array = [NSMutableArray array];
[array addObject: [NSNull null]];
NSLog(@"Array contains: %@", array);
```

The preceding code produces this output:

```
Array contains: (
    "<null>"
)
```

Other than its mere existence as an object, the NSNull object does absolutely nothing. It has no instance methods. (This may remind you of some people who you knew in high school.) Because NSNull doesn't do anything, there is no need to have more than one instance of it. It is a singleton; each call to [NSNull null] returns the same object. You can use it as many times in as many places as you want without incurring any program bloat.

NSData

It's not always possible to stay within the world of objects. There may be occasions when you have to process a block of bytes. Perhaps the bytes are the contents of a file in some format that you have to parse yourself, or raw image data. NSData provides a convenient way to wrap a block of bytes and treat it as an Objective-C object.

Using NSData raises some inevitable questions: "Who owns those bytes?" "Where do they come from?" NSData offers several options. You can ask NSData to create an instance by copying some existing bytes:

```
unsigned howManyBytes = 100;

char *someBytes = (char*) malloc( howManyBytes );

NSData *data = [NSData dataWithBytes: someBytes length: howManyBytes];
```

The preceding code copies someBytes into a buffer created and owned by the NSData object. The buffer is freed when the NSData object is deallocated. You are still responsible for eventually freeing the original someBytes. If you don't want to incur the cost of a copy, you can do the following:

```
unsigned howManyBytes = 100;

char *someBytes = (char*) malloc( howManyBytes );

NSData *myData =
    [NSData dataWithBytesNoCopy: someBytes
            length: howManyBytes
            freeWhenDone: YES];
```

The NSData object uses the existing bytes (allocated by malloc) as its buffer. If the freeWhenDone: argument is YES, the NSData object takes ownership of the bytes and frees them when it is deallocated. (If you did not malloc someBytes yourself, freeWhenDone: should be NO. Passing YES in that case will cause your program to crash.)

Accessing NSData's Bytes

You can get read-only access to an NSData object's byte buffer with the bytes method. The return value of the bytes method is const void*, so it should be assigned to a variable that is typed as pointer to constant:

```
NSData *data = ...
const char *constantBytes = [data bytes];
```

If you want to modify the data in an NSData object after creating it, or if you want to create the contents of a byte buffer from scratch, you must use NSData's mutable subclass **NSMutableData**. Both the number and contents of **NSMutableData**'s bytes are changeable.

You can get a pointer to an **NSMutableData** object's byte buffer with the method **mutableBytes**:

```
NSMutableData *mutableData = [NSMutableData dataWithLength: 100];
char *mutableBytes = [mutableData mutableBytes];
```

The first line of the preceding example creates an **NSMutableData** object with a 100-byte-long buffer. The second line obtains a pointer to the first byte in the buffer. Of course, **mutableBytes** is a bare C pointer. It would be a very bad idea to use it to write to an address beyond the address of the following byte:

```
mutableBytes[[myMutableData length] - 1]
```

File to NSData and Back

NSData has methods for moving your bytes in and out of files:

```
NSString *pathToFile = ...

NSData *myData = [NSData dataWithContentsOfFile: pathToFile];

NSString *pathToOutputFile = ...

[myData writeToFile: pathToOutputFile atomically: YES];
```

If the **atomically:** argument is **YES**, the bytes are written to a backup file. When the write is complete, the backup file is renamed to the name specified by the path argument.

NSURL

Apple is moving toward using URLs to specify file resources as well as network resources. Methods that refer to a file by path are being replaced with methods that refer to the file with a file URL:

```
file://pathToFile
```

Instead of using an **NSString** to hold a URL, Foundation wraps the URL string in an **NSURL** object. **NSURL** is used for both file URLs and network URLs:

```
NSURL *someFile = [NSURL fileURLWithPath: @"/Users/rclair/notes.txt"];
NSURL *website =
    [NSURL URLWithString:  @"http://www.chromaticbytes.com"];
NSLog(@"Host: %@ URL: %@",
    [someFile host], [someFile absoluteString]);
NSLog(@"Host: %@ URL: %@",
    [website host], [website absoluteString]);
```

The preceding code creates a file `NSURL` from a path and a network `NSURL` from an `NSString` version of a network URL. Then, for each `NSURL` object, it logs the host using the `host` method and the URL's string using the `absoluteString` method. When the code is executed, it produces the following output:

```
Host: localhost URL: file://localhost/Users/rclair/notes.txt
Host: www.chromaticbytes.com URL: http://www.chromaticbytes.com
```

Objective-C Literals and Object Subscripting

Starting with Xcode 4.4, Apple has introduced some new syntax for the container classes `NSArray` and `NSDictionary`, and for `NSNumber`. In analogy with literal `NSString`s, the new additions are called *literals*. There is also new syntax that allows you to use the C language subscripting operator with Objective-C objects.

These new additions are just "syntactic sugar"—convenient shorthand notation for existing functionality. They are easier to type, but they do not add any new capabilities to the language.

NSArray Literals

`NSArray` literals are constructed like this:

```
@[object0, object1, ...]
```

The following code creates an array with three objects:

```
NSArray *array = @[@"Ralph, @"Norton", @"Alice"];
```

The preceding line of code is *exactly* equivalent to

```
NSArray *array =
  [NSArray arrayWithObjects: @"Ralph", @"Norton", @"Alice", nil];
```

The important points about `NSArray` literals are:

- The literal is just a shorthand notation that creates a normal `NSArray` object. Once the array is created, it has no memory that it was created with a literal.
- Each item placed in the array must be an Objective-C object. An item cannot be `nil`.
- The literal creates an immutable array (an `NSArray`). There is at present no literal to produce an `NSMutableArray`. You can always create an `NSArray` with the literal and then create a mutable copy of the original array.
- Unlike the argument list for the `arrayWithObjects:` method, the list of objects between the square brackets in the literal is *not* terminated with a `nil`.
- Like a convenience constructor, the literal does not transfer ownership to the calling code. You do not own the array created by a literal.

NSDictionary **Literals**

There is also a literal for creating an NSDictionary. It has the form

```
@{key : object, anotherKey : anotherObject, ...}
```

The following example creates an NSDictionary with two objects:

```
NSDictionary *drawingColors =
    @{ @"fillColor" : [UIColor redColor],
       @"outlineColor" : [UIColor blackColor] };
```

The preceding code is *exactly* equivalent to

```
NSDictionary *drawingColors =
    [NSDictionary dictionaryWithObjectsAndKeys:
        [UIColor redColor], @"fillColor",
        [UIColor blackColor], @"outlineColor",
         nil];
```

The important points about dictionary literals are:

- Each key and each object used in the dictionary literal must be an Objective-C object. Neither the key nor the object may be nil. The keys are typically NSString objects.
- Any object used as a key must be capable of being copied. The object's class must implement the method copyWithZone:.
- The literal creates an immutable dictionary (an NSDictionary). There is at present no literal to produce an NSMutableDictionary. You can always create an NSDictionary with the literal and then create a mutable copy of the original dictionary.
- When you specify the contents of a dictionary literal, the order of the elements in a pair is the key followed by the object being stored under that key. Note that this is the reverse of the order required by the method dictionaryWithObjectsAndKeys:.
- The list of key : object pairs between the curly brackets in the literal is *not* terminated with a nil.
- Like a convenience constructor, the dictionary literal does not transfer ownership to the calling code. You do not own the dictionary created by a literal.

NSNumber **Literals**

NSNumber literals allow you to create an NSNumber object by placing an @ character before a numeric or Boolean constant:

```
NSNumber *tromboneCount = @76;
```

The preceding line of code is equivalent to

```
NSNumber *tromboneCount = [NSNumber numberWithInt: 76];
```

Like array and dictionary literals, **NSNumber** literals do not transfer ownership. You do not own the **NSNumber** created by a literal.

The compiler decides whether to create an integer or floating-point **NSNumber** based on the presence or absence of a decimal point in the numeric constant.

```
NSNumber *cmPerInch = @2.54;
```

is equivalent to

```
NSNumber *cmPerInch = [NSNumber numberWithDouble: 2.54];
```

You can control the size of the **NSNumber** created with a literal by using a suffix on the numeric constant:

```
NSNumber *anInt  = @76;
NSNumber *anUnsignedInt = @76U;
NSNumber *aLong  = @76L;
NSNumber *aLongLong = @76LL;

NSNumber *aFloat = @2.54F;
NSNumber *aDouble = @2.54;
```

You can also use **NSNumber** literals to create **NSNumber** objects with Boolean values:

```
NSNumber *boolYes = @YES;
NSNumber *boolNo = @NO;
```

are equivalent to

```
NSNumber *boolYes = [NSNumber numberWithBool: YES];
NSNumber *boolNo = [NSNumber numberWithBool: NO];
```

You may use a minus sign to indicate a negative number:

```
NSNumber *negativeThree = @-3;
```

However, you cannot use a literal to create an **NSNumber** from an expression, even if the expression involves only constants:

```
NSNumber *rootTwo = @sqrt(2);  // WRONG!
```

The preceding line of code will not compile. To get an **NSNumber** from an expression you must *box* it. Boxed expressions are covered in the next section.

Boxed Expressions

Boxing an expression evaluates the expression and places the result in an appropriate object. As of Xcode 4.4, numeric types (including **BOOL** and enum types) and C strings can be boxed, resulting in **NSNumber** and **NSString** objects, respectively.

The syntax for boxing an expression is

```
@( expression )
```

To box an expression you surround it with parentheses and precede it with an @.

```
NSNumber *total = @(12+4);
```

```
// same as NSNumber *total = [NSNumber numberWithInt: (12+4)];
```

Recall that in C single variables are valid expressions. The following code works correctly:

```
CGFloat a = 3.0;
CGFloat b = 4.0;
CGFloat c;
```

```
c = sqrt( a*a + b*b );
NSNumber *hypotenuse = @( c );
```

Single numeric constants are also expressions.

```
NSNumber *twentyFive = @(25);
```

produces the same result as

```
NSNumber *twentyFive = @25;
```

> **Note**
>
> Boxed expressions provide a convenient shorthand syntax for creating **NSNumber** objects. But there is no special syntax for unboxing **NSNumber** objects. You still have to use the **NSNumber** methods **intValue**, **floatValue**, **boolValue**, and so on to recover the original numeric value held in the **NSNumber** object.

Boxing Enum Constants

Enum constants are generally treated as integer constants. But you cannot use them directly as **NSNumber** literals. If you have occasion to store an enum constant in an **NSNumber**, you must box it:

```
enum {
    PetDog,
    PetCat
    PetGoldFish
} pets;
```

```
NSNumber *favoritePet = @( PetDog );
```

Boxing C Strings

The boxing syntax can also be used to create **NSString** objects from C strings:

```
NSString *str = @("Here comes the sun.");
```

If your C string is a literal C string as in the previous example, the exercise is rather pointless. You would just code the following directly:

```
NSString *str = @"Here comes the sun.";
```

However, the boxing syntax is quite useful if you are passed a pointer to a C string or use a function that returns a C string:

```
NSString *str = @( functionThatReturnsCString() );
```

The boxing syntax has a few restrictions when used with C strings: A C string used for boxing must be \0 terminated and UTF-8 or ASCII encoded. Attempting to box a **NULL** pointer causes an exception.

> **Note**
>
> Like a convenience constructor, a boxed expression does not transfer ownership to the calling code.

Objects and Subscripting

Xcode 4.4 also introduced subscripting for arrays and dictionaries. This allows you to set and retrieve objects from Objective-C array and dictionary classes using the conventional C subscript syntax.

Array Subscripting

For arrays, the subscript is an unsigned integer:

```
NSArray *names =
   @[@"Ralph", @"Norton", @"Alice", @"Trixie"];


id item = names[1]; // item is now @"Norton"
```

Accessing an array with subscripting is equivalent to using the **objectAtIndex:** method.

If you have an **NSMutableArray**, you may use subscripting to replace or add objects to the mutable array.

```
NSMutableArray *consultants = ...
consultants[0] = @"Joseph";
```

The preceding example is equivalent to

```
NSMutableArray *consultants = ...
[consultants insertObject: @"Joseph" atIndex: 0];
```

> **Note**
>
> Despite having the same syntax as a regular C array, subscript expressions for **NSArray** and **NSMutableArray** are just syntactic sugar for the array instance methods described earlier in this chapter. The index used in an array subscript expression is bounds checked. The legal values for the index are the same as the legal values for an index used with the equivalent method: If the length of an **NSArray** or **NSMutableArray** is count, you may use subscripts to access objects only at indices between zero and count-1. If you are adding or replacing an object in an **NSMutableArray**, you may use subscripts only at indices between zero and count.

Dictionary Subscripting

While you are probably familiar with the concept of subscripting an array, subscripting a dictionary may be a new idea. When subscripting is used with dictionaries, the subscript is a dictionary key rather than an array index.

```
NSDictionary *drawingColors =
    @{ @"fillColor" : [UIColor redColor],
       @"outlineColor" : [UIColor blackColor] };

UIColor *colorToUse = (UIColor*) drawingColors[@"fillColor"];
```

The last line of the preceding example is equivalent to

```
UIColor *colorToUse =
    (UIColor*) [drawingColors objectForKey: @"fillColor"];
```

If you have an **NSMutableDictionary**, you may use the subscript notation to insert a new key-value entry or replace an existing object in your dictionary:

```
NSMutableDictionary *otherColors = ...
otherColors[@"backgroundColor"] = [UIColor greenColor];
```

The last line of the preceding example is equivalent to

```
[otherColors setObject: [UIColor greenColor]
            forKey: @"backgroundColor"];
```

> **Note**
>
> While container literals and subscripting are often discussed together, they are independent extensions to Objective-C. You can use subscripting whether or not your container object was created with a literal.

Adding Subscripting to Your Own Classes

Subscripting works by translating the subscript expression into a message expression. The selector used for the message depends on whether you are reading or writing to the container and whether the subscript is an integer or an Objective-C object. When reading from an array,

```
id object = array[index];
```

is translated to

```
id object = [array objectAtIndexedSubscript: index];
```

When writing to a (mutable) array,

```
mutableArray[index] = newObject;
```

is translated to

```
[mutableArray setObject: newObject atIndexedSubscript: index];
```

Similarly for dictionaries, the lines

```
id object = dictionary[key];
mutableDictionary[key] = newObject;
```

are translated into the message expressions

```
id object = [dictionary objectForKeyedSubscript: key];
[mutableDictionary setObject: newObject forKeyedSubscript: key];
```

If you are creating a custom class where subscripting would make sense, you can add integer-indexed subscripting to your class by implementing the methods

```
-(id) objectAtIndexedSubscript:(NSUInteger) index;

// for mutable classes only

- (void) setObject:(id) object atIndexedSubscript:(NSUInteger) index;
```

Or you can add object-indexed subscripting by implementing

```
-(id) objectForKeyedSubscript:(id) key;

// for mutable classes only

- (void) setObject:(id) object forKeyedSubscript:(id)key;
```

Structures

Foundation, like Objective-C in general, is not a dogmatic purist about object-oriented programming. A few small entities are just plain structures rather than objects. The structures that you will probably meet are the following:

- **NSPoint** defines a point in two-dimensional space:

```
typedef struct _NSPoint
{
  CGFloat x;
  CGFloat y;
} NSPoint;
```

- **NSSize** defines the size of a rectangular area. You will occasionally see it mis-used as an offset.

```
typedef struct _NSSize
{
  CGFloat width;
  CGFloat height;
} NSSize;
```

- **NSRect** defines a 2-D rectangle by its origin (the corner with the minimum values of **x** and **y**) and its size:

```
typedef struct _NSRect
{
  NSPoint origin;
  NSSize  size;
} NSRect;
```

- **NSRange** defines a starting index (called location here) and a length:

```
typedef struct _NSRange
{
  NSUInteger location;
  NSUInteger length;
} NSRange;
```

> **Note**
>
> Core Graphics (the low-level graphics framework) and iOS use a differently named, but identically defined, set of structures for points, sizes, and rectangles. The structures **CGPoint**, **CGSize**, and **CGRect** have the same memory layout and member names as **NSPoint**, **NSSize**, and **NSRect**. However, there is no **CGRange** structure. Both iOS and Mac OS X use **NSRange**.

NSRange is used extensively in string processing to denote substrings:

```
NSString *string = @"abcdefghijklmnopqrstuvwxyz";
NSRange  range = NSMakeRange( 5, 10 );
NSString *substring = [string substringWithRange: range];
NSLog( @"Substring is %@", substring );
```

The preceding code uses the Foundation function **NSMakeRange** to create an **NSRange** structure beginning at 5 with a length of 10. The range structure is used as an argument to the **NSString** method **substringWithRange:** to create a substring beginning at character index 5 and extending for 10 characters. When the code is executed, it produces the following output:

```
Substring is fghijklmno
```

Although they are declared in Foundation, **NSPoint**, **NSSize**, and **NSRect** are used throughout the AppKit to define the size and position of views, controls, and windows, and in the course of drawing graphics.

NSPoint, **NSSize**, and **NSRect** have the same memory layouts as their Core Graphics equivalents, **CGPoint**, **CGSize**, and **CGRect**. If you have to descend to the Core Graphics level for some of your drawing, you can go back and forth between the Foundation and Core Graphics structures by using the Foundation functions **NSRectToCGRect** and **NSRectFromCGRect**, **NSPointToCGPoint** and **NSPointFromCGPoint**, and **NSSizeToCGSize** and **NSSizeFromCGSize**.

```
NSRect nsRect = NSMakeRect( 0.0, 0.0, 100.0, 100.0 );
CGRect cgRect = NSRectToCGRect( nsRect );
```

In the other direction:

```
CGRect cgRect = CGRectMake( 0.0, 0.0, 100.0, 100.0 );
NSRect nsRect = NSRectFromCGRect( cgRect );
```

Besides the creation functions, Foundation defines a number of other functions for working with NSRange, NSPoint, NSSize, and NSRect.[2]

Geometry Structures on iOS

NSPoint, NSSize, and NSRect are not defined in the iOS version of Foundation. iOS uses the equivalent Core Graphics structures CGPoint, CGSize, and CGRect. Apple has also removed the functions for working with NSPoint, NSSize, and NSRect from the iOS Foundation. But beware! The functions were "removed" by removing their declarations. The code for these functions is still present (as of iOS 5). If you try to use one of these functions, you will get a compiler warning:

```
/Users/rclair/testApp/AppDelegate.m:19:14:
warning: implicit declaration of function 'NSIntersectsRect' is
invalid in C99 [-Wimplicit-function-declaration,3]
```

If you ignore the compiler warning, the code works as expected. However, you will get an unpleasant surprise when you go to submit your app to the App Store. It will be rejected for using a private API. Be aware of this issue if you are moving existing code from the desktop to iOS.

Summary

This chapter covered some of the most commonly used Foundation classes: NSString, NSArray, NSDictionary, NSSet, NSNumber, NSData, and NSURL. NSString and NSArray are safer than their plain C analogs because they are bounds checked. The NSDictionary class implements associative arrays similar to those found in other languages. The NSNumber class provides a wrapper for numeric values so that numbers can be treated as objects when necessary. NSData provides similar wrapping services for blocks of bytes. The last section of the chapter examined some Foundation entities that are plain C structures: NSRange, NSPoint, NSSize, and NSRect.

---

2. See https://developer.apple.com/library/mac/#documentation/Cocoa/Reference/Foundation/
Miscellaneous/Foundation_Functions/Reference/reference.html.

Exercises

1. Verify that the Foundation array classes are bounds checked:

   a. Create an **NSMutableArray** and populate it with three **NSString** objects.

   b. Using the method **objectAtIndex:**, try to retrieve an object from index −1. Try again with index 3. What happens?

   c. Using the method **insertObject:atIndex:**, try to insert another **NSString** at index −1. What happens?

   d. Now try to insert the new string at index 3. Explain your results.

2. Practice using dictionaries:

   a. Create an empty **NSMutableDictionary**.

   b. Add the names of some of your family and friends (as **NSString**s) to the dictionary. Use strings representing their relationships to you as the keys:
   [friendsAndFamilyDict setObject: @"Martin" forKey: @"Father"];

   c. Verify that you can insert the same object into the dictionary more than once using different keys.

   d. Try to insert a different object using a key that you have already used. What happens?

   e. Using **objectForKey:**, try to retrieve the value for a non-existent key. Does the program crash?

3. Create an **Adder** class with a class method that takes two **NSNumber** objects as arguments and returns their sum as an **NSNumber**. (Assume for the exercise that the **NSNumber** objects contain **float** values.) Write a small program to test your method.

4. Sort an **NSArray**:

   a. Create an **NSArray** that holds the following strings: @"Raspberry", @"Peach", @"Banana", @"Blackberry", @"Blueberry", and @"Apple".

   b. Obtain a sorted version of the array using the **NSArray** method **sortedArrayUsingSelector:**. Use the selector for the **NSString** method **caseInsensitiveCompare:** as the argument. You should read the documentation for **sortedArrayUsingSelector:** and **caseInsensitiveCompare:** before proceeding.

   c. Log the contents of the newly created sorted array.

5. Practice working with **NSData**:

   a. Create an **NSMutableData** object with a buffer of 50 bytes.

   b. Get a pointer to the object's buffer.

   c. Use the pointer to write the first 50 integers into the buffer.

     d. Write the contents of your **NSMutableData** object to a file.

     e. In a second program, use the file to initialize an **NSData** object.

     f. Get the pointer to the **NSData** object's buffer.

     g. Use the pointer to log the values stored in the buffer and verify that everything worked correctly.

6. Create a class that logs its **retain** and **release** messages. You can do this by overriding **retain** and **release**. In both methods, insert an **NSLog** statement as the first line in the method, and then call the superclass version of the method. Use your class with an **NSMutableArray** and an **NSMutableDictionary**, and verify that

     a. An object is retained when it is placed in the collection

     b. An object is released when it is removed from the collection

     c. An object is released if it is in the collection when the collection is deallocated

7. Try out **NSNumber** literals and boxed expressions. Write a program that creates some **NSNumber** objects using both literals and boxed expressions. Retrieve and log the stored numeric values to verify that you get back the original values.

8. Try out array and dictionary literals and subscripting:

     a. Create an **NSArray** object using literals. You can just use **NSString** objects for the objects.

     b. Verify that the resulting **NSArray** is immutable by attempting to add an object to the array.

     c. Access an item from the array using the subscripting notation and verify that it is working correctly.

     d. Make a mutable copy of the array. Add to the array using the subscripting notation. What happens if you use a subscript beyond the current bounds of the array?

9. Repeat Exercise 8 (except for the last item that refers to array bounds) with an **NSDictionary**.

Control Structures in Objective-C

Chapter 1, "C, the Foundation of Objective C," covered the basic C language control statements used for looping and branching: `if`, `for`, and `while`. This chapter examines how these statements are typically used in an Objective-C setting. It also covers some additional Objective-C looping constructs, including the *Fast Enumeration* feature that is new with Objective-C 2.0. Finally, it covers Objective-C's exception system.

`if` Statements

As noted in Chapter 3, "An Introduction to Object-Oriented Programming," Objective-C defines its own Boolean type, `BOOL`, and the constants `YES` and `NO` to represent true and false. A message expression using a method that returns a `BOOL`, such as the `NSArray` method `containsObject:`, can go into the condition part of an `if` statement, as shown here:

```
NSArray *employeeNames = ...
NSString *nameOne = @"Ralph";

if ( [employeeNames containsObject: nameOne] )
  {
    ...
  }
```

You can use expressions that return a `BOOL` with the usual logical operators to make compound conditions:

```
NSArray *employeeNames = ...

NSString *nameOne = @"Ralph";
NSString *nameTwo = @"Alice";
```

```
if ( [employeeNames containsObject: nameOne] &&
     [employeeNames containsObject: nameTwo] )
  {
    ...
  }
```

Remember that C uses short circuit evaluation with compound conditions. If `nameOne` isn't contained in `employeeNames`, the second message expression in the condition is not executed. It doesn't make any difference in the preceding example, but it could make a difference if your message expressions have side effects.

A Warning about Explicit Comparisons

Be very careful when making explicit comparisons to YES and NO. The following is merely verbose:

```
NSArray *employeeNames = ...
NSString *nameOne = @"Ralph";

// Technically OK, but verbose

if ( [employeeNames containsObject: nameOne] == NO )
  {
    NSLog( @"%@ doesn't work here.", nameOne );
  }
```

However, an explicit comparison to YES is a slippery slope that can lead to bugs:

```
NSArray *employeeNames = ...
NSString *nameOne = @"Ralph";

// Not yet a bug, but dangerous

if ( [employeeNames containsObject: nameOne] == YES )
  {
    NSLog( @"%@ works here.", nameOne );
  }
```

The explicit comparison is OK in the preceding example because `containsObject:` will return only one of the two values, YES or NO. But if you get in the habit of making explicit comparisons to YES, the practice can get you into trouble. Let's say you have an `NSString` and you want to do something with it only if the string has a non-zero length. If you write the following, thinking "non-zero means true," you are in trouble:

```
NSString *nameOne = @"Ralph";

// WRONG!

if ( [nameOne length] == YES )
  {
```

```
        // Do something with non-zero length string
    }
```

The condition is false.

Recall that BOOL is actually an integer type and that YES is a defined constant with a value of one:

```
#define YES  (BOOL)1
```

The length of the string in the preceding example is five. Five does not equal one.

This is the proper way to write the preceding if statement:

```
// Correct

if ( [nameOne length] )
  {
     // Do something with non-zero length string
  }
```

If you want to be more explicit, you can write

```
// Also correct

if ( [nameOne length] > 0 )
  {
     // Do something with non-zero length string
  }
```

Testing Objects for Equality

A common use of if statements is to check to see if two expressions are the same. This is simple and uncontroversial with primitive numeric types:

```
int b = ...
int a = 9;

if ( a == b )
  {
    printf("The same!\n");
  }
```

When b is set to 9, the expression in parentheses is true; otherwise, it is false.

Be Careful of == and =

Be careful when you type comparisons. == is the test for equality, and = is the assignment operator. Accidentally leaving out one of the = signs and typing

```
  if ( a=b )
```

when you mean to type

```
if ( a==b )
```

is a classic C mistake. The first expression assigns the value of **b** to **a** and then determines the expression's truth value by looking to see if **a** is zero or non-zero. The second expression checks to see if **a** and **b** are equal.

The Clang compiler will help you out by flagging constructs like

```
if ( a=b )
```

with a warning. If, like Horton the elephant, you meant what you said, you can silence the warning by using an extra set of parentheses:

```
if ( (a=b) )
```

Also, note that Clang has been taught to understand certain common Objective-C idioms and will *not* complain about code such as

```
if ( self = [super init] )
```

and

```
NSEnumerator *enumerator = ...
while ( id object = [enumerator nextObject] )
```

When you compare objects, you have to think about what it means to be "the same." You have to distinguish between *pointer identity* and *equality*. Pointer identity is easy. Two objects—and by *object* I mean "pointer to an instance of a class"—are identical if both point to the same memory location. You can check for pointer identity the same way you compare primitive types:

```
SomeClass *object1 = ...
SomeClass *object2 = ...

if ( object1 == object2 )
  {
    NSLog( @"The objects are identical" );
  }
```

For some classes, it is possible for instances of the class to be equal without being identical. For example, you could have two distinct **NSString** objects that contain the exact same text. You could also have two distinct **NSColor** objects that have the same color space and color components.

NSObject defines an instance method, **isEqual:**, that lets you check for equality. **NSObject**'s implementation of **isEqual:** just checks for pointer identity. If **SomeClass** doesn't override **isEqual:**, the following example has the same effect as the previous example:

```
SomeClass *object1 = ...
SomeClass *object2 = ...

if ( [object1 isEqual: object2] )
  {
    NSLog( @"The objects are equal" );
  }
```

Many classes do override **isEqual:**. For example, **NSColor**'s implementation returns **YES** if both objects are instances of **NSColor** and have the same color space and color components.

A few Cocoa classes define special methods to test for equality that you can use when you know something about the objects being tested. **NSString** defines the method **isEqualToString:**, which is faster than using **isEqual:** when you know both objects are strings:

```
NSString *string1 = ...
NSString *string2 = ...
if ( [string1 isEqualToString: string2] )
  {
    NSLog( @"The strings are the same." );
  }
```

> **Note**
>
> Don't confuse the method **isEqual:** with **isEqualTo:**. The method **isEqualTo:** is part of a Cocoa scripting protocol for ordering objects.

for **Statements and Implicit Loops**

One of the most common programming tasks is to loop over a collection of objects.

for **Statements**

You can use a standard C **for** loop to iterate over an Objective-C array; for example:

```
NSArray *displayList = ... // Array of graphic objects to draw
NSUInteger j;

NSUInteger numToDraw = [displayList count];

for (j=0; j < numToDraw; j++ )
  {
    [[displayList objectAtIndex: j] draw];
  }
```

The objects returned by **objectAtIndex:** are returned typed as **id**. As long as each of them can respond to a **draw** message, the loop will behave properly.

Implicit Loops

You can make the code in the preceding example a bit cleaner by creating an implicit loop using `NSArray`'s `makeObjectsPerformSelector:` method:

```
NSArray *displayList = ...
[displayList makeObjectsPerformSelector: @selector( draw )];
```

The implicit loop does the exact same thing as the explicit loop. A `draw` message is sent, in order, to each object in `displayList`.

NSSet also implements a `makeObjectsPerformSelector:` method:

```
NSSet *aSet =  ...
[aSet makeObjectsPerformSelector: @selector( doSomething )];
```

Each object in **aSet** receives a **doSomething** message exactly once. The order in which the objects are messaged is unspecified.

NSArray and NSSet also implement the method `makeObjectsPerformSelector:withObject:`. This method allows you to make implicit loops using a selector that takes a single object argument:

```
NSMutableArray *displayList = ...
[displayList makeObjectsPerformSelector: @selector( drawWithColor: )
            withObject: [NSColor blueColor]];
```

Each object in **displayList** is sent a **drawWithColor:[NSColor blueColor]** message.

If you need to iterate over a set or an array with a selector that takes a primitive type as an argument or more than one argument, you will have to go back to an explicit loop.

> **Note**
>
> The selectors used as arguments for
>
> `makeObjectsPerformSelector:`
>
> or
>
> `makeObjectsPerformSelector:withObject:`
>
> should not modify the array or set used as the receiver.

Implicit Loops with Blocks

Beginning with Mac OS X Snow Leopard (version 10.6), Apple has added a number of methods that iterate over Foundation collection objects using *blocks*. Blocks are similar to functions, but unlike functions, they carry a context with them. Blocks and the new iteration methods that use blocks are covered in Chapter 17.

while **Statements and** NSEnumerator

Using a while loop in conjunction with an instance of the NSEnumerator class is a more idiomatic way to iterate over an Objective-C collection. An NSEnumerator takes the objects in a collection and hands them out, one at a time, with the method nextObject. When all the objects have been dispensed, any further calls to nextObject return nil.

You don't create NSEnumerator objects yourself. NSEnumerator is an abstract class with no public interfaces for creating instances. Instead, you obtain an enumerator object from the collection class that it enumerates.

The following example reuses the code from the previous section, but it has been rewritten using a while loop:

```
NSMutableArray *displayList = ... // Array of graphic objects to draw
GraphicObject *graphicObject;

NSEnumerator *myEnumerator = [displayList objectEnumerator];

while ( graphicObject = [myEnumerator nextObject] )
  {
    [graphicObject draw];
  }
```

The truth value of the assignment expression (note the single =) in the parentheses is the value of graphicObject. Each time through the loop, the return value of nextObject is assigned to graphicObject, and then graphicObject is tested to see if it evaluates to true or false. If nextObject returns an object, graphicObject is some non-nil value that counts as true. The body of the loop is executed. When the collection is exhausted, nextObject returns nil. The truth value of graphicObject is then false (remember, nil is just an alias for zero) and the loop ends.

At this point, the enumerator object is depleted. If you want to loop over the collection again, you must obtain a fresh NSEnumerator object before beginning the second loop:

```
myEnumerator = [displayList objectEnumerator];
```

The enumerator for an array enumerates the array's objects in order. The order of enumeration for sets and dictionaries is unspecified. Some collection classes also have specialized enumerators: NSArray provides reverseObjectEnumerator, which goes through the array backward, starting with the object at the highest index. NSDictionary provides keyEnumerator, which iterates over the set of keys used for the dictionary rather than over the objects that the dictionary contains.

Modifying a Mutable Collection While Enumerating

It is not safe to modify (add objects to or remove objects from) a mutable collection that is being enumerated. The results may be unpredictable. There are two ways to work around this problem:

- Obtain a new array that contains all the objects in the collection and enumerate the new array while modifying the original collection.

- Enumerate the collection and create a list of the required changes. When you are finished enumerating the collection, you can proceed and make your changes.

Assume that a `GraphicObject` class implements an `isBitmap` method that tells whether the receiver is a bitmap graphic. Here is how you would remove all the bitmap graphics from an array `displayList` by enumerating a copy of `displayList`:

```
1   NSMutableArray *displayList = ... // Array of graphic objects
2   GraphicObject *graphicObject;
3
4   NSEnumerator *enumerator =
5     [[NSArray arrayWithArray: displayList] objectEnumerator];
6
7   while ( graphicObject = [enumerator nextObject] )
8   {
9       if ( [graphicObject isBitmap] )
10       {
11           [displayList removeObject: graphicObject];
12       }
13   }
```

The statement on Lines 4 and 5 creates an (immutable) copy of `displayList` and obtains the copy's object enumerator. The enumerator is then used to loop over the copy array while making changes to the original collection.

The important point is that the array that is being enumerated (the copy of `displayList`) is not being modified during the enumeration.

> **Note**
>
> You can obtain an array of all the objects in an `NSSet` (or `NSMutableSet`) by using the method `allObjects`. You can obtain an array of all the objects in an `NSDictionary` (or `NSMutableDictionary`) by using the method `allValues`. In both cases, the order of the objects in the resulting array is unspecified.

The following example shows how to accomplish the previous task by enumerating the original `displayList` array and building up a temporary array of objects that should be removed:

```
NSMutableArray *displayList = ... // Array of graphic objects
```

```
GraphicObject *graphicObject;
NSMutableArray *tmpArray = [NSMutableArray array];

NSEnumerator *enumerator = [displayList objectEnumerator];

// Build an array of objects to remove

while ( graphicObject = [enumerator nextObject] )
  {
    if ( [graphicObject isBitmap] )
      {
        [tmpArray addObject: graphicObject];
      }
  }

// Remove the objects

[displayList removeObjectsInArray: tmpArray];
```

tmpArray must be an **NSMutableArray** so that objects can be added to it. After the enumeration is complete, the objects in **tmpArray** can safely be removed from **displayList**.

Fast Enumeration

Objective-C 2.0 adds a new syntax, called **for ... in**, for enumerating over collections. The **for ... in** construction is easier to code and runs faster than traditional loops based on **NSEnumerator**. With these advantages, you should use this syntax instead of **NSEnumerator**-based **while** loops. But as you will see later in this section, **NSEnumerator** is still useful as a helper class in some situations.

The basic form of a **for ... in** loop is

```
for ( type loopVariable in expression )
  {
    // Statements
  }
```

expression must evaluate to an object (usually a Cocoa collection class of some sort) that conforms to the **NSFastEnumeration** protocol. (A class conforms to a protocol if it implements a specified set of methods. Protocols are covered in Chapter 13.)

When the **for ... in** loop executes, *loopVariable* is set to the first item in the collection and then the statements in the body are executed. These steps are then repeated in turn for each item in the collection.

The following example reuses code from the previous sections, but it has been rewritten to use a **for ... in** loop:

```
NSMutableArray *displayList = ... // Array of graphic objects to draw

for ( GraphicObject *graphicObject in displayList )
  {
  [graphicObject draw];
  }
```

You can also use an existing variable as the loop variable in a **for ... in** loop:

```
NSMutableArray *displayList = ... // Array of graphic objects to draw
GraphicObject *graphicObject;

for ( graphicObject in displayList )
  {
    [graphicObject draw];
  }
```

Some important things to note about **for ... in** loops:

- You can break out of the loop with a **break** statement or use a **continue** statement to skip to the next iteration.
- If *loopVariable* is declared as part of the **for ... in** statement, it is undefined outside the body of the loop.
- If *loopVariable* is an existing variable declared outside of the **for ... in** statement, its value after the **for ... in** loop depends on how the loop ends. If the loop executes to completion, *loopVariable* is set to **nil**.
- If a **break** statement is encountered, an existing *loopVariable* is left at whatever value it had when the **break** statement was executed.

The Cocoa collection classes **NSArray**, **NSDictionary**, and **NSSet**, as well as **NSEnumerator**, conform to **NSFastEnumeration**. Why **NSEnumerator**? Sometimes classes provide subclasses of **NSEnumerator** that perform special tasks. For example, to iterate and draw **displayList** in reverse order, you could do this:

```
NSMutableArray *displayList = ... // Array of graphic objects to draw

for ( GraphicObject *graphicObject in
      [displayList reverseObjectEnumerator] )
  {
  [graphicObject draw];
  }
```

Fast Enumeration makes your code look cleaner, but it also provides several additional advantages, one of which is speed. It is "fast." It is optimized to execute more efficiently than loops written by hand. It does this by effectively in-lining parts of the loop: Under the hood, it asks for many objects at a time, which eliminates many message dispatches or function calls.

Fast Enumeration is also safe in the sense that it prevents you from modifying a collection while it is being iterated. The following code:

```
NSMutableArray *displayList = ... // Array of graphic objects


for ( GraphicObject *graphicObject in displayList )
  {
    if ( [graphicObject isBitmap] )
      {
        [displayList removeObject: graphicObject];
      }
  }
```

causes a runtime exception:

```
*** Terminating app due to uncaught exception 'NSGenericException',
    reason:
*** Collection <NSCFArray: 0x1032b0> was mutated while being enumerated.
```

To modify a collection, you must do something similar to what was shown in the previous section; for example:

```
NSMutableArray *displayList = ... // Array of graphic objects

NSArray *allObjects = [NSArray arrayWithArray: displayList];

for ( GraphicObject *graphicObject in allObjects )
  {
    if ( [graphicObject isBitmap] )
      {
        [displayList removeObject: graphicObject];
      }
  }
```

NSDictionary and Fast Enumeration

This is a potential "gotcha" if you don't read the fine print. When `for ... in` is used with an `NSDictionary` object, it enumerates over the dictionary's *keys*, not its objects. To fast enumerate over a dictionary's objects, you must use the dictionary's object enumerator, as shown here:

```
NSDictionary *myDictionary = ...
for ( id objectInDictionary in [myDictionary objectEnumerator] )
  {
    ...
  }
```

An Example Using Fast Enumeration

Here is a more extensive example that uses some of the constructs that we've just discussed. It's a program, `myls`, that mimics the basic behavior of the Unix `ls` command.

> **Note**
>
> `ls` is the Unix command for listing files and directories. If you're not familiar with `ls`, open the Terminal program (*/Applications/Utilities/Terminal.app*) and type `man  ls`. Or just experiment: Type `ls` and press Return to see the results.

After you build the example in Listing 10.1, you can type `myls` at the Unix prompt:

%myls

and `myls` will list the files in the current directory. If you type

%myls foo

`myls` will

- List `foo`, if `foo` is a directory
- Echo "foo" if `foo` is a file
- Give an error message if `foo` doesn't exist

If there is more than one argument, `myls` repeats the process for each argument.

`myls` uses `printf` rather than `NSLog` to send the output to the standard output (the terminal window) rather than the console. In a couple of places, it is necessary to use the `NSString` methods `stringWithUTF8String:` and `UTF8String` to go from C strings to `NSString` instances and back.

> **Note**
>
> You should use `NSString` objects rather than C strings wherever possible. Unfortunately, the OS uses C strings, so it is necessary to convert back and forth when talking to the OS.

`myls` also requires one Foundation object that hasn't been covered: `NSFileManager`. `NSFileManager` is an example of a Foundation object that wraps interactions with the OS. It is a singleton object that provides methods to programmatically manipulate the filesystem. After it has the file manager object, the program can do most of the things with the filesystem that you can do sitting at a terminal window. The file manager can create, move, and delete files and directories, list directories, copy files, check to see if a file exists, check on permissions, create symbolic links, and get the current working directory.

> **Note**
>
> Before proceeding, you may want to look at the documentation for the `NSFileManager` class: http://developer.apple.com/library/mac/#documentation/Cocoa/Reference/ Foundation/Classes/nsfilemanager_Class/Reference/Reference.html.

The first thing to do is use the `NSFileManager` class method `defaultManager` to get the single instance of the file manager:

```
NSFileManager *fileManager = [NSFileManager defaultManager];
```

You can then use the file manager to get the contents of a directory as an array of `NSString` objects:

```
NSArray *directoryContents =
[fileManager contentsOfDirectoryAtPath: @"/Users/you" error: nil];
```

> **Note**
>
> The `error:` argument in `contentsOfDirectoryAtPath:error:` is used to return a pointer to an `NSError` object. If you are interested in receiving error information, you pass in the address of a pointer to an `NSError` object:
>
> ```
> NSError *returnedError;
> NSArray *directoryContents =
> [fileManager contentsOfDirectoryAtPath: @"/Users/you"
>             error: &returnedError];
> ```
>
> If invoking `contentsOfDirectoryAtPath:error:` results in an error, the returned `NSError` object will contain information about the error. You can obtain a localized description of the error by using the `localizedDescription` method of `NSError`:
>
> ```
> NSString *errorMessage =
>    [returnedError localizedDescription];
> ```
>
> In this example `myls` checks to make sure the path it passes to `contentsOfDirectoryAtPath:` exists and is a directory. It isn't equipped to handle other error conditions, so it passes `nil` for the error argument.

The complete program is shown in Listing 10.1.

Listing 10.1   *myls.m*

```
1   #import <Foundation/Foundation.h>
2
3   int main (int argc, const char *argv[])
4   {
5     @autoreleasepool {
6
7       BOOL isDirectory;
8
9       NSMutableArray *pathsToList =
```

```
10                   [NSMutableArray arrayWithCapacity: 20];
11    NSFileManager *fileManager = [NSFileManager defaultManager];
12
13    // argv[0] is the command name
14    // Any others are directories or files to list
15
16    if ( argc == 1 ) // Just command name so list the current directory
17      {
18        [pathsToList addObject:  [fileManager currentDirectoryPath]];
19      }
20    else
21      {
22          // Convert input arguments to NSString and
23          // add them to the array
24        int j;
25        for ( j=1; j < argc; j++ )
26          {
27            [pathsToList addObject:
28                 [NSString stringWithUTF8String: argv[j]]];
29          }
30      }
31
32    for ( NSString *path in pathsToList )
33      {
34        if ( [fileManager fileExistsAtPath: path
35                           isDirectory: &isDirectory] )
36          {
37            if ( isDirectory ) // List the files in the directory
38              {
39              NSArray *directoryContents =
40                [fileManager contentsOfDirectoryAtPath: path
41                             error: nil];
42                for ( NSString *contentPath in directoryContents )
43                  {
44                    printf( "%s\n", [contentPath UTF8String] );
45                  }
46              }
47            else  // It's a file, just list it
48              {
49                printf( "%s\n", [path UTF8String] );
50              }
51          }
52        else    // Oops, no file or directory with that name
53          {
54            printf("myls: %s:  No such file or directory\n",
55                    [path UTF8String]);
56          }
```

```
57     }
58   }
59   return 0;
60 }
```

`argv` is a C array, not an object, so `myls` must use a regular `for` loop (starting on Line 25) to convert any arguments into `NSString` objects and store them in an `NSMutableArray`.

`pathsToList` and `directoryContents` are `NSMutableArray` instances, so the program can use the `for ... in` syntax to loop through them (Lines 32 and 42).

The `NSFileManager` method `fileExistsAtPath:isDirectory` (Line 34) is interesting. Its second argument is typed `BOOL*` (pointer to `BOOL`). The second argument must be the address of a `BOOL` declared in the method's caller. This is because the method needs to return two `BOOL` values, one for whether there is an entry at the specified path, and another for whether the entry is a directory. It returns the first `BOOL` as the return value of the method. It returns the second `BOOL` by setting the value of the `BOOL` variable whose address is passed in as the second argument.

Exceptions

Exceptions are abnormal conditions that prevent a program from continuing with execution. Creating an exception is referred to as *raising an exception* or *throwing an exception*. Common situations that will raise an exception are actions such as sending a message to an object that doesn't respond to that message, or attempting to retrieve an object from an `NSArray` with an index that is outside the bounds of the array. If you don't do anything to handle an exception, the exception causes the program to terminate.

Objective-C provides a mechanism to handle exceptions with the compiler directives `@try`, `@catch`, and `@finally`. Each of these directives introduces a block of code as shown in Listing 10.2.

> **Note**
>
> Versions of Mac OS X prior to 10.3 don't support exceptions. If you do use them, your program will run only on Mac OS X 10.3 or later.

Listing 10.2   **Exceptions**/*SimpleExceptionHandler.m*

```
1  id hamburger = @"hamburger";
2
3  @try
4  {
5    hamburger = [hamburger addCheese];
6  }
7  @catch( NSException *exc )
```

```
 8  {
 9    NSLog(@"Exception: %@ : %@", [exc name], [exc reason]);
10  }
11  @finally
12  {
13    NSLog(@"This block is always executed.");
14  }
```

The code that might cause a problem goes in the **@try** block. In Listing 10.2, executing the line

```
hamburger = [hamburger addCheese];
```

raises an exception because in this example **hamburger** is an **NSString** and **NSString** doesn't implement the method **addCheese**.

The **@catch** block catches the exception. Exceptions are always thrown with an *exception object*, which becomes the argument to the **@catch** block. The runtime and the Cocoa frameworks use instances of the class **NSException** as exception objects. Here, the **@catch** block just uses information from the **NSException** object to log the exception.

The code in the **@finally** block is always executed. If the **@try** or **@catch** blocks contain a **return** statement, the return is delayed until after the code in the **@finally** block is executed. In Listing 10.2, the **@finally** block logs a message, and the program continues executing with the statement after the **@finally** block.

> **Note**
>
> In a multithreaded program, exceptions are caught only if the code raising the exception is executing on the same thread as the **@try/@catch/@finally**.

Throwing Your Own Exceptions

The runtime system and the Cocoa frameworks throw exceptions for you in various unfortunate situations. However, you can also throw your own exceptions using the **@throw** compiler directive, as shown in the following example:

```
- (void) addOnion
{
  if ( [pantry numOnions] <= 0 )
    {
      NSException *exception =
          [NSException exceptionWithName:@"OutOfOnionException"
                      reason:@"PantryEmpty" userInfo:nil];

      @throw exception;
    }
```

```
  else
    {
      ...   // Add the onion
    }
}
```

NSException

NSException is a Foundation class that packages up useful information about an exception. When you create an **NSException**, you can specify the name of the exception and the reason for the exception and provide an **NSDictionary** that holds additional information. Although you can use any object as the exception object when throwing your own exceptions, the runtime and the Cocoa frameworks always use **NSException**.

The preceding examples use an **NSException** object (see the sidebar *NSException*), but you can use any Objective-C object as an exception object. For example, you can use a custom subclass of **NSException** or an **NSString** as an exception object:

```
@throw  @"Sorry. We're out of Onions";
```

The **@catch** block that is used to catch an exception must have an argument type that matches the type of object used with the **@throw** statement. If, as in the preceding line of code, you throw an **NSString** as the exception object, the corresponding **@catch** must look like this:

```
@catch( NSString *s )
{
  ...
}
```

Multiple @catch Blocks

You can set up your code to throw different types of exception objects for different situations. Then, you can use multiple **@catch** blocks, each typed for a different type of exception object, with a single **@try** block, as shown in the following example:

```
@try
  {
    ...
  }
@catch (NSString *myString)
  {
    // Process exceptions thrown with an object that is an
    // NSString or a subclass of NSString
  }
```

```
@catch (NSException *myException)
   {
      // Process exceptions thrown with an NSException object
   }
@finally
   {
      ...
   }
```

When there are multiple `@catch` blocks, an exception is caught by the first `@catch` block (going in program order) that matches the exception object. The condition for a match is that the exception object is a member of, or a member of a subclass of, the class used as the type in the `@catch` block. If the code throws an exception using an object that doesn't match any of the `@catch` blocks, the exception is not caught. The program terminates immediately and the code in the `@finally` block is not executed.

Nested Exception Handling

The code inside a `@try` block may itself contain a `@try/@catch/@finally` set, the equivalent of

```
@try
   {
      @try
         {
         }
      @catch( NSException *exc )
         {
         }
      @finally
         {
         }
   }
@catch( NSException *exc )
   {
   }
@finally
   {
   }
```

> **Note**
>
> This is a just a simple illustration. The inner `@try/@catch/@finally` may actually be buried further down in code placed in the outer `@try` block.

When an exception is raised, it is caught by the first `@catch` block (working upward in the stack from the point where the exception was raised) whose argument type matches the exception object type. The `@catch` block itself may throw an exception (either the original or a new one) that can be caught for further processing by another `@catch` block contained in a routine located higher on the stack.

Note

Any code in the `@finally` block corresponding to the original `@catch` block is executed before the new exception is handled.

What Types of Exceptions Are in the Frameworks?

The Apple documentation doesn't have a comprehensive list of all the exceptions that the runtime and the Cocoa frameworks can raise. The exceptions that can be raised by various individual framework methods are described in the documentation for those methods.

Using Exceptions

To use exceptions in your program, you must tell the compiler that you are using them. If you are compiling from the command line, you must pass the flag `fobjc-exceptions` to Clang. If you are using Xcode, you do this by setting the *Enable Objective-C Exceptions* item to *Yes* in the *Apple LLVM compiler - Language* section of the *Build Settings*, as shown in Figure 10.1.

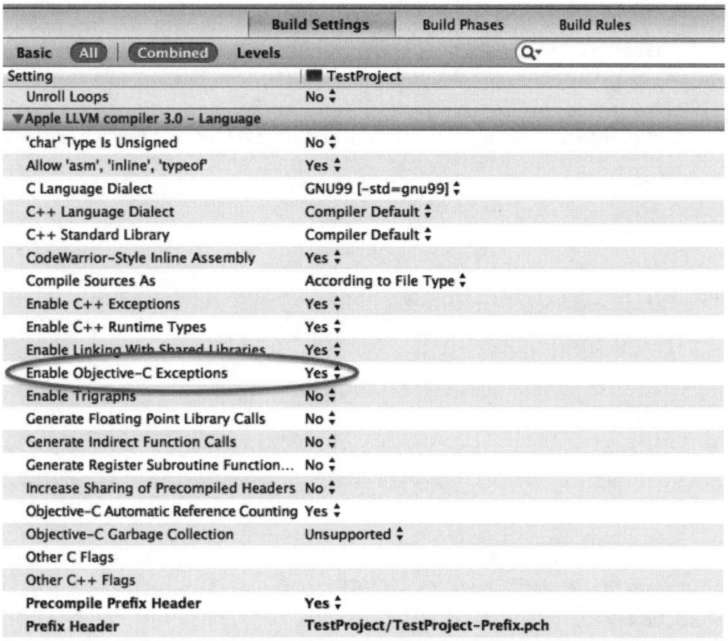

Figure 10.1   Enabling exceptions in Xcode

Should You Use Exceptions?

Now that you've learned all about exceptions, I have to tell you that they are rarely used in Objective-C. In particular, you shouldn't use them for ordinary flow control. Some languages, like Python, are optimized for exception handling. Objective-C is not. Exception handling in Objective-C is expensive.

Exceptions in Objective-C were primarily designed for catching programmer errors and other non-recoverable problems. In situations where you can test for an error condition in advance, you should do so rather than adding code to catch a potential exception.

As an example, if you are given an object typed as id, and you want to send it a particular message, you can see if the object is able to respond to the message by using the method respondsToSelector, as shown in the following example:

```
id someObject;

if ([someObject respondsToSelector: @selector(addCheese)])
  {
     [someObject addCheese];
  }
else
  {
     NSLog(@"Sorry. Can't add cheese to %@", [someObject description]);
  }
```

The preceding is a much better approach than placing the line

```
[myObject addCheese];
```

in a @try block.

Normal error conditions should be passed out by return values:

```
- (BOOL) addOnion
{
  if ( [pantry numOnions] <= 0 )
    {
      return NO;
    }
  else
    {
      ... // Add the onion
      return YES;
    }
}
```

If you need more information about the error condition, you can add an argument to the method to pass back a reference to an NSError object, which encapsulates information about the error.

One of the problems with using exceptions is that the code raising an exception may be several levels down in the stack from the `@catch` block that will catch it. When the exception is raised, execution jumps to the `@catch` block, bypassing all the intermediate routines on the stack. If the bypassed code contains cleanup code or other code that was expected to execute, the program may be in an inconsistent state when it continues after the `@finally` block. The program can continue, but it may produce incorrect results or crash at a later point. This is particularly problematic if, as is the case with the Cocoa frameworks, the code that is bypassed was not designed to work in this manner.

Summary

This chapter looked at looping and branching in an Objective-C context. The main points are:

- You can use the Objective-C Boolean type `BOOL` anyplace a truth value is needed in an ordinary C control construct. However, you should avoid making explicit comparisons to `YES` and `NO`.

- When comparing two objects, you need to decide whether you require pointer identity (the two objects are the same object) or equality (the two objects are distinct but are equal for your purposes).

- You can use an ordinary `for` loop for looping over a collection, but if the collection is an `NSArray` or `NSSet`, and the loop body is a single message, an implicit loop using `makeObjectsPerformSelector:` results in cleaner code.

- Prior to Objective-C 2.0, the best way to loop over a collection was to use a `while` loop in conjunction with an `NSEnumerator` object. An `NSEnumerator` object, obtained from the collection object, dispenses the collection's objects one at a time with its `nextObject` method. When all the objects in the collection have been dispensed, `nextObject` returns `nil`.

- Objective-C 2.0 adds Fast Enumeration and the `for ... in` syntax. Fast Enumeration has better performance than the traditional looping constructs.

- Objective-C implements an exception handling system with `@try`/`@catch`/`@finally` directives. Objective-C exceptions are expensive. They should be used only for truly exceptional situations and not for ordinary flow control.

The next chapter, Chapter 11, "Categories, Extensions, and Security," shows you how to add methods to an existing class and discusses Objective-C's (somewhat limited) security features.

Exercises

1. Write a program that includes these lines of code:

```
NSArray *arrayOfStrings =
    [NSArray arrayWithObjects: @"", @"Objective-C", nil];
for ( NSString *string in arrayOfStrings )
  {
    if ( [string length] == YES )

      NSLog( @"%@ has non-zero length!", string );
    else
      NSLog( @"%@ has zero length!", string );
  }
```

   Verify that your program behaves badly, and then fix the program so that it works correctly.

2. Create an array of NSString objects (use whatever strings you like). Using a plain C for loop and NSArray's objectAtIndex: method, calculate the total number of characters held by the strings in the array.

3. Rewrite your program from Exercise 2 to use a while loop and an NSEnumerator object.

4. Rewrite your program from Exercise 3 to use a for ... in loop.

5. Create the following mutable array:

```
NSMutableArray *animalArray =
    [NSMutableArray arrayWithObjects: @"Lion", @"Tiger",
        @"Elephant", @"Duck", @"Rhinoceros", nil];
```

   Iterate over animalArray using a for ... in loop and try to remove all the strings that are more than five characters long from the array. Do this directly from within your for ... in loop. What happens?

6. Using the array from the previous exercise, write a program that correctly removes any string that is longer than five characters from the array. Show that your code works by logging the animalArray before and after removing the strings with a statement like
   NSLog(@"%@", [animalArray description]);

   Your solution should still use a for ... in loop.

7. Create an array that holds three strings; for example:

```
NSArray *duckArray =
    [NSArray arrayWithObjects: @"Huey", @"Dewie",
                               @"Louie", nil];
```

a. Next, set up @try/@catch/@finally blocks. The @catch block should catch an NSException object and log the exception name and reason. The @finally block should contain a logging statement so you can tell if it has been block executed. Put another logging statement after the @try/@catch/@finally blocks.

b. Put a statement that accesses the array inside the @try block. Try to access the array element at index 2. Verify that the code in the @finally block is executed.

c. Next, change your code and attempt to access the array element at index 3. What happens?

Categories, Extensions, and Security

In Chapter 6, "Classes and Objects," you learned the basics of defining classes and allocating, initializing, and copying object instances. But there is more to life than simple object creation. This chapter shows you how to add a method to an existing class even if you don't have the source code for that class, how to hide the existence of methods and instance variables from (at least some) prying eyes, and how to limit access to an object's instance variables. It also discusses Objective-C security (and the lack thereof).

Categories

Categories let you add additional methods to an existing class without subclassing it, and without requiring access to the class's source code. Using a category to extend the behavior of a class is a much lighter-weight procedure than subclassing.

As an illustration, suppose you want to take a string like "Four score and seven years ago" and turn it into "FourScoreAndSevenYearsAgo." A string like that, in which each word in the original string is capitalized and then squashed together into a single block of characters (with no spaces), is called a *CamelCase* string. (It is named after the obvious visual analogy to camel humps.)

> **Note**
> Objective-C class names that follow the usual convention are CamelCase. Objective-C method names are usually a variant of CamelCase where the first letter of the first word is lowercase.

The first thing you should do is to look at the documentation for `NSString` and see if `NSString` already has a `-camelCase` method. Unfortunately, it doesn't.

Your next thought might be to add a `camelCase` method by subclassing `NSString`. This is a bad idea for a couple of reasons:

- As you saw in Chapter 9, "Common Foundation Classes," `NSString` is a class cluster. Although not impossible, subclassing a class cluster is a non-trivial enterprise and requires some serious thought to do correctly.

- If you add the method `camelCase` by subclassing, every string that you want to turn into a `CamelCase` string would have to be an instance of the `CamelCase` subclass instead of a plain `NSString`. This requirement could be a burden if you receive strings from other classes. Most classes that deal in strings return plain `NSString` objects.

All in all, subclassing is too blunt an instrument for this task. In contrast, using a category is very easy. The only thing that you have to do is provide the method declaration in an `@interface` section and the code for the method in an `@implementation` section. The runtime will then add your category method to the class. After it has been added by the runtime, a category method behaves exactly as if it had been coded in the class by the original programmer.

Here is an example of a `CamelCase` category method for `NSString`. The header file for a category is very similar to a regular class header file, as shown in Listing 11.1.

Listing 11.1   *NSString+CamelCase.h*

```
#import <Foundation/Foundation.h>

@interface NSString (CamelCase)

-(NSString*) camelCaseString;


@end
```

Your category header file must import the header file for the class you are extending. In this example, the header file for `NSString` is imported by *Foundation/Foundation.h*. The `@interface` line contains the name of the class you are adding to (here `NSString`) and the name of the category (`CamelCase` in this example). The category name is arbitrary (you could call it `InitialCase` or whatever you like instead). However, you can't use the same name for two different categories on a given class. This example follows the common naming convention for category files, which is `ClassName+CategoryName`—the name of this header file is *NSString+CamelCase.h*.

> **Note**
>
> One big difference between a category and a subclass is that a category cannot add any variables to a class. The header file reflects this: It has no instance variable section.

Now look at the category implementation. The category implementation file (shown in Listing 11.2) looks like an ordinary class implementation file. It must import the corresponding header file. The method implementation(s) go between an @implementation directive and an @end directive. The only difference is that the @implementation line has the category name in parentheses after the class name.

Listing 11.2   *NSString+CamelCase.m*

```
1   #import "NSString+CamelCase.h"
2
3   @implementation NSString   (CamelCase)
4
5   -(NSString*) camelCaseString
6   {
7     NSString *capitalizedString = [self capitalizedString];
8
9     NSArray *components =
10      [capitalizedString componentsSeparatedByCharactersInSet:
11         [NSCharacterSet whitespaceCharacterSet]];
12
13    NSString *output = @"";
14
15
16    for ( NSString *word in components )
17      {
18        output = [output stringByAppendingString: word];
19      }
20
21    return output;
22  }
23  @end
```

Now let's take a look at the code in Listing 11.2:

- Line 7 uses the **NSString** method **capitalizedString** to get a new string that capitalizes the first letter of every word in the text of the original string and sets the other letters in the string to lowercase. Notice that, just as with any other method, a category method can use **self** to refer to the receiver for which it was called. A category method also has the same access as a regular method to a class's instance variables.

- Line 9 creates an array containing each word in the original string as a separate string. The loop beginning in Line 16 concatenates the individual words together as a single string. (It runs the strings together and removes the spaces between the words.)

- Line 21 returns the final product. The string returned by `stringByAppendingString:` is already autoreleased, so you can just return it directly.

You can now use the category on any `NSString`, as shown in the following code:

```
#import "NSString+CamelCase.h"

NSString *string = @"Four score and seven years ago";
NSLog( @"%@", string );
string = [string camelCaseString];
NSLog( @"%@", string );
```

If you run code containing the preceding code fragment, you will see the following result:

```
Four score and seven years ago
FourScoreAndSevenYearsAgo
```

Overriding Methods with Categories

You can also use a category to override an existing method declared by a class. There are some subtleties and dangers in doing this.

- Unless you are very sure you know exactly what the method does in all situations where the method is used, you may wind up breaking something.
- When you use a category to override a method, the new version replaces the original one. There is no way for the category version to call the original method. But, if the original version was itself an override of a superclass version, the category version can still call the superclass version of the method via **super**.
- You can have as many categories as you like for a given class, but each category has to have a distinct name.
- You can't use a category method to override another category method. If you declare methods with the same name in different categories, it doesn't cause a compiler or linking error, but the version of the method that is used depends on the order in which the categories are loaded.

Should I Use a Category or a Subclass?

As R. Crumb's Mr. Natural would say, "Get the right tool for the job!"[1] But what is the right tool? Because jobs vary, I can't give you a definite answer. But here are some things that you should consider:

- **Simple is good.** If a category method will do the job, use it. Lengthening the inheritance chain of a class can make the code more difficult to maintain.

1. http://en.wikipedia.org/wiki/Mr._Natural_(comics).

- **Classes that are implemented as class clusters, such as NSString, require a lot of work to subclass.** Use a category if you can.
- **Categories have wide visibility.** A method added to a class in a category can be used by any instance of that class and any instance of a class that inherits from that class. This may make the method available on a wider scale than you intended. If you find yourself about to add a category on NSObject, you should pause and perhaps rethink your design. Such a category is rarely a good idea as it will affect every object in your program.
- **Overriding with a category can be dangerous.** Be especially careful when using a category to override an existing method in a class. You should make sure that you understand what the original method did and where it is used before you replace it.
- **Adding instance variables requires subclassing.** If you need to add instance variables to extend a class, you will have to create a subclass.
- **Sometimes you have no choice but to subclass.** If you need to extend the same class in different ways in different parts of your program, you will probably have to subclass.
- **Some classes are intended to be subclassed.** Some classes are partially or completely abstract and require that you subclass them to make them fully functional. An example is NSView: In order to do custom drawing or respond to mouse gestures, you must subclass NSView.
- **Try object composition.** You can also extend a class by object composition. Using object composition (which is a design pattern rather than a language feature), you create an entirely new class and hold an instance of the class you are extending in one of the new class's instance variables. Messages that can be handled by the original class are passed to it by the enclosing class. Messages that invoke new functionality are handled by the enclosing class.

This is a long list, but all the items are really variants of the same idea: Think before you code.

Other Uses for Categories

Categories have a number of other uses:

- A large class might have several hundreds of methods and thousands of lines of code to implement them. (To see an extreme example, look at the header file for the AppKit class NSWindow, */System/Library/Frameworks/AppKit.framework/ Headers/NSWindow.h*.) You can use categories to break such a class into several, more manageably sized files. The instance variables and basic methods go in the normal interface and implementation files. The other methods, broken into sensible groups, go in a series of category files. This allows more than one programmer to work on the class simultaneously.
- Categories can also be used to control which of a class's methods are publicly visible to users of the class. To do this, you divide the class's methods into public

and private. The declarations for methods that you want to be public go in the normal header file. The methods that form the class's private API go in a category file.

You then distribute only the public header file to potential users of the class. But keep in mind that this is only an information hiding scheme. If someone discovers the name of a private method by doing some snooping, there is nothing that you can do to prevent him or her from calling it.

- Finally, category header files (without corresponding implementation files) can be used to declare informal protocols (see Chapter 13, "Protocols"). You use the category header to tell the compiler that the methods in the protocol exist and are implemented in classes that adopt the protocol.

Category Methods Are First-Class Citizens

Methods that are defined in a category have all the rights and privileges of methods defined in the class interface. In fact, at run time, there is no difference between the two. They have full access to any of the class's instance variables. They are inherited if the class is subclassed.

Associative References

As you have seen in the preceding section, categories allow you to add methods to a class, even if you do not have the source code for that class. It would be nice if you could do the same thing with instance variables. You can't. But Objective-C 2.0's associative reference feature lets you do something almost as good. Imagine that Apple had designed Objective-C so that every object had a hidden dictionary where you could store other objects. Storing something in an object's hidden dictionary would serve the same purpose as storing it in an instance variable. The difference is that you wouldn't need a new instance variable to store something in the dictionary. Associative references work like this hypothetical dictionary.

Let's say you wanted to add an **NSString** variable to a **UIImage** (the iOS image class) to hold a caption for the image. Since you are (probably) not Apple, you don't have the source code to **UIImage**. So you can't add an instance variable to **UIImage**. But you can create an *association* between **UIImage** and **NSString** objects. The following code shows how to create an association:

```
#import <objc/runtime.h>
...
static char captionKey;

UIImage *myImage = ... // get an image
NSString *caption = ... // get the caption
```

```
objc_setAssociatedObject (
    myImage,
    &captionKey,
    caption,
    OBJC_ASSOCIATION_COPY_NONATOMIC
);
```

The first thing to notice is that Apple has not wrapped associative references in an Objective-C interface. Associative references use low-level C functions that are implemented in the runtime. To use associative references you must import the runtime header *objc/runtime.h*.

The function that sets the association is **objc_setAssociatedObject()**. It takes four arguments:

1. The first argument is the source object, the object you are adding the association to. In this case the source object is a **UIImage**.

2. The second argument is the key for the association. This functions just like a dictionary key. It will be used to identify the associated object when you want to retrieve it. The key is typed as **void***. Any pointer will do, but typically you define a static variable and use its address as the key.

3. The third argument is the value that is being associated with the source object. Here an **NSString** holding a caption is being associated with the **UIImage**, using the address of **captionKey** as the key.

4. The fourth argument is the *association policy*. This is one of a set of defined constants. The association policy determines if the source object retains the associated object, copies it when the association is made, or just holds the associated object without retaining or copying it. The association policy also determines whether making the association is an atomic operation.

The possible values of the association policy constant are

```
OBJC_ASSOCIATION_ASSIGN
OBJC_ASSOCIATION_RETAIN_NONATOMIC
OBJC_ASSOCIATION_COPY_NONATOMIC
OBJC_ASSOCIATION_RETAIN
OBJC_ASSOCIATION_COPY
```

If the constant does not contain the word **NONATOMIC**, the association is created using an atomic operation. Atomic operations are used in some multithreaded environments. They require the use of a lock and are slower than nonatomic operations. They are not needed in most cases.

> **Note**
>
> A source object can have more than one associative reference as long as each reference has its own unique key.

To retrieve the associated object, you use the same key that you used to create the association:

```
UIImage *image = // Image with an associated NSString
NSString *caption =
    (NSString*) objc_getAssociatedObject(image, &captionKey);
```

> **Note**
>
> The key is a pointer—a number representing an address—not the name of the pointer. If you make the association in one file, using the address of a variable as the key, and you want to retrieve the associated object in a different file, you must arrange to have the pointer value available in the second file. You cannot just define a new variable with the same name in the second file, take its address, and use the address of the new variable for the key.

To remove an association just set a `nil` object using the same key that you used to make the association:

```
objc_setAssociatedObject(image, &captionKey, nil,
                         OBJC_ASSOCIATION_ASSIGN);
```

You could also use

```
objc_removeAssociatedObjects( image );
```

However, this function is dangerous—it removes *all* of an object's associative references and returns the object to its original state.

> **Note**
>
> Associative references are a one-way reference (just like storing an object in an instance variable). The source object knows that it has associated values, but the value objects do not know that they are part of an association.

Associative references are available on Mac OS X 10.6 or later and iOS 3.1 or later.

Extensions

Suppose you're writing a class that other programmers will use. You'd like to have some methods that are for your internal use only. If you declare the methods in your class's header file, they will be visible to anyone using the class. Extensions let you declare methods, properties, and instance variables—out of public view—by adding an interface section in the class's implementation file. (Extensions *extend* the interface declaration into the *.m* file.)

Another common use for extensions is to provide an internal setter method for an instance variable that you want to be publicly read-only. Listing 11.3 shows the header file for a class like that. The class declares a getter for the instance variable

readOnlyBool, but it does not declare a setter method. This makes readOnlyBool
effectively a read-only variable (at least for those who do not go snooping; see *Security*
later in this chapter).

Listing 11.3   *ClassWithExtension.h*

```
@interface ClassWithExtension : NSObject
{
  BOOL readOnlyBool;
}

- (BOOL) readOnlyBool;

@end
```

Extensions look exactly like category declarations, except that they have no name.
The extension goes in the class's implementation file, before the @implementation
directive, as shown in Listing 11.4. Note that the empty parentheses are required on
the @interface line.

Listing 11.4   *ClassWithExtension.m*

```
#import "ClassWithExtension.h"

@interface ClassWithExtension ()

- (void) setReadOnlyBool: (BOOL) newValue;

@end

@implementation ClassWithExtension

- (BOOL) readOnlyBool
{
  return readOnlyBool;
}

- (void) setReadOnlyBool:(BOOL) newValue
{
  readOnlyBool = newValue;
}

- (id) init
{
  if (self = [super init] )
    {
      [self setReadOnlyBool: YES];
```

```
    }
  return self;
}

@end
```

You can think of an extension as an anonymous category, but there are a couple of differences:

- The implementation of the extension methods must be in the `@implementation` section of the same file.

- Unlike the case with a category, the compiler checks up on you; if you declare a method in an extension but forget to implement it, you'll get a warning.

Instance Variable Scope (Access Control)

Objective-C provides four directives to control access to an object's instance variables:

- `@private`

  The instance variable is accessible only in methods of the class that declared it. Trying to access it from a subclass results in an error.

- `@protected`

  The instance variable is accessible in methods of the class that declared it and in the methods of any class that inherits from that class. This is the default and the normal case. You usually want to hide a class's instance variables from unrelated classes but allow them to be accessed by any subclasses that the class may have.

- `@public`

  The instance variable is accessible anywhere, even in code outside of the class that declared it or any of that class's subclasses.

- `@package`

  The instance variable is `@public` if accessed from code within the same library or framework where it is defined and `@private` otherwise. `@package` works only with the modern (64-bit) runtime. If it is used with the legacy (32-bit) runtime, it has the same meaning as `@public`.

In addition to being allowed to access the instance variable from methods inside the declaring class or one of its subclasses, `@public` enables you to treat a pointer to an instance of the class as if it were a pointer to a C structure. You can access the instance variable like this:

```
instance->instance variable;
```

> **Note**
>
> But now that I've told you that you can access instance variables directly, let me tell you not to do it. Accessing the internals of a class violates encapsulation, one of the basic principles of object-oriented programming. If you access the inner workings of a class directly and the implementation of that class changes, your code may break.

The directives go before the instance variables they describe, in the class's interface section. When given, a directive is in effect until a different directive replaces it. The default, if you don't provide a directive, is `@protected`, as shown in Listing 11.5.

Listing 11.5   *DinnerDish.h*

```
@interface DinnerDish : NSObject
{
    Chef *chef;
  @private
    Recipe *recipe;
    int     calories;
  @protected
    BOOL lowFat;
    BOOL spicy;
  @public
    NSString *description;
}

@end
```

In Listing 11.5, `DinnerDish`'s instance variables `chef`, `lowFat`, and `spicy` are `@protected`; `recipe` and `calories` are `@private`; and `description` is `@public`.

Historically, Objective-C programmers have been fairly lax about using these directives (although this is changing). Most programmers seem content to go with the default `@protected` (see the upcoming section *Security*). However, if you find yourself using a class that has instance variables marked `@private`, you should take the hint and not try to use or modify them in a category or subclass. (You would have to subvert the `@private` directive with a category to access private instance variables in a subclass.) The original programmer is telling you that those instance variables are not part of the class's public interface and might be subject to change in a future version of the class.

Hiding Your Instance Variable Declarations

One persistent criticism of Objective-C has been that it does an inadequate job of hiding the inner workings of a class. A class's interface file, which must be distributed to any code that wants to use the class, contains *too* much information. You have to declare all the class's instance variables in the interface section, even ones that were strictly for internal use only. While it has been possible to hide declarations of private methods in a class extension or private header file, all of a class's instance variables are exposed to the entire world.

This has now changed with the Clang compiler. Starting with Xcode 4.2, you can declare instance variables and properties in a class extension:

```
#import "ClassWithExtension.h"

@interface ClassWithExtension ()
{
    SomeClass *variableYouWouldRatherNotExpose;
}

@property (nonatomic, retain) SomeOtherClass *privateProperty;

@end

@implementation ClassWithExtension

@synthesize privateProperty;

...

@end
```

In fact, you don't even need a class extension. Using the Clang compiler, you can declare instance variables (but not properties) directly inside the implementation section of a class by enclosing the declaration in a pair of curly brackets:

```
#import "VariableHidingClass.h"

@implementation VariableHidingClass

{
  SomeClass *variableYouWouldRatherNotExpose;
  OtherClass *anotherVariableYouWouldRatherNotExpose;
}

- (void) someMethod;
...
@end
```

Note

The curly brackets are necessary. If you omit them, you are declaring ordinary file-scope variables, not instance variables.

This is a great improvement in encapsulation. Your class's public interface file now needs to expose only those methods and properties that you consider part of the public interface to the class. Any methods or variables that you consider part of the internal workings of your class can be hidden from public view by declaring them in a class extension or, for variables, in the class's implementation section.

Note

Instance variables that are declared in a class extension or an @implementation section are @private. The compiler won't complain if you put @protected or @public before such a declaration, but those statements do not have any effect.

Because they are declared in the class's .m file, instance variables that are declared in a class extension or an @implementation section are not visible to subclasses or categories of the original class. If you attempt to access one of these variables from a subclass or a category, you receive an undeclared symbol error. You can get around this by redeclaring these variables in a class extension section for the *original class* that is placed in your subclass or category implementation file.

Here is a class extension section for a class **MyClass**. It declares some instance variables.

```
@interface MyClass ()
{
  NSstring *instanceVariableOne;
  NSArray  *instanceVariableTwo;
}
@end
```

To make **instanceVariableOne** and **instanceVariableTwo** accessible in a subclass or category on **MyClass**, you redeclare the variables in another class extension section inside the implementation file of your subclass or category. For example, if your subclass is called **MySubclass**, place the following at the beginning of *MySubclass.m*:

```
@interface MyClass ()
{
  @protected
  NSstring *instanceVariableOne;
  NSArray  *instanceVariableTwo;
}
@end
```

Note

Although a @protected directive has no effect if it is used in the original class extension in the superclass file, when it is used in the class extension added to the subclass file, it overrules the original @private accessibility of the instance variables. The @protected is not needed if you are writing a category file. Categories have direct access to @private variables.

Access Control for Methods

There are none.

Objective-C doesn't have any notion of private, protected, and public for methods. You can send any message to any object. If the compiler thinks (by looking at the method declarations in the current scope) that the object won't respond to the message, you get a warning. But the ultimate test is at run time: If the object can respond to the message, it does. Otherwise, the object either forwards the message (if the designer of the class has arranged for that) or raises an exception.

You can try to prevent users of a class from calling methods that you consider private by putting their declarations in extensions or private category files. But, in the end, this approach functions like the lock on your front door. It keeps the honest people honest, but if someone is determined to call one of your "private" methods, there is nothing you can do to stop him or her.

> **Note**
>
> Don't use a leading underscore character to indicate private methods. Apple reserves the use of method names beginning with an underscore. If you declare a method with a name beginning with an underscore, you may inadvertently override a superclass method.

Namespaces

Objective-C doesn't have namespaces at present.

Namespaces in other languages are used to prevent name collisions between objects defined in different libraries. (Libraries in Objective-C are called *frameworks*; see Chapter 8.) If you try to link against two separate frameworks, both of which define a class `Button`, you would have problems. Most Objective-C frameworks solve this on an ad hoc basis by prepending two or three letters to the beginning of all the classes in the framework. The Cocoa frameworks use `NS` (for NeXTSTEP, of course); the button class in the AppKit framework, for example, is named `NSButton`.

Programmers (or the companies they work for) frequently define their own prefixes for all the classes defined in a project or all the cases defined in the company's code. For example, I use `CB` for classes that I write for my own company, Chromatic Bytes. However, there is no central registry or mechanism to ensure that your prefix is unique.

Security

Attempts to hide instance variables or restrict access to them are easily defeated by using a category.

Listing 11.6 shows a class with a secret:

Listing 11.6   *ClassWithSecret.h*

```
#import <Foundation/Foundation.h>

@interface ClassWithSecret : NSObject
{
  @private
    int secretNumber;
}

@end
```

The compiler doesn't allow a subclass to access the instance variable `secretNumber`—if you try, you get an error. But if you really want to get at `secretNumber`, all you have to do is define some accessor methods in a category on `ClassWithSecret`,[2] as shown in Listings 11.7 and 11.8.

Listing 11.7   *ClassWithSecret+Cheating.h*

```
#import "ClassWithSecret.h"

@interface ClassWithSecret (Cheating)

- (int) revealSecretNumber;
- (void) changeSecretNumber:(int) newSecretNumber;

@end
```

Listing 11.8   *ClassWithSecret+Cheating.m*

```
#import "ClassWithSecret+Cheating.h"

@implementation ClassWithSecret (Cheating)

- (int) revealSecretNumber;
{
  return secretNumber;
}
```

---

2. I didn't use the standard naming convention for accessors here. This is because `ClassWithSecret` might have defined methods with those names for its own internal use in a private header or extension. I don't want to accidentally replace those because if they have side effects, replacing them might break the class.

```
- (void) changeSecretNumber:(int) newSecretNumber
{
  secretNumber = newSecretNumber;
}

@end
```

The category methods work exactly as if the original creator of `ClassWithSecret` had supplied them to you as part of the `ClassWithSecret`. Using them, you can make a subclass of `ClassWithSecret` that reads and writes the `@private` variable `secretNumber` without even a warning from the compiler, as shown in Listings 11.9 and 11.10.

Listing 11.9   *CheatingNosySubclass.h*

```
#import <Foundation/Foundation.h>
#import "ClassWithSecret.h"

@interface CheatingNosySubclass : ClassWithSecret
{
}

- (void) revealSecret;
- (void) resetSecretNumber:(int) newSecretNumber;

@end
```

Listing 11.10   *CheatingNosySubclass.m*

```
#import "CheatingNosySubclass.h"
#import "ClassWithSecret+Cheating.h"

@implementation CheatingNosySubclass

- (void) revealSecret
{
  printf("The secret number is... %d\n", [self revealSecretNumber]);
}

- (void) resetSecretNumber:(int) newSecretNumber
{
  [self changeSecretNumber: newSecretNumber];
}

@end
```

> **Note**
>
> If `secretNumber` had been declared in a class extension or in the `@implementation` section of `ClassWithSecret`, you would have to redeclare it in a class extension added to *ClassWithSecret+Cheating.m*, as discussed in the section *Hiding Your Instance Variable Declarations* earlier in this chapter.

To do the preceding, you have to know the name of the instance variable. But suppose that the creator of a class hides its instance variables in a class extension or in the class's `@implementation` section. Even this doesn't really keep things secret. The information in an Objective-C executable that the runtime uses to fill its structures (including the names of instance variables) is available and can be read by any program.

Dumping a Class

The command line tool `otool` (part of the standard Mac OS X distribution) can display the instance variables and methods from an Objective-C program or framework, albeit in a somewhat cryptic format. Even better is `class-dump` (www.codethecode.com/projects/class-dump), which prints out the same information nicely formatted as Objective-C interface sections, one for each class.

`otool` and `class-dump` are useful for educational purposes, but you shouldn't use any private methods, instance variables, or frameworks that you discover. Private methods and undocumented APIs are subject to change without notice. If you do use them and they change or disappear, your program will probably break.

As noted earlier, Objective-C doesn't provide any access control for method names. You can try to hide the declaration of private methods in a class extension in the implementation file. But if somebody roots out the name and signature with `class-dump` (see the sidebar *Dumping a Class*), he or she can successfully call the method. The compiler will complain with a warning, but that problem can be evaded by crafting a custom category header file that declares the methods using the information from `class-dump`.

I certainly don't recommend that you do any of this, but you should be aware that it exists. Some newcomers find it a bit shocking, but in practice it doesn't cause much trouble—most people learn to live by the maxim that it's a bad idea to write code that depends on the undocumented internals of other people's code or libraries.

> **Note**
>
> Apple will reject an app from the OS X or iOS App Stores if it uses a private or undocumented Apple method.

However, there are some areas where you should be careful. One example is licensing code: Although it is probably inevitable that your app will be cracked, you don't want to make it any easier for a cracker, so you should probably write your licensing code or anything similarly sensitive in straight C.

Calling C Functions from Objective-C

A common question that newcomers ask is "Can I call C functions from within an Objective-C method?" I'll divide the answer into three parts: technical, practical, and philosophical.

Technical

Absolutely. Objective-C is a superset of C. You can place a call to a C function anywhere that you can put a statement or in any expression (as long as the function returns a value of the appropriate type for the expression). You can also use an object pointer as an argument to a C function, message an object (one passed in as an argument or one created inside the function) in the body of the function, or use an object pointer as a return value.

Practical

Sometimes you may have to use C functions. If you are writing a Mac OS X or iOS application, you may need to use Apple C language libraries for some tasks. A prime example is graphics. The UIKit and the AppKit provide basic drawing capabilities. To do more sophisticated drawing, you have to use the Core Graphics C API. Looking further than the world of Apple, there is a universe of third-party C libraries that do assorted useful tasks. Because Objective-C interoperates with plain C, you can link and use these libraries even if you don't have access to their source code.

Philosophical

Now we are in dangerous territory. Some object-oriented programming practitioners aren't entirely happy with using C functions. They feel you should shun straight C as much as possible. Not everyone agrees. A good way to start a long thread on an Objective-C mailing list is to ask a question like the following: "I have a mathematical routine that I need as a helper in my class. Should I just write it as a C function, place the code in my implementation file, and then call the C function from my methods?" The hard-line, object-oriented programming contingent would tell the questioner to wrap the C code and make it one of the class's methods.

It is really a matter of taste (the code will work either way), but I have the opposite view. For me, one of the wonderful things about Objective-C is that it does not require everything to be handled in a strictly object-oriented fashion. At the risk of taking some flak, I would say, "Object-oriented programming is a methodology, not a religion." It is extremely useful for a very large number of tasks, but for some tasks other methodologies are more appropriate. Many mathematical calculations are inherently procedural. There isn't really anything to be gained by putting them in an Objective-C wrapper just to say they are "object oriented." If you need to write a mathematical helper function, go ahead and write it in C. If you need to use such a function in more than one place, put the source in a separate *.c* file (or *.m* file if it refers to Objective-C objects), and place the function declaration in a matching header file. You can then include the header file and use the function wherever it is required.

Summary

Categories allow you to add methods to an existing class without requiring access to the class's source code. This provides a way to extend classes without subclassing them; the new methods become a part of the existing class. Category header files, which are just lists of method declarations, can be used to split large classes into several files or to provide separate header files for public and private methods.

Extensions provide another way to hide declarations of private methods. Objective-C methods can be private only in the sense of the visibility of their declarations. A programmer who knows the name of a method can call it successfully even if the method's declaration isn't visible.

Objective-C provides access control for instance variables with the `@public`, `@protected`, and `@private` compiler directives; however, it is possible to go around them and access `@private` variables by using a category method.

You may also hide the declarations of instance variables by placing the declarations in a class extension or between a set of curly brackets in the `@implementation` section of a class.

Exercises

1. Write a category method on `NSString` that reverses the order of words in a string. Your `-reverseWords` category method should turn the string "dog bites man" into the string "man bites dog." (The original string is the receiver and the reversed string is the method's return value.) Write a small program to test `-reverseWords`.

2. Write a class that has an extension and a program to test it. (Your class doesn't have to do anything useful; you can just put in `printf` or `NSLog` statements for the method bodies.)

    a. Temporarily omit the implementation of the method that you declare in the extension. Verify that the compiler warns you of the omission.

    b. Add the implementation of the extension method and try to call it from the test program. Verify that the compiler warns you that it cannot find the method. Then notice that you can successfully call the method anyway.

3. Verify the instance variable scope rules. Define a class that has one each of `@private`, `@protected`, and `@public` instance variables. Then:

   a. Try to access each instance variable directly (`object->instance variable`) from outside the class.

   b. Create a subclass of the original class. Try to access each instance variable from within a subclass method.

4. Write a category that snoops on the `@private` instance variable in the class you defined in Exercise 3. Use the approach shown in Listings 11.7 and 11.8.

5. Download the program **class-dump** (www.codethecode.com/projects/class-dump). Run it against some of the Objective-C programs that you have written for the exercises in this book to see what its output looks like. **class-dump** is a command line program that you run from a terminal window with this command:

   `%class-dump` *executable name*

6. Try hiding your instance variables:

   a. Write a small class that declares an instance variable inside a class extension and another instance variable directly inside your class's `@implementation` section.

   b. Write and compile a small test program that uses your class. Then run **class-dump** on the resulting executable program. Verify that, although you have hidden the class's instance variables from users of the class's interface file, they are still visible in the output of **class-dump**.

   c. Create a subclass of your class. Try accessing one of the superclass instance variables in a subclass method. What happens?

   d. Fix the problem by redeclaring the superclass instance variables in a class extension (on the original class) added to your subclass's *.m* file.

12

Properties

One of the most common programming tasks is to set or retrieve a value held in one of an object's instance variables. Although it is possible in some cases to access the instance variable directly, doing so is a bad practice. The correct way to access an instance variable is to write accessor methods. An accessor method that sets an instance variable's value is called a *setter*, and one that returns an instance variable's value is called a *getter*.

For example, if your object has the integer instance variable `numberOfDogs`, you should declare and implement the following two methods:

```
// returns the current value

-(NSInteger) numberOfDogs;

// sets a new value

-(void)setNumberOfDogs:(NSInteger) newNumberOfDogs;
```

> **Note**
>
> Naming the getter `instanceVariableName` and the setter `setInstanceVariableName` is a convention, not a requirement of the Objective-C language. But it is a convention that you should learn to follow, because certain advanced Cocoa features such as *key-value coding* depend on the convention. Key-value coding allows you to set and get the value of an instance variable by using an `NSString` key to identify the variable being accessed.
>
> Key-value coding is covered in Chapter 7 ("Key-Value Coding; Key-Value Observing") of *Cocoa Programming for Mac OS X* by Aaron Hillegass.[1]

1. Aaron Hillegass, *Cocoa Programming for Mac OS X, Third Edition* (Boston: Addison-Wesley, 2008).

The one drawback to using accessors is that they are tedious to code, especially if the class has a large number of instance variables. Objective-C 2.0 introduces a new feature called *declared properties*. It adds two new statements that reduce the work required to code and implement accessors:

- The `@property` statement provides a shorthand way to declare accessor methods.
- The `@synthesize` statement causes the compiler to write designated accessor methods for you.

> **Note**
>
> Apple refers to the feature as *declared properties* but for brevity the rest of the chapter will use the simpler *properties*.

> **Note**
>
> Most of the discussion in this chapter assumes manual reference counting. The section *A Look Ahead at Automatic Reference Counting* discusses the additional property attributes used with Automatic Reference Counting (ARC). ARC is covered fully in Chapter 16.

The chapter begins by showing you how *not* to access instance variables and then shows you the proper way to code accessor methods. The chapter continues with detailed coverage of the new declared properties feature. It covers how to declare properties, how to get the compiler to create the accessor methods and instance variables for you, and when you might want to forgo the convenience and code the accessor yourself. The final section of the chapter covers *dot syntax*, another new feature of Objective-C 2.0. Dot syntax provides an alternative to using traditional bracketed message expressions to invoke accessor methods.

Accessing Instance Variables Outside of an Object (Don't Do It)

Assume you've been asked to build a part of a business system that tracks a company's employees. Start with a very simple class that stores an employee's name, ID number, supervisor, and salary.

Listing 12.1 shows an `Employee` class that declares instance variables to hold this information.

Listing 12.1   *Employee.h*

```
@interface Employee : NSObject
{
  NSInteger   employeeNumber;
  NSString   *name;
  Employee   *supervisor;
```

```
    NSInteger  salary;
}

...

@end
```

Suppose you want to use instances of this class to calculate the total annual payroll. (You work for a responsible company and management wants to see if the company has enough money to make it through the year.) A refugee from C who is just learning object-oriented programming might be tempted to try to access the salary instance variable directly inside a loop that sums the total payroll, as shown in Listing 12.2.

Listing 12.2 **Accessing an instance variable outside of an object**

```
NSArray  *allEmployees = // ...
NSInteger payroll = 0;

for ( Employee *employee in allEmployees )
  {
    payroll += employee->salary; // BAD PRACTICE!
  }
```

This will not work as coded. The Clang compiler gives you an error for trying to access a protected variable from outside the class.[2] (Recall, from Chapter 11, "Categories, Extensions, and Security," that instance variables are protected by default. Instance variables that are protected may be accessed only by methods belonging to the class or one of the class's subclasses.)

You could eliminate the error and get the code to compile by going into *Employee.h* and declaring the instance variables `@public`. But please don't do that. It's a terrible way to do things. One of the principles of object-oriented programming is encapsulation. You should be able to use an `Employee` object without knowing anything about its internal workings. That way, if something in the class's implementation changes, code that uses that class won't break.

Declaring and Implementing Accessors

Because you are not going to access `Employee` instances' instance variables directly, you have to write some accessor methods (that is, setters and getters) to manipulate the

---

2. The gcc compiler only gives a warning for trying to access a `@protected` instance variable directly. The error message notes that in the future direct access of a `@protected` instance variable will be an error. The future is now here: The Clang compiler gives an error for directly accessing a `@protected` instance variable.

instance variables. Listing 12.3 shows a revised version of *Employee.h* that adds declarations for the accessor methods.

Listing 12.3   *Employee.h* (accessors)

```
@interface Employee : NSObject
{
  NSInteger  employeeNumber;
  NSString  *name;
  Employee  *supervisor;
  NSInteger  salary;
}

- (NSInteger) employeeNumber;

- (void) setName:(NSString*) newName;
- (NSString*) name;
- (void) setSupervisor:(Employee*) newSupervisor;
- (Employee*) supervisor;
- (void) setSalary:(NSInteger) newSalary;
- (NSInteger) salary;


...


@end
```

Notice there is no setter for the `employeeNumber` instance variable. An employee's salary, supervisor, and even name may change, but presumably the employee number is assigned when a person is hired and it never changes. (The `employeeNumber` instance variable is initialized in an `init` method when the `Employee` instance is created.)

The Form of Accessors

The typical form of a getter just returns the instance variable, as shown in Listing 12.4.

Listing 12.4   **Form of a getter**

```
- (Employee*) supervisor
{
  return supervisor;
}
```

For primitive types a typical setter is just an assign, as shown in Listing 12.5.

Listing 12.5   **Form of a setter for a primitive instance variable**

```
- (void) setSalary:(NSInteger) newSalary;
{
   salary = newSalary;
}
```

In most cases, objects that are stored in an instance variable should be retained when they are stored and released when they are replaced by a new object. The typical form of a setter that accomplishes this is shown in Listing 12.6.

Listing 12.6   **Form of a setter for an object instance variable using** `retain`

```
- (void) setSupervisor:(Employee*) newSupervisor
{
  [newSupervisor retain];
  [supervisor release];
  supervisor = newSupervisor;
}
```

Sending a **release** message to the current object stored in **supervisor** balances the **retain** message that it received when it was stored. The order of the statements in the preceding code is important. If **supervisor** and **newSupervisor** are the same object, releasing **supervisor** before retaining **newSupervisor** could cause the object to be deallocated before it can be retained. In this case a pointer to a deallocated object is stored in **supervisor** and results in a crash if **supervisor** is later used as the receiver in a message expression.

In some cases you may want to store a copy of an object rather than retaining it. This is done when you want to preserve a snapshot of the current state of the object. The form of a setter that uses **copy** is shown in Listing 12.7.

Listing 12.7   **Form of a setter using** `copy`

```
- (void) setName:(NSString*) newName
{
  NSString *oldName = name;
  name = [newName copyWithZone: nil];
  [oldName release];
}
```

Note

You must make sure that any object you copy belongs to a class that implements `copyWithZone:`.

The form of simple accessors is just boilerplate, but it can be a *lot* of boilerplate. The code to implement the accessors for just the four variables in the **Employee** class occupies almost an entire page. The properties feature of Objective-C 2.0 eliminates this drudgery in many cases, as you'll see in the next section.

Accessors Using Properties

The `Employee` class from the previous section can be recoded using `@property` statements to declare the accessors in the interface section and the `@synthesize` directive in the implementation section to tell the compiler to create their implementations. Listing 12.8 shows the revised interface section. The changes are shown in **bold**.

Listing 12.8   *Employee.h* **coded using** `@property` **statements**

```
#import <Foundation/Foundation.h>

@interface Employee : NSObject
{
  NSInteger employeeNumber;
  NSString *name;
  Employee *supervisor;
  NSInteger salary;
}

@property (nonatomic, readonly) NSInteger employeeNumber;
@property (nonatomic, retain)  NSString *name;
@property (nonatomic, retain)  Employee *supervisor;
@property (nonatomic, assign)  NSInteger salary;


...


@end
```

The `@property` statements replace the declarations for the accessor methods. This is an improvement. It's less code: A single line declares both the getter and setter (if there is one). It's also easier to read, and as a bonus, it contains some information about how the accessors are constructed. (The different attributes—the items in the parentheses—are covered in the next section.)

The real surprise is the amount of code in the implementation file, shown here in Listing 12.9.

Listing 12.9   *Employee.m*

```
#import "Employee.h"

@implementation Employee

@synthesize employeeNumber;
@synthesize name;
```

```
@synthesize supervisor;
@synthesize salary;

...

@end
```

That's all there is. The `@synthesize` statement goes in the `@implementation` section. It causes the compiler to create the accessor methods for you. End of drudgery.

To be more specific, the following line in the example causes the compiler to create the code for the two methods `setName:` and `name`, as shown here:

```
@synthesize name;
```

These two methods will exist at run time. You can call them just as if you had coded them yourself.

You may also use a single `@synthesize` for more than one property:

```
@synthesize employeeNumber, name, supervisor, salary;
```

Synthesizing the accessor methods isn't required. In some cases you may want to code them yourself to perform additional processing beyond a simple set or get. In that case, you tell the compiler that you are supplying the accessors with a `@dynamic` statement:

```
@dynamic propertyName;
```

> **Note**
>
> If you `@synthesize` a property, and also provide an implementation for one or both of the property's accessors, the compiler will use the code that you provide. For example, if you use `@synthesize` and provide an implementation for the corresponding setter, the compiler will use your implementation of the setter and synthesize the getter.

The Instance Variable Name Can Be Different from the Property Name

It is possible to use different names for a property and the instance variable that represents it. If you want to use different names, you must inform the compiler in your `@synthesize` statement:

```
@synthesize propertyName = instanceVariableName;
```

You could rename the **supervisor** instance variable in the **Employee** example (refer to Listings 12.8 and 12.9) **boss** but retain the name **supervisor** for the property. The revised interface section looks like this:

```
#import <Foundation/Foundation.h>

@interface Employee : NSObject
{
```

```
    NSInteger  employeeNumber;
    NSString  *name;
    Employee  *boss;
    NSInteger  salary;
}

@property (nonatomic, readonly) NSInteger employeeNumber;
@property (nonatomic, retain)  NSString *name;
@property (nonatomic, retain)  Employee *supervisor;
@property (nonatomic, assign)  NSInteger salary;

...

@end
```

And the implementation looks like this:

```
#import "Employee.h"

@implementation Employee

@synthesize employeeNumber;
@synthesize name;
@synthesize supervisor = boss;
@synthesize salary;
...

@end
```

The synthesized accessors are still `supervisor` and `setSupervisor:`. The name `boss` is only used internally.

Synthesized Instance Variables

If you are writing programs that will use the modern runtime (anything other than a Mac OS X program compiled as a 32-bit program), you can eliminate another bit of typing. You can omit the instance variable declaration between the curly brackets, and the compiler will automatically create the instance variable for you, using the specification in the property statement. If all your instance variables are synthesized, you may also omit the curly brackets:

```
@interface Greeter : NSObject

@property (nonatomic, retain) NSString *greetingText;

...

@end
```

When you @synthesize the property greetingText, the compiler creates both accessor methods *and* the instance variable. Again, this works only with the modern runtime. If you try to compile the preceding code for the legacy runtime, you get the following error:

```
error: synthesized property 'greetingText' must either be named
the same as a compatible instance variable or must explicitly
name an instance variable
```

The synthesized instance variable is just as good as one explicitly declared between the curly brackets of an @interface section. It even shows up in the output of class-dump.

Synthesized instance variables can be accessed directly only in the main implementation section of a class or in a category or subclass that is coded in the same *.m* file as the class's main implementation section. Attempting to access a synthesized instance variable directly in any other situation causes an error message that the variable is an undeclared identifier. If you want to access a synthesized instance variable in a subclass or in a category that is coded in a separate file, you should use the variable's accessor methods.

@synthesize **by Default**

Prior to Xcode 4.4 the default compiler directive for property synthesis was @dynamic. If you didn't explicitly code either @synthesize or @dynamic for a property, the compiler assumed @dynamic. You were expected to provide the code for the property's accessor methods. Xcode 4.4 reverses this. The default compiler directive for property synthesis is now @synthesize. If you don't specify @synthesize or @dynamic, the compiler assumes @synthesize, and it will synthesize both the accessor methods *and the instance variable* for you.

There is a slight wrinkle in this. If the name of the property is myProperty, the name of the synthesized variable is _myProperty, that is, myProperty with a leading underscore. To clarify: If you don't specify @synthesize or @dynamic, it is equivalent to coding

```
@synthesize myProperty = _myProperty;
```

Now for a bit of potential confusion. To be backward compatible with code written before Xcode 4.4, if you specify @synthesize but don't declare an instance variable, the synthesized instance variable for the property myProperty is named just myProperty. Coding

```
@synthesize myProperty;
```

in this case is equivalent to coding

```
@synthesize myProperty = myProperty;
```

Of course, if you use an explicit @synthesize, you can still use any name you like for the synthesized instance variable:

```
@synthesize myProperty = someOtherName;
```

> **Note**
>
> If you have explicitly coded the setter, getter, or both for a property, the compiler will use your accessor rather than synthesize one. An explicitly coded accessor always prevents the compiler from synthesizing the same accessor.

Doesn't Apple Reserve Leading Underscores for Themselves?

This has been a point of confusion and misinformation over the years. The official policy is: Apple doesn't reserve variable names with leading underscores for their own use. You are free to start variable names with an underscore. In fact, Apple encourages you to do so for instance variables. Apple *does* reserve method names that begin with an underscore for their own use. If you name one of your methods with a leading underscore, you run the risk of colliding with or accidentally overriding one of Apple's private methods.

Synthesis Summary

The following two sections summarize the behavior of @dynamic, @synthesize, and synthesize by default for a property named myProperty.

Explicit Declaration

If you code @dynamic or @synthesize:

- For @dynamic, you are on your own. You must code the accessors yourself, and you must declare an instance variable for myProperty (if it is to be backed by an instance variable; see the section *Properties without Instance Variables* later in this chapter).

- For @synthesize, the compiler synthesizes any accessor that you have not coded yourself. It synthesizes an instance variable if you have not explicitly declared one. The synthesized instance variable is named myProperty unless you set another name in @synthesize. If you code
  ```
  @synthesize myProperty = someOtherName;
  ```
  the synthesized instance variable is named someOtherName.

Synthesize by Default

If you don't code either @dynamic or @synthesize:

- If you don't supply either accessor, the compiler synthesizes both accessors and synthesizes an instance variable named _myProperty.

- If you code one accessor, the compiler synthesizes the other accessor and synthesizes an instance variable named _myProperty.
- If you code both accessors, the compiler does not synthesize anything. This means that you must also supply an explicitly declared instance variable if one is required.

> **Note**
>
> There is one quirk here. If you are doing synthesize by default and you let the compiler synthesize one or both accessors *and* you declare an explicit myProperty instance variable, the compiler still synthesizes the instance variable _myProperty. Your class then has *two* instance variables: myProperty and _myProperty. The accessor methods -setMyProperty and -myProperty set and get the instance variable _myProperty.

Private Properties

You may have properties that represent some private state of your class. If you don't want to expose these properties to users of your class by declaring them in the class's interface file, you can declare these properties in a class extension in the class's implementation file:

```
@interface MyClass ()

@property (nonatomic, assign) NSInteger private_1;
@property (nonatomic, retain) NSString* private_2;

...

@end
```

> **Note**
>
> Declaring properties in a class extension hides the property *declarations* from users of your class. But it does not prevent someone who does not want to play by the rules from invoking the accessors for those properties if he or she discovers the properties by using otool or class-dump on your class.

The @property Statement

The form of a property declaration is

```
@property ( attributes )   type name;
```

type and *name* are self-explanatory. The *attributes* provide information about how the accessors are coded. They are described in the subsections that follow.

assign, retain, copy

These attributes affect how the synthesized setter is constructed. If you use `assign`, the setter simply assigns the new value to your property:

```
myProperty = newValue;
```

The `assign` attribute is the only choice allowed for a non-object property.

For an object property under reference counting, `assign` creates a *weak reference* (see Chapter 15, "Reference Counting").

If you use `retain` and ask the compiler to `@synthesize` your accessors, it creates a setter equivalent to the one shown in Listing 12.6 earlier in the chapter. If you use `copy` and ask the compiler to `@synthesize` your accessors, it creates a setter equivalent to the one shown in Listing 12.7.

> **Note**
>
> To use `copy`, the type of the property must be a class that can be copied. The class must adopt the `NSCopying` protocol by implementing `-copyWithZone:` (see Chapter 6, "Classes and Objects").

If you don't explicitly specify `assign`, `retain`, or `copy`, the compiler assumes a default value of `assign`. This isn't a problem for primitive types. However, for object properties under reference counting, you will get a compiler warning if you don't specify one of the three.

How do you decide between copying and retaining? It depends on the design of your objects and what the property represents. If the property is meant to be a snapshot of the current state of an object that is mutable, you should copy it.

If the object used to set a property is meant to model an entity itself rather than the entity's current state, you should retain it. Imagine that the business system has various objects with properties (`president`, `vicePresident`, `employeeOfTheMonth` . . .) of type `Employee`. You don't want to chase through the entire system to update all the copies of `Employee` if something (`name`, `salary`, `...`) about the employee changes. Using `retain` (or `assign` if you want a weak reference) in this case ensures that all instance variables that are meant to hold a given employee refer to the same instance of `Employee`.

readwrite, readonly

If a property is declared `readwrite`, the property's value can be set as well as retrieved. Both accessors are synthesized. This is the default. If the property is declared `readonly`, only a getter is synthesized. If you attempt to use the (non-existent) method `setMyProperty:`, your program crashes with a "does not respond to selector" exception.

nonatomic

Properties that are not declared **nonatomic** are atomic by default. When you specify **nonatomic**, the compiler synthesizes accessors without regard for thread safety.

> **Note**
>
> When properties were first introduced, there was no **atomic** keyword. Properties were declared atomic by leaving out the **nonatomic** keyword. There is now an **atomic** keyword. It is not mentioned in most of the current documentation, but it is present and works as expected. However, most people still create atomic properties by leaving out the **nonatomic** keyword.

When accessing a property in a multithreaded program, it is possible for a thread to be interrupted by another thread before a set or get is completed. This can result in mayhem such as over-releases, objects with an incorrect reference count, or getters that return a pointer to a deallocated object.

To prevent this, you can declare the property **atomic** (or omit the **nonatomic** keyword). Then, the synthesized accessors will be atomic; a set or a get will complete correctly without interference from another thread.

For a non-object property the getter is a simple **return** statement and the setter is a simple assignment that is always atomic. For object properties under reference counting, life is more difficult. The synthesized setter and getter use locks to prevent another thread from interrupting the set or get. In addition, the getter retains and then autoreleases the returned object.

> **Note**
>
> This behavior on the part of the getter prevents another thread from releasing the object, potentially causing the object's retain count to go to zero before your thread has a chance to use or retain it.

The locks come at a cost in performance, so if you are not writing multithreaded code, you should declare your properties **nonatomic**. Then, the synthesized accessors won't use locks. The getter simply returns the object, and the setters look like the examples shown in Listings 12.6 and 12.7.

setter=name, getter=name

Normally, the synthesized names for the property **myProperty** would be **setMyProperty** and **myProperty** for the setter and getter, respectively. **setter=name** and **getter=name** allow you to provide alternate names. The primary use for this is to allow the getter for a Boolean property, such as **caffeinated**, to be named **isCaffeinated**, as shown here:

```
@property (nonatomic, getter=isCaffeinated) BOOL caffeinated;
```

This improves the readability of your code.

attributes and @dynamic

If you provide your own implementation of the accessor methods, the compiler does not check to see that the methods you supply agree with the attributes in the corresponding @property declaration. It silently lets you do unwholesome things such as assign to a property that you have declared copy, or provide a setter method for a property declared as readonly.

More about @dynamic

The opposite of @synthesize is @dynamic. When you specify @dynamic for a property, the compiler expects you to supply your own implementation of the accessor methods for that property. If you don't, you'll get a warning at compile time, and then an error at run time when you try to use the property. Declaring a property to be @dynamic also tells the compiler not to synthesize an instance variable for the property, even if you have not explicitly declared an instance variable for that property. As you will see in the following section, it is possible to have a property that does not have a corresponding instance variable.

Why would you want to write the accessor methods when the compiler can do the work for you? The compiler synthesizes only relatively simple accessors that just set or return the property. Sometimes you may need to do more. You might need to take some other actions when a property is set. For example, you might want to filter the input to make sure the property being set stays within an acceptable range.

Consider a property that holds the volume setting for a speaker:

```
#define kMaxVolume 1.0
#define kMinVolume 0.0
{
  float speakerVolume;
}
@property (atomic, assign) float speakerVolume;
```

If the acceptable values run from 0.0 to 1.0, you can write a setter that clamps the new value to that range:

```
- (void) setSpeakerVolume: (float) newVolume
{
  // protect against out of range input
  if (newVolume > kMaxVolume)
    {
      speakerVolume = kMaxVolume;
    }
  else if (newVolume < kMinVolume)
    {
      speakerVolume = kMinVolume;
    }
```

```
      else
        {
          speakerVolume = newVolume;
        }
    }
```

Properties without Instance Variables

Another reason to code your own accessors is that there might not even *be* an instance variable corresponding to a property. Properties are actually a generalized description of an object's public interface. They represent the characteristics or state of an object that you expose to a user of the object. But properties don't necessarily specify the object's internal structure. Properties are usually stored in instance variables (and most of the discussion in this chapter focuses on this case), but they don't have to be. They could be stored in a helper object that your object owns, stored externally in a file, or even calculated on the fly. It doesn't matter as long as the getter returns the property and the setter (if there is one) sets it.

Here's an example where the property returned by the getter is calculated. Consider a `RestaurantEmployee` class:

```
#import <Foundation/Foundation.h>

@interface RestaurantEmployee : NSObject
{
  NSInteger age;
  ...
}

@property (nonatomic, assign) NSInteger age;
@property (nonatomic, readonly) BOOL canServeBeer;
...

@end
```

In some places there is a law that an employee must be above a certain age to serve alcohol, so you should define a read-only Boolean property `canServeBeer`. You don't have to actually store `canServeBeer` in its own instance variable; you can compute it from the `age` instance variable as follows:

```
#import "RestaurantEmployee.h"

@implementation RestaurantEmployee

@synthesize age;
@dynamic canServeBeer;
```

```
- (BOOL) canServeBeer
{
  if ( [self age] >= 21 )
    return YES;
  else
    return NO;
}

...

@end
```

Properties and Memory Management

Using properties and synthesized setters or correctly hand-coded setters takes a lot of work out of reference counting. As long as you make sure that you always use an instance variable's setter method to set its value, most of your reference counting takes place without any further work on your part.

> **Note**
>
> It is good practice to use the accessor methods, even when accessing an instance variable from within a method. A possible exception to this rule is when you refer to an instance variable in an `init` or `dealloc` method. Some experienced Objective-C programmers (myself included) feel that these are purely internal operations. Your object is in the process of being constructed in an `init` method or torn down in a `dealloc` method. The object may not be in a consistent state when these methods are executed. Also, in typical cases of initialization or deallocation, you may not want or need the side effects that may be caused by invoking accessor methods. In an `init` method, you should set the instance variable directly (retaining the object you are storing if that is required). In a `dealloc` method, you should release the instance variable directly instead of invoking the instance variable's setter with a `nil` argument.
>
> However, this is one of those issues where people disagree. You will find people who argue the other way and insist that you should always use the accessor methods even in `init` and `dealloc`.

dealloc

It would be nice if you could go out and get a latte while the compiler does all your work for you. Although properties are a step in that direction, you still have to do some work yourself. The compiler can synthesize your accessor methods, but if you are not using ARC, it doesn't completely take care of memory management. If your class has any properties that are retained or copied, you have to remember to release those objects in the class's `dealloc` method. Even here, properties are helpful. Looking at the property declarations reminds you which objects need releasing.

The `dealloc` method for the `Employee` class from Listing 12.9 looks like this:

```
- (void) dealloc
{
  [name release];
  [supervisor release];
  [super dealloc];
}
```

A Look Ahead at Automatic Reference Counting (ARC)

As mentioned earlier, when you use the Clang compiler's new ARC feature, the compiler takes care of your memory management for you. It analyzes your code and inserts `retain`, `release`, and `autorelease` messages for you. You can still use properties, but there are a couple of alternate names for existing property attributes and one new attribute.

strong

The `strong` attribute is a synonym for `retain`.

```
@property (nonatomic, strong) NSArray *myArray;
```

When you declare a property as `strong`, the compiler makes sure that the synthesized setter retains the incoming object.

weak

A property with the `weak` attribute makes its corresponding instance variable a *zeroing weak reference*.

```
@property (nonatomic, weak) NSArray *myArray;
```

The object held in `myArray` is not retained. If that object is deallocated, `myArray` is automatically set to `nil`. This prevents you from accidentally using a pointer to a deallocated object.

unsafe_unretained

The `unsafe_unretained` attribute is a synonym for `assign`.

```
@property (nonatomic, unsafe_unretained) NSArray *myArray;
```

An `unsafe_unretained` property is also a weak reference. However, the corresponding instance variable is *not* automatically set to `nil` when the object stored in it is deallocated. It is unsafe because it may hold a reference to a deallocated object.

You'll learn more about ARC in Chapter 16.

Subclassing and Properties

A subclass inherits any properties (and their accessors) from its superclass. You can repeat the property statement in the subclass header (for the purposes of documentation), but the compiler complains unless the property statement is the same in both the original and subclass header files.

There is one exception: You can redeclare a **readonly** property to be **readwrite** in the subclass. This allows you to follow the common design pattern of having a mutable subclass of an immutable class.

For example, start with a **Shape** object that is given a permanent color at creation time:

```
@interface Shape : NSObject
{
  NSColor *color;
  ...
}

@property (nonatomic, retain, readonly) NSColor *color;

  ...
@end
```

Now, let's define a subclass of **Shape**, **ColorableShape**, that permits color changes:

```
@interface ColorableShape : Shape
{
}
@property (nonatomic, retain, readwrite) NSColor *color;

...

@end
```

This is the corresponding **@implementation** section:

```
@implementation ColorableShape

@dynamic color;

- (void) setColor:(NSColor*) newColor
{
  if (color != newColor)
    {
      [newColor retain];
      [color release];
```

```
        color = newColor;
    }
}

@end
```

You have to be careful here. If you use @synthesize in ColorableShape instead of using @dynamic, you get an error:

```
Property 'color' attempting to use ivar 'color' declared
in super class 'Shape'
```

Hidden Setters for readonly Properties

You can use a similar strategy to provide a hidden setter (for internal use) for properties that are publicly declared as readonly. You do this by redeclaring the readonly property in an extension in the class's *.m* file (see Chapter 11, "Categories, Extensions, and Security"). To make employeeNumber in the Employee class from Listings 12.8 and 12.9 writable internally, you can modify Listing 12.9 to look like this:

```
#import "Employee.h"

@interface Employee ()
@property (nonatomic, readwrite) int employeeNumber;
@end

@implementation Employee

@synthesize employeeNumber;
@synthesize name;
@synthesize supervisor;
@synthesize salary;
...

@end
```

Now the compiler synthesizes both accessors. setEmployeeNumber: is visible for internal use in the implementation file, but not visible to users of the Employee class.

> **Note**
>
> As noted in Chapter 11, "Categories, Extensions, and Security," there is nothing to prevent a user of the Employee class from calling setEmployeeNumber if he or she discovers its existence by guessing or dumping the class.

Properties as Documentation

In addition to their other virtues, properties serve as a form of documentation for your classes. They are more compact and more readable than the method declarations they replace, and they carry more information. They tell you if a property is read-only, something about how the property is stored, and whether its accessors are thread safe.

Look at the property declaration for the `employeeNumber` property in the `Employee` class:

```
@property (nonatomic, readonly) NSInteger employeeNumber;
```

It tells you immediately that `employeeNumber` is read-only. You don't have to go looking through the entire header file to see if the getter has a matching setter.[3] This is obviously a trivial point for the small example classes in this chapter, but the header files in real systems can be much larger. *NSWindow.h*, the header file for Cocoa's `NSWindow` class, is more than 650 lines and has almost 250 method declarations.

Dot Syntax

Along with properties, Objective-C 2.0 also introduces a new syntax, called *dot syntax*, which is shorthand syntax for calling accessor methods.

Instead of writing code like this:

```
Employee *employee =  // ...

NSInteger currentSalary = [employee salary];
[employee setSalary: 100000];
```

you can write

```
Employee *employee =  // ...

NSInteger currentSalary = employee.salary;
employee.salary = 1000000;
```

At run time, the dot syntax is pure "syntactic sugar." These two examples produce exactly the same executable code.

Syntactic Sugar

Syntactic sugar is syntax added to a computer language to make code written in that language more readable for human programmers. It has no effect on the binary that a compiler produces or the execution of the resulting program. For example, as you saw

---

3. The order of method declarations in a header file has no effect on the resulting binary, but for the sake of anyone looking at the file, related methods should be placed in close proximity. Unfortunately, like other ideals, not everyone lives up to this one.

in Chapter 1, "C, the Foundation of Objective-C," the elements of a regular C array are actually accessed by pointer. The following two statements do the same thing. Both set the third element of an array of integers `someArray` to 17:

```
*(someArray + 2) = 17;
someArray[2] = 17;
```

The second form, which uses brackets, is syntactic sugar. It results in the same executable code as the pointer expression, but it is easier to read.

Although using dot syntax makes no difference at run time, it has advantages when you write programs. Using dot syntax requires less typing when you write code—an advantage for the impatient and those with tendon problems. And when you are familiar with the dot syntax, it can make the code easier to read. This is more apparent when you need to refer to a property of a property (of a property . . .). Define a `Manager` subclass of `Employee` with an additional `assistant` property:

```
@property(nonatomic, retain) Employee *assistant;
```

Setting the assistant's salary like this:

```
Manager *manager = //...
manager.assistant.salary = 50000;
```

is easier to type and read than

```
Manager *manager = //...
[[manager assistant] setSalary: 50000];
```

When you use dot syntax, the compiler is stricter when checking your code. If you try to set a read-only property like this:

```
Employee *employee = // ...
[employee setEmployeeNumber: 999];
```

you will get a warning:

```
warning: 'Employee' may not respond to '-setEmployeeNumber:'
```

And if you then try to run the program, it will crash because the property is `readonly` and there is no `-setEmployeeNumber:`.

However, if you try to set a read-only property using dot syntax, like this:

```
Employee *employee = // ...
employee.setEmployeeNumber = 999;
```

compiling results in an error instead of a warning:

```
error: object cannot be set - either readonly property or no setter found
```

By flagging this as an error rather than a warning, the compiler saves you from a future crash by forcing you to fix the problem before you can run your program.

Similarly, trying to set a property that doesn't exist like this:

```
[employee setCaffeinationLevel: 100];
```

only gets you a compiler warning (and, again, a runtime crash), whereas the following gets you a compiler error:

```
employee.caffeinationLevel = 100;
```

> **Note**
>
> Warnings about unknown method names become errors under ARC. See Chapter 16, "ARC."

Dot Syntax and Properties

This chapter has discussed dot syntax in terms of properties, but the two concepts are actually independent of each other. Dot syntax is not dependent on properties. You can use the accessors defined by property statements directly without using dot syntax. Conversely you can use dot syntax with accessors that are defined without a @property declaration. If you code this:

```
NSInteger raise = // ...
Employee *employee = // ...

NSInteger salary = employee.salary;
salary += raise;
employee.salary = salary;
```

all that counts is whether `Employee` defines and implements the two methods `salary` and `setSalary:`. It doesn't care whether the methods are declared with a `@property` statement or the traditional way. It also doesn't care whether the method implementations are synthesized or coded explicitly.

Dot Syntax and C Structures

The dot syntax has caused a lot of grumbling in some quarters. Some people just don't like syntactic sugar. Others point out that the dot already has a perfectly good meaning in C: It's how you access members of a structure. Their objection is that the dot syntax *hinders* readability because correctly interpreting an expression like the following:

```
foo.bar.baz
```

requires that you know for each—`foo`, `bar`, and `baz`—whether it is an object or a structure. They further object that this apparent ambiguity makes it difficult for newcomers to learn the language. There have been a lot of bits spilled on both sides of this topic in various blogs. The subject has the makings of yet another (small-scale) computer science religious war. Apple's official position on whether or not to use dot syntax is that it is a personal preference. You can use it or you can use the traditional bracket notation. Either works. But whether or not you choose to use the dot syntax in your own code, you should be able to read and understand it, as Apple is using dot syntax extensively in their sample code.

I can't do anything for *saccharophobia*,[4] but, as for the ambiguity issue, you (and the compiler) can properly parse a dot expression by examining the type of each component in the expression. If you define a structure:

```
struct vector3
{
    float x, y, z;
};
```

you can use it as a property in a class:

```
@interface Rocket : NSObject
{
    vector3 velocity;
    ...
}

@property (nonatomic) vector3 velocity;
    ...
@end
```

To get the vertical component of a rocket's velocity, you can write

```
Rocket *rocket = // ...
float verticalVelocity = rocket.velocity.z;
```

Working from left to right, `rocket.velocity` is a `vector3` structure. Therefore, the next dot is the structure member operator.

Dot Syntax Doesn't Access Instance Variables Directly

The similarity between the dot syntax for accessor methods and the syntax for referencing an element of a C structure leads some people to assume that the dot syntax is accessing instance variables directly. If that were true, it would be a gross violation of the "information hiding" principle, but it's not true. The dot syntax just invokes the appropriate accessor method. Any side effects (`retain`, `release`, `copy`, or anything else) happen just as if you had coded the statement using the traditional syntax.

One situation where you have to pay attention to this is when you use an object's instance variables inside its own methods. Consider the `Employee` class from Listing 12.1. Coding the following:

```
name = newName;
```

---

4. *saccharophobia*: Fear of sugar.

inside one of `Employee`'s methods sets the instance variable `name` directly with an assign.

Using the dot syntax like this:

```
self.name = newName;
```

sets `name` using the `setName:` method. This is not a trivial difference: In the second example, `newName` is retained, whereas it isn't in the first example.

If you don't pay attention to this issue, you might make the following classic mistake. Imagine that you have synthesized a retained property:

```
@property (nonatomic, retain) Foo *myFoo;
```

Then, in your `init` method you code the following:

```
self.myFoo = [[Foo alloc] init];
```

The object stored in the instance variable `myFoo` now has a retain count of two: one from the `alloc` and one from the `retain` message in the synthesized setter. When you send `myFoo` a `release` message in your `dealloc` method, the retain count of the object held in `myFoo` does not go to zero and the object is leaked. Either of the following lines fixes the problem:

```
self.myFoo = [[[Foo alloc] init] autorelease];
myFoo = [[Foo alloc] init];
```

Note that the first line of the preceding code uses the property's setter while the second line bypasses the setter. If the setter has other side effects besides retaining the object, you must decide whether you want those side effects to occur when the object is assigned.

Summary

The main focus of this chapter has been how to set and retrieve the values stored in an object's instance variables using the new Objective-C 2.0 declared property feature. These are the main points to remember about accessing instance variables and using properties:

- You should access an object's instance variables by using accessor methods to set and get the instance variables' value. You shouldn't access the instance variables directly from outside the object.

- The `@property` statement lets you declare the accessor methods in a convenient shorthand form.

- Property declarations provide extra information about the accessor methods such as whether object instance variables are assigned, retained, or copied, and whether the accessors use locks to ensure atomicity.

- When accessors are declared with a property declaration, you can ask the compiler to create the code for the accessor methods for you by using a @synthesize directive. The synthesized accessor reflects the attributes specified in the @property statement.

- If you don't declare an instance variable for a synthesized property, the compiler will synthesize an instance variable for you.

- Starting with Xcode 4.4, the default, if you don't specify either @synthesize or @dynamic, is @synthesize.

- Using @synthesize creates very basic accessors that only set or retrieve the property value. If you need to do extra processing when accessing a property (for example, clamping an input value to a specified range), you can use @dynamic and code the accessor for the property yourself.

- Objective-C 2.0 also introduces the dot syntax, a shorthand way to call accessor methods.

Exercises

1. Design and code a **TripDuration** class that has instance variables for a trip's distance, the speed at which the trip is traveled, and a name for the trip. **TripDuration** should include a method for returning how long the trip will take based on the formula **time = distance/speed**. Declare and implement the accessor methods without using properties.

   When you are finished, write a small test program that uses the **TripDuration** class. It should allocate a trip **TripDuration** object; set the distance, speed, and trip name; and then retrieve the trip duration. It should also log the **TripDuration** by printing out the distance, speed, time, and trip name.

2. Rewrite the **TripDuration** class using properties. Make **duration** a **readonly** property (even though it has no corresponding instance variable). Use @synthesize where it is appropriate.

3. Comment out your @synthesize statements and build your program. What happens?

4. You don't want to get a speeding ticket, so rewrite **TripDuration** to limit the speed to some reasonable value. Also, if the speed is zero, the trip will take an infinite amount of time. Computers don't like infinities, so make sure that speed has some minimum value. (This means that speed has to be @dynamic and that you have to write those accessors yourself.)

5. Leave the previous version of **TripDuration** alone, but rewrite your test program to use dot syntax when calling **TripDuration**'s accessors.

13

Protocols

A *protocol* is a defined set of methods that a class can choose to implement. Protocols are useful when an object needs to talk to one or more other objects but doesn't know (or particularly care about) the class of those other objects. Objective-C protocols are the equivalent of Java interfaces. In fact, the designers of Java borrowed the concept from Objective-C. Protocols are used throughout the Cocoa frameworks. Objective-C has both *formal* and *informal* protocols. A formal protocol declares a set of required methods and perhaps some optional methods. A class can then *adopt* the protocol by implementing all the protocol's required methods. When a class declares that it adopts a formal protocol, the compiler checks to see that the class implements all the protocol's required methods. An informal protocol is merely a list of method declarations in a category header that a class could choose to implement. Most uses of informal protocols in the Cocoa frameworks are being replaced by formal protocols.

> **Note**
>
> In this chapter, except in the section titled *Informal Protocols* at the end, the word *protocol* refers to a formal protocol.

In this chapter you will learn when to use a protocol, how to declare a formal protocol, and how to code a class that adopts a formal protocol. The chapter then goes through a complete example, a `TablePrinter` class. A `TablePrinter` object can print data from another object in the form of a table. A `TablePrinter` does not need to know the class of the object that is supplying the data. The only thing a `TablePrinter` needs to know is that the object supplying its data belongs to a class that adopts the `TablePrinterDataSource` formal protocol.

The Rationale for Protocols

As an example, suppose you want to design a drafting (mechanical drawing) system. You could ask your users to draw everything from scratch with lines and arcs, but it would be much more convenient if you could supply them with libraries of common components, like nuts and bolts, that know how to draw themselves. Let's call these components *drawable items*.

The view object that is doing the drawing doesn't really care about what class a drawable item belongs to. It cares only that an object that is a drawable item can respond to a specified set of messages. A drawable item should be able to return a bounding rectangle (so you can see if it is visible on screen), set and get its color, and draw itself. An instance of any class that implements these methods will work as a drawable item.[1]

If you gather these methods together and give the collection a name, you have a protocol. A class that implements a protocol's methods is said to *adopt* the protocol. As you will see later in the chapter, a class advertises the protocols that it adopts in its interface section.

Why Not Just Use Inheritance?

Why not just have all the drawable items in the program inherit from a single `DrawableItem` abstract class that declares the necessary methods?

That's possible, and you might even do it that way if you were designing a small system with a limited number of drawable items. However, under other circumstances, subclassing is an awkward solution: The classes that represent various components that you need to draw might have been created (for other purposes and with their own object hierarchy) before you started your program. They may have been supplied to you by a third party. Adding functionality to implement a protocol is a much cleaner solution than refactoring an entire class hierarchy to push in an abstract class near the top. The beauty of protocols is that only functionality matters, not class.

Using Protocols

In this section I'll continue with the drawable item example to show you the mechanics of declaring and using protocols. Later in the chapter I'll go through a different example protocol in detail.

Declaring a Protocol

You declare a protocol by declaring its methods between `@protocol` and `@end` compiler directives. By convention, protocol names follow the same naming scheme as class names. They are CamelCased with the first letter capitalized.

---

1. This is obviously a highly simplified example. In a real drafting system you would need methods to set a component's position and orientation, and methods for obtaining dimensioning and other information.

For the `DrawableItem` protocol, the declaration looks like this:

```
@protocol DrawableItem
- (void) drawItem;
- (NSRect) boundingBox;
- (NSColor*) color;
- (void) setColor:(NSColor*) color;
@end
```

The protocol declaration goes in a header file, so you could put this declaration in a header file named *DrawableItem.h*. There is no corresponding implementation file. Each class that adopts the protocol provides its own implementations of the protocol methods.

Prior to Objective-C 2.0, a class that adopted a protocol was required to implement all of the protocol's declared methods. Objective-C 2.0 allows you to mark protocol methods as either optional or required:

- A class that adopts a protocol must implement all of the protocol's required methods.

- A class that adopts a protocol is free to implement or not implement any of the protocol's optional methods.

- Optional and required methods are marked off with the `@optional` and `@required` directives, respectively. The methods are considered in the order that they are declared in the file. Methods declared following a `@required` directive are required.

- `@required` is the default. If you do not specify either `@required` or `@optional`, the methods are required.

In the drafting example, some drawable items might supply text to use as a label. For example, you could use an optional method to get the text, as shown here:

```
@protocol DrawableItem

@required
- (void) drawItem;
- (NSRect) boundingBox;
- (NSColor*) color;
- (void) setColor:(NSColor*) color;

@optional
- (NSString) labelText;

@end
```

If a particular `DrawableItem` class has some label text, it implements the `-labelText` method; otherwise, it doesn't. It is up to any class using a `DrawableItem` to check if a given `DrawableItem` implements `-labelText`.

Adopting a Protocol

A class adopts a protocol by implementing all the protocol's required methods and any or none of the protocol's optional methods. You tell the compiler that your class is adopting a protocol by adding the protocol name, enclosed in angle brackets, to the class's @interface line:

```
@interface AcmeUniversalBolt : AcmeComponent <DrawableItem>
```

A class conforms to a protocol if it adopts the protocol or if it inherits from a class that adopts the protocol.

A class can adopt more than one protocol. The protocols are listed, separated by commas, between a single set of angle brackets. If AcmeUniversalBolt conforms to the NSCopying protocol (by implementing copyWithZone:) as well as to DrawableItem, its @interface line would look like this:

```
@interface AcmeUniversalBolt : AcmeComponent <DrawableItem, NSCopying>
```

The order in which the protocols are listed is not important.

Protocols as Types

You can declare a variable to be a type that holds an object conforming to a protocol by adding the protocol name to the type declaration:

```
id <DrawableItem> currentGraphic;
```

This tells the compiler nothing about what class currentGraphic is, only that it conforms to the DrawableItem protocol. If you try to assign an object that doesn't conform to the DrawableItem protocol to currentGraphic, the compiler complains.

It's also possible to be more restrictive:

```
AcmeComponent<DrawableItem> *currentGraphic;
```

This tells the compiler that currentGraphic is an instance of the AcmeComponent class or one of its subclasses and that its class implements the DrawableItem protocol.

> **Note**
>
> This construction is rarely seen. The whole point of protocols is that users of a conforming object don't have to know anything about its class, only that it conforms to the protocol.

Properties and Protocols

If some of your protocol methods are accessor methods, you can declare them in the protocol header using property statements. In the DrawableItem example, the protocol declaration might look like this:

```
@protocol  DrawableItem

@required
- (void) drawItem;
@property (nonatomic, readonly) NSRect boundingBox;
@property (nonatomic, retain) NSColor *color;

@optional
@property (nonatomic, retain) NSString *labelText;

@end
```

Any class adopting the protocol would have to either synthesize the accessors corresponding to the properties or provide implementations for them, just as if the properties were declared in the class's `@interface` section.

Starting with Mac OS X 10.6, you may declare properties in a protocol as `@optional`. If you use this example on Mac OS X 10.5, you have to use regular method declarations to declare the optional setter and getter for `labelText`.

TablePrinter **Example**

Let's look at another example in detail. The `TablePrinter` class provides a table printing service for other objects. It prints a single-column table of strings with an optional title and optional line numbers. A `TablePrinter` can create a table for *any* object as long as the object conforms to the `TablePrinterDataSource` protocol. This is an attractive way to do business. The `TablePrinter` itself never stores any of the data used in the table. It doesn't have to know what class the data source is or anything about it, only that the data source can answer certain questions (via a message) like "How many rows are in this table?" or "What information goes in row j?"

> **Note**
>
> The `TablePrinter` class mimics, in a simplified fashion, the behavior of the AppKit's `NSTableView` (on the desktop) and the UIKit's `UITableView` (on iOS). `NSTableView` and `UITableView` are more complicated classes than `TablePrinter`, but both get the data they display in the same way as a `TablePrinter`. They take a `dataSource` object that is expected to conform to a protocol and then query the data source using methods from the protocol.

The code for the `TablePrinter` example is described in the next several sections and consists of the following files:

- *TablePrinterDataSource.h* defines the `TablePrinterDataSource` protocol (see Listing 13.1).
- *TablePrinter.h* and *TablePrinter.m* are the interface and implementation files for the `TablePrinter` class (see Listings 13.2 and 13.3).

- *FruitBasket.h* and *FruitBasket.m* are the interface and implementation files for a FruitBasket class (see Listings 13.4 and 13.5). This is a simple class that is used to test the TablePrinter.
- *TablePrinterExample.m* is the main routine for a program that creates a FruitBasket and uses a TablePrinter to print a table of the FruitBasket's contents (see Listing 13.6).

When you are done reading this section, you should build and then run the program.

TablePrinterDataSource

The TablePrinter can print a table for any object that conforms to the TablePrinterDataSource protocol that is shown in Listing 13.1.

Listing 13.1   TablePrinter/*TablePrinterDataSource.h*

```
#import <Foundation/Foundation.h>

@protocol TablePrinterDataSource

@required
- (int) numberOfRowsInTable;
- (NSString*) stringForRowAtIndex:(int) index;


@optional
- (NSString*) tableTitle;
- (BOOL) printLineNumbers;

@end
```

The protocol has two required methods:

- numberOfRowsInTable tells the TablePrinter the number of rows in the table.
- stringForRowAtIndex: supplies the data (an NSString) for the requested index.

There are also two optional methods: one to provide the table's title (tableTitle) and one to specify whether the TablePrinter should use line numbers (printLineNumbers). If these two methods are not implemented, the TablePrinter uses "Table" for the title and skips the line numbers.

TablePrinter

Listing 13.2 shows the header file for the `TablePrinter` class:

Listing 13.2   TablePrinter/*TablePrinter.h*

```
#import <Foundation/Foundation.h>

@protocol TablePrinterDataSource;

@interface TablePrinter : NSObject
{
    id <TablePrinterDataSource> dataSource;
}

@property(nonatomic, assign)  id <TablePrinterDataSource> dataSource;
- (void) printTable;

@end
```

It has a single instance variable to hold the data source, accessor methods for the data source, and a method to actually print the table. The instance variable and property are typed as `id <TablePrinterDataSource>` to indicate that whatever object is stored there is expected to conform to the protocol. The following line is a forward declaration:

```
@protocol TablePrinterDataSource;
```

It tells the compiler that, yes, `TablePrinterDataSource` is a protocol. That's all the compiler needs to know in the header file.

> **Note**
>
> Notice that the property declaration for `dataSource` is `assign` rather than `retain`. This is because in a more realistic program the data source is the primary object, which continues to exist, and the table printer is just a (possibly temporary) accessory used to display the primary object's contents. Holding an object in a variable without retaining the object is called making a *weak reference* to the object (see Chapter 15, "Reference Counting").

The implementation file for the `TablePrinter` class is shown in Listing 13.3.

Listing 13.3   TablePrinter/*TablePrinter.m*

```
#import "TablePrinter.h"
#import "TablePrinterDataSource.h"

@implementation TablePrinter
```

```
@synthesize dataSource;

- (void) printTable
{
  NSString *separator = @"-------------------------";
  NSString *title = @"Table";

  if ( [dataSource respondsToSelector: @selector( tableTitle )] )
    {
      title = [dataSource tableTitle];
    }
  printf( "\n%s\n%s\n", [title UTF8String],
                         [separator UTF8String] );

  int numRows = [dataSource numberOfRowsInTable];
  int j;
  BOOL printLineNumbers = NO;

  if ( [dataSource respondsToSelector: @selector(printLineNumbers)] )
    {
      printLineNumbers = [dataSource printLineNumbers];
    }

  for ( j=0; j < numRows; j++ )
    {
      NSString *outputString = [dataSource stringForRowAtIndex:j];

      if ( printLineNumbers )
        {
          printf( "%d | %s\n", j+1, [outputString UTF8String] );
        }
      else
        {
          printf( "%s\n", [outputString UTF8String] );
        }
    }
}

@end
```

The `printTable` method prints the header, asks for the number of rows in the table, and then loops, asking the data source for the string to print in each row.

There are several things to notice:

- You have to import the protocol header file so the compiler can check that you are calling methods that the protocol defines.

- printTable uses NSObject's respondsToSelector: to see if dataSource implements the optional protocol methods tableTitle and printLineNumbers before invoking them. If dataSource does not implement the optional methods, printTable uses default values for tableTitle and printLineNumbers.

- printf() is used instead of NSLog()purely for aesthetic reasons. printf() doesn't distract us with the date, time, and process information that NSLog() adds to each line. However, because printf() doesn't know anything about NSStrings, you have to convert the output strings to C strings with the UTF8String method before giving them to printf().

FruitBasket

FruitBasket is a very simple class; it just stores some fruit names in an array. It is used here to test the TablePrinter class. It declares that it adopts the TablePrinterDataSource protocol by adding TablePrinterDataSource to the @interface line in its header file, as shown in Listing 13.4.

Listing 13.4 TablePrinter/*FruitBasket.h*

```
#import <Foundation/Foundation.h>
#import "TablePrinterDataSource.h"

@interface FruitBasket : NSObject <TablePrinterDataSource>
{
  NSArray *fruits;
}
@end
```

The *FruitBasket.m*, shown in Listing 13.5, has the implementations of the protocol methods. The two optional methods are commented out to simulate a class that implements only the protocol's required methods. Leave them that way for the moment.

Listing 13.5 TablePrinter/*FruitBasket.m*

```
#import "FruitBasket.h"
@implementation FruitBasket

- (id) init
{
  if (self = [super init])
    {
      fruits =
        [[NSArray alloc] initWithObjects:
            @"Apple", @"Orange", @"Banana",
            @"Kiwi", @"Pear", nil];
    }
  return self;
}
```

```
- (void) dealloc
{
  [fruits release];
  [super dealloc];
}


- (int) numberOfRowsInTable
{
  return [fruits count];
}


- (NSString*) stringForRowAtIndex:(int) index
{
  return (NSString*)[fruits objectAtIndex: index];
}


/*- (NSString*) tableTitle
{
  return @"Available Fruits";
}*/


/*- (BOOL) printLineNumbers
{
  return YES;
}*/


@end
```

main

Listing 13.6 is the testbed for the project. It creates a **TablePrinter** object, and then it creates a **FruitBasket** object and gives it to the **TablePrinter** as its data source. Finally, **TablePrinter** is asked to print the table.

Listing 13.6   TablePrinter/*TablePrinterExample.m*

```
#import <Foundation/Foundation.h>
#import "TablePrinter.h"
#import "FruitBasket.h"

int main (int argc, const char *argv[])
{
  @autoreleasepool
    {
      TablePrinter *myTablePrinter = [[TablePrinter alloc] init];
      FruitBasket *myFruitBasket = [[FruitBasket alloc] init];
```

```
        [myTablePrinter setDataSource: myFruitBasket];
        [myTablePrinter printTable];

        [myTablePrinter release];
        [myFruitBasket release];
    }
    return 0;
}
```

When the program is run, you should see the following as the result:

```
Table
------------------------
Apple
Orange
Banana
Kiwi
Pear
```

Where Does a Protocol Declaration Live?

A protocol declaration must be visible to the interface section of a class that adopts that protocol. In the current example, the declaration of the `TablePrinterDataSource` protocol is placed in its own header file, *TablePrinterDataSource.h* (see Listing 13.1), which is then imported into *FruitBasket.h* (see Listing 13.4). As an alternative, the declaration of `TablePrinterDataSource` could be placed in *TablePrinter.h* (see Listing 13.2). *FruitBasket.h* would then need to import *TablePrinter.h*. Typically, in the Cocoa frameworks, a formal protocol is declared in the header file of the class that is the primary user of objects conforming to that protocol. However, a few Cocoa formal protocols are declared in their own header files.

A Problem

Although the program worked, you should have noticed a small problem when you built it: some compiler warnings such as the following:

```
TablePrinter.m:29:8: warning: instance method
'-respondsToSelector:' not found (return type defaults to 'id')
```

The compiler is complaining that `respondsToSelector:` isn't part of the `TablePrinterDataSource` protocol. It isn't, but it shouldn't matter because `respondsToSelector:` is implemented by `NSObject`, and every object (including the object passed in as the data source) inherits from `NSObject`. And it doesn't matter—the program worked just fine, didn't it? Well, yes, but it's a bad idea to get in the habit of ignoring compiler warnings, even semi-spurious ones. If you start ignoring warnings, one day, as sure as the sun rises, you'll ignore one that isn't spurious and there will be trouble.

You can fix this in one of two ways. In *TablePrinter.h*, you can change the type in the instance variable and property declarations to

```
NSObject <TablePrinterDataSource> *dataSource;
```

This tells the compiler explicitly that `dataSource` is a subclass of `NSObject` as well as implementing `TablePrinterDataSource`. A more elegant solution is to change the `@protocol` line in *TablePrinterDataSource.h* to be

```
@protocol TablePrinterDataSource <NSObject>
```

This means that anything that adopts `TablePrinterDataSource` also adopts the `NSObject` protocol. (This illustrates the important point that one protocol can adopt another.) `NSObject` is a protocol that `NSObject` adopts (see the sidebar *NSObject Class and NSObject Protocol* below). Again, because `NSObject` implements `respondsToSelector:`, you don't have to do any work beyond making the compiler understand that everything is OK.

NSObject Class and NSObject Protocol

This can be a bit confusing. There is both an `NSObject` class and an `NSObject` protocol. `NSObject` (the class) is the root class for almost all Objective-C objects. `NSObject` (the protocol) is a formal protocol that lists the methods that any class must implement to be a good Objective-C citizen. These are some of the very basic methods such as `respondsToSelector:`, `superclass`, and the reference counting `retain` and `release`. (For a complete list, see the header file *NSObject.h*.) `NSObject` (the class) adopts `NSObject` (the protocol), and then most classes acquire these methods by inheriting, directly or indirectly, from `NSObject`. `NSProxy`, Foundation's other root class (used for building distributed systems), also adopts `NSObject` (the protocol).

Implement the Optional Methods

Now implement the two optional methods in `TablePrinterDataSource` by uncommenting them in *FruitBasket.m*. This adds a title for the table and row numbers. If you build the program again and run it, the result should be

```
Available Fruits
------------------------
1 | Apple
2 | Orange
3 | Banana
4 | Kiwi
5 | Pear
```

Protocol Objects and Testing for Conformance

Protocol objects are objects that represent protocols. They are members of the class
`Protocol`. You obtain a protocol object from the protocol's name with the
`@protocol()` directive:

```
Protocol myDataSourceProtocol = @protocol( TablePrinterDataSource );
```

Unlike class objects, protocol objects have no methods, and their use is confined to
being an argument to the `NSObject` method `conformsToProtocol:`. This method
returns `YES` if the receiver implements all the required methods in the protocol and `NO`
otherwise. You could use a protocol object to build a safer version of `TablePrinter`
by coding the accessor methods for the `dataSource` instance variable yourself and
doing a bit of extra work. A safer setter is shown in Listing 13.7.

Listing 13.7   **A safer setter for the `TablePrinterDataSource`**

```
- (void) setDataSource: (id <TablePrinterDataSource>) newDataSource
{
   if ( ! [newDataSource
             conformsToProtocol: @protocol(TablePrinterDataSource)] )
     {
       dataSource = nil;
       NSLog(@"Error: TablePrinter: non-conforming data source.");
     }
   else
     dataSource = newDataSource;
}
```

The preceding version of **setDataSource:** prevents assigning an object that does not
conform to the `TablePrinterDataSource` protocol as the `dataSource`. If such an
object were assigned as the `dataSource`, it would likely cause a crash when one of
the protocol methods was invoked.

NSObject also has a class method, `conformsToProtocol:`, that you can use to
test if a class (rather than an instance of a class) conforms to a protocol. The following
would return `YES`:

```
[FruitBasket conformsToProtocol: @protocol(TablePrinterDataSource)];
```

Testing for protocol conformance is an example of defensive coding. With a few extra
lines of code, you can prevent a runtime crash.

Informal Protocols

The protocols discussed so far in this chapter are called *formal* protocols. A formal protocol is declared with a `@protocol` statement. Classes that adopt a formal protocol are
marked with a `<ProtocolName>` on the class's `@interface` line. Objective-C also

has *informal* protocols. Like formal protocols, informal protocols are groups of related methods that a class might want to implement. An informal protocol declares its methods in a category (usually a category on **NSObject**), but without a corresponding category implementation:

```
@interface NSObject (MyInformalProtocol)

- (void) informalProtocolMethod;

@end
```

An informal protocol is actually in the nature of a gentleperson's agreement on the part of the programmer writing a class that adopts the protocol. The programmer agrees to implement the informal protocol's methods when coding that class, but the compiler does nothing to check that he or she follows through on the agreement. The category functions as a piece of documentation listing the methods in the protocol. There is no type checking at compile time and no way of determining at run time if a class implements an informal protocol. Classes that adopt an informal protocol must declare the protocol methods in their interface section and put the code for those methods in their implementation section.

> **Note**
>
> When you code a class that adopts an informal protocol, the protocol method implementations must go in the *class's* **@implementation** section, *not* in a category **@implementation** section. If you place the implementations in a separate category **@implementation** section, your method implementations are added to *all* classes (assuming the protocol is declared as a category on **NSObject**). This is unlikely to be what you intended to do.

So what's the point of using informal protocols? Before Objective-C 2.0, all the methods in a formal protocol were required. The only way to have optional methods in a protocol was to use an informal protocol and note the optional methods in the documentation. With the advent of **@optional** and **@required**, there isn't much reason to use an informal protocol: You can have optional methods and still enjoy the benefits of a formal protocol.

You can see this progression in the Apple frameworks: In earlier versions of the AppKit, **NSTableDataSource** (the data source protocol for AppKit's **NSTableView**) was an informal protocol. Beginning in Mac OS X Snow Leopard (version 10.6), **NSTableDataSource** has been replaced with the **NSTableViewDataSource** formal protocol.

Summary

Protocols add flexibility to program design by letting you type objects by behavior rather than by class. There are many situations where all that is required of an object is that it implements a particular set of methods. In these situations, the object's class and other behavior are immaterial. Protocols let you formalize this pattern:

- You declare a protocol by giving it a name and declaring its methods between `@protocol` and `@end` directives.

- Protocol methods may be either required or optional. The default, if you do not specify, is required.

- A class *adopts* a protocol by implementing all of the protocol's required methods and, perhaps, some or all of the protocol's optional methods. The class advertises that it has adopted the protocol by appending the protocol name inside angle brackets after the superclass name on the class's `@interface` line. The header file containing the protocol declaration must be visible to the adopting class's `@interface` section.

- You can add a protocol name to the type declaration of an instance variable or a method argument. If you do this, the compiler checks to see that an object that you assign to the instance variable or use as the method argument adopts the specified protocol.

- You can use the class or the instance version of `conformsToProtocol:` to see if a given class or a given object adopts a particular protocol.

- Before calling an `@optional` method, you should use `respondsToSelector:` to make sure the receiver has implemented the method.

The protocols described in the preceding points are called formal protocols. There are also informal protocols, which are just a list of methods that a class might choose to implement. There is no compiler support for checking informal protocols. They were originally used to declare protocols that had optional methods. With the introduction of the `@optional` directive in Objective-C 2.0, there is no reason to use an informal protocol instead of a formal protocol.

Exercises

1. Design and declare a `StockKeepingUnit` protocol for an inventory system. An instance of a class that adopts `StockKeepingUnit` should be able to report things like product name, manufacturer, list price, and SKU number.

2. Define a `CheeseBasket` class that can hold the names of cheeses. Make sure that it adopts the `TablePrinterDataSource` protocol. Add an instance of `CheeseBasket` to the `TablePrinter` example (see Listing 13.6) and use the same `TablePrinter` instance to print both the fruits in the `FruitBasket` and then the cheeses in the `CheeseBasket` by changing the `TablePrinter`'s data source. This is a simple exercise, but it emphasizes the point that the `TablePrinter` can use any class as its data source as long as the class implements the required methods in the `TablePrinterDataSource` protocol.

3. Define a class that does *not* implement the required methods in
   `TablePrinterDataSource`. Try to use an instance of this class as the
   data source for a `TablePrinter` in Listing 13.6 instead of an instance of
   `FruitBasket`. What happens when you compile the program? What happens
   when you run the program?

4. Modify the `TablePrinter` source to use the safe setter (shown in Listing 13.7)
   for the `dataSource` instance variable and repeat the previous exercise.

Part III

Advanced Concepts

The first four chapters in Part III cover Objective-C memory management in detail. Chapter 14 is an overview of Objective-C memory management. Chapter 15 covers manual reference counting. Manual reference counting is a memory management system that keeps a count of the number of places an object is used. It requires the programmer to explicitly code various memory management methods. Chapter 16 covers Automatic Reference Counting (ARC). ARC automates the reference counting system described in Chapter 15.

Chapter 17 covers Objective-C 2.0's blocks feature, which is a central part of Apple's Grand Central Dispatch concurrency mechanism.

Chapter 18 covers a few recently introduced items that seemed not to fit anywhere else in the book.

- Chapter 14, "Memory Management Overview"
- Chapter 15, "Reference Counting"
- Chapter 16, "ARC"
- Chapter 17, "Blocks"
- Chapter 18, "A Few More Things"

Memory Management
Overview

People who live in apartments often face a storage problem: They have more stuff than places to put stuff. Solving this problem requires shuffling possessions in and out of basement storage lockers and periodically going through the apartment and throwing out things that are no longer needed. Managing memory usage is the computer science equivalent of the apartment dweller's problem.

Memory management is important because memory is a limited resource. Although it is true that current computers can have amounts of physical memory that would have seemed like an intoxicated dream only a few years ago, the average program's memory requirements and the users' expectations have also increased. Keeping a program's memory footprint as small as possible improves its performance by reducing the chances that the computer's virtual memory system will have to swap part of the program out to disk and then later read it back in from the disk. It also improves the overall performance of the system by reducing competition for physical memory among all the running programs.

Memory management is important on Mac OS X; however, it is critical on iOS devices. iOS devices have virtual memory (every process has its own address space), but they do not have a full paging system. Read-only pages of memory such as program text may be swapped out, but there is no paging for writable areas of memory. In addition, the amount of physical memory on some iOS devices is severely constrained. Early versions of the iPhone and iPod touch have only 128 MB of RAM. (The iPad 2 and iPhone 4S have 512 MB; the third-generation iPad has 1 GB.) When the remaining amount of unused memory drops below a threshold, iOS sends all the running programs a low memory warning. It is expected that your program will respond to such a warning by releasing as much memory as it can. If you ignore the warning and the low memory condition persists, iOS will terminate your program.

The Problem

In Objective-C terms, memory management means tracking objects that have been created and freeing them (returning their memory to the system) when they are no longer needed. All Objective-C objects are dynamically allocated; their bytes come from the heap. If you try to create an object on the stack by declaring an automatic variable that holds an object instead of a pointer to an object:

```
NSString aString;
```

the compiler reprimands you and refuses to compile the file:

```
error: statically allocated instance of Objective-C class 'NSString'
```

The proper way to create an object is to declare a pointer variable and use the method **alloc** to allocate memory for your object on the heap. The following line creates an NSString:

```
NSString *aString = [[NSString alloc] initWithString: @"Hi!"];
```

After you've created some objects and used them, the question arises: How do you return them when you're finished? The Golden Rule of memory management is "When you're finished with something that you allocated, you have to give the bytes back to the heap." One possibility would be for Objective-C to provide a method that, when called, would just free the bytes used for an object:

```
[aString freeObject];
```

However, this is not a very satisfactory solution. It requires you to keep track of every place, in the entire program, that an object is used, and to call the **freeObject** method when you are sure you are completely finished with that object. This is clearly impractical for anything other than a trivial program. It's beyond impractical for a program that might contain hundreds of objects, which are used in a large number of files worked on by a team of programmers.

Memory Leaks

A memory leak occurs when a program allocates memory from the heap and then does not return that memory to the heap when the program is finished with it. Leaks waste a scarce system resource. The leaked bytes are no longer used for their original purpose and are unavailable for any other use.

A memory leak causes the memory footprint of a program to be bigger than it should be, with adverse implications for performance. The effects of a leak can range from insignificant, if the loss is just a few bytes here and there, to running the system out of memory and crashing the program, if the leak is inside a loop or the program executes for an extended period of time.

The Solutions: Objective-C Memory Management

Objective-C 2.0 provides two systems for memory management: *reference counting* (also called *manual reference counting, retain counting,* or *managed memory*) and *Automatic Reference Counting (ARC).* Each of these systems is described briefly in the sections that follow and treated in detail in subsequent chapters.

> **Note**
>
> Another memory management system, *garbage collection*, was introduced with OS X 10.5 in 2007. However, garbage collection did not perform as well as had been expected. Garbage collection is deprecated as of OS X 10.8 and is not covered in this book.

Reference Counting (Manual Reference Counting)

In a program that uses reference counting each object keeps a count, called the *retain count,* of the number of places it is being used. When an object is created (allocated from the heap), it has a retain count of one. The programmer is responsible for correctly maintaining the retain count by sending a `release` message to that object when it is no longer needed. If that object is used elsewhere in the program, the programmer must send it a `retain` message to indicate the additional usage and send the object a corresponding `release` message when that usage is over.

An object may be used in more than one place so it may receive more than one `retain` message and more than one `release` message. Each `retain` message increments the object's retain count; each `release` message decrements the retain count. When an object's retain count drops to zero (indicating that it is no longer being used), the object is deallocated and the object's bytes are returned to the heap.

Reference counting is the source of more confusion and bugs than any other part of Objective-C. Nevertheless, it is important to learn and understand reference counting, even if you choose to use ARC. Why is that?

- Until 2007 reference counting was the only memory management system available in Objective-C. Also, there are some people who do not care for ARC and continue to use reference counting for their new code. If you wind up working on an existing code base, you are very likely to encounter manual reference counting.

- Many real-world OS X and iOS programs require the use of objects from the C language Core Foundation–level frameworks. Core Foundation objects use a manual reference counting system that is very similar to the Objective-C reference counting system. But, unlike Objective-C, there is no alternative to reference counting for Core Foundation objects.

- Even if you use ARC (described in the next section) to automate reference counting, there are some situations that require manual intervention and a good understanding of how reference counting works.

Reference counting is treated in detail in the next chapter.

Automatic Reference Counting (ARC)

ARC is a new system of memory management that was introduced with OS X 10.7 and iOS 5. ARC automates the existing manual reference counting system. When you compile code with ARC, the compiler analyzes your code and inserts `retain` and `release` messages for you. This eliminates most of the effort and headaches involved in using reference counting. Since ARC automates the existing system, it can interoperate with code that uses manual reference counting. An executable can combine code from files that were compiled with ARC and traditional manual reference counting.

> **Note**
>
> ARC requires Xcode 4.2 or later and the LLVM 3.0 (Clang) compiler or later. OS X programs that use ARC must be built with the OS X 10.7 or later SDK. They may be deployed back to OS X 10.6. iOS programs that use ARC must be built with the iOS 5 or later SDK. They may be deployed back to iOS 4.

ARC is the subject of Chapter 16.

Onward

This completes our overview of Objective-C memory management. The next chapter begins an excursion through the details of the Objective-C memory management systems.

15

Reference Counting

With the introduction of Automatic Reference Counting in the spring of 2011, Apple has begun referring to the traditional Objective-C reference counting system as *manual reference counting*. For the sake of brevity I will use the term *reference counting* to refer to the manual system and the term *ARC* to refer to Automatic Reference Counting. This chapter covers manual reference counting.

Reference Counting Basics

Reference counting is very simple in principle. Each object stores a count, called the *reference count* or *retain count*, of the other objects that are using it. When you first create an object using **alloc**, its retain count is one. You own the object. When you no longer need the object, you indicate that you are finished with it by sending the object a **release** message:

```
[anObject release];
```

The **release** message subtracts one from the object's retain count. If the new retain count is zero, the object is dismantled and its memory is returned to the heap. This point is worth repeating: A **release** message doesn't deallocate the receiver; it decrements the retain count. As you will see in the next section, there are situations where an object's retain count is higher than one. The object is recycled to the heap only if the **release** message causes the retain count to fall to zero.

The entire trick of using reference counting is making sure that you keep the retain count correctly. When you use manual reference counting (the subject of this chapter), this requires some work on your part.

The following code shows the simplest reference counting pattern:

```
1  -(void) simpleMethod
2  {
3     NSMutableArray *anArray = [[NSMutableArray alloc] init];
4
```

```
 5    // Code that uses anArray goes here
 6
 7    // Finished with anArray
 8    [anArray release];
 9    anArray = nil;
10
11    ...
12  }
```

Now let's examine that code:

- Line 3: `anArray` is created with `alloc` (its retain count is one).
- Line 5: `anArray` is used for something (its retain count is still one).
- Line 8: The method is finished with `anArray`. It sends `anArray` a `release` message. `anArray`'s retain count goes from one to zero, which causes `anArray` to be deallocated.
- Line 9: Remember that object variables hold pointers to objects. When the object that `anArray` points to is deallocated, the object's bytes are returned to the heap. The pointer held in the variable `anArray` is no longer valid; the heap is free to use those bytes for another object. This line sets `anArray` to `nil` to prevent accidentally using the invalid pointer later in the method and potentially corrupting some other object.

You can see the beginnings of some rules here. Think of it as a contract: If you create an object, you own it. You are responsible for correctly balancing that object's creation with a matching `release` message. The methods that return an object that you own are methods whose name begins with `alloc`, `new`, `copy`, or `mutableCopy`.

Something like the following is a guaranteed memory leak:

```
-(void) badlyCodedMethod
{
    NSMutableArray *anArray = [[NSMutableArray alloc] init];

  // Do stuff with anArray

  ...

  // Return without releasing anArray

  return;
}
```

The variable `anArray` is an automatic variable. When the method exits, the variable is gone forever. The object the variable was pointing to still has a retain count of one, but nothing holds a pointer to it. The object can never be released; it stays around, doing nothing, but occupying memory that could be used for something else, until the program exits.

Receiving Objects

So far, reference counting may seem like just a fancy name for "remember to free what you have allocated." Its real usefulness becomes apparent when you start passing objects around from one method to another.

An object received from another method is presumed to remain valid for the remainder of the receiving method. In the following example, NSDate's date method returns an object that represents the current time and date:

```
- (void) doSomethingWithTheCurrentDate
{
  NSDate *currentDate = [NSDate date];

  // currentDate is used, but not stored in an instance variable
  ...
}
```

The method doSomethingWithTheCurrentDate can use currentDate until it returns, without worrying that currentDate will be deallocated.

> **Note**
>
> This condition is true only in a single-threaded program. In a multithreaded program, it is possible for another thread to cause the received object to be deallocated (by sending that object a release message that decrements the received object's retain count to zero) before the method that received the object returns. Methods that return objects in a multithreaded environment require special care if you want them to meet this condition. (See the section *Multithreading* later in this chapter.)

If you want to store a received object in an instance variable and continue to use it after the receiving method returns, you must take an active step to ensure that the object remains valid and is not deallocated. You must send it a retain message. To illustrate this, imagine, as you did in Chapter 6, "Classes and Objects," that you are creating some classes for a rock-and-roll simulation game. A RockStar object needs a Guitar object:

```
@Class Guitar;

@interface RockStar : NSObject
{
  Guitar *guitar;
  ...
}
  -(Guitar*) guitar;
  -(void) setGuitar:(Guitar*) newGuitar;

  ...

@end
```

When a game controller object sets up the game, it allocates a `RockStar` instance and a `Guitar` instance and passes the `Guitar` instance to the `RockStar` by invoking `RockStar`'s `setGuitar:` method. The obvious way to code the `setGuitar:` method has a problem:

```
- (void) setGuitar:(Guitar *) newGuitar
{
  guitar = newGuitar;   // WRONG
}
```

The game controller created the `Guitar` with an `alloc`. What happens if at some later time the controller balances its `alloc` with a `release`? The `Guitar` object's retain count goes to zero and it is deallocated. The `RockStar` is left holding a pointer to an invalid object. To prevent this from happening, the `RockStar` should send a `retain` message to `guitar:`

```
[guitar retain];
```

The `retain` message is the opposite of `release`: It increments the receiver's retain count. When the `RockStar` sends a `retain` message to `guitar`, the message raises the retain count of the object held in `guitar` to two. This prevents the object from being deallocated, even if the code that originally allocated it sends it a `release` message.

Listing 15.1 shows the final form of the `setGuitar:` method.

Listing 15.1 `setGuitar:`

```
1  - (void) setGuitar:(Guitar*) newGuitar
2  {
3    if ( newGuitar != guitar )
4      {
5        [guitar release];
6        guitar = newGuitar;
7        [guitar retain];
8      }
9  }
```

The `setGuitar:` method must allow for the possibility that the `guitar` instance variable already contains an object (perhaps the `RockStar` is switching guitars because the original one has been smashed on stage). The `Guitar` instance currently held in the `guitar` variable received a `retain` message when it was stored; it must now receive a `release` message when it is being replaced.

Notice in the preceding code:

- Line 5: The object currently held in `guitar` is released. If `guitar` is currently `nil`, this line has no effect.
- Line 6: The new object is stored in `guitar`.

- Line 7: The new `Guitar` instance is sent a `retain` message. A `retain` message returns its receiver as the return value. Lines 6 and 7 could be combined and written as

```
guitar = [newGuitar retain];
```

- Line 3: If both `guitar` and `newGuitar` point to the same object, and Lines 5 and 7 were executed, they would send that object a `release` message and a `retain` message in succession. The `release` message might cause the object to be deallocated. The `retain` message would then have an invalid receiver, and the program would probably crash the next time it tried to use the `guitar`. The `if` statement in Line 3 prevents this from happening.

> **Note**
>
> The preceding code is essentially what is generated when the compiler synthesizes the following property statement:
>
> ```
> @property (nonatomic, retain) Guitar *guitar;
> ```
>
> It is written out here as an illustration; in a real program, it is cleaner to use `@property` and synthesize the setter. See Chapter 12, "Properties."

Ownership

Objective-C reference counting is often discussed in terms of *ownership*:

- If you create an object, you own it.
- You take ownership of an object that something else created by sending the object a `retain` message. Objective-C ownership is not exclusive ownership. It registers an interest in keeping the object alive. An object can have many owners. Taking ownership of an object by sending it a `retain` message does not remove anyone else's ownership of that object.
- When you are finished with an object that you own, you must relinquish your ownership of that object by sending it a `release` message.
- When an object has no more owners (which means that its retain count is zero), the object is deallocated.

For methods that return objects, ownership follows a naming convention:

- If you create an object by invoking a method whose name begins with `alloc`, `new`, `copy`, or `mutableCopy`, you own the returned object.
- If you receive an object from any other method, you do *not* own the returned object. If you want to use the object beyond the scope of the method that received it (by storing it in an instance variable or a global variable), you must take ownership of the object.

> **Note**
>
> The naming rule has changed recently. Before 2011 the naming rule was "You own an object returned by a method that begins with `alloc` or `new` or contains the word `copy`." The change was made to make the rules more uniform for ARC. Note that, since the change was recent, there are a large number of books, blogs, and forum posts floating around that cite the old version of the rules.

Taking Ownership by Copying

You can also take ownership of an object by copying it instead of retaining it.

> **Note**
>
> You must make sure the object's class supports copying before you attempt to copy it. A class that is capable of being copied must adopt the `NSCopying` protocol by implementing `copyWithZone:` or the `NSMutableCopying` protocol by implementing `mutableCopyWithZone:`.

Strictly speaking, when you take ownership by copying, you are taking ownership of the newly created copy, not the original object.

Should you use `copy` or `retain` when taking ownership? It depends on the design of your program and objects. If the object is mutable, there is the possibility that something else retaining the object might modify it. If what you need for the current context is a snapshot of the way the object is now, you should copy it; otherwise, you should retain it. Copying is more expensive in execution time and memory than simply retaining, particularly if the object in question is complicated and has implemented a deep copy.

> **Note**
>
> Some immutable classes implement `copy` as an additional `retain`. The `copy` method simply returns the receiver with an incremented reference count instead of allocating a new object. Since the object is immutable, there can never be any difference between the original object and a copy. There is no point in having more than one instance of such an object.

dealloc

When a `release` message drops an object's retain count to zero, the object is deallocated. But what happens to the objects that the deallocated object stored in its own instance variables? When a `RockStar` object is deallocated, what happens to the `Guitar` object stored in its `guitar` instance variable? The `Guitar` object received a `retain` message when it was stored (see Listing 15.1). If the `RockStar` object just disappears, the `Guitar` object never gets a balancing `release` message; it will be leaked.

To prevent leaks, an object that stores other objects in its instance variables must release those objects in a `dealloc` method. As an example, `RockStar` overrides `NSObject`'s `dealloc` method with its own implementation:

```
- (void) dealloc
{
  [guitar release];

  // Release any other objects held in instance variables.
  ...

  // Don't forget this
  [super dealloc];
}
```

The full deallocation sequence is shown in Figure 15.1.

1. `release` is implemented in `NSObject`. `RockStar` inherits that implementation. If a `release` message results in a zero retain count, `release` invokes `dealloc`.

2. Because `RockStar` overrides `dealloc`, it is `RockStar`'s implementation of `dealloc` that is executed.

3. `RockStar` sends `guitar` a `release` message to balance the `retain` message `guitar` received when it was stored. If no other object has ownership of the object held in `guitar`, it is also deallocated. `RockStar` also sends `release` messages to any other objects that it owns that are stored in its instance variables.

4. `RockStar`'s `dealloc` method uses `super` to invoke its superclass's implementation of `dealloc`. Since `RockStar`'s superclass is `NSObject`, it is `NSObject`'s implementation of `dealloc` that is invoked. When you have an object with a

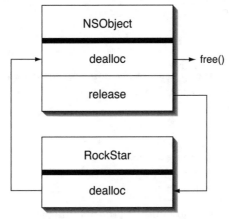

Figure 15.1   Deallocating an object

deeper inheritance chain, each class's **dealloc** method invokes its superclass's **dealloc** method until, eventually, **NSObject**'s **dealloc** method is invoked.

5. **NSObject**'s implementation of **dealloc** starts a chain of events that eventually calls the system library function **free()**, which does the work of returning **RockStar**'s bytes to the heap.

The **[super dealloc]** line is very important. If you forget it, **NSObject**'s implementation of **dealloc** is not executed, and the object's bytes are leaked. It is also important that the **dealloc** message to **super** be the last line in a **dealloc** method. When **[super dealloc]** returns, the object has been deallocated and is no longer valid.

> **Note**
>
> You should not invoke **dealloc** directly (except when invoking **[super dealloc]** as the last line of a **dealloc** method). It is invoked for you automatically when an object's retain count becomes zero.

Returning Objects

There is one situation where reference counting doesn't work quite as smoothly as you might like. Imagine that the **Guitar** class has a class method that returns instances of **Guitar**:

```
@interface Guitar : NSObject
{
  // Instance variables
}

+ (Guitar*) guitar;

  // Other methods

@end
```

This type of method is called a *convenience constructor*. Convenience constructors are very common in the Cocoa frameworks. Your first impulse might be to code the **guitar** method like this:

```
+ (Guitar*) guitar
{
  Guitar *newGuitar = [[Guitar alloc] init];
  return newGuitar;
}
```

The preceding code creates and returns a properly initialized **Guitar** instance, but it has a memory management problem: It creates a **Guitar** object with **alloc**, but it never balances the **alloc** with a **release**. As it stands, the **guitar** method leaks the newly allocated object.

> **Note**
>
> You might argue that the code that invokes the **guitar** method and accepts the returned object should be responsible for releasing the object. But that doesn't follow the rules. **guitar** doesn't begin with **alloc**, **new**, **copy**, or **mutableCopy**, so the invoker does not own the returned object. If the invoking code takes ownership of the returned object by sending the object a **retain** message, it would have to eventually balance that **retain** with a **release**. But that **release** doesn't balance the **alloc** in the **guitar** method.

A quick attempt at a repair doesn't work:

```
- (Guitar*) guitar
{
  Guitar *newGuitar = [[Guitar alloc] init];
  [newGuitar release]; // WRONG!
  return newGuitar;
}
```

The preceding code balances the **alloc** with a **release**, but it creates a much bigger problem. The **release** drops **newGuitar**'s retain count to zero, causing it to be immediately deallocated. What is returned is a pointer to a now non-existent object. The stale pointer eventually causes a crash or corrupts another object.

Fixing this problem requires Objective-C's autorelease mechanism, which is described in the next section.

Autorelease

The problem a convenience constructor, or a similar method, faces is that it creates an object, but it has no way to track that object and then balance the object's creation by sending it a **release** message at an appropriate time.

Objective-C solves this problem with the *autorelease* mechanism. Autorelease is a way of handing an object to a trusted third party, called an *autorelease pool*, for release at a future time. The name *autorelease* is a bit of a misnomer; it should really be called *delayed release*.

Autorelease Pools

You create an autorelease pool by using the **@autoreleasepool** compiler directive along with a pair of curly brackets. The curly brackets define the scope (block of code) where the autorelease pool created by the compiler directive is in effect.

```
@autoreleasepool
{

}
```

When you send an object an **autorelease** message, the object is placed in the auto-release pool:

```
[anObject autorelease];  // Places anObject in the autorelease pool
```

When the program exits the scope of the autorelease pool (the block of code between the pool's curly brackets), every object placed in the pool by an **autorelease** message receives a **release** message.

The **autorelease** method returns the receiver as its return value. This allows an **autorelease** message to be nested with other messages or used as the argument of a return statement:

```
SomeClass *autoreleasedObject =
    [[[SomeClass alloc] init] autorelease];
```

In the preceding code, the object created by **[[SomeClass alloc] init]** is sent an **autorelease** message. The return value of the **autorelease** message is the original object, which is then stored in the variable **autoreleasedObject**.

Sending an object an **autorelease** message is just a form of registration. It adds the object to the pool's list of objects, but it does not cause any messages to be sent to the object. After the **autorelease** message is executed, the receiver is still fully alive and valid.

Some key points about autorelease:

- Sending an **autorelease** message to an object that you own fulfills your contract to eventually relinquish ownership of that object. An autorelease is a release; it's just one that happens in the future.

- It is possible to send an object an **autorelease** message more than once. When the autorelease pool is emptied, such an object receives multiple **release** messages, one for each time it was autoreleased.

- When the program exits the autorelease scope, it doesn't necessarily mean that all the objects in the pool are deallocated. All the objects in the pool are sent a **release** message. If that **release** message causes an object's retain count to go to zero, that object is deallocated.

Managing Autorelease Pools

The runtime maintains a stack of autorelease pools. Creating a pool pushes it onto the stack; exiting the pool's scope pops it off the stack. Objects receiving an **autorelease** message are placed in the pool that is on the top of the stack.

> **Note**
> Don't confuse the stack of autorelease pools with the program stack.

Calling `autorelease` on an object with no pool on the stack is a mistake. The runtime will complain to you, because the lack of an autorelease pool causes a memory leak, but the program will continue executing. A message like the following is written to the console log (and to the terminal window if it is a command line application):

```
__NSAutoreleaseNoPool(): Object 0x100001050 of class Guitar
        autoreleased with no pool in place - just leaking
```

Even if you do not code any **autorelease** messages, many of the Cocoa classes use autorelease internally.

If you are writing a GUI program, the AppKit or UIKit creates autorelease pools for you. GUI programs have an *event loop*. The event loop waits for some user interaction (a mouse click or a keystroke, for example), packages information about the interaction as an event object, and distributes the event object to other parts of the program. The loop then returns to the top and waits for the next interaction. The AppKit or UIKit creates an autorelease pool at the beginning of each pass through the event loop (which pushes the pool onto the stack). The scope of the pool lasts until the bottom of the event loop, where the pool is popped off of the stack.

Figure 15.2 shows the lifecycle of an object created and then autoreleased during one pass through the event loop. The object's life can be extended if another object retains it before the bottom of the event loop.

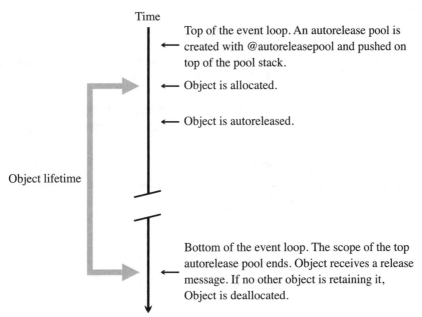

Figure 15.2   Lifecycle of an autoreleased object in a GUI program

If you are writing a Foundation (non–GUI) program, you must create at least one autorelease pool yourself:

```
main ()
{
  @autoreleasepool
    {
  ...
  // Whatever your program does
  ...
    }
return 0;
}
```

Autorelease Pools the Old Way

Prior to the Clang compiler, the autorelease mechanism was disguised as an Objective-C object. To create an autorelease pool the old way you allocate an `NSAutoreleasePool` instance:

```
NSAutoreleasePool *pool  = [[NSAutoreleasePool alloc] init];
```

The preceding line of code creates an autorelease pool and pushes it onto the stack. The pool is on the stack until it is removed and emptied by a `drain` message:

```
[pool drain];
```

Contrary to some of the (mis)information currently circulating, `@autoreleasepool` is not a part of ARC. It is a separate addition to the Objective-C language. When you compile with Clang, you may use either `@autoreleasepool` or `NSAutoreleasePool` for non-ARC code. (But you should use `@autoreleasepool`. It is more efficient than creating an `NSAutoreleasePool` object.)

Code compiled with ARC (see Chapter 16) must use `@autoreleasepool`.

Back to Convenience Constructors

You now have the means to design a convenience constructor that does not cause memory management problems. The following code shows the correct form of a convenience constructor for the `Guitar` class:

```
+ (Guitar*) guitar
{
  Guitar *newGuitar = [[Guitar alloc] init];
  [newGuitar autorelease];
  return newGuitar;
}
```

The `autorelease` message balances the `alloc` message, so this method obeys the memory management rules. Code that invokes the `guitar` method has an opportunity to retain the returned `Guitar` object because the `release` message implied by the autorelease is not sent until the autorelease pool is emptied at a future time.

Autorelease and iOS

If you are writing an iOS application, you should avoid using autorelease for large objects. Objects sitting in an autorelease pool count toward your program's memory footprint and can contribute to a situation where your program receives a low memory warning. Instead of using a class's convenience constructors (which generally return autoreleased objects), you should allocate large objects directly with `alloc` and release them as soon as you are finished with them.

Using Extra Autorelease Pools to Control Memory Usage

There are situations where it is useful to create your own autorelease pools. If you have a method that creates and autoreleases many objects, and you execute that method in a loop, those objects accumulate in the top-level autorelease pool, uselessly taking up memory until the loop exits and the pool can be released.

```
int j;
id  myObject = ...

for (j=0; j < MANY_TIMES; j++)
   {
     // Do something that creates and autoreleases many objects

     [myObject prolificAllocatorAndAutoreleaser];
   }
```

In situations like this, you can reduce your program's memory footprint by providing a new pool for each pass through the loop and releasing it at the bottom of the loop, as shown here:

```
int j;
id myObject = ...

for (j=0; j <  MANY_TIMES; j++)
  {
    // Create a new pool each time through the loop

    @autoreleasepool
      {
        // Do something that creates and autoreleases many objects

        [myObject prolificAllocatorAndAutoreleaser];
```

```
        // Exiting the autorelease scope sends a release message to
        // all the objects that were autoreleased during this pass
        // through the loop
    }  // pool
}  //loop
```

The Retainer and the Retained Don't Know about Each Other

This is a subtle and often misunderstood point: When Object A retains Object B, the two objects don't know about each other in any meaningful sense. All that an object knows is how many objects have an ownership of it (that is, its retain count). The object doesn't have a list of pointers to the objects that retain it. Similarly, an object doesn't have a list of objects it has retained. There is nothing in the Objective-C language or runtime that does the equivalent of saying to an object that is being discarded, "Hey! You! You're holding retains on the following objects. Release them before you go away!"

You, the programmer, have to keep track of your `allocs`, `copys`, and `retains` when coding and balance them with a `release` or `autorelease`.

retainCount

`NSObject` implements the `retainCount` method, which returns the current value of an object's retain count:

```
NSUInteger currentRetainCount = [anObject retainCount];
```

At first sight, it seems like `retainCount` could be useful for debugging memory management problems. However, in a real program using the Cocoa frameworks, many framework objects retain and release objects by passing them around in arrays and dictionaries. The result is that an object's reported retain counts are very often higher than what you would expect from tracking the object through your own code. Also, some constant objects, such as `NSString` literals, may report meaningless retain counts. In practice, the `retainCount` method is rarely helpful.

Multithreading

Reference counting becomes a bit more complicated in a multithreaded program. The typical setter pattern, shown in Listing 15.1, is problematic in a multithreaded environment. If two threads attempt to invoke `setGuitar:` at approximately the same time, the second thread can interrupt the first thread before the first thread finishes executing the method. This can result in an object with an incorrect retain count, or a crash if the object that was originally stored in `guitar` receives two `release` messages, one from each thread.

Preventing threads from interfering with each other while using the setter method requires the use of a lock, as shown in Listing 15.2.

Listing 15.2 `setGuitar:` **with lock**

```
-(void) setGuitar:(Guitar*)newGuitar
{
  @synchronized(self)
    {
      if ( newGuitar != guitar )
        {
          [guitar release];
          guitar = newGuitar;
          [guitar retain];
        }
    }
}
```

The `@synchronized()` compiler directive sets up a locking mechanism that allows only one thread at a time to execute the code in the compound statement (code block) that follows it. If a thread attempts to enter the code block while another thread is executing it, the second thread will block until the first thread has finished executing. In the preceding code, the `@synchronized` block guarantees that setting `guitar` is an atomic operation.

> **Note**
>
> The argument to `@synchronized()` is used to identify the lock. It can be any Objective-C object; `self` is a convenient choice here. If several different blocks of code are synchronized using the same argument to `@synchronized()`, the blocks are all locked with the same lock. Once a thread acquires the lock and enters one of those blocks, other threads are prevented from entering any of those blocks until the first thread gives up the lock by exiting the block.

The code in Listing 15.2 is equivalent to the code that the compiler creates when it synthesizes a setter method from this property statement:

```
@property (retain) Guitar *guitar;
```

Recall that until recently there was no **atomic** attribute for property declarations. You usually declare a property to be atomic by omitting the **nonatomic** attribute.

In a multithreaded program, getters also require modification. The following simple getter can cause problems in a multithreaded program:

```
- (Guitar*) guitar
{
  return guitar;
}
```

By convention, an object returned by a getter should remain valid until the method that invoked the getter returns. In a multithreaded program, another thread could cause the object held in `guitar` to be deallocated at any time after the getter returns. The original thread may not even get a chance to retain the object. Rewriting the getter to use the following pattern eliminates the problem:

```
- ( Guitar*) guitar
{
  @synchronized(self)
    {
      return [[guitar retain] autorelease];
    }
}
```

Sending `guitar` a `retain` message followed by an `autorelease` message does not give the receiving method ownership of the `guitar` object. But, by putting the `guitar` in the invoking thread's autorelease pool, it ensures the `guitar` object will remain alive, at least until the end of the current autorelease scope. The receiving method can then take ownership if it wants to use the object beyond the scope of the current autorelease pool. The `@synchronized` block is required to make sure that another thread does not interrupt the pair of messages.

> **Note**
>
> The preceding patterns for an instance variable's setter and getter guarantee that the getter will return either `nil` or a valid object—**but only if both the setter and getter are synchronized on the same object.** If the setter and getter use different objects as the argument to their respective @**synchronized** directives, it is possible for the getter to be interrupted by another thread using the setter. This can result in the getter returning a dead object or one with an incorrect retain count.

> **Note**
>
> The code shown in this section makes setting and getting an instance variable atomic in a multithreaded environment. But making your accessors atomic won't by itself make your code thread safe. Thread safety is more than just atomic operations; it requires *very* careful analysis and design. See https://developer.apple.com/library/ios/#documentation/General/Conceptual/ConcurrencyProgrammingGuide/Introduction/Introduction.html.

When Retain Counts Go Bad

Reference counting depends on following the rules and balancing each object creation and **retain** message with an appropriate **release** or **autorelease** message. What happens if you make a mistake? Under-releasing an object causes a memory leak. The object is not deallocated when it should be, and its memory is never returned to the heap.

The results of over-releasing are more immediate and dire. If you send an object an extra `release` message, or send a `release` message to an object that you do not own, one `release` message causes the object to be deallocated. When the program sends the next `release` message, it is sending a message to a deallocated object. The result is usually a crash. This type of problem can be difficult to hunt down if the correct `release` and the spurious `release` are sent in widely separated sections of the code.

NSZombie

One way to track down over-release problems is to use Foundation's `NSZombie` feature. When `NSZombie` is enabled, objects that are deallocated are not returned to the heap. Instead, they are turned into `NSZombie` objects. `NSZombie` objects log any messages that are sent to them. You can also set a debugger break point on `[NSZombie release]` and `[NSZombie autorelease]`. This allows you to see where the extra release is coming from. To enable `NSZombie`, set the environment variable `NSZombieEnabled` to `YES`. To set this up in Xcode, choose *Edit Scheme* from the *Scheme* pop-up on the upper left of the Xcode window's toolbar. When the sheet appears, click the *Diagnostics* tab and then check the *Enable Zombie Objects* check box (Figure 15.3).

The best way to use `NSZombie` is with the new version of the Instruments application. In Xcode, choose *Profile* (⌘-I) from the *Product* menu. This builds a version of your program for use with Instruments. When the build is finished, Xcode starts

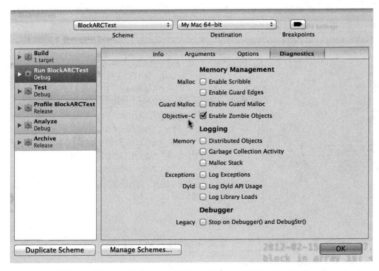

Figure 15.3   Enabling `NSZombie` objects in Xcode 4

Instruments for you. When Instruments shows its initial panel, select *Zombies* and then click the *Profile* button (or press the Return key). Instruments then runs your application and shows you any places where you have sent a message to a deallocated object. Instruments also shows you the lines of code that are most likely to be the source of your problem (see Figure 15.4).

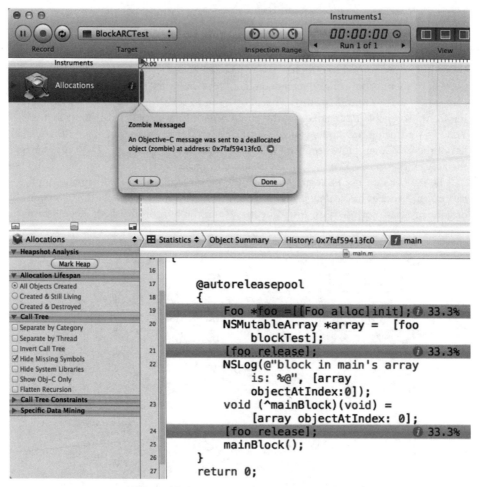

Figure 15.4 Instruments and NSZombie

Retain Cycles

There is one other potential problem with retain counting. It occurs if you create two or more objects that mutually retain each other. Suppose that the rock-and-roll game has a `Band` object. The `RockStar` has an instance variable `band` that retains the `RockStar`'s `Band`, as shown in Listing 15.3.

Listing 15.3   *RockStar.h*

```
@class Band;

@interface RockStar : NSObject
{
  Band *band;
  ...
}
@property (nonatomic, retain) Band *band;

  ...

@end
```

The `RockStar` releases the object held in `band` in its `dealloc` method, as shown in Listing 15.4.

Listing 15.4   *RockStar.m*

```
@implementation RockStar

@synthesize band;
...

- (void) dealloc
{
  [band release];

  ...

  [super dealloc];
}

@end
```

Similarly, the `Band` object has a `RockStar` variable, `leadSinger`, as shown in Listing 15.5.

Listing 15.5   *Band.h*

```
@class RockStar;

@interface Band : NSObject
{
  RockStar *leadSinger;
  ...
}
@property (nonatomic, retain) RockStar *leadSinger;

  ...

@end
```

The **Band** also follows the rules. It releases the object held in **leadSinger** in its **dealloc** method, as shown in Listing 15.6.

Listing 15.6   *Band.m*

```
@implementation Band

@synthesize leadSinger;
...

- (void) dealloc
{
  [leadSinger release];

  ...

  [super dealloc];
}

@end
```

Both **RockStar** and **Band** follow the memory management rules, but there is still a problem. When a **RockStar** object and a **Band** object are connected to each other, neither can be deallocated. This is true even if no other object owns either of them. The **RockStar**'s retain count can't go to zero, because the **Band** owns it. The **Band** will never release the **RockStar** because the **RockStar**'s ownership of the **Band** prevents **Band**'s **dealloc** from being called. When the game controller tries to release the two objects, the memory for both objects is leaked.

This unfortunate state of affairs is called a *retain cycle*. It is the simplest example of a retain cycle. You can create much more elaborate retain cycles: Object A retains Object B, which retains Object C, which retains . . . , which retains Object A.

The only way out of the problem is to change the code so at least one of the objects responsible for the retain cycle does not retain the other. For example, change the property statement in the interface section of `RockStar` to the following:

```
@property (nonatomic, assign) Band *band;
```

Because the **band** object is no longer retained, you must also remove the [band release] statement from `RockStar`'s `dealloc` method. These changes break the cycle; the objects can now be deallocated.

An object that holds a reference to another object without retaining it is said to make a *weak reference* to that object. The normal case, where an object retains an object held in one of its instance variables, is called a *strong reference*. Coding objects with weak references requires some care. When a `Band` object is deallocated, it relinquishes its ownership of the `RockStar` object held in its `leadSinger` instance variable. If there is any possibility that the `RockStar` object will continue to exist after the `Band` object is deallocated (if, for example, some other object also owns the `RockStar`), the `Band`'s `dealloc` method should be modified to set the `RockStar`'s `band` variable to `nil`, as follows:

```
- (void) dealloc
{
  [leadSinger setBand: nil];
  [leadSinger release];

  ...

  [super dealloc];
}
```

Setting the `RockStar`'s band variable to `nil` prevents the `RockStar` from inadvertently using a pointer to a deallocated object.

Objective-C has no automatic way to detect retain cycles. The only way to prevent a retain cycle is to code carefully. Use your knowledge of the structure of your classes, and do not create one. When two objects need to know about each other (the `Band` and `RockStar` in the preceding example) by holding a reference to each other, at least one of the references must be a weak reference. At least one of the pair must not retain the other.

The Final Goodbye: When Programs Terminate

When a program terminates, all the system resources the program used are reclaimed by the operating system. The virtual memory pages that back any memory you used or allocated go back onto the operating system's free list. The bad effects of forgetting to release a block of memory do not persist beyond the execution of a program. Because of this, the `dealloc` methods of any objects that are still alive when the program terminates may never be called. Everything is disappearing anyway—there is no need to go through the motions of unwinding an object graph and releasing each object individually. But there is a trap here: If you get in the habit of doing other kinds of cleanup in your `dealloc` methods, the code for those cleanups may never be called.

For example, suppose you have code that is supposed to write out some state information to a disk file when your program terminates. If you put that code into some object's `dealloc` method, you may be unpleasantly surprised. The code will never be executed.

The AppKit on Mac OS X and the UIKit on iOS provide a mechanism for handling this situation. Both provide an object (`NSApplication` and `UIApplication`, respectively) that represents the application. In both cases, the application object allows you to register a custom object, which you define and create, as the application object's delegate. When the application is about to terminate, the application object sends the delegate an `applicationWillTerminate:` message. Your delegate object does the cleanup by providing an implementation of `applicationWillTerminate:` that contains any necessary cleanup code.

If you are writing a non-GUI Foundation program, you simply place any cleanup code just before the `return` statement in your `main` routine.

Some programmers don't bother with a `dealloc` method for objects that last the entire time span of a program's execution. These are objects such as inspector panels in a GUI application. Omitting a `dealloc` method is a bad practice. If you get in the habit of always providing a `dealloc` method when an object is holding on to other objects, you're less likely to forget it in a case where it is needed. And if you reuse the code from one of your "permanent" objects in a different context in another program, one where the object doesn't last the execution life of the program, the proper `dealloc` will already be in place.

Summary

These are the key points of Objective-C's reference counting memory management system:

- An object's retain count keeps track of the number of other objects that are using the object. The retain count is frequently expressed as the number of owners an object has.
- Objects are created with a retain count of one.
- Sending an object a `retain` message increases its retain count by one.
- Sending an object a `release` message reduces its retain count by one.
- An `autorelease` message has no immediate effect, but it arranges to send a `release` message to its receiver at some future time.
- When an object's retain count reaches zero, the object is deallocated.

Reference counting is an effective way to manage memory, but you have to follow the rules, which are:

- You own any object that you have created with a method that begins with `alloc`, `new`, `copy`, or `mutableCopy`.

- You do *not* own an object returned to you by any other method. The returned object might be autoreleased; however, it might not be. You don't care. The only thing that counts is that you do not own the object.

- You can take ownership of an object by sending it a `retain` message.

- When you are finished using an object that you own, you must relinquish ownership by sending the object a `release` message or an `autorelease` message. If you don't own an object, you must not send it a `release` message or an `autorelease` message.

Some auxiliary rules:

- If you receive an object from a method that is not one of the creation methods, and you want to store it in an instance variable for future use, you must take ownership of the received object. (This rule has an exception for weak references.)

- If you have an object that has taken ownership of any of the objects stored in its instance variables, your object must implement a `dealloc` method to release those objects when it is being deallocated.

Exercises

1. Write a small program that creates an object and then sends the object a `retain` message followed by two `release` messages: one to balance the creation and one to balance the `retain`.

   a. Add statements that log the object's retain count (using the method `retainCount`) after the creation, the `retain` message, and the first `release` message. Verify that the retain counts are what you expect.

   b. Why would it be a bad idea to try and verify that the object's retain count is zero after the second `release` message?

   The `retainCount` method works for illustrative purposes in this simple exercise, but, as noted in the chapter, it isn't of much help when you are debugging a real program.

2. This exercise looks at the autorelease sequence:

   a. Define a class that overrides `release` and `dealloc` with implementations that log when the method is being executed. In both cases, the `NSLog` statement goes at the beginning of the override implementation, and a call to the superclass implementation goes at the bottom of the implementation. (Note that the return type of **release** is **oneway void**. Cocoa supports a system of distributed objects where an object in one process can message an object in a different process. When using distributed objects, the **oneway** declaration tells the originating process not to block while waiting for a return from the target process. The declaration has no meaning or effect in programs like the ones covered in this book where distributed objects are not used. (For more information see https://developer.apple.com/library/mac/#documentation/Cocoa/Conceptual/DistrObjects/DistrObjects.html#//apple_ref/doc/uid/10000102i.)

b. Write a small program that allocates and then autoreleases an instance of your class. Place **NSLog** statements just before and after the **autorelease** message, and just before and after the message that releases the autorelease pool. These log statements should just tell you that you have reached a particular point in the program. For example:

```
NSLog( @"Just before the autorelease." );
```

c. Run the program. Make sure that you understand and can explain the output.

3. Make a retain cycle:

a. Implement skeleton versions of the **RockStar** class and the **Band** class, as shown in Listings 15.3, 15.4, 15.5, and 15.6.

b. Add log statements to both classes' **dealloc** method.

c. Write a program that allocates a **RockStar** object and a **Band** object. Set the **Band**'s **leadSinger** instance variable to the **RockStar** object, and the **RockStar**'s **band** instance variable to the **Band** object.

d. Send **release** messages that balance the allocation to both objects. Verify that neither object is deallocated.

e. Change your code so that **RockStar** now makes a weak reference to its **band**. Run the program again and verify that both objects now deallocate.

4. The following two lines of code both create an empty mutable array. What is the difference between them?

```
NSMutableArray *ar1 = [[NSMutableArray alloc] init];
NSMutableArray *ar2 = [NSMutableArray array];
```

What are the memory management implications? (Hint: Neither of your answers should contain the word *autorelease*.)

ARC

Memory management is the bane of programming in Objective-C. Beginners find it confusing and difficult to learn. Even experienced Objective-C programmers seem to have trouble following the rules from time to time. The result is often memory leaks, crashes, and hours spent chasing memory bugs. Over the past years Apple has made several attempts to make the task of memory management less onerous.

The first attempt was garbage collection (GC). In a program that uses garbage collection a separate thread wakes up periodically, examines the program's memory, and returns objects that are not being used to the heap. Unfortunately, GC impacts performance and has other issues. GC was never available on iOS, and it is deprecated in OS X beginning with OS X 10.8 (Mountain Lion).

The next step was the development of the Clang Static Analyzer. The Analyzer, part of the open-source LLVM compiler project, is a program that examines code and flags a number of potential errors, including memory management issues.

The current attempt at pain-free memory management, and the subject of this chapter, is ARC. ARC stands for Automatic Reference Counting. Built on experience gained from developing the Clang Analyzer, ARC is a part of the compilation process that examines your code and *inserts* `retain, release,` and `autorelease` *messages for you* wherever they are required. This means that you no longer have to write code like the following:

```
- (void) setBigCheese:(NSString*) newBigCheese
  {
    if ( newBigCheese != bigCheese )
      {
        [newBigCheese retain];
        [bigCheese release];
        bigCheese = newBigCheese;
      }
  }
```

With ARC you can just write

```
- (void) setBigCheese:(NSString*) newBigCheese
  {
    bigCheese = newBigCheese;
  }
```

ARC takes care of releasing the old value of `bigCheese` and retaining the new value for you. Much of the work (and pain) of memory management simply disappears. If that were all there was to ARC, this chapter could end here. Unfortunately, ARC is not completely automatic in all cases. There are still a few situations where you must understand the details of reference counting and give ARC some additional information. There are also some new rules that you have to learn to abide by. The details of ARC form the content of the rest of this chapter.

What ARC Is and Is Not

Here are some basic points about ARC:

- The RC in ARC stands for reference counting. ARC is not a completely new and different memory management scheme. It automates the existing Objective-C reference counting system.

- ARC manages memory for Objective-C objects. It does *not* manage Core Foundation objects (which have their own reference counting system) or raw bytes allocated with `malloc`. If you directly `malloc()` some bytes, you must remember to `free()`them. If you create some Core Foundation objects, you must remember to release them.

- ARC's work is performed as part of the compilation process. However, it requires a runtime that implements a prescribed set of functions.

- ARC can interoperate with files and libraries that are compiled with manual reference counting. When compiling a project, you can turn ARC on and off on a file-by-file basis.

- ARC does not find or correct retain cycles. The new weak reference system (covered in a later section of this chapter) gives you a tool to help prevent retain cycles, but you still must take care with the design of your classes to ensure that you do not create retain cycles.

- ARC works on both iOS and OS X, but on OS X ARC works only with the 64-bit (new) runtime.

How ARC Works

ARC works by carefully analyzing your code, applying a set of local rules, and then inserting **retain** and **release** messages according to those rules. The *local* is important; it is what lets ARC interoperate with code that uses manual reference counting. After it inserts the memory management calls, ARC does an extensive optimization. The optimizations can be as simple as removing a **retain** immediately followed by a **release**, or as complex as creating code that looks up the call stack at run time to see what the invoking code is going to do with an object that the currently executing method returns. In some cases looking at the invoking code allows ARC to remove additional redundant messages or to avoid placing objects in the autorelease pool.

Unless you tell it otherwise by specifying one of the new variable qualifiers (see the section *New Variable Qualifiers* later in this chapter), ARC considers all variables that hold Objective-C objects to be strong references. A strong reference to an object means that the object is in use and needs to be kept alive. When assigning an object to a strong reference variable (referred to as creating a *strong reference*), ARC releases the current contents of the variable and retains the new value. When a strong reference disappears (because the object whose instance variable holds the strong reference is being deallocated, or because a local variable holding the strong reference goes out of scope), the retain count of the object held in the disappearing strong reference is decremented. In this way ARC ensures that objects stay alive as long as they are needed and disappear when they are no longer needed. When the last strong reference to an object disappears, the object's retain count drops to zero and the object is deallocated. The object's memory is returned to the heap.

ARC Reasons Correctly about More Complicated Situations

ARC behaves correctly in situations that are more complicated than simple assignment. For example, suppose that you want a method that removes an object from a position in a mutable array and then returns the object to you. **NSMutableArray** has a method to remove an object at a given index:

```
- (void)removeObjectAtIndex:(NSUInteger)index;
```

But that method doesn't return the removed object. To get what you want you'll have to write a category method for **NSMutableArray**. With ARC the category method would look like this:

```
- (id) removeAndReturnObjectAtIndex: (NSUInteger*) index
{
  id myObject = [self objectAtIndex: index];
  [self removeObject: myObject];
  return myObject;
}
```

Under manual reference counting the preceding code might cause a crash. If the only thing retaining **myObject** is the mutable array (**self** in the example), **myObject** will be deallocated when it is removed from the mutable array. The **return** statement would return a dead pointer.

ARC handles this situation correctly. It automatically inserts `retain` and `autorelease` messages into the code so that the result is the equivalent of

```
- (id) removeAndReturnObjectAtIndex: (NSUInteger*) index
{
  id myObject = [[self objectAtIndex: index] retain];
  [self removeObject: myObject];
  return [myObject autorelease];
}
```

ARC understands that an object returned by `objectAtIndex:` may not have an owner after it is removed from the array, so it immediately retains that object. ARC balances the `retain` with an `autorelease` at the last moment when the variable holding the object is going out of scope.

ARC is extremely conservative. It inserts more `retains` and `releases` than a skilled programmer might use and then relies on a sophisticated optimization pass to remove any redundant messages.

ARC Imposes Some Rules

To do its work reliably ARC imposes a few new rules and makes a few things that were conventions under manual memory management into rules. These are described in the next several sections.

You Can't Invoke the Memory Management Methods Yourself

You cannot send any `retain`, `release`, `autorelease`, or `retainCount` messages yourself in a file compiled with ARC. In fact, if you try to code one of these messages, pushy Xcode, compiling in the background, will complain with a red stop sign in the margin and an error message as soon as you type the message expression. This makes sense if you think about it. If you were able to send `retain` and `release` messages, you would be, in essence, fighting ARC for control of the memory management. You can think of the rule as "only one cook at a time." If ARC is managing an object's memory, it can't do its work correctly if you are meddling behind its back.

Similarly, ARC does not allow you to create your own custom `retain`, `release`, `autorelease`, or `retainCount` methods. You cannot override `NSObject`'s implementation of these methods. If you try to override them, your code will not compile.

ARC and `dealloc`

Under manual reference counting the main business of a `dealloc` method is to release any objects held in retained instance variables. Your object is going away, and `dealloc` is the last chance you have to relinquish your object's ownership of any other objects held in your object's instance variables. If that is all you are doing in dealloc, you no longer need the dealloc method under ARC. ARC will take care of releasing any objects held in instance variables. You don't have to do anything. But some classes may do other things in their dealloc method. Your class may have bytes acquired with malloc, or references to Core Foundation objects that need to be released. Or it may have a network connection that has to be closed. If your class had to use dealloc to do any non-Objective-C cleanup under manual reference counting, you will still need a dealloc to do that cleanup under ARC. There is one important difference: Under ARC you no longer need to call [super dealloc]. The compiler handles that for you. Invoking [super dealloc] yourself results in a compile error.

> **Note**
>
> ARC releases objects held in a class's instance variables as one of the last things it does while tearing down the object. At the point your dealloc method (if there is one) is called, all of the objects held in instance variables are still alive and valid, even if your object is the last thing holding a strong reference to them.

Method Naming Conventions

ARC formalizes some of the Cocoa naming conventions. The convention in manual reference counting is that methods whose names begin with alloc, new, copy, or mutableCopy return objects with a +1 retain count. You own any object returned by such a method. You don't own objects that are returned by methods with any other type of name. The convention is almost universally adhered to—it's one of the memory management rules—but the compiler does not enforce the convention for programs that do not use ARC. Although you shouldn't, you can violate the convention in a program that does not use ARC if you are careful and know what you are doing.

> **Note**
>
> The phrase *+1 retained object* or *+1 retain count* is commonly used to indicate that ownership of a returned object is being transferred to the calling code. Whatever the object's total retain count is, there is an unbalanced ownership from a creation or copy (the +1) that is being transferred to the calling code. The calling code is then responsible for eventually balancing the creation or copy with a release or an autorelease. ARC takes care of this obligation for you.

ARC makes the convention an official rule: Methods that begin with alloc, new, copy, or mutableCopy must pass ownership to the invoking code. Methods with other names do not pass ownership. You might have a question about this. If ARC is putting in retain and release calls hidden from your eyes, how do you know the retain status of an object at the point it is returned from a method? The surprising answer is that it doesn't matter if all of your code is compiled under ARC. ARC has complete information and will manage to do the right thing even if you violate the rule. The rule comes into play when you combine ARC files with non-ARC files or with libraries or frameworks that are not compiled with ARC. In those cases the only way

ARC can know the status of a returned object is to look at the method name. If, for example, in a non-ARC file you code a method that begins with the word **new** but returns an autoreleased object, you will confuse ARC's bookkeeping and cause an over-release and probably a crash.

What if you need (or want) to use one of these words in a method name? When checking the method name, ARC breaks the name into separate words using Camel-Cased capitalization. It then checks to see if the first word is **alloc**, **new**, or **copy** or if the first and second words are **mutable** and **copy**. As an example, ARC would expect

```
-(id) newYorkBagel; // create a YorkBagel instance
```

to return a +1 retained object. But it would expect

```
-(NewyorkBagel*) newyorkBagel; // return an existing NewyorkBagel
```

to return an object without ownership transfer.

If you find that the preceding rules are interfering with your creativity in naming methods, you can bypass them by adding the annotation **NS_RETURNS_NOT_RETAINED** or **NS_RETURNS_RETAINED** to your method declaration.

```
-(id) newYorkBagel NS_RETURNS_NOT_RETAINED;
```

should return an unretained instance of a **NewYorkBagel**.

These rules also mean that if you are going to ask the compiler to generate accessor methods for a property, you cannot give that property a name that begins with **alloc**, **new**, **copy**, or **mutableCopy**. Why? The name of the synthesized accessor will be the same as the name of the property.

```
@property (nonatomic) NSString *newEmployeeName;
```

The synthesized accessor for **newEmployeeName** is

```
- (NSString *) newEmployeeName;
```

It begins with **new** but the accessor doesn't transfer ownership to the invoking code, so it violates the rules. You can get around this by renaming the property's getter:

```
@property (nonatomic, getter=getNewEmployeeName) NSString *newEmployeeName;
```

> **Note**
> The rules are a slight change from the original Cocoa conventions. The original Cocoa conventions referred to names that "*contain* the word **copy**." The ARC rules say "names that *begin* with the word **copy** (or **mutableCopy**)."

ARC Needs to See Method Declarations

ARC needs to see a method declaration for every method that it encounters in a message expression. *See* means that the method has been declared in the same file as the message expression or in a file that is ultimately imported into that file. Under manual reference counting, using a method whose declaration is not visible at the point of the message expression, such as

```
Foo *foo  = [[Foo alloc]init];
[foo undeclaredMethod];
```

results in a warning:

```
Instance method '-undeclaredMethod' not found
(return type defaults to 'id')
```

The code may in fact execute properly if `Foo` actually implements `undeclaredMethod` and you have merely forgotten to put its declaration in `Foo`'s interface section.

Using ARC, the warning becomes an error:

```
No visible @interface for 'Foo' declares the
selector 'undeclaredMethod'
```

This is because ARC cannot determine whether the method returns an object or a primitive type from a method name. And, despite all the rules, ARC also cannot tell what the memory status of a returned object is by looking at the method name alone. You may have changed the method's expected retain status by adding an `NS_RETURNS_NOT_RETAINED` or `NS_RETURNS_RETAINED` to the method declaration.

ARC needs to see a method declaration even if the receiver is typed as `id`.

```
NSArray *list = ...
for ( id item in list )
{
  [item doSomething];
}
```

The preceding code won't compile under ARC unless the compiler can see a method declaration for `doSomething`. The declaration can be anywhere (a class header, a category header, or in some cases a protocol header) as long as it is visible to the compiler at the point of the message expression.

Obective-C Pointers and C Structs

You can't put a pointer to an Objective-C object in a C struct or union. Code like the following is not allowed under ARC:

```
struct  _sentence
  {
    NSString *noun;
    NSString *verb;
  } sentence;
```

ARC has no way of reliably following the lifetime of a C struct, so it has no way of knowing when it can safely release any objects assigned to structure members. It's

possible to get around this by declaring structure members that hold objects to be
`__unsafe_unretained`.

```
struct _sentence
  {
    __unsafe_unretained NSString *noun;
    __unsafe_unretained NSString *verb;
  } sentence;
```

`__unsafe_unretained` is a new variable qualifier introduced in ARC (see the following section). When a variable is declared as `__unsafe_unretained`, it tells ARC
to forgo any memory management when assigning an object to that variable. If you do
this, you are implicitly promising that a strong reference somewhere else is keeping the
objects held in the structure members alive, at least until those structure members are
no longer referenced.

A better solution is to turn your structure into a class:

```
@interface Sentence : NSObject
{
    NSString *noun;
    NSString *verb;
}

@property (nonatomic) noun;
@property (nonatomic) verb;

@end
```

For the price of a little bit of extra work, ARC will now manage the lifetimes of
`Sentence` and its subparts.

New Variable Qualifiers

ARC introduces some new qualifiers for variable declarations. Chapter 15, "Reference
Counting," introduced the concept of strong and weak references in the abstract. ARC
makes the notion of strong and weak references explicit.

__strong

When you store an object in a `__strong` variable, you create a strong reference to
that object. A strong reference keeps an object alive: When ARC stores an object in a
`__strong` variable, it sends the object a `retain` message. If the variable already holds
an object, ARC sends the current object a `release` or an `autorelease` message.
(ARC creates the `retain` and `release` messages for you.) An object also receives a
`release` or `autorelease` message when a `__strong` variable that holds a reference
to it goes out of scope.

When the last strong reference to an object goes away, the object's retain count goes to zero, the object is deallocated, and its bytes are returned to the heap.

> **Note**
>
> Technically the qualifier is supposed to go just before the variable name:
> ```
> NSString * __strong employeeName;
> ```
>
> However, the compiler will accept other placements:
>
> ```
> NSString __strong *employeeName;
> __strong NSString * employeeName;
> ```

Variables without a qualifier are **__strong** by default. As a consequence, you will rarely see **__strong** actually coded.

```
NSString * __strong employeeName; //employeeName is a strong reference
NSString *managerName;            // managerName is also strong reference
```

This saves you roughly 7 × (the number of variables in your project) keystrokes.

Stack local variables (variables declared in a method or function) and function and method parameters that hold objects are also **__strong** by default. And, in a change from non-ARC Objective-C, stack local variables that hold objects (except variables declared as **__unsafe_unretained**) are initialized to **nil**. (Local variables that hold ordinary C types and non-object pointers are still not initialized and initially contain junk.)

Since instance variables are also initialized to **nil**, this means that every Objective-C object strong variable is either **nil** or holds an object that was retained when it was stored in the variable. This is an important guarantee: **Every strong variable contains either a valid object or nil**. No dangling pointers. Say goodbye to one large class of bug.

> **Note**
>
> ARC has an extensive optimization phase. Depending on what is going on in the surrounding code, the exact pattern of **retain** and **release** or **autorelease** messages that are inserted when assigning an object to a **__strong** variable may not be exactly as described in the preceding text, but it is equivalent.

Memory Warnings and ARC

When you start programming for iOS, you will have to learn how to handle memory warnings. If free memory becomes scarce on a device running iOS, the system sends a memory warning to all running apps. When your app receives a memory warning, you are expected to release any objects that are not currently being used. But how can you do this if you've turned over the memory management to ARC? It's simple. Just assign **nil** to any variables holding objects that are not currently needed. ARC stores the **nil** and sends a **release** message to the object currently stored in the variable.

__weak

A __weak variable implements a zeroing weak reference. This definition has two parts. The *weak* part means that ARC does not retain an object when it is stored in a __weak variable, nor does ARC send a release message to the previous contents of the variable. Unlike a strong reference, a weak reference to an object does not prevent that object from being deallocated.

The *zeroing* part means that when an object held in a __weak variable is deallocated because the last strong reference to the object has gone away, the __weak variable and any other __weak references to the object are set to nil. The variable becomes nil as soon as the deallocation process starts. This is a great safety feature. It prevents you from accidentally sending a message to a deallocated object and causing a crash.

> **Note**
>
> It is the *reference* to the object that is weak. Objects themselves have no attribute that is strong or weak. A given object can have both strong and weak references to it. In fact, an object held in a weak reference must have a strong reference to it somewhere else, or it will be deallocated and the __weak variable set to nil.

As you might imagine, all of this requires an extensive amount of bookkeeping to work. This bookkeeping is handled by a separate bit of the runtime called (are you ready?) the *weak system*. Unfortunately, while Apple was able to make most ARC work with OS X10.6 and iOS 4 by linking in a compatibility library, the same was not possible for the weak system. __weak variables are available only starting on OS X 10.7 (Lion) and iOS 5.

> **Note**
>
> A few, mostly older, Cocoa classes such as NSWindow and NSViewController cannot be used with the weak system. Unfortunately, this is not currently noted in the reference documents for these classes. However, your application will be happy to inform you that a class doesn't work with the weak system by crashing when you assign an instance of one of these classes to a __weak variable. A list of classes that do not currently work with the weak system can be found in the Frequently Asked Questions section of http://developer.apple.com/library/mac/#releasenotes/ObjectiveC/RN-TransitioningToARC/Introduction/Introduction.html.

__autoreleasing

When an object is assigned to an __autoreleasing variable, ARC first retains the object and then autoreleases it. ARC does nothing to the previous value that was stored in the variable.

You will almost never need to use __autoreleasing. Its primary use is for variables that return objects by reference in a method parameter. The Cocoa convention is that returning an object by reference does *not* transfer ownership of that object to the calling code. Objects returned by reference are expected to be autoreleased.

The most common examples of `__autoreleasing` variables are the many Cocoa methods that return an `NSError` value by reference.

```
NSError *err;
BOOL worked = [someObject doSomethingWithPossibleError: &err];
if ( ! worked )
   {
       NSLog(@"Oops: %@", err);
   }
```

The `NSError` object passed back in the variable `err` is autoreleased. Strictly speaking, the signature of the method in the preceding code should be

```
- (void) doSomethingWithPossibleError:(__autoreleasing NSError**) error;
```

However, the compiler recognizes the situation and treats the returned error object as `__autoreleasing` even if the qualifier is not there:

```
-(void) doSomethingWithPossibleError:(NSError**) error;// don't need it
```

Actual `__autoreleasing` declarations are extremely rare.

> **Note**
>
> Only automatic variables (stack local variables and parameters) may be declared as `__autoreleasing`.

__unsafe_unretained

This scary-sounding qualifier is just another name for "assign." It means that ARC does no memory management when an object is assigned to a variable declared as `__unsafe_unretained`. An `__unsafe_unretained` variable is a form of weak reference, but one that is unsafe because it may wind up holding a dangling pointer. Like a `__weak` variable, it doesn't retain its contents. But, unlike a `__weak` variable, its value is not automatically set to `nil` when the object it holds is deallocated. This means that you must be careful to set its value to `nil` yourself when the object it is holding is no longer needed. If you forget to do this, you may wind up sending a message to a deallocated object and cause a crash.

The main use of `__unsafe_unretained` is to create weak references and break retain cycles in code that must function on OS X 10.6 or iOS 4.2 where the weak system is not available.

> **Note**
>
> Stack local variables declared as `__unsafe_unretained` are not initialized.

Properties

The new qualifiers can be used with Objective-C declared properties. The variable representing the property is given the same qualifier that is used in the property declaration:

```
@property (nonatomic, strong) NSArray *anArray;
// anArray is __strong

@property (nonatomic, weak) ADelegateClass *delegate;
// delegate is __weak

@property (nonatomic, unsafe_unretained) NSString *name;
// name is __unsafe_unretained
```

In property declarations compiled with ARC, **strong** and **retain** are synonyms. Properties without a qualifier are strong by default. **assign** and **unsafe_unretained** are also synonyms. The following two statements produce the same result:

```
@property (nonatomic, strong) NSArray *anArray;
@property (nonatomic, retain) NSArray *anArray;
```

These two statements also produce the same result:

```
@property (nonatomic, unsafe_unretained) NSString *name;
@property (nonatomic, assign) NSString *name;
```

As a matter of documentation clarity you might prefer **strong** over **retain** and **unsafe_unretained** over **assign**.

A Potential Problem with Older Code

The new variable qualifiers mean that there is an essential difference between variable declarations under ARC and variable declarations under manual reference counting. Under ARC variable declarations also carry memory management semantics, while under manual reference counting they don't. This can create some issues when moving older code to ARC. Consider this bit of code from Chapter 13, "Protocols":

```
@interface TablePrinter : NSObject
{
    id <TablePrinterDataSource> dataSource;
}

@property(nonatomic, assign)
        id <TablePrinterDataSource> dataSource;
...

@end
```

```
@interface TablePrinter
@synthesize dataSource;
...
@end
```

This code gives an error at the `@synthesize` line when compiled with ARC. The problem is that the `dataSource` instance variable has no qualifier, so it is now strong by default. But the property declaration says `assign`, which ARC takes as a synonym for `__unsafe_unretained`. The discrepancy causes an error.

To fix this problem simply change the code so that both the variable declaration and the property indicate that `dataSource` is a weak variable:

```
@interface TablePrinter : NSObject
{
    __weak id <TablePrinterDataSource> dataSource;
}

@property(nonatomic, weak)
      id <TablePrinterDataSource> dataSource;
...

@end

@interface TablePrinter
@synthesize dataSource;
...
@end
```

Alternatively, you can omit the explicit declaration of `dataSource` and let the compiler synthesize the instance variable for you.

Retain Cycles

Retain cycles are a problem with reference counting systems. Retain cycles occur when two or more objects mutually retain each other. To refresh your memory take a moment and review the section on retain cycles in the previous chapter. The simplest example of a retain cycle occurs when two objects hold strong references to each other. A holds a strong reference to B, and B holds a strong reference to A. The result is a memory leak. Neither can ever be deallocated, even if there are no other strong references to either A or B.

> **Note**
>
> The terminology can vary a bit. Some people refer to retain cycles as *reference cycles* or simply *cycles*. Under ARC Apple has taken to calling them *strong reference cycles*. These names all mean the same thing.

ARC does not catch or fix retain cycles for you. In fact, ARC makes it slightly easier to accidentally create retain cycles. Since references under ARC are strong (retaining) by default, it is easy to inadvertently create a retain cycle if you are not paying attention. The solution, as in Chapter 15, "Reference Counting," is to use a weak reference to break the cycle. With ARC, that means declaring one of the variables in the cycle to be __weak.

Using the example from Chapter 15, consider a game that has a **Band** object and a **RockStar** object that refer to each other. Rewritten for ARC, the @interface sections for the **Band** and **RockStar** classes should look like Listings 16.1 and 16.2.

Listing 16.1 *RockStar.h*

```
@class Band;

@interface RockStar : NSObject
{
    __weak Band *band;
    ...
}
@property (nonatomic, weak) Band *band;

    ...

@end
```

Listing 16.2 *Band.h*

```
@class RockStar;

@interface Band : NSObject
{
    RockStar *leadSinger;
    ...
}
@property (nonatomic, strong) RockStar *leadSinger;

    ...

@end
```

This breaks the cycle. If there are no other strong references to **Band** and **RockStar**, the **Band** object is deallocated (since **RockStar** does not have a strong reference to it). As part of its deallocation process, the **Band** object releases its strong reference to the **RockStar** object, permitting the **RockStar** object to be deallocated.

Finding Retain Cycles with Instruments

While ARC doesn't help you with retain cycles, the Instruments application that comes with the developer tools will show you any retain cycles that are causing leaks in your program. You can run Instruments from within Xcode. Under the *Product* menu in Xcode choose *Profile* (⌘-I). After your project builds, you will see the Instruments startup screen, as shown in Figure 16.1. Select the *Leaks* instrument and hit Return. Instruments will run your application and report any leaks it finds as vertical orange bars in the *Leaks* trace. (There are two traces: *Leaks* and *Allocations*. The *Allocations* instrument comes along for free when you choose the *Leaks* instrument.)

If you have any leaks, choose *Leaks* in the column heading above the lists of leaks to display a pop-up, and then choose *Cycles & Roots* as shown in Figure 16.2. (Make sure that you have the *Leaks* Instrument selected and not the *Allocations* Instrument.) Instruments will list any cycles that are causing leaks.

When you select one of the items in the list of cycles, Instruments shows you a graph of the references that are causing the cycle. In Figure 16.2 Instruments shows a cycle caused by using versions of the `Band` and `RockStar` classes that have not been fixed to eliminate the retain cycle by using a weak reference.

Figure 16.1   Instruments startup screen

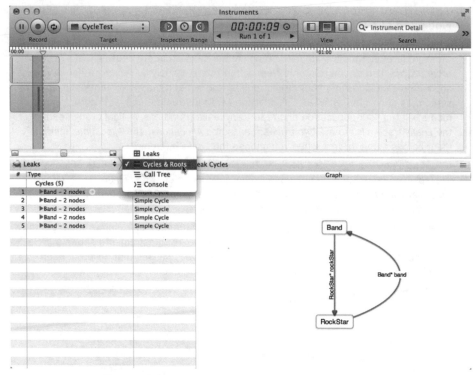

Figure 16.2   Instruments at work finding a retain cycle

ARC and Core Foundation

It would be ideal if you could write all your OS X and iOS programs with pure Objective-C. In the real world, however, it is often necessary to use objects and code from the Core Foundation framework (see Chapter 8, "Frameworks") or one of the other plain C frameworks that are built on top of Core Foundation (for example, Core Graphics, Image I/O, or the iOS AddressBook framework). For convenience I will refer to these frameworks collectively as Core Foundation (or CF).

To review, the Core Foundation frameworks use a handcrafted object system written in plain C. CF objects have their own separate reference counting system. Objects obtained from functions that have the words **Create** or **Copy** in their names are returned with a +1 retain count. The function **CFRetain(aCFObject)** increases the retain count of **aCFObject** by one, and **CFRelease(aCFObject)** decreases the retain count by one. When an object's retain count drops to zero, it is deallocated. If you receive a CF object from a **Create** or **Copy** function, you must eventually balance the creation or copy with a call to **CFRelease**. If you fail to do that, you have a leak. This should all seem familiar at this point.

ARC does *not* automate this separate reference counting system. Let me repeat that. If you are using CF objects, you are responsible for understanding manual reference counting and properly retaining and releasing your CF objects.

If your Objective-C objects never meet your CF objects, things are relatively simple. ARC manages the Objective-C objects, and you manually manage the CF objects. However, there are a couple of situations where ARC and CF cross paths: Objective-C framework methods that return CF objects and toll-free bridging (see Chapter 8, "Frameworks"), where a given object (a particular set of bytes) can be treated as an Objective-C object or as a CF object depending on how you choose to look at it. We'll look at these two situations in the next two sections.

> **Note**
>
> Recall from Chapter 8 that all Core Foundation objects are toll-free bridged at the level of `NSObject`. This means that at a minimum they can be cast to `id` and they will respond correctly to Objective-C `retain` and `release` messages.

CF Objects Returned from Methods

Some Cocoa methods return CF-level objects. For example, the Cocoa Touch color class, `UIColor`, has a getter method that returns a `CGColorRef`, the Core Graphics color object. When a CF object is returned by an Objective-C method, ARC allows a cast to `id`:

```
UIColor *aUIColor = ...
NSMutableArray *colorArray = [NSMutableArray array];
id aCGColor = (id)[aUIColor CGColor];
[array addObject: aCGColor];
```

ARC lets you do this because it understands the Cocoa naming conventions. Since the method `CGColor` doesn't begin with `alloc`, `new`, `copy`, or `mutableCopy`, ARC knows that the method doesn't transfer ownership.

Toll-Free Bridging

In all other situations a cast from one side of the toll-free bridge to the other is a problem for ARC. When you cast an object from CF to Objective-C (or the other way around), the result is a single object whose retain count can be manipulated by two different systems that don't talk to each other. ARC knows nothing about CF memory management conventions. To make matters worse, you have direct control over one of the systems (CF) but not the other (ARC). Like a soup made by two cooks, this is a recipe for trouble. The compiler's way of avoiding trouble is to disallow casts between Objective-C and CF objects. If you try to cast directly from a Core Foundation type to its toll-free bridged equivalent (or vice versa), the compiler flags the cast as an error.

The problem is fixed by supplying ARC with some additional information via a special type of cast called a *bridging cast*. There are three possible cases:

- The cast does not transfer ownership.
- The cast transfers ownership out of CF and into ARC.
- The cast transfers ownership out of ARC and into CF.

We'll consider each in turn.

Cast Does Not Transfer Ownership

In this case one side is just temporarily "borrowing" the object from the other side. There is no transfer of ownership.

```
CFStringRef cfString =
    CFStringCreateWithCString( NULL,
                              "Four score and seven years ago...",
                              kCFStringEncodingASCII );
NSString *nsString = (__bridge NSString*) cfString;
NSLog (@"%@", nsString);
CFRelease( cfString );
```

The `__bridge` tells ARC that there is no ownership transfer in the cast. The object was created on the CF side. Because there is no ownership transfer, a balancing call to `CFRelease()` must occur on the CF side.

Cast Transfers Ownership out of CF and into ARC

A `__bridge_transfer` cast transfers ownership from CF to ARC. It tells ARC that there is an unbalanced retain count on the CF side (from a **Create** or **Copy**) that must eventually be balanced by a **release**. ARC takes responsibility for sending that **release**.

```
// Create object in CF code
CFStringRef cfString =
    CFStringCreateWithCString( NULL,
                              "Four score and seven years ago...",
                              kCFStringEncodingASCII );

// cast and transfer ownership of the object to ARC

NSString *nsString = (__bridge_transfer NSString*) cfString;

// ARC takes ownership of the object

NSLog (@"%@", nsString);
...
// ARC will send nsString a release message when it is no longer needed
```

Cast Transfers Ownership out of ARC and into CF

A `__bridge_retained` cast goes the other way. It transfers ownership from ARC to CF. It tells ARC that responsibility for balancing the creation of an object is being passed to CF. When the CF code is finished with the object, it must call `CFRelease()` with the object as an argument.

```
// Create an ARC managed NSString
NSString *nsString = [NSString stringWithUTF8String: "Four score"];

//cast and transfer ownership to CF

CFStringRef cfString = (__bridge_retained CFString*) nsString;

// ARC no longer manages nsString
// Use cfString
...
// CF owns cfString, it must release it
CFRelease ( cfString );
```

Hide Your Casts with Macros

You can improve the aesthetics of your code by hiding `__bridge_transfer` and `__bridge_retained` casts with the macros `CFBridgingRelease()` and `CFBridgingRetain()`, respectively. These two lines of code do the same thing:

```
NSString *nsString = (__bridge_transfer NSString*) cfString;
NSString *nsString = CFBridgingRelease( cfString );
```

as do these two lines:

```
CFStringRef cfString = (__bridge_retained CFString*) nsString;
CFStringRef cfString = CFBridgingRetain( nsString );
```

Casting to and from `void*`

ARC forbids direct casts between object pointers and variables typed as **void***:

```
NSArray *array = [NSArray arrayWithObject: @"Dog"];
void *cPointer = (void*) array; //WRONG - gives a compile error
```

The reason is the same reason that ARC forbids most direct casts between object pointers and Core Foundation types. If you cast an object pointer to **void***, you are giving that object to an unknown quantity. ARC doesn't manage non-Objective-C pointers, so it has no way of following what happens to an object stored in a **void*** variable. Going the other way, if you cast a **void*** pointer to an Objective-C object (assuming that what was stored in the **void*** variable was, in fact, an Objective-C object), ARC has no way to determine that object's ownership status.

If you are sure you know what you are doing, you can overrule ARC by using one of the bridge casts:

```
NSArray *array = [NSArray arrayWithObject: @"Dog"];
void *cPointer = (__bridge void*) array; // OK
```

But beware! A __bridge cast has no memory management implications, and void* is not a strong reference. If all the strong references to your object go away, it will be deallocated and your void* variable may be left holding a pointer to a dead object. In the following code the value returned by getPointer is an invalid pointer. Using it may cause a crash.

```
- (void*) getPointer
{
  NSArray *array = [NSArray arrayWithObject: @"Dog"];
  void *cPointer = (__bridge void*) array; // OK
  return cPointer;   // WRONG!
}
```

> **Note**
>
> It is hard to predict whether using the pointer returned by the preceding example will actually cause a crash. The answer depends on exactly when you use the pointer. If ARC has autoreleased array and the current pool has not yet been emptied, you may not have a crash. But that is purely an accident. What is certain is that using an invalid pointer is *very* bad practice. At some point in time it will very likely cause a crash.

Casting back and forth to void* is a bad idea. You shouldn't do it. Unfortunately, there are a few places in the Cocoa frameworks where you are forced to cast to and from void*. Most of these are cases where you are setting up a callback. You pass the system a selector to use as a callback and a context to be used as the selector's argument when it is called. Usually you want to use an NSDictionary or an NSArray as the context argument. But, for reasons lost in the history of Cocoa, these context arguments are typed as void* rather than id.

A typical example is the code used to display a sheet in OS X.

> **Note**
>
> Sheets are the small temporary panels that drop from the top of the window frame in an OS X program. They are used for tasks like file selection or letting the user set values.

This method has an argument for a delegate, a didEnd selector that the delegate implements, and an argument for a context object, which is typed as void*. When the sheet is dismissed, the delegate invokes the didEnd method with the context object as the argument.

The context object, typically an NSDictionary, is used to pass information from the object creating the sheet to the code handling the user's input. Properly modified for ARC, the code looks like this:

```
@implementation SheetController

-(IBAction)showTheSheet:(id)sender
{
  // This code sets up and displays the sheet

  NSDictionary *contextObject = [NSDictionary dictionary]
    ...
    // fill the dictionary with context information
    ...

  [NSApp beginSheet:sheetWindow
         modalForWindow: window
         modalDelegate: sheetControllerDelegate
         didEndSelector:
           @selector(sheetDidEnd:returnCode:contextInfo:);
         contextInfo:(__bridge_retained void*) contextObject];
}
@end


@implementation SheetControllerDelegate

- (void)sheetDidEnd:(NSWindow*) sheet
         returnCode:(int)returnCode
         contextInfo:(void*) contextObject
{
  // This method is invoked when the user dismisses the sheet

  NSDictionary *contextDict =
      (__bridge_transfer NSDictionary*) contextObject

  // Do something with contextDict
  ...
}
@end
```

Note the use of `__bridge_retained` and `__bridge_transfer` casts. The
`__bridge_retained` cast passes ownership to the sheet code. This is balanced when
ownership of the dictionary is passed back to ARC with a `__bridge_transfer` cast
in the callback. (The sheet code does no actual memory management.) Using plain
`__bridge` casts in the preceding code could cause a crash. When the context dictionary
is created, it is stored in a local variable. That local variable goes out of scope when
`showTheSheet:` returns. Without the `__bridge_retained` there are no longer any
strong references to the dictionary and it is deallocated. The `contextObject` argument passed to the callback now contains a pointer to a deallocated object and can
cause a crash when it is referenced.

> **Note**
>
> Apple is in the process of replacing this type of code with code that uses blocks (see Chapter 17) for callbacks.

ARC and Extra Autorelease Pools

Using ARC, you don't know whether a particular object will be released or auto-released, or exactly when it will be deallocated. However, you can still use additional autorelease pools to limit your memory footprint when you have code that make lots of objects that are needed for only a short time:

```
id myObject = ...
for ( int j = 0; j < MANY_TIMES;; j++ )
  {
    @autoreleasepool
      {
      // code that allocates many objects
      // that are used only temporarily
      [myObject makeLotsOfObjects];
      }
  }
```

The additional `@autoreleasepool` scope in the preceding example ensures that any temporary objects created during a single pass through the loop receive a **release** message no later than the point at the bottom of the loop where the `@autoreleasepool` scope ends and the corresponding autorelease pool is emptied. ARC may decide to send a **release** message to such objects at an earlier point rather than autoreleasing them, but the extra `@autoreleasepool` scope prevents the case where the number of objects in the current autorelease pool increases with each iteration of the loop.

ARC and Exceptions

ARC does not handle exceptions cleanly. After an exception has been thrown, there is no guarantee that the memory management bookkeeping is in a consistent state. Objects held in strong variables that should be released when an exception is thrown are not released. This is not a serious problem: As noted in Chapter 10, "Control Structures in Objective-C," Objective-C exceptions are for truly exceptional conditions, not for flow control. They are used to catch programmer errors and situations where the program is about to crash. Recoverable error conditions (things like a missing data file) are handled by passing an **NSError** object back to the calling code.

> **Note**
>
> If you must use exceptions and want ARC to do a better job of cleaning up when an exception is thrown, you can compile your code with the `-fobjc-arc-exceptions` flag.

Using ARC

OK, you're sold! ARC is for you. Where can you use it and how do you turn it on?

ARC on Mac OS X

ARC works only with the 64-bit (new) Objective-C runtime. You cannot use ARC for 32-bit programs or for fat binaries that include both a 32-bit version and a 64-bit version of the program. This means that programs using ARC will not run on some of the very early Intel Macs that are 32-bit only.

Using OS X 10.7 (Lion) or later, you can build ARC programs for deployment back to 10.6 (Snow Leopard). Note, however, that the weak system is not available on 10.6. If your program must run on 10.6, use __unsafe_unretained instead of __weak for weak references.

You cannot build ARC programs for OS X on 10.6.

ARC on iOS

You can build ARC programs for iOS (both simulator and device) on OS X 10.6 or later. ARC programs can be deployed back to iOS 4, but the weak system is not available on iOS 4.

Building with ARC

ARC requires the Clang compiler that is included with the Xcode 4 (or later) distribution. The compiler flag -fobjc-arc tells the compiler to use ARC; the flag –fno-objc-arc turns ARC off. These flags may be set on a file-by-file basis.

The easiest way to use ARC is to let Xcode set the flags for you. To start a new project in Xcode choose *File > New > Project...* (Shift-⌘-N). Xcode shows you a sheet that offers a choice of the type of application to build. When you have made a selection and clicked *Next* (or used the Return key), the next sheet includes a check box labeled *Use Automatic Reference Counting* (Figure 16.3). If that box is checked, Xcode will use ARC for all your files.

If you want to turn ARC off for a particular file, do the following:

1. Click on your project in the *Project Navigator.* Xcode will show you a column with your project and all its targets in the main window.

2. Click on the target that you are building.

3. Click on *Build Phases* in the menu strip that runs along the top of the main window.

4. Click on the disclosure triangle labeled *Compile Sources.*

5. Xcode shows you a scrolling list of all the files that will be compiled when the target is built.

6. Double-click on the file that you want compiled without ARC.

7. Xcode pops up a box. Enter **–fobjc-no-arc** and click *Done* (see Figure 16.4).

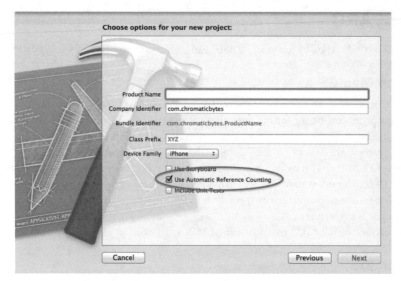

Figure 16.3   Enabling ARC for a new project

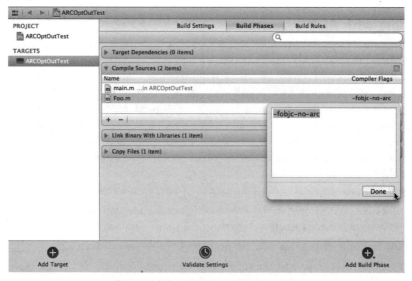

Figure 16.4   Disabling ARC for a file

ARC Uses Runtime Functions

Let me tell you a secret: ARC doesn't directly invoke `retain`, `release`, or `autorelease` on objects. It calls one of a set of runtime C functions. For example, instead of inserting

```
[yourObject retain];
```

into your code, ARC inserts the C function `objc_retain()`:

```
objc_retain( yourObject );
```

There are similar functions for `release` and `autorelease` as well as additional functions that are optimized for special situations.

The function `objc_retain()` eventually invokes `yourObject`'s `retain` method. Remember that under ARC you are not allowed to override `retain`, `release`, or `autorelease`. So unless `yourObject` belongs to or is a subclass of a class that was compiled without ARC, it is `NSObject`'s implementation of `retain` that is invoked. As part of the ARC project Apple has moved `NSObject`'s implementation of the memory management methods directly into the Objective-C runtime. This results in a considerable performance improvement.

I mention these functions so you will understand what they are if you see them in a stack trace or a disassembly, but they are not part of a public API. You should never call them yourself. They are reserved for the compiler's use. If you try to use them yourself, the code will compile, but it will confuse ARC's bookkeeping with very likely unpleasant results.

More Information

The online Apple documentation on ARC is rather thin. If you have access to the WWDC 2012 videos, I recommend viewing session 406, *Adopting Automatic Reference Counting*.

If you want to know more about how ARC works, you can read the ARC specification at http://clang.llvm.org/docs/AutomaticReferenceCounting.html. Note that this is a specification, not user documentation. Parts of the specification are difficult reading if you are not a compiler geek.

Summary

ARC takes much of the pain out of memory management by automating the existing manual reference counting system. Instead of having to code `retain`, `release`, and `autorelease` messages yourself, ARC figures out where they are needed and inserts them for you.

In return for lifting this burden ARC asks you to obey a few new rules:

- You are not allowed to send `retain`, `release`, `autorelease`, or `retainCount` messages yourself.

- You are not allowed to override `retain`, `release`, `autorelease`, or `retainCount` with your own implementation of these methods.

- You no longer need a `dealloc` method to release objects held in instance variables. If you have other business to conduct when an object is being deallocated (such as freeing bytes obtained from `malloc` or releasing Core Foundation objects), you may still use `dealloc`. If you have a `dealloc` method, ARC calls `[super dealloc]` for you. Including `[super dealloc]` in your `dealloc` method is a compile error under ARC.

- You can't store Objective-C objects in C structs.

- The Cocoa naming conventions for methods that return retained objects are now rules.

Most of the time coding for ARC just means not having to code `retain`, `release`, and `autorelease`. But there are still some situations that require care and thought:

- Casting between Objective-C objects and `void*` and casting between Objective-C and Core Foundation objects require the use of special casts called bridging casts.

- ARC does not detect or remove retain cycles. It does help you avoid retain cycles by providing weak zeroing references with the new `__weak` variable qualifier. Objects stored in `__weak` variables are not retained. When the object held in a `__weak` variable is deallocated, the variable is automatically set to `nil`. The `__weak` qualifier is not available on iOS 4 or OS X 10.6.

ARC requires Xcode 4. Programs compiled with ARC can be deployed back to OS X 10.7 and iOS 5 with the weak system, and back to OS X 10.6 and iOS 4 without the weak system.

Exercises

1. Revisit your HelloObjectiveC program from Chapter 4, "Your First Objective-C Program."

   a. Try compiling the program with ARC. (Search for *Objective-C Automatic Reference Counting* in your Xcode *Build Settings* and set its value to *Yes*.) Verify that it does not compile and note the various error messages.

   b. Fix the program so that it does compile under ARC and verify that it still works correctly.

2. Apple's official position is that you shouldn't worry about where the compiler is inserting `retain`, `release`, and `autorelease` messages for you. You should just trust the compiler to do the correct thing. That's probably a good idea for the most part. However, if you, like me, are curious, it is interesting to see what the ARC is actually doing.

   a. Create a class that does something trivial. Exactly what your class does doesn't matter; it could, for example, have no instance variables and a single method that logs itself. We are more interested in what happens to instances of this class than in what it does.

   b. Add a `dealloc` method that logs itself and then invokes `[super dealloc]`.

   c. In your class override `retain`, `release`, and `autorelease`. Your overrides of these methods will log that they were called and then call the corresponding superclass implementation.

   For example, here is what the override of `release` looks like:

   ```
   - (oneway void) release
   {
     NSLog( "Releasing a %@", [self class] );
     [super release];
   }
   ```

   The return type for both `retain` and `autorelease` is `id`. Your versions should log themselves and then return the result of sending the same message to `super`. Yes, this class won't compile under ARC, but you are going to take advantage of ARC's interoperability with manual reference counting and compile this one file without ARC.

   d. Add a convenience constructor for your class:

   ```
   + (MyClass*) myClass
   {
       return [[[myClass alloc] init] autorelease];
   }
   ```

   e. Write a test program that exercises your class. For example, create an instance of your class by using `alloc`, and create another by using your convenience constructor. Try passing an instance of your class to another class that stores it in an instance variable.

f. Set your project to compile with ARC, but compile your logging class without ARC as described in the section *Building with ARC* earlier in this chapter.

g. Build and run your program. Look at the output of your logging class and note where it is retained, released, and autoreleased by ARC. Try rearranging your code and see what effect that has on the various messages. (There is no "right" answer for this exercise—the idea is to just get a feel for what ARC is doing.)

Blocks

Blocks provide a way to package up some executable code and a context (various variables) as a single entity so they can be handed off for execution at a later time or on a different thread. In other languages, blocks or similar constructs are sometimes called *closures* or *anonymous functions*. Blocks are an Apple-supplied extension to C, Objective-C 2.0, and C++. Apple has submitted blocks to the C standards working group as a proposed extension to C. Blocks are available on Mac OS X 10.6 or later and iOS 4.0 or later.

> **Note**
>
> You can use blocks on iOS 2.2+ and on Mac OS X Leopard (10.5) if you install *Plausible Blocks* (PLBlocks). Plausible Blocks, a reverse-engineered port from Apple-released open-source Darwin OS code, provides the compilers and runtime required to use blocks. You can obtain Plausible Blocks from http://code.google.com/p/plblocks/.

Handing off a package of work is useful in many situations, but one of the main driving forces behind the adoption of blocks is Apple's *Grand Central Dispatch* (GCD) feature. GCD is designed to make concurrency easier to program and more efficient to execute. Essentially, GCD is a thread pool that is managed for you by the operating system. The idea behind GCD is that the operating system has a global view of all the processes running on your Mac or iOS device and allocates resources (CPU, GPU, and RAM) as needed to make things run more efficiently. GCD can make better decisions than a user space program can make about the number of threads to use and when to schedule them for execution. You can use blocks to submit units of work for GCD to execute.

> **Note**
>
> GCD provides a C interface for submitting blocks. The Foundation framework provides a higher-level interface to GCD through the classes `NSOperationQueue`, `NSBLockOperation`, and `NSInvocationOperation`.
>
> `NSInvocationOperation` allows you to submit units of work as `NSInvocation` objects instead of blocks, but as you will see in the section *NSInvocation*, `NSInvocation` objects are somewhat difficult to set up. Blocks are much easier to use.

This chapter is an introduction to blocks. You will learn how to define a block, how a block has access to variables in its surrounding context, how to use a block in your own code, and about the somewhat tricky topic of memory management for blocks. The chapter also explores some pitfalls that can befall an unwary user of blocks. As with the rest of the book, we will look at how to use blocks in a manual reference counting environment first and then cover how to use blocks under ARC. Understanding how blocks interact with memory management is important because there is one area where ARC is not quite automatic.

Before looking at blocks in detail, the chapter takes a pair of detours and looks at two earlier ways of packaging up functionality: *function pointers* and the Foundation class `NSInvocation`. These detours illustrate how awkward it was to package up functionality in the pre-blocks era and should motivate you to learn to use blocks instead.

Function Pointers

When the compiler encounters a function call, it inserts a jump instruction to the code that performs the function. (A jump instruction causes the program execution to jump to the specified code instead of executing the line of code directly after the jump instruction.) To return, the function executes a jump instruction back to the line of code following the original function call. In a normal function call, the landing point of the jump instruction (and hence the function that is called) is static. It is determined at compile time. But a function call can be made dynamic through the use of a *function pointer.*

The following line declares `myFunctionPtr` as a pointer to a function that takes two `int`s as arguments and returns an `int`:

```
int (*myFunctionPtr) (int, int);
```

Figure 17.1 shows the anatomy of a function pointer.

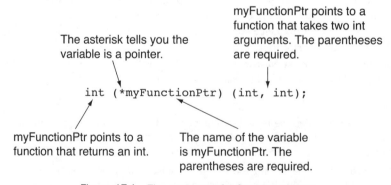

Figure 17.1 The anatomy of a function pointer

The general form of a function pointer is

```
return_type (*name)(list of argument types);
```

Function pointers are a low point in C syntax. Instead of reading left to right or right to left, they read from the inside out. More complicated function pointer declarations can quickly turn into puzzles, as you will see in Exercise 17.1.

A Syntax Quirk in Objective-C

The "from the inside out" declaration style of function pointers doesn't fit with Objective-C's syntax for method arguments. Recall that Objective-C requires the type for a method argument to be enclosed in parentheses *before* the argument name. This conflict is resolved in favor of the syntax for method arguments.

When declaring a method argument that is a function pointer, the name comes outside. For example, a pointer to a function that has no arguments or return value is normally declared as follows:

```
void (*funcPtr)(void);
```

A *function* that takes a function pointer of the preceding type as an argument is declared like this:

```
void functionWithFPArg(void (*funcPtr)(void));
```

But a *method* with the same argument type is declared like this:

```
-(void) methodWithFPArg:(void(*)(void)) funcPtr;
```

Putting the name of the function pointer last in a function pointer declaration works only when declaring the type of a method argument. Putting the name last results in a compiler error in any other situation.

You can also declare arrays of function pointers. The following line declares **fpArray** as an array of 10 pointers to functions. Each function takes a single argument, a pointer to a **float**, and returns **void**:

```
void (*fpArray[10])(float*);
```

A function pointer can point to a function that has another function pointer as an argument or a return value:

```
void (*(*complicatedFunctionPointer)(void))(void);
```

complicatedFunctionPointer is a pointer to a function that takes no arguments and returns a pointer to a function that takes no arguments and returns **void**.

Declarations like the preceding one are ugly, but you can make your code cleaner by hiding the ugliness with a typedef:

```
typedef void (*(*complicatedFunctionPointerType)(void))(void);
```

```
complicatedFunctionPointerType myFunctionPtr;
```

Calling a Function with a Function Pointer

The following example shows how to assign a function to a function pointer and how to call the function using the function pointer:

```
void logInt( int n )         // Code a function
  {
    NSLog(@"The integer is: %d", n);
  }


void (*myFunctionPtr)(int); // Declare a function pointer

myFunctionPtr = logInt;      // Make it point to logInt
myFunctionPtr( 5 );          // Execute the function through the pointer
```

To make the function pointer refer to a function, you simply assign it the name of the function. The function must be defined or visible by a forward declaration at the point it is assigned.

To call a function through a function pointer, you simply add the arguments, encased in parentheses, to the function pointer. A function call through a function pointer is just like a normal function call except that you use the name of the function pointer variable instead of the function name, as shown in the previous code snippet.

Note

There is no need to use the address-of operator (&) or the dereferencing operator (*) with function pointers. The compiler knows which names are functions or function pointers and which names are regular variables.

Using Function Pointers

One of the primary uses of function pointers is for *callbacks*. Callbacks are used in situations where you have a function or method that is going to do some work for you, but you would like the opportunity to insert your own code somewhere in the process. To do this, you pass the working function or method a pointer to a function containing the code you want executed. At the appropriate time, the working function or method will call your function for you.

For example, **NSMutableArray** provides the following method for use in custom sorting:

```
- (void)sortUsingFunction:
          (NSInteger (*)(id, id, void *))compare
              context:(void *)context
```

When you invoke **sortUsingFunction:context:**, the method sorts the contents of the receiver. To perform the sort, **sortUsingFunction:context:** must examine pairs of array elements and decide how they are ordered. To make these decisions, sortUsingFunction:context: calls the compare function that you passed in by pointer when the method was invoked.

The compare function must look at the two objects it receives and decide (based on whatever criterion you require) whether they are ordered as NSOrderedAscending, NSOrderedSame, or NSOrderedDescending.

> **Note**
>
> NSOrderedAscending, NSOrderedSame, and NSOrderedDescending are integer constants defined by the Foundation framework.

The sortUsingFunction:context: method also passes the compare function the void* pointer that the method received as its context argument. This is a pure pass-through; sortUsingFunction:context: doesn't look at or modify context. context may be NULL if compare doesn't require any additional information.

Listing 17.1 sorts an array containing some NSNumber objects. The address of a BOOL is passed in to control the direction of a numerical sort.

Listing 17.1   *ArraySortWithFunctionPointer.m*

```
#import <Foundation/Foundation.h>

NSInteger numericalSortFn( id obj1, id obj2, void *ascendingFlag )
{
  int value1 = [obj1 intValue];
  int value2 = [obj2 intValue];
  if ( value1 == value2 )  return NSOrderedSame;
  if ( *(BOOL*) ascendingFlag )
    {
      return  ( value1 < value2 ) ?
          NSOrderedAscending : NSOrderedDescending;
    }
  else
    {
      return  ( value1 < value2 )
        ? NSOrderedDescending : NSOrderedAscending;
    }
}

int main (int argc, const char *argv[])
{
  @autoreleasepool
    {
      // Put some number NSNumber objects in an array
      NSMutableArray *numberArray =
        [[NSMutableArray alloc] initWithCapacity: 5];
      [numberArray addObject: [NSNumber numberWithInt: 77]];
```

```
        [numberArray addObject: [NSNumber numberWithInt: 59]];
        [numberArray addObject: [NSNumber numberWithInt: 86]];
        [numberArray addObject: [NSNumber numberWithInt: 68]];
        [numberArray addObject: [NSNumber numberWithInt: 51]];

        NSLog( @"Before sort: %@", [numberArray description] );

          // This flag controls the sort direction.
          // Change it to NO to sort in descending order.
          BOOL ascending = YES;

        // Sort the array
        [numberArray sortUsingFunction: numericalSortFn
                          context: &ascending];

        NSLog( @"After sort: %@", [numberArray description] );
        [numberArray release];
    }
  return 0;
}
```

Notice:

- `ascendingFlag` is passed in as `void*`. It must be cast as `BOOL*` before it can be dereferenced to get the `BOOL` value.

- The name of a function, in this case `numericalSortFn`, can serve as a properly typed pointer to that function. Here, it is used as the argument when invoking `sortUsingFunction:context:` without defining a separate function pointer variable.

The Trouble with Function Pointers

There is one large inconvenience with using function pointers as callbacks or in any situation where you are trying to hand off some code for execution by another part of the program or another thread. Any context that the function requires must be packed up and submitted as a separate collection of variables.

Most designs using callback functions or methods use the pattern shown in Listing 17.1. The function or method that is passed the callback function accepts a blind pointer as an additional argument and then passes that pointer back to the callback function, as shown in Figure 17.2. This is only a minor inconvenience when the context is a single variable as in the preceding example. However, if your function requires a more complicated context, you must create and load a custom `NSDictionary`, `NSArray`, or other object to hold the context and then pass the pointer to that dictionary, array, or object as the context variable. Either way is awkward if the context involves many variables.

void (*callbackFnPtr) (callbackContext*) = ... ;
callBackContext* someContext = ... ;

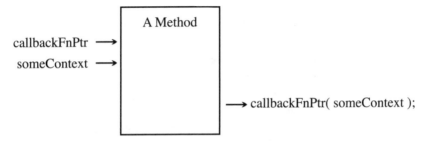

1. A pointer to a callback function and a pointer to some context information are passed into the method.

2. At some later time, the method calls the function (using the passed-in function pointer) with the passed in context as the argument.

Figure 17.2   Passing a callback function to a method

NSInvocation

NSInvocation objects are a second way of packaging up functionality for later use. An NSInvocation object takes an Objective-C message and turns it into an object. Some people refer to an NSInvocation as a *freeze-dried* message expression. The invocation object stores the message's receiver (called the *target* in invocation speak), selector, and arguments. An invocation object can be saved for later execution or passed on to another part of your code. When you send the invocation object an invoke message, the invocation sends the target object a message using the stored selector and arguments.

As an example, consider a LineGraphic class with a method drawWithColor:width: that draws a line with a specified color and line width:

```
LineGraphic *graphic = ...
[graphic drawWithColor: [NSColor redColor] width: 2.0];
```

Listing 17.2 shows how to turn the preceding message into an invocation.

Listing 17.2   **Constructing an NSInvocation**

```
LineGraphic *graphic = ...

NSInvocation *drawInvocation =
    [NSInvocation invocationWithMethodSignature:
        [graphic methodSignatureForSelector:
            @selector(drawWithColor:width:)]];
```

```
[drawInvocation setTarget: graphic];
[drawInvocation setSelector: @selector(drawWithColor:width:)];

[drawInvocation retainArguments];

NSColor *color = [NSColor redColor];
float linewidth = 2.0;

[drawInvocation setArgument: &color atIndex: 2];
[drawInvocation setArgument: &linewidth atIndex: 3];
```

To set up an invocation, `NSInvocation` needs to know the method signature of the message being encapsulated—its return type and its argument types. The message's selector is just a name and doesn't carry any type information, so you must obtain the type information by calling the target's `methodSignatureForSelector:`. This is a method that all classes inherit from `NSObject`. It returns an `NSMethodSignature` object, which is an encoded representation of the selector's return type and argument types. Finally, you pass the returned `NSMethodSignature` to `NSInvocation`'s `invocationWithMethodSignature:` class method to create the invocation.

Note

In Listing 17.2, the call to `methodSignatureForSelector:` is nested inside the call to `invocationWithMethodSignature:`, so there is no explicit `NSMethodSignature` variable.

Next, you set the invocation's target and selector with `setTarget:` and `setSelector:`.

An `NSInvocation` does not retain its target or any of its arguments by default. If you are going to save an invocation for future execution, you should ask the invocation to retain its target and arguments by sending the invocation a `retainArguments` message. This prevents the target and arguments from being released before the invocation is invoked. This is true even if you are using ARC. ARC doesn't (at least as of this writing) follow the progress of the objects held in an `NSInvocation` object. If you don't send the invocation a `retainArguments` message and the last strong reference to the invocation's target or any of its arguments goes away, you will probably have a crash when you send the invocation an `invoke` message.

The arguments for the encapsulated message are set with the `setArgument:atIndex:` method:

- You pass the *address* of the variable being used for the argument, not the variable itself. You can't use a value directly in a `setArgument:atIndex:` message:

```
[drawInvocation setArgument: 2.0 atIndex: 3];  // WRONG!
```

- If the selector has an argument that is not an object (an argument that is a primitive C type such as `int` or `float`), you may use the address of the primitive type directly. There is no need to wrap the `width` argument in an `NSNumber` object.
- The arguments are identified by their position in the message. Notice that indices start at 2. Indices 0 and 1 are reserved for the hidden method arguments `self` and `_cmd`. (For an explanation of a method's hidden arguments, see Chapter 5, "Messaging.")

Now that you have created `drawInvocation`, you can store it or hand it off to other code. When you are ready to draw the line, you simply execute the following line of code:

```
[drawInvocation invoke];
```

An invocation like the preceding one could be used as part of a display list scheme in a drawing program. Each invocation, stored in an array, encapsulates the message required to draw an element in the final scene. When you are ready to draw the scene, you loop through the array of invocations and invoke each one in turn:

```
NSMutableArray *displayList = ...
for NSInvocation invocation in displayList
{
  [invocation invoke];
}
```

Two additional points:

- An `NSInvocation` can be invoked any number of times.
- It is possible to encapsulate a message with a return value in an `NSInvocation`. To get the return value, send the invocation a `getReturnValue:` message, as illustrated here:

```
double result;
[invocationReturningDouble getReturnValue: &result];
```

The argument to `getReturnValue:` must be a pointer to a variable of the same type as the invocation's return type. If you send a `getReturnValue:` message to an invocation object before it has been sent an `invoke` message, the result is undefined. The value is garbage.

`NSInvocation` objects are used in the Cocoa framework to schedule an operation to be performed after a time interval (`NSTimer`), and in the Cocoa undo mechanism (`NSUndoManager`). `NSInvocation` objects solve one of the problems of using function pointers; they carry at least some of their context with them in the form of the arguments to the encapsulated message. That said, `NSInvocation` objects have a major drawback—as you have seen in Listing 17.2, they are difficult to construct.

Blocks

Blocks are similar in many ways to functions, with the important exception that blocks have direct access to variables in their surrounding context. Blocks also take the value of any of those variables that they are using with them if the block is passed out of the current context. "Direct access" means that a block can use variables declared in its surrounding context even though those variables are not passed in to the block through an argument list. Blocks are declared as follows:

```
^(argument_list){ body };
```

Blocks begin with a caret (^), followed by an argument list enclosed in parentheses and one or more statements enclosed in curly brackets. This expression is called a *block literal* and has the following characteristics:

- Blocks can return a value by using a **return** statement in the body.
- You don't have to specify the return type; the compiler determines the return type by looking at the body of the block.
- If the block doesn't have arguments, the argument list is written as **(void)**.
- Block literals don't have a name; that is why they are sometimes called *anonymous functions*.

The following is a simple block example that takes an integer, doubles it, and returns the doubled value:

```
^(int n){ return n*2; };
```

You can call a block literal directly by appending values for its arguments surrounded by parentheses:

```
int j = ^(int n){ return n*2; }( 9 ); // j is now 18
```

This works, but it is a bit silly; you could get the same result by simply coding the following:

```
int j = 2 * 9;
```

In normal use, a block literal is assigned to a variable typed as a pointer to a block, or used as an argument to a function or a method that takes a pointer to block argument.

Block Pointers

A variable that is a block pointer (a pointer to a block) is declared as follows:

```
return_type (^name)(list of argument types);
```

This should look familiar; it has exactly the same form as the declaration of a function pointer, except that the * has been replaced with a ^.

> **Note**
>
> Don't refer to a variable that holds a block pointer as a block variable. As you will see later in the chapter, the term *block variable* is reserved for a different entity.

The following example illustrates how to declare a block pointer, assign a block to it, and then call the block through the block pointer:

```
int (^doubler)(int);   // doubler is typed as a pointer to a block
                       // that takes an int argument and returns an int

doubler = ^(int n){ return n*2; };

int j = doubler( 9 );  // j is now 18
```

You can use block pointers as arguments to a function or a method:

```
// someFunction is a function that takes a block pointer as an argument

void someFunction( int (^blockArg)(int) );

int (^doubler)(int)= ^(int n){ return n*2; };

someFunction( doubler );
```

You can also use a block literal directly in a function call or an Objective-C message expression:

```
void someFunction( int (^blockArg)(int) );

someFunction( ^(int n){ return n*2; } );
```

> **Note**
>
> Objective-C method declarations have the same quirk with block pointers as they do with function pointers: When declaring a method that takes a block pointer argument, the name comes outside the type declaration:
>
> ```
> - (void) doSomethingWithBlockPointer:
>          (int (^)(int)) blockPointer;
> ```

Access to Variables

A block has

- Read-only access to automatic variables visible in its enclosing scope[1]
- Read/write access to static variables declared in a function or method
- Read/write access to external variables
- Read/write access to special variables declared as *block variables*

---

1. The scope of various classes of variables is discussed in Chapter 2, "More about C Variables."

Here is a simple example of a block accessing a local variable in its enclosing scope:

```
int j = 10;

int (^blockPtr)(int) = ^(int n){ return j+n; };

int k = blockPtr( 5 );  // k is now 10 + 5 = 15
```

The value that a block uses for a local variable from its context is the value that the local variable has when the flow of execution passes over the block literal, as shown here:

```
1   int j = 10;
2
3   int (^blockPtr)(int) = ^(int n){ return j+n; };
4
5   j = 20;
6
7   int k = blockPtr( 5 );  // k is 15, not 25 as you might expect
```

Note in the preceding code:

- Line 1: The local variable j is set to 10.
- Line 3: The block **blockPtr** is defined. **blockPtr** has access to the local variable j. The value of j that **blockPtr** uses is bound to the value that j has when the program execution passes over this line. In effect, **blockPtr** now has a private copy of j that is set to 10.
- Line 5: To show that **blockPtr**'s value of j was bound in Line 3, j is reset to 20.
- Line 7: The **blockPtr** is evaluated with an argument of 5, resulting in a return value of 10 (the value of j at the time Line 3 is executed) + 5 (the argument) = 15.

A block's access to local variables is read-only. The following code, which attempts to set the value of j from inside **blockPtr**, results in a compiler error because **blockPtr**'s access to the local variable j is read-only:

```
int j = 10;

void (^blockPtr)(void) = ^(void){ j = 20; };
```

> **Note**
>
> If a local variable holds a pointer to an object, a block cannot change the variable to point to a different object. But the object that the variable points to can still be modified by the block:
>
> ```
> NSMutableArray *localArray =  ...
>
> void (^shortenArray)(void) = ^(void){ [localArray removeLastObject]; };
>
> // Removes the last object in localArray
> shortenArray();
> ```

The compiler gives blocks read/write access to function and method `static` variables and external variables. The value the block sees for this type of variable is the value the variable has when the block is executed, not when the block is defined:

```
static int j = 10;

int (^blockPtr)(int) = ^(int n){ return j+n; };

j = 20;

int k = blockPtr( 5 );   // k is 25
```

Block Variables

Variables declared with the new type modifier `__block` are called *block variables*:

```
__block int integerBlockVariable;
```

Block variables are shared by any blocks defined in their scope—any block defined in the scope of a block variable can read and write to that variable.

For example:

```
1  __block int j = 10;
2
3  void (^blockPtr_1)(void) = ^(void){ j += 15; };
4  void (^blockPtr_2)(void) = ^(void){ j += 25; };
5
6  blockPtr_1(); // j is now 25
7  blockPtr_2(); // j is now 50
```

Note in the preceding code:

- Line 1: j is declared as a `__block` variable and set to 10.
- Line 3: `blockPtr_1` is defined. Because j has been declared as a `__block` variable, `blockPtr_1` is permitted to set the value of j.
- Line 4: Similarly, `blockPtr_2` is permitted to set the value of j. Both `blockPtr_1` and `blockPtr_2` share read/write access to the variable j.
- Line 6: `blockPtr_1` is evaluated, incrementing j by 15, resulting in a value of 25 for j.
- Line 7: `blockPtr_2` is evaluated, incrementing j by 25, resulting in a value of 50 for j.

Block variables start out on the stack like any other automatic variable. But if you copy a block that references a block variable, the block variable is moved from the stack to the heap along with the block (see the section *Copying Blocks*).

> **Note**
>
> The term *block variable* refers to a variable that is declared with the __block modifier, as described in the preceding paragraphs. Don't confuse "block variable" and "variable that holds a pointer to a block." A block variable is not a block.

Blocks Are Stack Based

When you define a block literal inside a function or method, the compiler creates a structure on the stack that holds the private copies of the values of any local variables that the block references, the addresses of read/write variables that it references, and a pointer to the block's executable code.

> **Note**
>
> The block structure is created on the stack, but the block's executable code is not on the stack. It is in the text portion of the program along with all the other executable code.

Blocks have the same lifetime as automatic variables. When the block literal goes out of scope, it is undefined, just like an automatic variable that has gone out of scope. Scope for a block literal is defined in the same way as scope for an automatic variable (see Chapter 2, "More about C Variables"): If a block literal is defined inside a compound statement (between a pair of curly brackets), the block literal goes out of scope when the program execution leaves the compound statement. If a block literal is defined in a function, it goes out of scope when the function returns. The following code is incorrect:

```
int (^doubler)(int);
{
    ...
    doubler = ^(int n){ return n*2; };
    ...
}
...
int j = doubler( 9 );   // WRONG! Bug!
```

In the preceding example, j is undefined. At the point where `doubler(9)` is executed, the block that the `doubler` variable points to has gone out of scope and the block may have been destroyed.

> **Note**
>
> If you try the preceding example, it may appear to work correctly. j may very well be set to 18. But that would be an accident of the way the compiler has arranged the code in this instance. After the block is out of scope, the compiler is free to reuse the space the block occupied in the stack frame. If the compiler has reused the space, the result of trying to execute the out-of-scope block would be an incorrect value of j or, more likely, a crash.

Global Blocks

You can also assign a block literal to a file-scope block pointer:

```
#import <Foundation/Foundation.h>

void (^logObject)(id) =
  ^(id obj){ NSLog( @"Object Description: %@", obj ); };

// logObject( someObj ) may be used anywhere in the file.
```

The compiler creates global-scope blocks in low memory like any other file-scope variable. Global blocks never go out of scope.

Blocks Are Objective-C Objects

It may seem surprising, but blocks are also Objective-C objects. A newly created block is the only example of an Objective-C object that is created on the stack. Blocks are instances of one of several private subclasses of **NSObject**. Apple doesn't provide the header for the block classes so you can't subclass them or do much of anything with them in an Objective-C sense except send them **copy**, **retain**, **release**, and **autorelease** messages. Copying and memory management for blocks are covered in the next sections.

Copying Blocks

One of the main uses of blocks is to pass a chunk of work (some code plus some context) out of the current scope for processing at a later time. Passing a block to a function or method that you call (passing the block down the stack) is safe (as long as that function or method is going to execute on the same thread). But what happens if you want to pass a block to a different thread or pass a block out of the current scope as a return value? When the current function or method returns, its stack frame is destroyed. Any blocks that were defined in its scope become invalid.

To preserve a block, you must copy it. When you copy a block, the copy is created on the heap. The heap-based copy is then safe to return up the stack to the calling function or pass off to another thread.

If you are coding in straight C, you can use the **Block_copy()** function, as follows:

```
int(^doublerCopy)(int) = Block_copy( ^(int n){ return n*2; } );
```

In Objective-C, you can send a **copy** message to the block:

```
int(^doublerCopy)(int) = [^(int n){ return n*2; } copy];
```

The two preceding examples are equivalent. In either statement, you could use a block pointer instead of the block literal.

When you copy a block, the new block gets copies of the values of any automatic variables that the block references. (The block accesses automatic variables by value. The value of the variable is copied into the block object when it is created.)

But What about Block Variables?

Block variables are accessed by reference. It wouldn't be very useful to copy a block and then leave the copied block referring to a variable that is destroyed when the program execution leaves the current scope.

To remedy this, when you copy a block, the compiler also moves any block variables that the block references from the stack to a location on the heap. The compiler then updates any blocks that reference the block variable so they have the variable's new address.

One consequence of the compiler's behavior in this situation is that it is a *very* bad idea to take the address of a block variable and use it for anything. After the copy operation, the original address refers to a memory location that may now be garbage.

Memory Management for Blocks

If you copy a block with `Block_copy()`, you must eventually balance that call with a call to `Block_release()`. If you use the Objective-C **copy** message and you are using reference counting, you must balance the **copy** message with a **release** or an **autorelease**:

```
int(^getDoublerBlock())(int)
{
  int(^doublerBlock)(int) = ^(int n){ return 2*n; };

  // The returned block is autoreleased. This balances the copy
  // and makes getDoublerBlock conform to the naming convention
  // for memory management.
  return [[doublerBlock copy] autorelease];
}
...

int(^doubler )(int) = getDoublerBlock();   // Get the block

int sevenDoubled = doubler(7); // Use the block
```

Don't mix calls to `Block_copy()` and `Block_release()` with Objective-C's **copy** and **release** messages.

If a block references a variable that holds an object, that object is retained when the block is copied and released when the block is released.

> **Note**
>
> If you are using manual reference counting, an object held in a __block variable is *not* retained when a block that references it is copied. However, __block variables behave differently under ARC. See the section *Blocks and ARC* later in the chapter.

When copying a block inside a method body, the rules are slightly more complicated:

- A direct reference to `self` in a block that is being copied causes `self` to be retained.

- A reference to an object's instance variable (*either directly or through an accessor method*) in a block that is being copied causes `self` to be retained. This is because a reference to an instance variable is really a reference through `self`, that is, `self->instanceVariable`.

- A reference to an object held in a local variable in a method causes that object, but not `self`, to be retained.

> **Note**
>
> The preceding rules are presented separately for blocks copied inside a method to emphasize the consequences of a block accessing an object's instance variable. But there is really no significant difference between copying a block inside and copying a block outside a method. The only difference is that outside of a method, there is no way to reference an object's instance variable without referencing the object itself.

Capturing `self`

You should be careful when copying a block. If the code that copies the block is inside a method and the block refers to any of the object's instance variables, the copy causes `self` to be retained. It is easy to set up a retain cycle that prevents both the object and the block from ever being deallocated.

Listing 17.3 shows the interface section for a class that has an instance variable **name** to store a name, and a method **logMyName** to log that name. **logMyName** uses a block stored in the instance variable **loggingBlock** to do the actual logging.

Listing 17.3   *ObjectWithName.h*

```
#import <Foundation/Foundation.h>

@interface ObjectWithName : NSObject
{
  NSString *name;
  void (^loggingBlock)(void);
}

@property (nonatomic, retain) NSString *name;
```

```
- (void) logMyName;
- (id) initWithName:(NSString*) inName;
```

@end

Listing 17.4 shows the corresponding implementation file.

Listing 17.4   *ObjectWithName.m*

```
1   #import "ObjectWithName.h"
2
3   @implementation ObjectWithName
4
5   @synthesize name;
6
7   - (id) initWithName:(NSString*) inputName
8   {
9     if (self = [super init])
10      {
11         name = [inputName copy];
12         loggingBlock = [^(void){ NSLog( @"%@", name ); } copy];
13      }
14    return self;
15  }
16
17  - (void) logMyName
18  {
19    loggingBlock();
20  }
21
22  - (void) dealloc
23  {
24    [loggingBlock release];
25    [name release];
26    [super dealloc];
27  }
28
29  @end
```

ObjectWithName is a very simple class. However, this version of ObjectWithName has a retain cycle. If you create an ObjectWithName object, it won't be deallocated when you release it.

The problem is Line 12 of Listing 17.4:

```
loggingBlock = [^(void){ NSLog( @"%@", name ); } copy];
```

To store the block in the instance variable `loggingBlock`, you must copy the block literal and assign the copy to the instance variable. This is because the block literal goes out of scope when `initWithName:` returns. Copying the block puts the copy on the heap (like a normal Objective-C object). However, the block literal references the instance variable `name`, so the `copy` causes `self` to be retained, setting up a retain cycle. The block now has ownership of the object and the object has ownership of the block (because it has copied the block). The object's reference count never goes to zero and its `dealloc` method is never called.

You can fix this problem in several ways. One way is by changing Line 12 of Listing 17.4 so it reads as follows:

```
loggingBlock = [^(void){ NSLog( @"%@", inputName ); } copy];
```

With this change, the block copying operation retains the input argument `inputName` rather than the instance variable `name`. Because the block no longer references any of the object's instance variables, `self` is not retained and there is no retain cycle. The object will still have the same behavior because `name` and `inputName` have the same content.

Another way to avoid the retain cycle is to assign the object held in the instance variable `name` to a `__block` variable, and then use the `__block` variable instead of the actual instance variable inside the block, like this:

```
__block NSString *tempName = name;
loggingBlock = [^(void){ NSLog( @"%@", tempName ); } copy];
```

Finally, you can assign `self` to a `__block` variable and use the `__block` variable with the instance variable's accessor method:

```
__block id tempSelf = self;
loggingBlock = [^(void){ NSLog( @"%@", [tempSelf name] ); } copy];
```

The preceding two code snippets work because an object held in a `__block` variable is not retained when the `__block` variable is copied to the heap.

Traps

Because blocks are stack-based objects, they present some traps for the unwary programmer. The snippet of code in Listing 17.5 is incorrect.

Listing 17.5

```
void(^loggingBlock)(void);

BOOL canWeDoIt = ...

// WRONG
```

```
if ( canWeDoIt )
  loggingBlock = ^(void){ NSLog( @"YES" ); };
else
  loggingBlock = ^(void){ NSLog( @"NO" ); };

// Possible crash
loggingBlock();
```

At the end of this snippet, `loggingBlock` is undefined. The `if` and `else` clauses of an `if` statement and the bodies of loops are separate lexical scopes, *even if they are single statements and not compound statements*. When the program execution leaves the scope, the compiler is free to destroy the block and leave `loggingBlock` pointing at garbage.

To fix this code, you must **copy** the block and then remember to release it when you are finished, as shown in the code snippet in Listing 17.6.

Listing 17.6

```
void(^loggingBlock)(void);

BOOL canWeDoIt = ...

if ( canWeDoIt )
  loggingBlock = [^(void){ NSLog( @"YES" ); } copy];
else
  loggingBlock = [^(void){ NSLog( @"NO" ); } copy];

// Remember to release loggingBlock when you are finished
```

This example is also incorrect:

```
NSMutableArray *array = ...

// WRONG!

[array addObject: ^(void){ doSomething; }];
return array; //
```

Recall that objects added to collection objects receive a **retain** message; however, in this case the **retain** doesn't help because **retain** is a no-op for a stack-based block. Again, to fix the problem, you must copy the block:

```
NSMutableArray *array = ...
[array addObject: [[^(void){ doSomething; } copy] autorelease]];
return array;
```

In the preceding code snippet, the **copy** message puts a copy of the block on the heap. The **autorelease** message balances the **copy**. The **retain** message that the copied block receives when it is placed in the array is balanced by a **release** message when the block is later removed from the array or when the array is deallocated.

Blocks and ARC

Blocks mostly just work when you use ARC, but there are a few special cases that need some attention. As you have seen in the preceding sections, if you want to pass a block out of the scope where it is defined, the block must be copied from the stack to the heap. ARC does this copy for you automatically. This means that the code shown in Listing 17.6 is unnecessary. You can use code like that shown in Listing 17.5. ARC will take care of the copy. ARC will also copy the block from the stack to the heap if you use a block as the return value of a function or a method.

But if you pass a block *in to* a method that expects to retain its argument, you must still use an explicit copy to move the block to the heap:

```
NSMutableArray *array = ...
[array addObject: [
^(void){ doSomething; } copy]];
return array;
```

ARC will *not* do this copy for you. (ARC will take care of balancing the **copy** with a **release** or an **autorelease**.)

> **Note**
>
> Requiring the programmer to code this copy is considered a bug in the current version of the Clang compiler. It may be fixed in some future version of Xcode.

The behavior of **__block** variables changes under ARC. Under manual reference counting, an object held in a **__block** variable is not retained when the variable is copied to the heap. With ARC, **__block** variables are strong (retained) references unless explicitly declared otherwise.

```
__block NSArray *array; // array is a strong reference under ARC
```

This means that using code like

```
__block SomeClass *tempSelf = self;
```

to break a retain cycle (as shown in the section *Capturing self* earlier in the chapter) does not work under ARC. In the preceding line of code, storing **self** in **tempSelf** causes **self** to be retained. You can restore the previous behavior of a **__block** variable (and its use in breaking retain cycles) by declaring it as **__weak**:

```
__weak __block SomeClass *tempSelf = self;
```

If you cannot use **__weak** because you are deploying your program to a version of iOS or OS X that doesn't support the weak system, you can use **__unsafe_unretained**:

```
__unsafe_unretained __block SomeClass *tempSelf = self;
```

Blocks in Cocoa

Beginning with Mac OS X Snow Leopard (version 10.6), Apple has started deploying blocks throughout the Cocoa frameworks. This section briefly describes three areas where Apple has added features that use blocks.

Concurrency with NSOperationQueue

Concurrent (multithreaded) programming is very difficult to do correctly. To make it easier for programmers to write error-free multithreaded programs, Apple has introduced Grand Central Dispatch (GCD). GCD implements concurrency by creating and managing a *thread pool*. A thread pool is a group of threads that can be assigned to various tasks and reused when the task is finished. GCD hides the details of managing the thread pool and presents a relatively simple interface to programmers.

The Cocoa class NSOperationQueue provides a high-level interface to GCD. The idea is simple: You create an NSOperationQueue and add units of work, in the form of blocks, for the queue to execute. Underneath NSOperationQueue, GCD arranges to execute the block on a separate thread:

```
NSOperationQueue *queue = [[NSOperationQueue alloc] init];

[queue addOperationWithBlock: ^(void){ doSomething; }];

// doSomething will now execute on a separate thread
```

- A block passed to GCD (either through NSOperationQueue or through the low-level C interface) must have the form

  ```
  void (^block)(void)
  ```

  It must not take arguments or return a value.

- The GCD mechanism takes care of copying blocks submitted to it and releases them when no longer needed.

> **Note**
>
> Programming concurrency is a complex topic. For a complete discussion of NSOperationQueue and GCD, see Apple's *Concurrency Programming Guide.*[2]

Collection Classes

The Foundation collection classes now have methods that enable you to apply a block to every object in the collection. NSArray has the following method:

```
- (void)enumerateObjectsUsingBlock:
        (void (^)(id obj, NSUInteger idx, BOOL *stop))block
```

2. https://developer.apple.com/library/mac/#documentation/General/Conceptual/ ConcurrencyProgrammingGuide/Introduction/Introduction.html.

This method calls **block** once for each object in the array; the arguments to **block** are

- **obj**, a pointer to the current object.
- **idx**, the index of the current object (**idx** is the equivalent of the loop index in an ordinary **for** loop).
- **stop**, a pointer to a **BOOL**. If the block sets **stop** to **YES**, **enumerateObjectsUsingBlock:** terminates when the block returns. It is the equivalent of a **break** statement in an ordinary C loop.

Listing 17.7 uses **enumerateObjectsUsingBlock:** to log a description of every object in an array.

Listing 17.7   *DescribeArrayContents.m*

```
#import <Foundation/Foundation.h>

int main (int argc, const char *argv[])
{
  @autoreleasepool
    {

      NSArray *array =
          [NSArray arrayWithObjects: @"dagger", @"candlestick",
              @"wrench", @"rope", nil];

      void (^loggingBlock)(id obj, NSUInteger idx, BOOL *stop) =
          ^(id obj, NSUInteger idx, BOOL *stop)
            { NSLog( @"Object number %d is a %@",
                idx, [obj description] ); };

      [array enumerateObjectsUsingBlock: loggingBlock];
    }
  return 0;
}
```

If you build and run this program, you should see the following result:

```
DescribeArrayContents [50642:a0b] Object number 0 is a dagger
DescribeArrayContents [50642:a0b] Object number 1 is a candlestick
DescribeArrayContents [50642:a0b] Object number 2 is a wrench
DescribeArrayContents [50642:a0b] Object number 3 is a rope
```

Did-End Callbacks

I haven't said much about AppKit in this book, but I'll assume that you are familiar with saving files on Mac OS X. You select *File > Save* in an app, and if this is the first time the file is saved, a *Save* sheet appears so you can name the file and select the location where it will be saved. You make your choices and click *Save*, or if you've changed your mind, you can click *Cancel*. After you click one of the buttons, the sheet slides up and disappears.

When you invoke the method that begins the sheet, Cocoa gives you the chance to register some code to be executed when the user dismisses the sheet. (This is where you put the code that actually saves the file to disk.)

Prior to Mac OS X 10.6, a *Save* sheet was started with this rather formidable method in the **NSSavePanel** class:

```
- (void)beginSheetForDirectory:(NSString *)path
        file:(NSString *)name
        modalForWindow:(NSWindow *)docWindow
        modalDelegate:(id)modalDelegate
        didEndSelector:(SEL)didEndSelector
        contextInfo:(void *)contextInfo
```

When the user dismisses the sheet, the sheet sends the object registered as **modalDelegate**, the message represented by the selector **didEndSelector**. Typically, the **modalDelegate** is the object that initiates the panel. **didEndSelector** has the form

```
- (void)savePanelDidEnd:(NSSavePanel *)sheet
            returnCode:(int)returnCode
        contextInfo:(void *)contextInfo;
```

- **sheet** is a pointer to the **NSSavePanel** object itself.
- **returnCode** is an integer that specifies which button the user clicked on.
- **contextInfo** is a blind pointer to the information passed to **beginSheetForDirectory:...** when it was invoked. This is how you pass information from the object that invoked the sheet to the code responsible for acting on the user's input.

For Mac OS X 10.6 and beyond, the preceding method has been deprecated and replaced with the following method:

```
- (void)beginSheetModalForWindow:(NSWindow *)window
            completionHandler:(void (^)(NSInteger result))handler
```

You simply pass in a block to be executed when the sheet is dismissed. The block can capture any required context so the blind **contextInfo** pointer is not required.

> **Note**
> The **file** and **directoryPath** arguments were removed as part of a separate cleanup that doesn't involve blocks.

Style Issues

Placing the statements of a block literal on a single line makes debugging difficult; for example:

```
^(void){doStuff; doMoreStuff; evenMore; keepGoing; lastStatement;}
```

You can set a debugger break point on **doStuff;**, but there is no way to step through or set a break point on any of the other statements in the block. If you stop on **doStuff;** and try to step, the debugger jumps to the line following the block literal—making it impossible to debug the subsequent lines in the literal. If your block literal is non-trivial and may require debugging, you should put the statements in the block's body on separate lines, as follows:

```
^(void){doStuff;
        doMoreStuff;
        evenMore;
        keepGoing;
        lastStatement;}
```

As noted earlier, you can place a block literal directly in a function or method call:

```
someFunction( otherArgs, ^(void){ doStuff;
                          doMoreStuff;
                          evenMore;
                          keepGoing;
                          lastStatement; } );
```

You could also assign the block to a block pointer variable and use the block pointer as the argument. Which you choose is a matter of preference: Some people are annoyed at creating an extra variable (which the compiler will probably optimize away), whereas others find that putting the block literal inside the function call makes the code hard to read.

Some Philosophical Reservations

Blocks are very versatile, and they are clearly an important part of Apple's plans for the future of Objective-C and Mac OS X. However, blocks come with a few issues that are worth a moment or two of thought:

- The term *block* was already in use. It is interchangeable with *compound statement* in almost every book on the C language. This might cause confusion in some circumstances.
- Blocks are *function oriented* and not very *object oriented*. This may be an issue if you are strongly attached to an ideal of object-oriented purity.
- Blocks completely break encapsulation. A block's access to variables that are not accessed through an argument list or an accessor method presents many of the same issues as using global variables.

Using __block variables and copying blocks can result in entangled objects: You can create separate objects (potentially belonging to different classes) communicating via a variable on the heap that is not visible to anything else.

- As with operator overloading in C++, blocks can be used in ways that lead to *Design Your Own Language Syndrome*, code that is very terse but very difficult for others (or yourself, several months later) to read and understand. This may not be an issue for independent developers, but it can be a problem if you are part of a programming team.

Summary

This chapter looked at several ways of packaging functionality to be executed at a later time or on a different thread. Function pointers let you hand off functions but require that you provide an extra variable to go with the function pointer if you need to pass some context to go along with the function. NSInvocation objects wrap the target, the selector, and the arguments of an Objective-C message expression in a single object that can then be stored or handed off for later execution. They are easy to use but difficult to construct.

Blocks, an Apple-added extension to C, Objective-C 2.0, and C++, wrap a series of statements and the variables in their surrounding context in a single entity. Grand Central Dispatch, Apple's system for managing concurrency, uses blocks as the medium for submitting tasks to be executed on other threads. Beginning with Mac OS 10.6, Apple is deploying blocks throughout the Cocoa frameworks to replace older methods that used NSInvocation objects or required separate target, selector, and context arguments for callbacks.

Exercises

1. This is more of a puzzle than anything else, but it will test your understanding of function pointer (and, by extension, block pointer) declarations. Consider the following declaration:

   ```
   int (*(*myFunctionPointer)(int (*)(int))) (int);
   ```

   What (in words) is myFunctionPointer?

2. Rewrite the HelloObjectiveC program from Chapter 4, "Your First Objective-C Program," to use an NSInvocation:

   Instead of passing the Greeter the greeting text as an NSString, create a Greeting class that encapsulates the greeting and a method that issues the greeting. (The method should take the greeting string as an argument and log it.)

   Package up issuing the greeting as an NSInvocation and pass it to the Greeter.

The `Greeter` should then issue the greeting by sending the invocation object the `invoke` message.

3. Write a program that uses some simple blocks and verify for yourself that

   a. The value for an ordinary automatic variable that a block sees is fixed when execution passes over the block literal and is unchanged if the value of the variable is changed later in the code

   b. A block cannot modify the value of an ordinary automatic variable in its scope

   c. A block can both read and set a variable declared with the `__block` type modifier

4. Rewrite the program in Listing 17.1 to use a block instead of a function. Use the `NSMutableArray` method:

   ```
   - (void)sortUsingComparator:(NSComparator)cmptr
   ```

   `NSComparator` is a typedef for a pointer to a block that takes two object arguments and returns the same integer constants as the function in Listing 17.1.

5. Write a program that looks for a name in an array of names and reports back the name's index in the array:

   a. Create an `NSArray` with some names (use `NSString` objects).

   b. Create a local `NSString` variable to hold the name you are searching for and an integer block variable to report back at what index the name was found.

   c. Search the array using `enumerateObjectsUsingBlock:`.

   d. Make sure your block uses the `stop` argument to stop looking when the name is found.

   e. If the name you are looking for isn't in the array, the block variable holding the index should have a value of −1.

6. Write a program that uses the `ObjectWithName` class (see Listings 17.3 and 17.4).

   a. Add a logging statement to `ObjectWithName`'s `dealloc` routine.

   b. In your `main` program, allocate an instance of `ObjectWithName`.

   c. Release `ObjectWithName` (or set your reference to it to `nil` if you are using ARC) and verify that it is never deallocated.

   d. Try the three suggested fixes in the text and verify that each of them will break the retain cycle.

A Few More Things

This chapter covers three small items that are new with Mountain Lion and Xcode 4.4. They are enums with a fixed underlying type and some type checking, the elimination of the need for forward declarations for methods in the `@implementation` section of a class, and a new piece of documentation that will help you keep track of when new Objective-C features were added to the language and what versions of OS X and iOS support those new features.

Enums with a Fixed Underlying Type

Standard C language enumeration constants or *enums* (see Chapter 1, "C, the Foundation of Objective-C") are a way of giving human-readable names to a set of integer constants.

```
typedef enum
{
    soup,
    pasta,
    chicken,
    cake
} foods;

...

foods mainCourse = chicken;
```

makes more sense to someone else reading your code (or to yourself, six months later) than

```
int mainCourse = 2;
```

But standard C enums have a couple of problems. The first problem is that there is no way of specifying the underlying integer type that is used for the enum. The compiler picks the size of the integer for you based on the values of the constants. (Recall that unless you specify the values explicitly, the values for the constants start at 0 and go in ascending numerical order.)

The second problem is that there is no type checking. If you add another enumeration to the preceding program:

```
typedef enum
{
    water,
    wine,
    beer,
    coffee
} drinks;
```

the compiler will silently let you make mistakes, such as coding

```
drinks currentDrink = chicken;
```

The code will run—under the hood `chicken` is an integer constant and `currentDrink` is some type of integer—but this is probably not what you intended. You might not notice the error until your program crashes or produces strange results.

Starting with Xcode 4.4, the compiler improves on standard C enums by letting you set the size of the underlying integer for your enums and providing a bit of type checking when you use them.

Setting the Underlying Type

Xcode 4.4 introduces a new syntax for declaring enums:

```
typedef enum  name :  type
{
    Constant_1,
    Constant_2,
...
    Constant_N
} name;
```

Using this new syntax, you can declare the **foods** enum like this:

```
typedef enum foods : unsigned char
{
    soup,
    pasta,
    chicken,
    cake
} foods;

foods mainCourse = chicken;
```

In the preceding code `mainCourse` is actually an `unsigned char`.

NS_ENUM Macro

To make declaring enumerations easier, Objective-C now provides a macro, `NS_ENUM`:

```
typedef NS_ENUM ( type, name )
{
    Constant_1,
    Constant_2,
...
    Constant_N
};
```

Using `NS_ENUM`, the declaration of the `food` enum looks like this:

```
typedef NS_ENUM( unsigned char, foods )
{
    soup,
    pasta,
    chicken,
    cake
};
```

Notice that the enumeration name does not appear on the last line when you use `NS_ENUM`. Putting it there:

```
typedef NS_ENUM( unsigned char, foods )
{
    soup,
    pasta,
    chicken,
    cake
} foods;
```

results in an error:

```
Redefinition of "foods" as a different kind of symbol
```

Type Checking Enums

You can ask the compiler to type check code using enumerations. To do this, add the –Wconversion flag to *Other Warning Flags* in the *Apple LLVM compiler - Warnings - All languages* section of your Xcode *Build Settings*.

When you have added the **-Wconversion** flag, code such as the following:

```
drinks currentDrink = chicken;
```

results in a warning:

```
Implicit conversion from enumeration type 'enum foods' to
different enumeration type 'drinks' (aka 'enum drinks')
```

Note that this is only a warning, not an error. If you ignore the warning, the code compiles and executes the underlying integer assignment.

The compiler warns only about conversions between enumeration types. Nonsense like the following line of code:

```
drinks currentDrink = 3 * beer + wine + 137;
```

compiles without any warnings.

Checking `switch` Statements with Enum Arguments

When you code a `switch` statement using an enum type as an argument, the compiler can check to see that you have handled all the possible values of the enum. To enable this checking, add the `-Wswitch` flag to your compiler settings. (You add `-Wswitch` in the same place you added the `-Wconversion` flag.)

When you have the flag set, this code:

```
drinks currentDrink = ...

switch (currentDrink)
  {
    case water:
      printf("Current drink is water !\n");
      break;

    case wine:
      printf("Current drink is wine !\n");
      break;

    case beer:
      printf("Current drink is beer !\n");
      break;
  }
```

results in the following warning:

```
Enumeration value 'coffee' not handled in switch
```

To eliminate the warning either add a case for the enumeration constant `coffee` or add a `default:` case to the `switch`.

Forward Declarations of Methods in the `@implementation` Block Are No Longer Needed

Let's say that you have a class, `Foo`, with a method, `doFoo`, that does something. Furthermore, assume that `doFoo` requires a helper method, `fooHelper`, to do its work. You might code your interface file as shown in Listing 18.1.

Listing 18.1   *Foo.h*

```
@interface Foo : NSObject
{
   ...
}

- (void) doFoo;
   ...
@end
```

And you might code your implementation file like Listing 18.2.

Listing 18.2   *Foo.m*

```
#import "Foo.h"

@implementation Foo

- (void) doFoo
{
   ...
  [self fooHelper];
   ...
}

- (void) fooHelper
{
  NSLog( @"Helping doFoo" );
   ...
}

@end
```

If you compile the preceding code using versions of Xcode prior to Xcode 4.4, you will get a warning if you are using manual reference counting:

```
warning: instance method '-fooHelper' not found
(return type defaults to 'id')
```

However, the code will still work because, while the compiler doesn't see a declaration for the method fooHelper, the method is there and the runtime method lookup can find it.

Using ARC, the situation is far worse. ARC needs to see the return type of any method at the point where the method is invoked. It can't see the return type of fooHelper, so ARC gives you a compilation error:

```
error: receiver type 'Foo' for instance message does not
declare a method with selector 'fooHelp'
```

You could fix this by putting the declaration of **fooHelper** in your class's interface section:

```
@interface Foo : NSObject
{
    ...
}

- (void) doFoo;
- (void) fooHelper;
    ...
@end
```

In most cases this is a bad idea. **fooHelper** is a private method and you don't want to advertise its presence to users of your class. (Remember that there is no way to prevent someone from invoking a method once he or she knows it exists.)

Another way to fix the problem is to rearrange the implementation file so that the implementation of **fooHelper** comes before the implementation of **doFoo**. This will work as long as you don't have mutually recursive methods that call each other.

A better solution is to place a forward declaration of **fooHelper** in a class extension:

```
#import "Foo.h"

@interface Foo ()
    -(void) fooHelper;
@end

@implementation Foo

- (void) doFoo
{
    ...
    [self fooHelper];
    ...
}

- (void) fooHelper
{
    NSLog( @"Helping doFoo" );
    ...
}

@end
```

With this change the compiler sees the declaration of **fooHelper** before it is invoked. The code compiles and works without a warning or error using either manual reference counting or ARC.

Now for the good news: When you use Xcode 4.4 or later, this problem simply goes away. You don't have to worry about it anymore. The compiler has been taught to look through the implementation file and gather information from all the method declarations and implementations in the file before it begins compiling.

Some New Documentation

The past several years have been a period of rapid change for Objective-C. Apple has added new features with almost every new version of OS X and iOS. It can be hard to keep track of what language features are available on what version of the operating systems. The situation is all the more confusing because Apple has stated that they are not going to increment the version number of Objective-C beyond 2.0. To specify a particular version of Objective-C you will have to say "Objective-C 2.0 as of Xcode 4.4" (for example).

The question of when and where you can use a language feature actually has two parts: Which version of Xcode can you use to compile code that uses a language feature, and which versions of OS X or iOS will run the resulting executable? The answers to the two questions are not necessarily similar. For example, a number of the new features introduced simultaneously with Mountain Lion (OS X 10.8) require Xcode 4.4 or later to compile, but the resulting binary will run on any version of OS X or iOS. These features include the enums described in this chapter, the elimination of the need for forward method declarations, and array and dictionary literals.

To make this all a bit easier to keep track of, Apple has added a new page of documentation called the *Objective-C Feature Availability Index*. This is a table with columns that list the feature, the versions of Xcode and the compiler where the feature was introduced, and what versions of OS X and iOS are required to run a program compiled using the feature.

The table is available at https://developer.apple.com/library/mac/#releasenotes/ObjectiveC/ObjCAvailabilityIndex/_index.html#//apple_ref/doc/uid/TP40012243.

Summary

This marks the end of both this chapter and the main text of the book. I hope you have enjoyed reading it. If you have persevered, read the chapters carefully, and done the exercises, you should have a good working knowledge of Objective-C 2.0. Your next step is to dive into Cocoa (for OS X) or Cocoa Touch (iOS) to learn the building blocks that you need for building apps. Good luck!

Exercises

1. Write a simple program that declares a standard C type enum. Declare a variable that is of this enum type and use the system `sizeof()` function to see what size integer the compiler assigns to the enum.

If you are unfamiliar with `sizeof()`, it returns, as a `long`, the size in bytes of its argument. For example:

```
int numTimes;
printf("size of numTimes is %ld\n", sizeof( numTimes ));
```

Now assign specific integers to your enumeration constants and make one of those constants 5000000000. What does this do to the size of the integer the compiler assigns to the enum?

2. Use the `NS_ENUM` macro to declare some enums. For the type use `char`, `short`, `int`, `NSInteger`, `long`. Verify with `sizeof()` that the size of the underlying integer for each of these enums is what you expect.

3. Write a program that uses the `Foo` class shown in Listings 18.1 and 18.2. (The program doesn't have to do anything.) Verify that the program compiles without an error or a warning on Xcode 4.4 or later. Try compiling the code with an earlier version of Xcode if you have one on your system. What happens?

Part IV

Appendices

The appendices contain additional useful information for Objective-C developers:

- Appendix A, "Reserved Words and Compiler Directives"
- Appendix B, "Toll-Free Bridged Classes"
- Appendix C, "32- and 64-Bit"
- Appendix D, "The Fragile Base Class Problem"
- Appendix E, "Resources for Objective-C"

Reserved Words and Compiler Directives

Table A.1 **C Reserved Words**

asm	auto	break	case
char	const	continue	default
do	double	else	enum
extern	float	for	goto
if	inline	int	long
register	restrict	return	short
signed	sizeof	static	struct
switch	typedef	union	unsigned
void	volatile	while	_Bool
_Complex	_Imaginary		

Beginning with Mac OS X Snow Leopard (version 10.6), Apple adds the keyword __block to C.

Table A.2 **Additional Objective-C Reserved Words**

id	Class	SEL	IMP
BOOL	nil	Nil	YES
NO	self	super	_cmd
__strong	__weak __autoreleasing	__unsafe_unretained	

The following words are used as type qualifiers in the Objective-C remote messaging system. Remote messaging is not covered in this book.

Table A.3 **Remote Messaging Reserved Words**

oneway	In	out	inout
bycopy	byref		

Table A.4 **Objective-C Compiler Directives**

@autoreleasepool	@interface	@implementation	@protocol
@end	@private	@protected	@public
@package	@try	@throw	@catch()
@finally	@property	@synthesize	@dynamic
@class	@selector()	@protocol()	@required
@optional	@encode	@"string"	@synchronized()

B

Toll-Free Bridged Classes

Core Foundation Type	Foundation Class	Availability (Listed OS and Later)
CFArrayRef	NSArray	Mac OS X v10.0
CFAttributedStringRef	NSAttributedString	Mac OS X v10.4
CFCalendarRef	NSCalendar	Mac OS X v10.4
CFCharacterSetRef	NSCharacterSet	Mac OS X v10.0
CFDataRef	NSData	Mac OS X v10.0
CFDateRef	NSDate	Mac OS X v10.0
CFDictionaryRef	NSDictionary	Mac OS X v10.0
CFErrorRef	NSError	Mac OS X v10.5
CFLocaleRef	NSLocale	Mac OS X v10.4
CFMutableArrayRef	NSMutableArray	Mac OS X v10.0
CFMutableAttributedStringRef	NSMutableAttributedString	Mac OS X v10.4
CFMutableCharacterSetRef	NSMutableCharacterSet	Mac OS X v10.0
CFMutableDataRef	NSMutableData	Mac OS X v10.0
CFMutableDictionaryRef	NSMutableDictionary	Mac OS X v10.0
CFMutableSetRef	NSMutableSet	Mac OS X v10.0
CFMutableStringRef	NSMutableString	Mac OS X v10.0
CFNumberRef	NSNumber	Mac OS X v10.0
CFReadStreamRef	NSInputStream	Mac OS X v10.0
CFRunLoopTimerRef	NSTimer	Mac OS X v10.0
CFSetRef	NSSet	Mac OS X v10.0
CFStringRef	NSString	Mac OS X v10.0
CFTimeZoneRef	NSTimeZone	Mac OS X v10.0
CFURLRef	NSURL	Mac OS X v10.0
CFWriteStreamRef	NSOutputStream	Mac OS X v10.0

> **Note**
> These are (currently) the only toll-free bridged classes. You should not use type or class names as a guide. If a class and type are not in the preceding table, they are not toll-free bridged, even if the class and type names are the same or similar.

See https://developer.apple.com/library/ios/#documentation/CoreFoundation/ Conceptual/CFDesignConcepts/Articles/tollFreeBridgedTypes.html#//apple_ref/ doc/uid/TP40010677-SW1.

C

32- and 64-Bit

At the time of the first edition of this book, Apple was in the process of moving OS X to 64-bit. That transition is now almost complete. Xcode and Clang build OS X programs as 64-bit by default. With Lion (OS X 10.7) new Macs boot a 64-bit kernel by default. While it is still possible to build 32-bit Objective-C programs for OS X, 32-bit OS X programs use the legacy runtime and cannot use the newer features of the Objective-C language such as ARC, synthesized instance variables, and instance variables that are declared in class extensions.

iOS and iOS devices are 32-bit only. The material in the rest of this appendix refers to OS X.

> **Note**
>
> The earliest Intel Macs (those with Core Duo or Core Solo processors) are 32-bit only.

The terms *32-bit* and *64-bit* refer to the number of bits used to address memory. A 32-bit program uses pointers that are 4 bytes wide and can address 2^{32} or about 4 gigabytes (GB) of memory. A 64-bit program can theoretically address 2^{64}, or about 1.8×10^{19}, bytes of memory. In practice, current Intel machines use only 48 of the 64 bits in an 8-byte pointer for addressing, giving a maximum address of about 280 terabytes. (A terabyte is about 10^{12} bytes.)

What is the point of such huge numbers? As computers have become faster, people in some disciplines have begun to write programs to work with very large data sets, large enough to run into the 4 GB limit on 32-bit addresses. On the hardware side, physical memory above 4 GB has become much more common. (Apple now sells laptops with up to 8 GB of physical memory and desktops with up to 32 GB of physical memory.) There is clear pressure to expand the size of addressable memory beyond 4 GB. Computer architectures work best with sizes that are powers of two, so the next logical pointer size after 4 bytes is 8 bytes.

> **Note**
>
> When thinking about this subject, remember that Mac OS X has a swap system and that each process has its own virtual address space. A process does not need to be loaded completely into physical memory in order to execute; the swap system takes care of moving memory pages between physical memory and the swap area on disk. A process that uses 2 GB of memory will run on a machine that has 1 GB of physical memory, albeit potentially much more slowly than it would run on a machine with 4 GB of physical memory (assuming that the 4 GB machine isn't running other large programs at the same time).

Kernel and User Programs in 64-Bit

The kernel and user programs are separate. Each can be either 32- or 64-bit. A 32-bit kernel can run both 32- and 64-bit user programs. So can a 64-bit kernel.

Programs must be entirely 64-bit or entirely 32-bit. If you compile a program for 64-bit, all the libraries and frameworks that you link against, and any plugins your program uses, must be available in 64-bit versions. This is not a problem for the system-supplied libraries and frameworks, such as the Cocoa frameworks, which are all available in 64-bit versions. However, if you are using other libraries, you may have to compile them yourself for 64-bit (if you have access to the source) or continue to build your program as a 32-bit application until 64-bit versions of the resources become available.

Coding Differences for 64-Bit Programs

The main difference between 32- and 64-bit executables is the size of some of the primitive types. In a 32-bit executable, `int`s, `long`s, and pointers are all 4 bytes. In a 64-bit executable, `int`s are still 4 bytes, but `long`s and pointers are 8 bytes. The primary point, the one that can cause you trouble, is that in a 64-bit executable, `long`s and pointers are no longer the same size as `int`s.

Assigning a type to a longer type is OK, but assigning a longer type to a shorter type truncates the value held in the longer type and may result in nonsense. This may seem an obvious point, but there is a long history in C programming of ignoring the difference between a pointer and an `int`, and ignoring the fact that many system calls actually return `long` rather than `int`. Glossing over the difference between a pointer and an `int`, or the difference between a `long` and an `int`, makes no real difference when they are all 4 bytes; but the same code compiled for 64-bit can cause real problems. When coding for 64-bit, you should be careful when doing pointer arithmetic; you should never cast a pointer to an `int` variable.

Performance

Does compiling a program as a 64-bit executable make it run faster? There is no way to tell without building the program as separate 32- and 64-bit executables and then comparing the execution times. When you move to a 64-bit executable, there are some competing effects. On one hand, when an Intel CPU runs in `x86_64` (64-bit) mode, it has access to more registers. It can use these registers instead of the stack to pass arguments during a function call, resulting in better performance. But moving from a 32- to a 64-bit executable can cause your programs' memory footprint to increase (because many 4-byte variables are now 8-byte variables), sometimes dramatically. The larger size can mean more instruction cache misses, which results in worse performance.

Compiling for 32-Bit and 64-Bit

New OS X projects in the current version of Xcode default to 64-bit. If you use the Clang compiler on the command line, it also defaults to 64-bit.

If you want to compile a program as 32-bit (if, for example, you are maintaining a program that must still run on older, 32-bit-only Macs), you can tell Clang to produce a 32-bit executable by using the `-arch` flag. The following command compiles *program.m* into a 32-bit executable:

```
clang -arch i386 program.m -framework Foundation
```

If you specify more than one `-arch` flag, Clang builds a universal binary that contains an executable for each of the architectures you specify. For example, the following line compiles *program.m* into a two-way *universal binary* (also known as a *fat binary*) with executables for 32-bit Intel and 64-bit Intel:

```
clang -arch i386 -arch x86_64 program.m -framework Foundation
```

Universal binaries let you build a program as 64-bit for users with recent Intel machines but retain compatibility for users with older Intel machines. The disadvantages of a universal binary are that the compile times are longer (the compiler has to build the program more than once), and the file size of the binary is larger (a universal binary is made up of a binary for each architecture, glued together as a single file). However, the in-memory footprint of a program executed from a universal binary is not larger than that of the same executable loaded from a single executable binary: The loader loads only the executable that is appropriate for the current environment.

> **Note**
>
> You cannot use ARC or the other recent additions to Objective-C in a 32-bit program or a universal binary that includes a 32-bit executable.

To compile a project as 32-bit or as a universal binary using Xcode, you set the architecture in your project's *Build Settings*, as shown in Figure C.1.

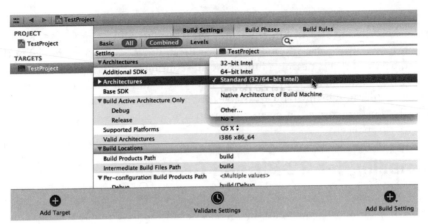

Figure C.1   Compiling for 32-bit with Xcode

More Information

The Apple documents on 64-bit Mac OS X are located at https://developer.apple.com/library/mac/#documentation/Darwin/Conceptual/64bitPorting/intro/intro.html.

The Cocoa-specific 64-bit documents are located at https://developer.apple.com/library/mac/#documentation/Cocoa/Conceptual/Cocoa64BitGuide/Introduction/Introduction.html.

The Fragile Base Class Problem

Many object-oriented languages suffer from what is called the *fragile base class* problem. If you add methods or instance variables to a class, you must recompile any classes that derive from the changed class. This is probably of no consequence for classes that you create in your own application code. Good practice requires that you make a clean compile before you release your program. But it is a problem for framework providers. For example, many of the classes in the Cocoa frameworks are intended to be subclassed. Imagine if you had to recompile all of your programs every time Apple wanted to change something in a Cocoa framework class. You (and everybody else) would also need fresh copies of any programs you didn't create yourself. People would be very unhappy.

The root of the fragile base class problem is a static (determined at compile time) memory layout for instance variables and methods. Because of Objective-C's dynamic method dispatch, it has never suffered from the method half of the fragile base class problem. You can always add methods to a class without requiring subclasses derived from it to be recompiled. You can even add methods to a class at run time (see Chapter 11, "Categories, Extensions, and Security").

In the past, Objective-C framework providers used various tricks to get around the instance variable part of the problem. These are strategies such as adding several instance variables reserved "for future use" when a class is first defined. This has the disadvantage that you don't know now what instance variables you may need in the future. It also wastes memory as long as the "future use" instance variables are not used. Another way of handling the problem is to provide a single extra instance variable that is a pointer to an `NSMutableDictionary`. The dictionary can be used to store additional values without changing the class's memory layout.

The modern runtime solves the instance variable part of the problem without any tricks. It locates instance variables by name rather than by static offsets in a structure.

This allows instance variables to be added to a class without requiring you to recompile any of the class's subclasses.

> **Note**
>
> The associative references feature (see Chapter 11, "Categories, Extensions, and Security") allows you to simulate adding instance variables to a single specified object. The association does not apply to any other instances of the object's class.

E

Resources for Objective-C

Apple Resources

If you are developing for Mac OS X or iOS, you should become a registered Apple Developer: https://developer.apple.com/programs/register/.

The registration is free. Registering as an Apple Developer allows you to download Xcode and the iOS SDK. It also allows you access to Mac and iOS online documentation, sample code, and Apple's online bug reporting system.

Apple also has two paid programs, the Mac Developer Program (https://developer.apple.com/programs/mac/) and the iOS Developer Program (https://developer.apple.com/programs/ios/). Each program costs US$99 per year.

The Mac Developer Program provides prerelease Mac OS X software, videos, and two Technical Support Incidents. Technical Support Incidents give you support from engineers on Apple's Developer Technical Support team. It also lets you submit apps for sale in the Mac App Store.

The iOS Developer Program provides prerelease iOS software, videos, documentation, and two Technical Support Incidents. It also lets you install apps on an iOS device and submit apps for sale in the iOS App Store.

> **Note**
>
> The free Apple Developer program allows you to use the iOS SDK to develop apps and test them on the iPhone/iPad simulator. To test apps on an iOS device and sell apps in the App Store, you must apply for, and be accepted into, the iOS Developer Program.

Membership in the Mac Developer Program or the iOS Developer Program also provides you with access to the Apple Developer Forums. Apple engineers answer many of the questions posted on these forums.

In addition, Apple hosts a number of mailing lists. Membership in one of the Developer Programs is not required to join these lists. The ones that are most useful for Objective-C development are the lists for Objective-C, Cocoa, and Xcode:

https://lists.apple.com/mailman/listinfo/objc-language

https://lists.apple.com/mailman/listinfo/cocoa-dev

https://lists.apple.com/mailman/listinfo/xcode-users

Although it isn't part of their official duties, a number of the Apple engineers read and post on these lists.

Internet Resources

The Apple Cocoa and Xcode mailing lists are archived in convenient form at CocoaBuilder.com: www.cocoabuilder.com.

The Cocoa list is also archived at www.mail-archive.com/cocoa-dev@lists.apple.com/.

The Omni Group, an independent Mac software company based in Seattle, makes a number of the frameworks that it has developed available as an open-source project. Even if you don't use these frameworks directly, they are well worth looking at as sample code: www.omnigroup.com/developer/.

GNUstep provides an open-source implementation of the AppKit and Foundation frameworks, based on the OpenStep API plus some additions based on Cocoa. GNUstep works on a number of systems, including OS X, Linux, and Windows: www.gnustep.org.

CocoaDev is a wiki site with a number of tutorials and links to articles on Objective-C and Cocoa: www.cocoadev.com/.

There are many other articles and blog posts about Objective-C on the Web, some better than others. As with so much else in the modern world, Google (or your favorite search engine) is your friend.

Groups

A number of cities have monthly CocoaHeads meetings: http://cocoaheads.org/. In addition to presentations, CocoaHead meetings are a good way to learn from more experienced developers.

Meetup.com lists a number of Objective-C-related *meetups*, particularly iPhone groups. Check to see if there is one near you: www.meetup.com/.

NSCoder nights are informal group coding sessions where you can exchange ideas and learn from other Objective-C programmers: http://nscodernight.com/.

Books

Buck, Erik M., and Donald A. Yacktman. *Cocoa Design Patterns*. Boston: Addison-Wesley, 2010.

Harbison, Samuel P., and Guy L. Steele. *C: A Reference Manual, Fifth Edition*. Upper Saddle River, NJ: Prentice Hall, 2002.

Kernighan, Brian W., and Dennis M. Ritchie. *The C Programming Language, Second Edition*. Upper Saddle River, NJ: Prentice Hall, 1988.

Singh, Amit. *Mac OS X Internals: A Systems Approach*. Boston: Addison-Wesley, 2006.

Index

Safari
Books Online

FREE
Online Edition

Your purchase of *Learning Objective-C 2.0: A Hands-on Guide to Objective-C for Mac and iOS Developers* includes access to a free online edition for 45 days through the **Safari Books Online** subscription service. Nearly every Addison-Wesley Professional book is available online through **Safari Books Online**, along with over thousands of books and videos from publishers such as Cisco Press, Exam Cram, IBM Press, O'Reilly Media, Prentice Hall, Que, Sams, and VMware Press.

Safari Books Online is a digital library providing searchable, on-demand access to thousands of technology, digital media, and professional development books and videos from leading publishers. With one monthly or yearly subscription price, you get unlimited access to learning tools and information on topics including mobile app and software development, tips and tricks on using your favorite gadgets, networking, project management, graphic design, and much more.

Activate your FREE Online Edition at
informit.com/safarifree

STEP 1: Enter the coupon code: JICCUWA.

STEP 2: New Safari users, complete the brief registration form.
Safari subscribers, just log in.

If you have difficulty registering on Safari or accessing the online edition,
please e-mail customer-service@safaribooksonline.com

 Addison Wesley Adobe Press ALPHA Cisco Press FT Press FINANCIAL TIMES IBM Press Microsoft Press New Riders O'REILLY

 Peachpit Press PRENTICE HALL que Redbooks SAMS SAS Publishing vmware PRESS WILEY wrox